AL CAPONE

AL CAPONE

His Life, Legacy, and Legend

DEIRDRE BAIR

NAN A. TALESE | DOUBLEDAY

NEW YORK LONDON TORONTO

SYDNEY AUCKLAND

Jacket design by Michael Windsor
Jacket image: Mugshot of Al Capone, November 1930 (detail).
PhotoQuest/Getty Images

LIBRARY OF CONGRESS CATALOGING-IN-PUBLICATION DATA
Names: Bair, Deirdre, author.
Title: Al Capone : his life, legacy, and legend / Deirdre Bair.
Description: First edition. | New York : Nan A. Talese/Doubleday, [2016] |
Includes bibliographical references and index.
Identifiers: LCCN 2016009367 (print) | LCCN 2016015716 (ebook) |
ISBN 9780385537155 (hardback) | ISBN 9780385537162 (ebook)
Subjects: LCSH: Capone, Al, 1899–1947. | Gangsters—United States—Biography.
| Criminals—United States—Biography. | Organized crime—United States—
History—20th century. | BISAC: BIOGRAPHY & AUTOBIOGRAPHY /
Criminals & Outlaws. | BIOGRAPHY & AUTOBIOGRAPHY / Historical. |
HISTORY / United States / 20th Century.
Classification: LCC HV6248 .C17 B34 2016 (print) | LCC HV6248 .C17 (ebook) |
DDC 364.1092 [B]—DC22
LC record available at https://lccn.loc.gov/2016009367

MANUFACTURED IN THE UNITED STATES OF AMERICA

1 3 5 7 9 10 8 6 4 2

First Edition

For John R. Ferrone

who always listened

CONTENTS

AL CAPONE

INTRODUCTION

———

This is the story of a ruthless killer, a scofflaw, a keeper of brothels and bordellos, a tax cheat and perpetrator of frauds, a convicted felon, and a mindless, blubbering invalid. This is also the story of a loving son, husband, and father who described himself as a businessman whose job was to serve the people what they wanted. Al Capone was all of these.

He died in 1947, and almost seven decades later it seems that anywhere one travels in the world, people still recognize his name and have something to say about who he was and what he did. Everyone has an opinion, and yet, within the deeply private world of his extended family, there is an ongoing quest to find definitive answers about its most famous member.

The saying goes that family history is often a mystery and that "all families are closed narratives, difficult to read from the outside." Attempting to reconstruct their truth is much like trying to solve the most complicated puzzle imaginable. In the case of those who bear a name that is famous or, as in the case of Al Capone's relatives and descendants, infamous, the task can be heavy indeed.

Some of his relatives found it easier to change their surname than to deal with its history, choosing to distance themselves and deny the relationship for a variety of reasons. Some merely wanted to lead ordinary private lives. Some said they feared reprisals from gangland Chicago, while still others who remained "connected" in varying degrees said they wanted to make their way in that world unencumbered by Al's long shadow. Still, there were those who kept the Capone name but said it was the reason why they had to lead peripatetic lives, some moving as far away as they could get, while others only moved cautiously from one town to another throughout northern Illinois, never far from the security and familiar environment of Chicago.

In recent years, the question of who has the right to claim a legitimate place within the family of Al Capone has resulted in some interesting pieces that may or may not fit into the puzzle of its history. "You who only know him from newspaper stories will never realize the real man he is," said his sister Mafalda in 1929, when he was in his prime. It is a remark echoed in so many other instances by his granddaughters, who have only recently become involved in sorting out what they call their "amazing family history." All four granddaughters (three of whom survive in 2015) called Al Capone "Papa." They loved him deeply as small children and still do as adults. With children and grandchildren of their own who ask about Papa, they now call him a "conundrum."

One of the questions they ponder repeatedly is how one man could embody so many vastly different personality traits. They talk among themselves about their family history; they argue and debate about whose memory is the most correct and the closest to the truth. They always strive to assess their grandparents and parents with honesty, objectivity, distance, and detachment, and they admit the difficulty, if not the impossibility, of arriving at definitive conclusions.

When they talk about their papa, they first put "Al Capone" in air quotes as they ask themselves what gave rise to the myth and legend. How did the grandfather they adored fit into all these stories? Where was the real person within the grandiose and exaggerated public personality, whose exploits continue to grow more outrageous seven decades after his death? What was it that makes the name of a man who died sick, broke, and demented in 1947 so instantly recognizable a decade and a half into a brand-new century? Are we fascinated with him today because of the so-called Roaring Twenties, the colorful time in which he lived? Is it because we now seek to understand the many ethnic histories that formed our country, and therefore the circumstances of his birth and family life as an Italian-American that might shed light on our own assimilation as Americans? Or, is it simply Al Capone's larger-than-life personality, the outsized figure who strutted across our historical stage for such a brief time that we did not have enough time while he was with us to assess him? After so many intervening years, can we figure him out? And after seven decades, is nothing left but the myth?

The members of his family agree with me that the enigma of Al Capone is a riddle to be solved and now is the time to try to do it. I was initially contacted by several members of the immediate family and the extended clan who were undertaking their own searches into the origins of their family and its subsequent history. I have been privileged to discuss my book with those people, and I have also benefited greatly from interviews and conversations with many other members of the extended Capone family whom I met throughout my research. Here, when I speak of the extended clan, I am including those who are definitely related, those who claim to be, and those who would just like to know whether or not they are.

While most prefer to keep their lives as private as possible and asked me not to reveal their true names or where they lived, they all agreed that everything they told me would be on the record. Those who asked me to keep their lives private often have children or grandchildren who don't mind being identified at all; they tell me it's "cool" to have a relative like Al Capone because he is far enough in their past that no onus is attached to their present circumstances. I have honored everyone's wishes because they all insisted that everything they told me was the truth as they knew it.

Mine is a curious hybrid of a book, because I concentrate more on the private man than the public figure. I admit that it is impossible to write about Al Capone without taking notice of the major events of his public life, but my aim was not to give yet another version of such well-trod ground unless I could provide new insights into it. Rather, my intention was to look at his public behavior within the context of his personal life, to see how the two might possibly be interrelated, and how the one might have had influence or bearing on the other. This was not an easy task, and like his family members I still wonder if it is possible to arrive at that curious postmodern concept of "the real truth." Starting in his lifetime, so many histories, biographies, articles, and profiles were written about Al Capone that even with today's technology it is impossible to arrive at an accurate tally of the secondary documents. All of them purported to be the truth, and perhaps they were at the time they were written. But as we know, what is true for one generation is usually subject to new and different interpretations by the next.

Whenever I speak to any member of the Capone family, our conversations always seem to end on the same note: the enigma of Al Capone is a riddle that our efforts may help to solve, and we share the consensus that our contributions to the task are beginnings but certainly not the final endings.

Chapter 1

THE EARLY YEARS

G abriele Capone was twenty-nine years old when he boarded the ship *Werra* that brought him to the United States in June 1895. With him were his wife, Teresa Raiola Capone, twenty-seven, and their two sons, three-year-old Vincenzo and seventeen-month-old Raffaele. Although they traveled as most other Italian immigrants did, in second class or steerage, Gabriele was unlike the majority who had to indenture themselves to pay for passage, for he had a trade that paid his family's way. He was a baker who had specialized in making pasta, which earned him a decent living in his native village of Castellammare di Stabia, just outside Naples. He was confident that his skills would easily lead to employment that would let him thrive in the New World. Gabriele was unlike his countrymen in another way: although Naples and its surrounding villages provided one of the largest contingents of Italian immigrants to America, and many bore the fairly common surname of Capone, none of his closest relatives had left their village, so no one was waiting on the dock to greet him and ease his way. A third distinction from most of the nearly fifty thousand other Italians who arrived that same year was probably most significant: he could read and write and had acquired a smattering of English that, coupled with a natural linguistic ability, he used from the beginning to navigate the teeming perils of life in New York.

A rumor surrounding his arrival has it that Gabriele did not enter the United States directly because he did not have enough money to pay the entrance fee imposed on immigrants at Ellis Island. Some of his descendants believe that he went instead to Canada and sneaked over the border, although they have no documentation to show how he would have found the money to go there if he did not have sufficient funds to leave Ellis Island. It is one of the earliest myths surrounding the origins of the Capone family in America; all that can be verified is that Gabriele Capone avoided New York's largest Italian settlement in Manhattan's crowded, crime-ridden Mulberry Bend on the Lower East Side and headed directly for Brooklyn. He had been forewarned of Mulberry Bend's dangers by the letters written by others from his village who came before him, but the tenement apartment he found in the area near the New York Naval Shipyard was not much better. Known locally as the Brooklyn Navy Yard, it was another gang-infested area of vice and crime where local thugs took turns hassling and assaulting the sailors who poured out of the main gate at the end of Navy Street. It was cheaper to live there than in Manhattan, and Gabriele thought it a possibly better place for a pasta maker to find work as a baker. However, this was not to be, and to find a way to support his family, he re-created himself as a barber.

His initial plan was to find work in someone else's shop until he could save enough money to set up one of his own, but he could find no one to hire him, so he had to take whatever work was offered. There is no mystery about why he abandoned baking, for it would have cost money he did not have to set up a shop of his own, which was the same reason he did not initially become a barber with his own shop. Other Italians who could not afford to set up a shop usually practiced their trades in their homes and made enough money to scrimp by, which Gabriele could have done as well. However, he was a cautious man, which was probably why he chose instead to find steady work alongside 90 percent of the city's Italian population, doing day labor whenever he could find it.

Much of it was the "dirty work" done under the auspices of the city's Public Works Department, the hard and dangerous physical labor building subways, sewers, and skyscrapers that no other ethnic group was desperate enough to take. Italians had replaced the Irish at the bottom of the ethnic influx by the 1890s, when an official in city government described the situation succinctly: "We can't get along without the Italians; we want someone to do the dirty work and the Irish aren't doing it any longer."

Gabriele fared better than most when he was hired as a grocery store clerk because the job enabled him to read, write, and speak English a little better every day. It was different for Teresa, who was already pregnant with her third child before the boat landed and who gave birth in 1895 to another son, Salvatore, in the Navy Street tenement. From the time they arrived, she helped her husband save money for a barbershop by taking in piecework for various garment factories. Because she worked at home and because everyone in her small enclosed world only spoke Italian, she had little reason to improve her English and throughout her life spoke it hesitantly. She was like most other Italian-American women of her generation, who all used the expression of going "down to America" when they had to venture beyond their known worlds of local tenements and shops; Teresa was representative of all their hesitations and fears because she insisted that her only safety came from within the sanctity of the family, which she always gathered close about her.

Whether by accident or design, there were no more children until 1899, when Gabriele was finally able to set up his own shop in a slightly better neighborhood at No. 69 on Brooklyn's elegantly named Park Avenue, a street whose quality of life was far removed from its Manhattan counterpart. He moved his growing family into an apartment above the shop where they were living when their first child conceived in the New World, Alphonse, was born on January 17, 1899. Teresa had hoped this pregnancy would result in a girl who would mark the end of her childbearing years, but neither was to be.

Alphonse was followed by five more children, the sons Erminio (1901), Umberto (1906), and Amadoe (1908) and the daughters Erminia (born and died 1910) and Mafalda (1912). At home, each child was called by the formal Italian baptismal name, but on the streets and at school the boys quickly adopted American versions. Vincenzo called himself Jimmy, and the others became (in the order of their birth) Ralph, Frank, Al, John (or sometimes Mimi), Albert, and Matthew (or Matty). Mafalda, who bore the pretentious name of King Victor Emmanuel's coddled princess daughter, never had a childhood nickname, for she liked the status her name gave and would not have tolerated one. Only as an adult were some of her favored nieces and nephews permitted to call her Aunt Maffie, and if she was in one of her bad moods, she might not respond until they used her full name.

Brooklyn's Park Avenue, unlike Manhattan's WASP enclave, was a curious mix of ethnic identities. Al came of age in the decade between 1910 and 1920, when the metropolitan area swelled with an immigrant influx that amounted to—according to the lawyer and patron of the arts John Quinn—"seven or eight hundred thousand dagos, a couple of hundred thousand Slovaks, fifty or sixty thousand Croats and seven or eight hundred thousand sweating pissing Germans." To Quinn, they were "nothing but walking appetites," and as he thought of so many other earlier arrivals, he despised them as well.

The Capones lived among them, on the fringe of the Italian section where it gave way to a mix of Irish, German, and eastern Europeans. Unlike other Italian ghettos in the New York area, where buildings were occupied by compatriots from the same province, sometimes segregated by floor based on families who came from the same tiniest villages, the Italian residents of this particular part of Brooklyn came from a variety of Italian homelands and spoke different dialects. Here, only the Sicilians kept to themselves in buildings of their own, but on the streets Al's playmates and school class-mates traced their origins throughout the poorest parts of southern Italy, from Sicily to Campania and Calabria. They all spoke "broken" English as he did, a mix of the dialects they heard at home and the heavily accented English that was pounded into them at school. The children of the other nationalities reflected the hodgepodge that was New York English, which made Al comfortable enough from his early childhood to move freely among other "Americans," as Italian-Americans dubbed anyone who had not come from their homeland. He was at ease among other ethnic groups and had no trouble relating to other nationalities, a quality that was appar-ent in the diverse group of people he hired as an adult gang leader.

Teresa stayed healthy and became the rock-solid foundation of the fam-ily despite bearing so many children and living one step up from hard-scrabble poverty in a small apartment with no heat and an outhouse down the stairs and out the back. They were even more crowded when they took in two boarders (one of whom worked as an assistant barber to Gabriele). Her word was law to her children, and it had to be, because, although she and Gabriele had a marriage based on love and mutual respect, his con-stitution was not as robust as hers. He would lay down family law, but she was the parent who enforced it. Whether he was weakened from the hard physical labor of the first grim years of their American life or whether he was simply prone to catch whatever illness came along, Gabriele was often not in the best of health. He did, however, work hard at his barbering, and he did have a steady enough clientele that allowed him to be the primary financial support for the family. It gave him great respect in the eyes of his children and the community.

Gabriele and Teresa seized every opportunity to prosper in their new life, and the extra income brought by her sewing and the two boarders was a great help in making them relatively comfortable in comparison with many of their fellow Italian immigrants. Unlike most, they did not expect their sons to quit school and go to work at the earliest opportunity, for although it was not actually said to the children, the parents valued education as a way to get ahead. Gabriele was a quiet man who liked to spend his evenings reading Italian newspapers or going to his social club just next door, where he enjoyed playing cards and billiards, while Teresa usually busied herself at home with some sort of sewing. With the exception of shopping, the only time she left the house was to go to daily Mass, for she was deeply religious, or for the evening meetings of the church's sodalities, as the women's groups were called. Whether or not Gabriele shared her devotion, he was like most other Italian men, for he (and the boys shortly after they received their first Communion) did not attend Mass on Sundays, let alone weekdays.

Both parents were highly respected within the Italian community, each known by the honorific titles of "Don Gabriele" and "Donna Teresa." By comparison to many of their neighbors, this extra degree of respect added to the general impression that they were reasonably secure and therefore, in the eyes of their countrymen and other neighbors, better off than most of them. The Capone family had come up in the world after 1906, when Gabriele took the oath to become an American citizen. The following year, they moved to a slightly better neighborhood when Gabriel (as he wrote his name now that he was an American) found commercial space for a barbershop with an apartment above it on a street called Garfield Place. The neighborhood was solidly traditional Italian, but the Capones once again lived on a street that was on its fringe, on the downhill side of Park Slope where Brooklyn's Little Italy abutted the solidly Irish Red Hook section. Italians were a minority in their building, which was mostly inhabited by Irish families or those relative rarities, native New Yorkers.

This was a household of some culture; Gabriel tried to share with his sons the ideas and interests he gleaned mainly from Italian and American newspapers and conversations with his clients, but none of the older boys were much interested. Jimmy just wanted to go to the movies to watch the cowboys, particularly his hero William S. Hart. His secret ambition was to go to Hollywood to become a cowboy movie star, but until he could get there, he went to Coney Island to hang around the stables of ponies he could not afford to ride. Ralph, who had no interest in anything at home, took up with street gangs as soon as he was old enough to do so. Frank, the best looking and most intelligent among all the brothers and possessed of more street smarts than the two older ones, soon followed Ralph but in a much more subdued manner. While Ralph often used his brawn to intimidate others into giving him what he wanted, Frank preferred not to risk harming his pretty-boy features, instead using charm and intelligence to persuade others to do his bidding. Despite being the third son who was supposed to defer to his two older brothers, Frank had such a way about him that he often took the lead in deciding what Jimmy and Ralph should do, and young Al looked up to him as well.

All the Capone boys respected their father and knew better than to oppose him in any way, for to do so would bring the wrath of Teresa down upon their heads—and their backsides. And yet, despite having parents who urged their sons to better themselves and rise to success through honest work and education, every one of the boys left school as early as he could and turned to crime in one form or another. Al was the only one who found extraordinary success through illegality and also the only son who, from the first, thought of himself as "American" rather than Italian or even Italian-American. His earliest memories were of the melting pot in which he grew up among different ethnic groups. As an adult, he grew angry when anyone called him Italian, saying repeatedly and angrily, "I'm no Italian, I was born in Brooklyn."

By the time they arrived on Garfield Place, the eight-year-old Alphonse had already established a reputation in both groups as a brawler to reckon with. As one of Al's many biographers said of an Irish kid in the neighborhood who was much like him, Al's mere *existence* presented a challenge."

This reputation was cemented after a fight that has gone down in Capone lore as "the incident of the washtub," or how Al rescued Mrs. Maria Adamo's stolen washtub and used it as a weapon in a fight with an Irish gang that disrespected Italian women. Nothing in that version of the story was true. What is true is that whenever the Italian matrons ventured out onto the streets to do their daily marketing, the Irish boys liked to sneak behind them and pull up their voluminous long skirts and petticoats to reveal their bare legs and the bloomers they wore underneath. Because none of the Italian boys had yet been brave enough to stop them, the Irish were boldly escalating their attacks by invading Italian neighborhoods, doing damage to property, and occasionally stealing whatever they could easily haul away. However, they did not steal Mrs. Adamo's washtub, because it was not something they needed or wanted. It was their arrogant demeanor that the Italian boys could not allow to go unchallenged.

The Italian boys were led by Frank Nitto, later to be known as Al's enforcer, Frank Nitti, who was then almost eighteen and a decade older than most of the others. Al was between the ages of eight and nine and already had a reputation for his fighting prowess, so Nitti made him the mascot of "the Boys of Navy Street," as they called themselves. The older boys "borrowed" the washtub and strapped it to Al, upside down and in front. They found two sticks and told him to be the gang's drummer who would lead their song as they marched to confront their Irish enemy, "We are the boys of Navy Street/touch us if you dare!" Once they engaged the other boys, the fight ensued, and throughout it Al stood in the midst of the fray, beating his drum and singing his song. After the fracas ended, the washtub was dutifully returned in time for Mrs. Adamo's next day's washing, and Al's reputation as a foot soldier who could be counted on in a fight was assured.

———

Al's school days were quite different. No matter their country of origin, all the recent immigrants found school a strange, dangerous, and often humiliating experience. Public school teachers were generally young and untrained, as harsh as most of the nuns who taught in the Catholic schools. Primary school was often a confusing experience for Italian children who were suddenly pushed from a warm and loving home, where mothers coddled their sons in the language they knew and understood, into the cold and clinical classroom, where they were treated rudely or ignored by teachers who did little to help them learn English. The general attitude was why bother, especially with Italians, who were considered the lowest of the low and who were only going to drop out at the earliest opportunity. In those days, Italians not only started out at the bottom; they stayed there.

Al was different from most of the people around him, starting with his big brothers Jimmy and Ralph (but not Frank) and extending to most of his classmates. He was a quick learner who soon spoke fluent English and was a good student, routinely earning the equivalent of B grades. He was especially quick with numbers and figures, but he was far more expert at playing hooky and seldom went to school long enough to demonstrate his natural ability. He always said he learned much more about life by being on the streets. He thrived there because he knew instinctively how to adapt to whatever he encountered, but in school there were so many rules and regulations that created frustrating situations in which he often found himself unable to control his behavior.

He was always big for his age, and as he grew, he developed a temper that matched his size. Between the ages of ten and twelve, he passed for a youth of sixteen to eighteen. He (and his brothers) were taller than most Italians, and as an adult, depending on who reported his size, he was either five feet ten inches or just about six feet tall. He weighed well over 200 pounds in his prime, somewhere around 250, and because he was so well-muscled, he carried his weight easily. He was well coordinated and graceful, and his contemporaries said he could have been a boxer or a professional dancer. As a ten-year-old, he liked to hang out around the gates of the Navy Yard and taunt sailors when they came through on their way to the bars and brothels that lined the street. There are numerous tales of his exploits, with some having him itching for fistfights with sailors twice his age; others have him actually fighting them and winning; and still others have him throwing rocks and bottles with other young boys who formed free-floating gangs for spur-of-the-moment battles that always brought the police. Neither police nor sailors ever caught young Al because he was so swift at running away.

In short, he was a brawler, and his propensity to fight culminated in his leaving school for good during the sixth grade—after the indignity of having to repeat it, thanks to extensive absences that led to frequent altercations with teachers who sometimes stopped at verbal abuse but more often allegedly hit him with sticks, rulers, or straps. He was a big kid going on fourteen when the sixth-grade teacher made the mistake of trying to punish him after another student stole his lunch and Al disrupted the classroom by demanding that it be returned. This particular story has come down through the years in two different versions: in one, the teacher (a very young woman) only wanted him to go into a coatroom and stand there with his face to the wall, which for Al was an unjust humiliation and the last straw; in another, the teacher (a highly respected older man) made the mistake of getting between Al and the boy who stole the sandwich and thus suffered a knockdown and knockout in the process.

There are also various versions of what Al did to retaliate after the encounter with whichever teacher it was: in one, after the young woman hit him, he hit her back before he walked out of the classroom, never to return. In another, she was unable to discipline him, so she sent him to the principal, who either took a stick to him or gave him such a tongue-lashing that here again he walked out and never went back. And if the teacher was indeed the man Al knocked down, he was supposedly angry enough to send the truant officer off on several unsuccessful hunts to find and return the boy to the classroom. This last version seems least likely, for truant officers were noted for turning in reports of "actively pursuing" an Italian child who left school, when in reality they cared so little that they did nothing.

No doubt there is a modicum of truth somewhere in all these stories, but when Al walked out, he was not doing anything different from what his older brothers had done before him: he was just quitting school, as they all did when they were around fourteen. Thus, to his parents, it seemed he was doing as his brothers did, and there was no conflict at home; they simply expected that because he was not going to school, he would go to work and contribute his wages to the family.

At first, Al had legitimate jobs. Various sources have him working behind the counter in a candy store, setting pins in a bowling alley, and working alongside his brother Ralph in a printing plant. One story that is certainly legend rather than reality says he earned $23 a week in a munitions factory, but even if he worked there during World War I, when he was in his late teens and wages were high, in 2015 dollars that would have been approximately $525, an astronomical sum that was certainly not the weekly salary of an average laborer. Other stories have him living as far away from Brooklyn as Buffalo, where he was said to have gone in search of work and where he held a variety of jobs. This never happened, for he was one of the typical Italian boys who always found work where they lived and who didn't leave the family home until they could marry and set up their own households. Although Al probably did work at many of the odd jobs that have come to be considered true parts of his life story, the only one that can be verified is that he did follow Ralph into a printing plant, where he worked as a box cutter alongside his brother between 1914 and 1916 and brought home $3 a week, approximately $68 in 2015 dollars and a good salary for a teenager with a sixth-grade education.

Al's paycheck became an important addition to the family's finances, for they had already lost two wage-earning sons, Ralph and Jimmy. Ralph moved to Manhattan when he married for the first time in 1915. His first wife of two (or three, depending on the legal status of his last companion) was Filomena Moscato, called Florence. She was born in Salerno, a city close to Naples in the province of Campania, and was a small child when her parents brought her to the United States. Ralph and Florence had a common background that should have resulted in a marriage that, if not based on love, should certainly have respected the traditional roles of an Italian husband and wife. It might have evolved like that if they were in their native Italy, but life in America had given Florence the idea that marriage did not need to be based on the old country's tradition of a wife's submission to her husband. She was quite a fighter, physically as well as verbally, and their first two years together were fractious. She liked to "go out," which most likely meant to bars and dance halls, so theirs was a household with broken crockery that often led to black-and-blue bruises on both of them. They did make peace long enough to have a son, their only child, Ralph junior, always called Ralphie, in 1917.

Shortly after "little Ralphie" was born, Ralph came home from work one day to find that Florence had run away, deserting both him and the baby. Teresa took them in and set about caring for Ralphie, while Ralph worked steadily to provide for the household. He was a good, dependable worker with a genial personality that made him popular with others who also learned quickly not to cross him; like Al, he had a temper that could turn violent with the least provocation. Ralph held a variety of jobs for the next several years, doing everything from being the front man who dealt with customers in the printing plant to selling penny insurance policies door-to-door. When he landed a job with a soft drinks bottling firm, he acquired the nickname by which he was known for the rest of his life, Bottles. It became highly appropriate when Al began bootlegging and Ralph was his right-hand man.

Jimmy contributed to the family by hanging around the farms and stables on Staten Island and bringing home what little money he could. He would have dressed as a cowboy had family finances permitted, and when he ran away from home sometime in 1905 at the age of thirteen, he intended to go to Hollywood and become a cowboy movie star. His whereabouts were unknown for the next three decades, and when he resurfaced years later, the family learned that he only got as far as Nebraska. He changed his name to Richard Hart, taking the surname of the silent movie star he most admired. Ironically, he became a well-known figure, Two Gun Hart, when he established a career as a sheriff in rural Nebraska who took delight in smashing bootleg stills and shipments of booze wherever he found them. Still, there was nothing to connect Two Gun Hart with Vincenzo Capone and his bootlegging brothers, and for many years the Capone family remained unaware of his existence.

———

Until Al was fourteen or fifteen, stories told by his contemporaries describe him as a nice boy who, after he quit school and went to work every day, always brought his entire paycheck home to his mother. He was well-known on the streets of his neighborhood because that was where everyone congregated for most of the year to escape the overcrowded, squalid, and fetid tenement apartments in which they had to live. In good weather, family life, from the oldest patriarch to the newest baby, was lived outside, on the stoops and on the streets. Everyone knew everyone else's business, so the memories of Al hanging around in pool halls or on the streets are true, but so too are the stories of how he had to be home every night at 10:30 or face the ire of his mother.

The writer Daniel Fuchs, who portrayed Brooklyn life with unstinting reality in his novels, knew Al and remembered him as someone unlikely to become a flamboyant gangster because, as a boy, he was "something of a nonentity, affable, soft of speech and even mediocre—in everything but dancing." Fuchs was most likely depicting Al before his first foray into criminality, which probably did not happen until after he quit school and was in his early teens, when his father set him up in what was meant to be an honest business.

Gabriel was aware of the fights that the Navy Street Boys led Al into, and he worried that the petty thefts and bad stunts they pulled might escalate into something far more serious. Al had taken to hanging out at one of the ubiquitous social clubs that dotted the neighborhood, this one called the Adonis, with a basement outfitted for target practice where he is believed to have held a gun for the first time. He was fourteen and big for his age, so to steer the boy away from a place where he could get into real trouble, Gabriel gave him a shoe-shine box and told him to stake out a position on the busy intersection of Union and Columbia Streets, where pushcarts lined the sidewalks and vendors hawked their wares in competition with the shops. Gabriel had tried earlier to set Frank up in the shoe-shine business, but the enterprising Frank sold his box to another boy for a handsome profit, then used the money to gamble and, with his winnings, to buy the flashy clothes he had begun to fancy. In the vernacular of the time, Frank was becoming a snazzy dresser and a ladies' man, and Al was eager to imitate him.

Although Gabriel had given up on his three older sons, he was trying to turn the next in line into a businessman who would see the wisdom of moving up in the world through honest labor. He told Al to park his box under the big clock that was the busiest spot on the street, where he would have the best chance of making the most money. It was also the location where some of Don Batista Balsamo's men conducted much of his business. Don Balsamo, whose informal but always respectful title was "the 'mayor' of Union Street," was also "the first godfather of Brooklyn." Al observed the don's minions as they made their weekly rounds to extort the local merchants into paying protection in exchange for doing business safely. Watching them gave Al the inspiration to go into the protection racket himself but on a much smaller scale that would escape Balsamo's notice and therefore his punishment.

Al's target was the other shoe-shine boys who brought their boxes to Columbia Street as soon as they saw what a lucrative spot it was for him. The first employees who did his actual collecting were two of his cousins, Charlie Fischetti and Sylvester Agoglia, and two of their friends, Jimmy DeAmato and Tony Scrapisetti. Al had learned the fine art of delegation from watching Frank, who, like the don, chose other boys to be his enforcers and seldom did the dirty work himself. He also noticed that Frank usually chose boys who were sometimes older than he but not nearly as intelligent or innovative and who were therefore content to be followers and not try to usurp him as leader. It was a practice Al followed throughout his adult career.

As this, his first business, grew, Al's helpers expanded to include other boys eager to make easy money. Soon this fairly large group began to think of themselves as a gang and gave themselves a name, the South Brooklyn Rippers. Their protection racket was ultimately unsuccessful when the Balsamo organization simply booted them off the street, but only after smiling at the boys' audacity and taking careful notice of who among them might become useful in the future. Eventually, it brought the boys, particularly Al, to the attention of two other rising stars in the criminal firmament, first Frankie Yale, né Ioele, and then Johnny Torrio. They watched as Al branched out from Brooklyn and strutted into Manhattan, where Ralph was now operating.

Ralph Capone left Ralphie with his mother, Florence, when she returned to claim him briefly before giving him up entirely to be raised by his grandmother Teresa. Ralph moved from his parents' home to Manhattan around 1917, where he had more opportunities to be with women, mostly the prostitutes and dance hall girls his mother would have frowned upon, and where he was doing deals that were just on the fringe of illegality. He was involved with the notorious adult gang called the Five Points, which specialized in selling stolen auto parts or sometimes actual cars, but more likely Ralph was just doing whatever odd jobs gang leaders assigned in order to pick up a quick buck. Al sometimes joined his brother in the city, where he became familiar with the streets of the Lower East Side, pulled pranks with other ruffians, and seized whatever opportunity he could to pick up a bit of change. Soon he was part of a loose affiliation who called themselves the Forty Thieves Juniors, and that brought him to the attention of his ultimate crime boss, Johnny Torrio.

One of the reasons the very young Al Capone thought Torrio presented such an attractive role model was that he operated in the mold of his admired older brother Frank, when in actuality Frank probably learned this technique from Torrio. He, too, was a snappy dresser, a short and slight man who never sullied his hands and whose preferred way of doing business was to use the biggest thugs he could find as his enforcers. Torrio must have had a silver tongue to go along with his considerable intelligence, for he "dominated his swollen-muscled thugs with a large brain abetted by a colossal nerve and will." This impressed young Al, as did Torrio's one consistent expression, that there were spoils out there aplenty and therefore no need for violent conflict because there was more than enough to go around.

Torrio and his gang gathered in one of the euphemistically titled "social clubs" that filled all the neighborhoods where they lived. The clubs had names that subtly identified which of two kinds they were: some bore the name of an Italian province, city, or hero, and law-abiding Italian men gathered there in the evenings to read newspapers, shoot pool, and talk among themselves; in others, such as the one bearing the name of the John Torrio Association, dangerous-looking men congregated all day long and stayed far into the night, not really doing very much of anything but always ready for whatever might arise. In pleasant weather, all the men hung out on the sidewalks in front of both kinds of clubs to watch the passing scene. Al was still in school when he had to walk past Torrio's every day, where men who did his bidding noticed the big kid just as he noticed them. Around the time he turned sixteen, he was mounting the stairs to Torrio's second-floor office and running numbers along with a host of other boys.

Here again, legend steps in: Before entrusting them with bags of money, Torrio allegedly would not be in his office when the boys arrived for their first interview. They would be invited to wait for him in his inner sanctum, where a large pile of money would be sitting on his desk in clear view. Some of the boys could not resist the temptation and took all or part of it, and they were immediately dealt with and dismissed. This tale is told about Al Capone in a variety of versions, but in each he was always a paragon of virtue who left the money untouched, thus earning Torrio's complete confidence in his trustworthiness.

In recent years, Torrio's importance in the annals of American crime has been diminished if not eclipsed because of Al Capone's near-mythical stature. It would be unfair to relegate him to the sidelines when he was, in the words of Herbert Asbury, an early and astute scholar of crime, "probably the nearest thing to a mastermind this country has yet produced." Torrio was active in Chicago criminal activity as early as 1909, going back and forth between there and New York until the late teen years, but by the 1930s, when he was an established figure and the word "crime" had become synonymous with the city of Chicago, the city's crime commission called him "an organizational genius," singularly responsible, as one of Capone's many biographers put it, "for the development of modern corporate crime ... casting traditional Italian racketeering in the American corporate mold, making its vices available to all, not just Italians, eventually extending its turf far beyond the streets of Brooklyn to the entire nation."

Johnny Torrio was indeed a formidable role model for a canny and intelligent boy looking to move up in the world, one who lived in a place where honest and upright role models were few and far between for the simple reason that their Italian surnames denied them so many opportunities within the American dream. In Al's case, it was easy for the young boy to have tremendous respect for the man who paid him handsomely for running numbers and carrying messages, work that was so much easier than bending over a shoe-shine box all day long. However, there seems to have been a gap in his thinking, a disconnect between the chores he did for Torrio and the money he was paid, which he dutifully brought home to his mother: the money was good, and it was probably better not to think about what he had to do to earn it.

There is no question that from the first he was unlike Torrio's other boy collectors and messengers, for at the beginning, and for reasons still unknown, he was the one whom Torrio never sent into the brothels. So what if Al collected bags of betting money from the saloons? He was only there in the daylight hours, when there didn't appear to be anything all that wrong with what he saw. He was not privy to beatings, shakedowns, and murders. He knew these things happened because everyone on the street talked about them, but they were done by men and boys so far down the Torrio organization's ladder that it seemed they went on in another world, one that did not touch its dandified leader, whose hands (literally as well as metaphorically) were scrupulously clean and who kept the hands of a small coterie of his best workers clean as well.

Al had a way with numbers and could add them up with such alacrity that he was soon one of the boys at the very top of Torrio's heap, often tapped to help the guys in the office who totted up the daily haul. He was still very young when he learned about Torrio's other businesses, everything from extortion to brothels, and he observed how Torrio never dealt with any of them directly. Al watched as he worked and waited eagerly to assume the ever increasing responsibilities Torrio delegated to him. These eventually included visiting the brothels and perhaps enjoying the girls while collecting the bags of money they earned. When he went into bars, businesses, or homes to intimidate people into paying up, he used a frighteningly unflinching stare that he learned by practicing in front of a mirror. As an earlier biographer astutely stated, "What Torrio, with his brilliant, analytical mind was able to conceive, Al would eventually be able to execute."

However, between the ages of sixteen and eighteen, even though he was fast rising in Torrio's organization in Brooklyn, not too many people would have thought of Al as much more than his brother Ralph's sidekick, the one who liked to shoot pool and go dancing with other Italian men who frequented the dance halls that lined the streets of lower Manhattan. These dance halls, for men only and where men danced with other men, held to the customs of the old country; no women, especially single, would risk their reputations by appearing in such places. Al soon became such a good dancer that he branched out to the non-Italian dance halls frequented by certain classes of women, some of them from good working-class families like his own, who were "American" enough to go out and enjoy themselves, others who were just unfortunate girls out to make a buck any way they could.

Al learned about women from Ralph, whose first reported bout with gonorrhea came around 1915, when Al was almost sixteen. His older brother was a good customer of the dance hall girls looking to pick up a quick trick or the prostitutes who worked openly on the streets, as well as those who worked in the many brothels. Ralph's gonorrhea was one of the fortunate varieties of the disease: at a time when there were no cures, his was the strain that healed quickly and never manifested itself later in life. Al never admitted to having had gonorrhea as a youth or to seeking treatment for a venereal disease such as the syphilis that first infected him in his twenties, but sex was abundant and readily available, and he indulged in it from a very young age. However, not with nice Italian girls, who were watched so carefully by their families that boys like Al had little opportunity to seduce them. And besides, he really wasn't interested in them.

The Italian girls he knew clung to the ways of the old country, and those ways were not his. Often they were taken out of school as early as the third or fourth grade while they were still children, because their overburdened mothers needed them to help raise younger siblings who seemed to be born every year. For these girls, forced to take on adult responsibilities so early, their lives consisted of the hard, grueling work of washing clothes, doing piecework, and becoming expert at housework far before their time. They clung to the ways of their mothers because it was all they knew, and this included the refusal—or the fear—of learning English and going out into the world beyond the stoop of their building or the corner of their street. Al wasn't interested in women like this, who, the minute they married, changed from willing sexual partners into the same Madonna-like beings as their mothers and had to be treated with the same kind of asexual respect. And neither was Frank.

Al watched as his older brother evaded Italian girls, and indeed all women, and how he skillfully sidestepped any talk of marriage, whether from his mother in the home or his friends on the street. Frank loved to dance and enjoyed taking the floor with dance hall girls, but he was almost too fastidious for sex, which he didn't even like to talk about and which gave rise to a few whispered rumors about his sexual orientation. This is where he and Al parted company: like Ralph, Al was entranced by women, and if they were prostitutes, it didn't matter; he embraced every opportunity for sex that came his way.

———

And so Al Capone reached adulthood like so many other boys in his neighborhood, with a future that seemed destined to consist of one violent scrape after another that would eventually bring him into conflict not only with others on the wrong side of the law but also with the law itself. Even though Torrio was spending so much time in Chicago that his move there was almost complete, stories still abound of how he increased Al's duties in New York by entrusting him to carry guns in brown paper bags (this one probably true) or to transport narcotics disguised as cans of tomatoes (this one highly unlikely, for Torrio carefully avoided dealing in drugs). Al did carry out threats—or worse—on those who thought they could refuse to pay extortion, or those who simply did not have the money to do so, and he was probably present when a few hits were made on some of the small-time mobsters who ran afoul of Torrio's organization. Whether he merely contributed to setting up the murders or actually carried them out depends on who is telling the tale, for if even some of the stories told by his many biographers are true, when they are added up, he was responsible for at least half a dozen killings before he was eighteen.

Reading about his youthful exploits is like reading a bildungsroman, not the traditional one of an artist or writer coming of age, but one of a young criminal coming into his manhood. There is, however, a basic question that is difficult to answer: Where does the life of the boy end and the life as a legend begin? Most likely for Al Capone, it happened somewhere between working for Johnny Torrio and working for Frankie Yale, and his marriage to the pretty Irish girl who said to anyone who would listen that he broke her heart but she loved him anyway.

Chapter 2

MAE

S he was a pretty Irish girl, a green-eyed blonde who hid from the public spotlight he relished even as it probed relentlessly into her private life, searching to find out how she stayed so deeply in love with and loyal to a man like Al Capone. Because she revealed so little about herself, the media invented ways to describe her, and what they wrote often depended on their mood of the moment: either she had hair like sunlight and eyes like the deep blue sea, or she was a peroxide blonde with buckteeth and bad taste in home furnishings. Neither was true: Mary Josephine Coughlin had startling green eyes, fair skin, and lustrous brown hair. No matter what they said about her and Al Capone, theirs was a love story, albeit one quite unlike the usual romantic tale of boy meets girl and lives happily ever after.

The circumstances of their courtship, marriage, and lifelong together-ness were entirely unorthodox, starting with the fact that they were actually able to marry at all; what remained constant was the lifelong devotion each partner brought to the marriage. The reality of their affection was almost storybook, despite his peccadilloes and predilections and the shame, embarrassment, and despair they repeatedly visited upon her. Strange as it might seem to outsiders, theirs was truly a love story, and they passed the love they showed each other on to their only son, who, in turn, showered it on his own four children.

Al was smitten from the first moment he saw Mary Josephine Coughlin (always called Mae) at the end of 1917, when he was a laborer in a box fac-tory and she worked in the office as a timekeeper. But why would a young woman two years his senior, and of her social station (proper lace curtain

Irish), even look twice at a street punk who seemed to have no future? Even more puzzling is how this nice girl got herself pregnant by this same punk and how her deeply religious Catholic family let her live openly in the family home without marrying the baby's father until after their child was born. Mae was a beautiful girl and later an elegant woman whose granddaughters remember as having the most radiant smile and a mellifluous laugh that brought her many admiring glances, even as an old woman. Although her teeth were large and white and straight, she had a pronounced overbite that her son and one of his four daughters inherited. It gave an interesting cast to her looks and one that made her son resemble her so much more than his father.

She was the second of five daughters: Muriel Anne was older, and she was the sister who became Mae's closest confidante; the younger girls were Veronica, Claire, and Agnes. Of her brothers, Walter was born just after Mae, and Dennis (called Danny) was the youngest of them all. Mae was sixteen when her father, Michael Coughlin, died suddenly and unexpectedly of a heart attack, but there was still enough money for her mother, Bridget Gorman Coughlin, to remain at home and send the older children out to work, and that was how the household survived. Despite the early passing of a beloved father, the Coughlin house was a happy one, with much laughter and music.

After her father's death, Mae was legally old enough to leave school. Her first (and only) job was the respectable one in the box factory that earned a decent salary, almost all of which she contributed to her family. She knew how to shop on a shoestring, and it helped that she had excellent taste; from her earliest days, she dressed with the style and verve of what was then called a classy dresser. When she met Al, he was eighteen, and he also had a legitimate job in the box factory, but most of his income came from working first for Johnny Torrio and then as Frankie Yale's jack-of-all-trades. He did whatever he was asked to do, and before he married, it allowed him to surrender his entire paycheck to his mother and still have money on the side for his own use.

Like Mae, Al was attentive to his dress, but there they parted company, for his taste was far flashier than hers. She dressed in muted pastels and neutrals, while he favored suits of brilliant colors, sometimes chartreuse or lemon yellow. He came under Frankie Yale's influence when Johnny Torrio recommended him as a good worker to the mobster who controlled the area around Coney Island. Al saw how Yale festooned himself with diamond pinkie rings, tiepins, and belt buckles, and as soon as he had the money to do the same, he did. None of this flashiness would endear him to Mae's mother, Bridget.

Their two-year age difference (Mae, born April 11, 1897; Al, born January 17, 1899) made their attraction and subsequent marriage unusual, for in those years marriages of Italian and Irish girls generally followed particular patterns. Italian girls often married as young as fourteen and usually to older men who had left school at the earliest possible date to begin stable working lives. They were seldom attracted to mere boys like Al who had not set off on a secure path of lifetime employment and who therefore could not set them up in their own homes. Irish girls married a bit later, usually between eighteen and twenty-one, and because Irishmen were slow to marry, they often found husbands among other nationalities, most often English or German. Men of those origins were grudgingly accepted by the parental generation, but when Irish girls began increasingly to accept husbands from eastern and southern European backgrounds, primarily Slavic or Italian, such unions were stigmatized. These brides were still looked down upon by other Irish girls who had succeeded in marrying one of their own kind.

Mae was twenty and a good catch for a nice fellow, but there was a bit of a problem with finding one in her Irish community. Most of the Irishmen in her milieu were well along in their thirties and still unmarried, leaving many of her girlfriends fretting that they might become old maids. It was no fun to be young, vital, and, truth be told, horny. In an era when birth control was risky, so many of the girls in her neighborhood found ready partners among the Italians, Germans, and Croats, whose ethnic enclaves abutted theirs and who were all keen to marry young. For some of these men, an Irish wife meant "marrying up" in social mobility, even though most of their Irish brides thought they were "marrying down," but it was enough for them that these husbands could be counted upon to treat them with respect and give them children. Their parents might have balked at such unions, but for Al and Mae's "American" generation there was a certain thrill attached to the otherness of the unknown.

For Al and Mae, the difference their nationalities made in their social standings was so pronounced as to make their marriage almost impossible. He lived among other Italian families in a crowded apartment above his father's barbershop in a building that was little more than a slum. She lived in a row house on a nice street of other Irish households just like hers, where lace curtains decorated windows that sparkled with cleanliness. He was a poor boy who was aware of the insults leveled against Italians, even though he was so big and tough that no one dared to say them to his face. The kindest slur Italians routinely faced was to be called garlic eaters, but the usual remarks were far uglier.

Although Al's father was a barber who had his own business, it was in an enclave where his only customers were poor Italians like himself. Mae's family was upwardly mobile Irish, well-off and proud of it, and when her father, Michael, was alive, he went to work every day in a starched white shirt to his job as a railroad clerk that brought him into daily contact with "Americans" of every ethnic stripe. Her mother stayed at home and tended to the family, while Al's mother spoke no English and took in piecework and boarders. Mae's mother came to New York from Ireland with her parents and as a young woman went directly from their home to her own without the usual stint as a housemaid. Bridget Gorman Coughlin never worked outside her married home, and the only people who ever lived in it were her husband and their seven children.

Irish girls were often better educated than their husbands, for even if they were not high school graduates, they usually stayed in school until they were sixteen and legally permitted to quit. English was their native language, they were known to keep themselves and their households clean, their children were well disciplined, and like their Italian mothers-in-law they went faithfully to the Catholic church. Also like Italian women, they were deferential to their husbands in all or most things; at least this was the surface impression they gave. Al Capone did not consciously follow this line of thinking about Irish girls, for his views on women, regardless of ethnic origin, were strongly colored by his rounds among prostitutes in the ubiquitous brothels where he collected earnings.

Like that of his brothers and everyone else who had reason to frequent brothels, his attitude was why not sample the wares. The women Al bedded represented many different nationalities and were all trained to be deferential to their male customers, leading him to believe that all women were naturally compliant and complacent. By the time he met Mae, he had been with many women but had never taken the time or had any reason to consider their individuality. Still, he was wise enough to know from the moment he met Mae that she was different.

His initial attraction was to her looks, but when he got to know her, he discovered that she was independent and quick-witted, had a keen sense of fun, and was as attracted to him as he was to her. She liked to laugh and have a good time, and her descendants use words like "spunky," "ambitious," and "fun loving" to describe her, citing how she got herself a good job and loved to go dancing, even if the only places in her part of Brooklyn qualified as dives where respectable girls usually didn't go. Mae loved that Al was as light on his feet and as good at trading quips as she was, but even more she recognized that he shared the qualities of determination and ambition and the desire to better oneself that she had. She found these traits—coupled with his fundamental intelligence—attractive. In later years, long after Al Capone's death, when the man had become an outsized legendary figure, some of the people who had known him during his early years in Brooklyn were asked for their memories of what he had been like as a young man. They told the same general story about him and Mae: that he only looked elsewhere for a mate because he had been spurned by the Italian girl he wanted to marry. In their interviews and conversations, they created a composite of several neighborhood candidates for the girl with whom Al was so besotted that she broke his heart. Al's second- and third-generation descendants find these accounts puzzling, for they have no family stories with even a vague resemblance to this legend. They know of none who could have been the paragon of virtue and beauty these old-timers remember. Mae hardly ever talked to her grandchildren about her memories of Brooklyn, and when she did, she only joked about pranks and escapades and never spoke of other girls.

According to those who knew young Al in Brooklyn, the family of the girl who allegedly spurned him came from a Neapolitan village near that of his parents. Although her parents had settled on the same street in Brooklyn, the story has it that they thought themselves a cut above the Capones, so when Al asked for the daughter's hand in marriage, the father rudely rejected him. As the story has been told and retold over the years, all sorts of details have been added to it: the girl was a great beauty, and her father was a person of substance and such community prominence that Al could not retaliate when his suit was spurned. He was supposed to have become so distraught by the rejection that he became morose and, when he met Mae, was depressed and on the rebound. None of this has ever been substantiated.

Al had indeed developed quite the eye for beautiful women of any age, and no doubt he was aware of anyone who was as attractive as this girl (or this composite of several Italian girls). Some did marry as young as fourteen, but the girl most likely to be at the origin of this story was barely thirteen if that. And for this episode to have fit into the time line of Al's life, it would have had to happen when he was fifteen or sixteen and in no position even to think of taking a wife. He probably did have a schoolboy crush on a nice-looking girl that over the years was turned into a tragic tale of unrequited love that threw him into the arms of an older woman who was practically a foreigner. In reality, Al Capone was not morose and depressed when he met Mae Coughlin: he was enchanted.

Mae, her sisters, and her older brother were so close in age that they all socialized together, and one of their favorite outings was to go to a neighborhood club on Saturday nights where they could have a few beers and dance. Al had learned how to treat women with politeness and respect by watching how Johnny Torrio behaved toward his "American" wife, Ann, a non-Italian from Kentucky of English-Irish descent. Torrio adored her and was famed among his criminal counterparts for honoring her by going home every night to eat dinner and spend the early evening, after which he went back to his social club to check on the nightly take of his bars and brothels.

Al copied Torrio's treatment of women as much as he could, but at first it was in his own clumsy fashion. He had an extra reason to turn on the charm with Mae, for he had begun to work for Frankie Yale early in their courtship and had been in a barroom brawl over a woman that left him with several ragged facial gashes, a sinister visage, and the nickname Scarface that he hated for the rest of his life. He tried never to be photographed in profile and always made sure to turn his head to his "good side," so any photographer who wanted to stay in his graces was swift to cooperate. In those early days, he had not yet begun to use the face powders and other cosmetic cover-ups that he favored in later years, so Mae saw him as he was and loved him anyway.

Torrio passed him on to Frankie Yale, who was born in Calabria as Francesco Ioele but whose name was pronounced so like the famed university that somewhere along the way he adopted the same spelling. Among his other attributes (all of them ruthless), Yale had a warped sense of humor, so when he set up a sleazy bar in Coney Island, he called it the Harvard Club. When he needed a shill to lure customers in, he asked his pal Torrio for a recommendation, which was how the almost-eighteen Al Capone got the initial job, after which he worked his way up to bouncer and finally bartender.

He learned from Yale just as he had learned from Torrio, but unfortunately for him Yale's approach to business was not nearly as refined. Torrio favored mediation, negotiation, and inclusiveness. He used reason to get his way, and if it failed, he let others use violence on his behalf. Yale dealt in brute force, instilling fear in everyone whose lives he touched as he terrorized whole neighborhoods with extortion, protection, loan-sharking, and kickbacks. Torrio was a small man who favored clothes in fine fabrics and quiet good taste; Yale was a big man who liked flashy clothes and jewelry that he completed with thick fat cigars and fedoras. Al admired Yale's clothing choices and made them his own as soon as he could afford them.

And so he went to work in a joint where cheap drinks led to nightly fracases on the tiny dance floor and where violence was the usual response to any real or imagined slight. On the night his face was slashed, Al thought he was paying a compliment to an attractive young Italian girl when he told her she had a nice ass. Her brother, who was very drunk, took it as an insult and thought he had no choice but to defend his sister's honor, even though he was much smaller than the big guy. One story has it that he slammed a bottle against the table and used the jagged edge to slice across Al's cheek. Others have him whipping out a knife to inflict the damage. Some argue that the scars were such that only a broken bottle could have made them because there were three scars and his attacker was too small to have reached him three separate times; others say he threw a chair at Al and, when his legs became entangled in it, whipped out the knife and struck three times.

Afterward, there was no reprisal by Al or anyone else on his behalf because the fellow who cut him was allegedly Frank Gallucio, another low-level employee in the Torrio-Yale criminal axis. Both bosses told Al to apologize for the insult and made Frank apologize for the cutting (however it happened), and the matter ended right there. The scars were real, but how Al got them is still debated almost one hundred years later.

—

Al and Mae were so attracted to each other that shortly after their first meeting they were sexually active, meeting in the darkest recesses of the box factory, as they had nowhere else to be alone. Mae became pregnant, and their first child, Albert Francis Capone, always called Sonny, was born two months prematurely on December 4, 1918, to Mae Coughlin in her family home at 117 Third Place, Brooklyn. She did not marry Alphonse

Gabriel Capone until December 30, and then not in his modest Italian parish but in hers, the large, impressive—and staunchly Irish—St. Mary Star of the Sea. Sonny was baptized there, even though baptisms of children who were conceived before their parents married were seldom permitted, never celebrated, and, if conducted at all, were without prior announcement in the parish bulletin; nor were the parents permitted to invite guests to the ceremony.

In that neighborhood and especially in that particular church, marriages between solidly working-class Irish girls and itinerant Italian men were especially frowned upon, and their different nationalities figured largely in why Al and Mae did not marry until after their only child's birth. Mae's widowed mother, Bridget Gorman Coughlin, was largely responsible for the delay, because she was adamantly against what was commonly considered a "mixed marriage." In the world of her church and her Irish culture, Italians were "colored" and never to be associated with, let alone married. It was a somewhat uneasy pregnancy that resulted in a premature birth, which leads Mae's grandchildren to think that Mrs. Coughlin was so against her favorite daughter's union that she deliberately set obstacles before the marriage, such as making the couple wait to see if the pregnancy would end with a live birth. In that Irish culture, there was always the possibility that if the child survived, it could be sent away for adoption, but both Mae and Al were determined that this would never happen.

Granted, most unmarried Irish-American girls were sent, like their counterparts in Ireland, to "relatives elsewhere" or to a convent where the nuns would quietly arrange for an adoption. All this was very different from the culture of Italian families, where illegitimate babies were often kept in the family even if their birth mothers had to pretend to be their sisters or where babies were given to childless relatives who adopted and raised them as their own.

If Mae's family had been in Ireland, they would have dealt with the shameful disgrace by following the tradition of sending her away until the infant could be adopted. But this was America, and immigrant parents, no matter what the country of origin, found that things were different here, because the values of the old country were often not respected by their children. Mae stayed determinedly in her home, and Al remained in his, hoping that Mrs. Coughlin would relent and let them marry before the child was born. She, in turn, stubbornly held to the belief that something— unspecified to be sure—would happen before the birth. However, there was a certain degree of timidity, if not fear, in her attitude toward Al Capone, who was already rumored to be starting his climb in the hierarchy of the criminal world, and that kept her from insisting on any overt and drastic action.

Even though they were unable to marry, once the pregnancy was recognizable, they managed to court sedately in the Coughlin house but only when Mrs. Coughlin was not at home. Family thinking is that if Mae's father had been alive, he would have permitted the marriage much earlier if only to save face. The resistance came from his widow, who was ferociously protective of her children and the larger reputation of her family within the community. She was in a quandary, because Mae made it clear that despite her mother's objections she was going to marry Al Capone. Of all her children, Mrs. Coughlin was closest to Mae, who was as much her friend and confidante as her daughter. Theirs was an enduring lifelong relationship in which they openly discussed topics that were not usually the stuff of conversations between the generations, and the topic of Mae wanting to marry Al was high among them.

Al visited the Coughlin house throughout the pregnancy whenever Mrs. Coughlin was out, when he was welcomed by Mae's siblings because they all enjoyed the exciting household drama their sister's boyfriend created. When Mrs. Coughlin finally agreed to see him, she was grudgingly tolerant at first, always polite and reserved, knowing of his terrible temper and probably preferring not to cross him. Mae's brother Walter was usually friendly, but he was always on his way out of the house and bent on following his own interests; only her sisters and the young Danny were enthralled by the exotic creature who was her boyfriend, and they usually tried to hang around while he was there. All the Coughlin girls were "musical," so Al's visits were often lively. Al didn't seem to mind if he and Mae were seldom alone on these evenings, for once she became pregnant, she was an object of respect more than a desirable sexual partner. Once her pregnancy began to show and she had to quit her job, Al contributed to the household.

Once Mrs. Coughlin realized how determined Mae was, she employed a new excuse about wanting them to wait until Al's future was more secure. She found another reason to stall the marriage when the United States entered World War I: as a single man, Al had to register for the draft, and he did so in September 1918, when Mae was in the early months of her pregnancy. Marriage would have brought a natural deferment, but Mrs. Coughlin still hesitated until after the baby was born. The marriage finally took place on December 30, almost four weeks after Sonny's birth. With Mae still weak and worried about her sickly baby, and both families uncomfortable and puzzled by the unorthodox union, it was not the happiest of occasions.

Contrary to some accounts, there was no wedding reception afterward, and Bridget and her children, including Mae, simply went home without inviting other friends or relatives (particularly Al's) to join them. Al did not move into a bedroom on the second floor of the Coughlin house until some time later, after his mother-in-law had begun to like him for the charming and attentive husband he was and also for the financial support he contributed to her family, for Mae followed the custom of the time and stayed at home to care for the baby. Al continued to work as a box cutter and do whatever other "odd jobs" he could find, which usually meant carrying out various tasks for the gangster Frankie Yale. Most likely, claiming the extra money came from vaguely described odd jobs was his way of keeping what he was really doing from his mother-in-law, and perhaps his wife as well.

Al loved Mae and demonstrated his affection with sweet talk and as many gifts as his limited financial circumstances permitted, but once Mae Coughlin became Mrs. Al Capone, there was a major change in their relationship: Al may have rejected an Italian girl as a possible wife, but he still held to the values Italian-American men expected from the women they married. For him, the vivacious and sexually active girl he fell in love with was expected to morph into what he believed should constitute respectable married behavior. The sexually attractive partner with whom he conceived a child somewhere within the darkened recesses of the box factory had to be treated as someone else entirely once they were married. The eager lover who had perhaps stopped just short of being a whore in his bed had to become a Madonna, and the fallen woman who bore her child out of wedlock became the revered angel in his house.

From mid-1918 to the end of 1919, Al's whereabouts and activities are not entirely clear. This was the period when some biographers and historians of crime say that he lived alone and on his own, away from his mother's home and Mae's. He was supposed to have taken a job in Baltimore before he and Mae were married, but exactly if or when he was there and how long he stayed are uncertain. The only point on which his many biographers agree is that if he did indeed go to Baltimore, it was the only "honest" job he ever held, as a bookkeeper in the legitimate construction business owned by Peter Aiello. It was probably the reason why he did not move into the Coughlin house immediately after the marriage, when Mae and the baby stayed there while he went back to Baltimore.

If he did go so far from home, some of his brothers' descendants who are old enough to remember their fathers' accounts believe it was because he took his responsibilities as a husband and father seriously and bookkeeping was a well-paying profession. Years later, long after Peter Aiello's death, his elderly son said his father often praised Al as a good and well-liked worker, one who arrived every day in white shirt, tie, and suit. In the firm's business office, he learned the intricacies of the double-entry system and polished the mathematical skills that he put to good use for the rest of his criminal career. Who knows how long he might have stayed there on the straight and narrow if his father had not died suddenly in 1919.

Chapter 3

———

THE NEED TO MAKE A LIVING

Gabriel was one month short of his fifty-fifth birthday when he died in November 1919, and, in a term of the times, had been in poor to middling health for a number of years. His shop had become relatively prosperous, and he now employed two assistant barbers, which allowed him to take his time arriving in the late morning and to leave in the early afternoon. His main activity while in the shop was chatting with customers as his assistants cut their hair, and he also spent a lot of time at his social club next door. It was there on November 14 that he collapsed and died of a massive heart attack, said to be from "chronic myocarditis" on his death certificate. Although he had had minor attacks before the one that killed him, they had not been severe enough for him to be hospitalized, so his death, though not entirely unexpected, still came as a shock.

Al rushed home from Baltimore as soon as he heard the news. Ralph came from Manhattan, where he was living with one of the succession of women he took up with after his first wife left him (five years had to pass before they were officially divorced). Frank was still technically living at home, although he spent most of his nights elsewhere; only Mafalda and the three younger boys, Erminio (Mimi or John), Umberto (Albert), and Amadoe (Matty), were still living under their mother's care. Mimi had quit school and was drifting sporadically from one occasional odd job to another, while the three younger children still went to school. Albert attended until shortly after his father died, using the death as the excuse to quit and find work to help support the family. He was a timid boy and the only brother who was relegated to the fringe of the world of gangs and rackets and who spent his life plodding from one legitimate (or semi-legitimate) low-paying job to another. Matty and Mafalda did go on to become high school graduates, and Matty even attended Villanova University for a while, but both only stayed in school because their big brother Al set a high value on the education he never had and insisted that they had to finish.

Teresa weathered her husband's death with dignity and equanimity. She did not change her routine in any way, keeping to her usual rounds of churchgoing and food shopping, nor did she make any attempt to learn English. Like most Italian matriarchs, her approach to life was based on the security of knowing that her sons would take care of her. Al immediately recognized that he would have to take full responsibility because his two older brothers could not be counted on to bring home the regular paychecks that were needed to keep the household afloat.

Ralph had his own rent to pay, his son to provide for, and the grandiose expenses of high living he incurred from entertaining women and gambling. He did hold a series of daytime blue-collar jobs but depended on his illegal connections for much of his income, and the tasks they sent his way were often low paying and sometimes far between. Frank's income came from the same sources, so it, too, often varied. Al had the only steady job, but besides his Baltimore expenses he had Mae and a sickly baby to support.

Al was a typical Italian boy who loved his family and needed to be in their midst and did not like being away from home. The death of his father gave him the excuse he needed to return, so he went back to Brooklyn and to Johnny Torrio and Frankie Yale. Al Capone needed a steady and good-paying job in a hurry, and they became the immediate answer to his needs.

He thought of moving Mae and Sonny into Teresa's apartment, but Mae quickly disabused him of that idea, and their first home together was a bedroom on the second floor of the Coughlin house. From the very beginning, there had been constant friction between Mae and her mother-in-law, and it only increased as years passed. Teresa spoke Italian to Mae—when she spoke to her at all—and she and the very young Mafalda formed a phalanx of two who scowled at or ignored the attractive blond foreigner who had been plunked down in their midst by their beloved and revered Al. Mafalda especially resented the woman she thought had usurped her place as the "spoiled brat family princess." All her brothers doted on her, but Al was the one she adored.

Mae did make several attempts to learn to cook Italian dishes, but she soon gave up trying because it was clear she was not wanted whenever she attempted to enter Teresa's kitchen. While they lived in her own mother's house, all Mae's attention was focused on Sonny, who was often cranky with colds and serious ear infections that required frequent (and expensive) doctor visits. Mae did not know it then, because she did not yet exhibit signs, but Al had infected her with syphilis, and she had passed it on to her child. It was not until they were living in Chicago that her symptoms erupted and she sought treatment at the Mayo Clinic.

Once back in Brooklyn, Al worked full-time for Johnny Torrio, which meant that he was out every night, often staying away from Mae for several days if not whole weeks at a time. Both in Brooklyn and then in Chicago, Torrio religiously went home for dinner every night, and Al tried but usually did not succeed in doing the same, so he made sure to telephone both houses every day, as much out of respect for his mother as out of love for his wife. Mae knew that he always called Teresa first because he would tell her Teresa's news of each member of the family, particularly of Mafalda, who liked to grab the phone as she approached her teen years.

Mae festered in silence, but she was canny enough to allow such slights to pass without comment or retaliation, signs of weakness that might get back to her in-laws and give them pleasure. She was secure in her husband's love and respect and knew how special she was, so she simply waited her turn. She also knew that one of Al's jobs was to collect money from Torrio's brothels and to make sure that the prostitutes did not get out of line, but if she knew that he routinely sampled their wares, she also kept that to herself. She made sure there were no arguments between them that he might inadvertently mention to Teresa for Mafalda to overhear. Even after they moved to Chicago and had separate phones installed in their house's two apartments, Al always phoned Teresa first.

Mae said nothing, and Al did not change his ways. They had overcome so many obstacles just to be able to marry that once they were man and wife, there were too many other, more serious issues they needed to resolve. The first was where, when, and how they would set up housekeeping, because the Coughlin house was bursting at the seams, but even more important was the question of how Al would support his little family on top of the larger extended one for which he had assumed major responsibility. He was just twenty-one, husband to a wife who wanted her own home and father of a sickly baby; Al Capone was a son, husband, and father who was looking for the best way to become a good provider for everyone. It was soon clear that the easiest route to financial stability was not through box factory or bookkeeping jobs, nor was it as Frankie Yale's bouncer. That route would come through Johnny Torrio, who valued young Al Capone's work and made it easy for him to go where he was wanted and appreciated.

————

Torrio was a gentleman, and although he was never a father, he was a model husband. He was an excellent role model, even a mentor, for an unformed, uneducated boy who wanted to become a good man, and Al Capone was soon working for him full-time. It was a symbiotic relationship that prospered from the start: Al needed someone to look up to, and Torrio needed someone he could trust. Torrio was branching out, and that meant more and greater responsibility for Al. Mae went along for the ride, and so did all the other Capones.

Torrio's frequent trips to Chicago had begun around 1909, when his reputation as a mediator and facilitator reached his cousin Victoria Moresco, and her husband, Giacomo "Big Jim" Colosimo. She was "the premier madam" of the crime- and racket-ridden area of Chicago known as the Levee, where she owned around one hundred (or somewhat fewer) brothels, and he, a much younger man about half her age, owned a restaurant that was a front for the rest of the graft and corruption that made them rich. But they were only one of the many gangs in the Chicago underworld, and what they controlled they wanted to keep. They contacted the Fox (as Torrio was nicknamed) after other gangs had the temerity to try to extort them, and he soon became everything they needed to keep their particular gangland empire secure. After Torrio had masterminded several murders and other less drastic forms of persuasion, Colosimo put him in charge of all his operations.

Realizing that Chicago provided a much larger arena than Brooklyn, Torrio decided to make a permanent move. However, when Big Jim balked at Johnny the Fox's plans for expansion, Torrio continued his usual pattern of keeping himself above the fray and quietly imported Frankie Yale from Coney Island to ensure his takeover. On May 11, 1920, Big Jim was murdered in his restaurant in broad daylight while his staff bustled about its business before the opening hour. There were so many workers rushing back and forth, and yet—what a surprise—no witnesses were found who dared to testify against Yale. He went back to his Harvard Club in Brooklyn, and Torrio got busy taking control of Chicago, from the highest levels of city government to the lowest of the mom-and-pop rackets.

The saga of how Torrio insinuated himself into Chicago gangland and how Al Capone became his successor has been told in fairly straightforward fashion by a multitude of biographers, historians of crime, and sociologists. They have all used the same public information, that is, newspaper stories, public records, government documents, and legal testimony taken from depositions and transcripts of court trials. All these accounts differ in some of the details, and arriving at the truths of what happened, and when and how, has never been absolute, but a good deal of truth can be found in the broad strokes.

At the start of his Chicago years, Torrio left Capone behind in Brooklyn to work primarily for Frankie Yale. Soon Capone was being entrusted with more and different responsibilities because he never hesitated to bash heads on Yale's behalf. From the prostitutes and other employees in the brothels to the bartenders at his pool halls and saloons, anyone who dared once to try to short Yale on money owed or protection paid knew better than to try it a second time while Al Capone was on the scene. His mere presence was enough to frighten people, especially after he was implicated in at least one murder with rumors of his complicity in several others, none of which could be pinned on him—again because no witnesses dared to identify him.

He was seemingly impervious, until he made the mistake of beating Arthur Finnegan, a low-level worker in Yale's rival gang, the Irish White Handers. Capone was making his rounds to collect money when he encountered Finnegan, who made insulting remarks about Irish girls who married Italians. Capone lost control and beat him so severely that he was hospitalized and close to death. A higher-up in the gang, Wild Bill Lovett, let it be known he was out for revenge and would kill Al Capone on sight. Lovett was a sharpshooter decorated for bravery in World War I, a psychotic who would murder without the least provocation, so this was a threat to take seriously. Yale was at war with the White Handers, and he knew retaliation was a certainty. He did not want to lose Capone, so he insisted that for the young brawler's own good he relocate to Chicago to work for Torrio and hide out until things cooled off. Both men thus ensured Al Capone's complete loyalty by saving him from certain assassination.

Al immediately recognized that Chicago offered a step up in the Torrio organization as well as the opportunity to live at last as a married man in his own household. But the domestic benefits didn't enhance his tough image, so he conveniently elided them when, in later years, he created the saga of how and why he left Brooklyn. Al claimed to reporters that he took all his worldly possessions: a change of clothes and $40. He did not add that he also took his wife and infant son. Once he got to Chicago, he did find a small apartment on Wabash Avenue, where he was not so lonely (as he claimed) that he had to send for Ralph and Frank. Quite soon after he and Mae were settled, he did send for Ralph, but only because he found it difficult to carry out all his duties for Torrio and needed help. Ralph came at once and moved into the tiny apartment with Al, Mae, and Sonny. After Ralph and Frank moved out, Al found a larger apartment for himself, Mae, and Sonny, where they lived for the better part of a year. Mae claimed it was one of the happiest periods of her life; it was small and not grand, but it was hers. Al was already looking for a house that would hold his entire family, which he found in 1922, the one on South Prairie Avenue that would hold them for the rest of their lives. By late 1921, Frank had come with two of the three Fischetti cousins, Rocco and Charlie, and they all went to work for Torrio; Al wanted his mother and the rest of her brood to come also, and by 1923, all the Capones were living there.

Many years later, when Al Capone was at the pinnacle of his criminal career, an interviewer asked him what impelled him to leave everything he had known all his life to go halfway across the continent and to a city he then regarded as the equivalent of a foreign country. He began his explanation by speaking first of Sonny and Mae, telling how he "loved [them] dearly," before inventing the story of how hard it had been to leave them behind in Brooklyn. He claimed that he knew he had to do it because if he disobeyed Torrio by refusing to go, he might have lost his job and would have had no means to support his family. He did not speak of how Torrio gave him enough money to bring his family with him, nor did he speak of his role in the Finnegan beating as the actual reason why he had to leave town. He did not even hint that this assault might have gotten him killed, in which case Mae would truly have been left with nothing. Thus, he was able to create a myth as he claimed one simple reason for going to Chicago: the need "to make a living." He told the truth, however, when he added that he was very young and filled with the brash self-confidence of youth, and "I thought I needed more."

Once he got to Chicago, his rise was spectacular: "Capone would go from a $15 a week mop boy (and occasional whore beater) to one of the most powerful and wealthy men in the world in a mere six years." His ascent in mobdom was phenomenal, his time at the top sensational, and his downfall meteoric. Indeed, his reign did last only six short years, but everything that happened in that brief time still commands worldwide attention, interest, and speculation.

What was there about Al Capone that captured so many different kinds of imagination? Some lives contain multitudes, and Al Capone's would seem to be one of them.

———

Chapter 4

AL COMES TO CHICAGO

l Capone began his life in Chicago, the "land of bilk and money," managing some of the brothels Johnny Torrio inherited after he arranged for Frankie Yale to get rid of Big Jim Colosimo. He was still several years away from (as a longtime Capone watcher put it) the "maneuver of the fates that made [him] the most influential man in Chicago . . . with the vast ramifications of business and industry paying tribute to him." In the beginning, his chores were much the same as they had been in Brooklyn; he collected the prostitutes' earnings, kept the books, and ensured that the premises stayed clean and ran smoothly, which meant he was often a combination of janitor, bouncer, and busker—the guy who stood out front and hustled the johns to come in and sample the wares.

He worked alone until Ralph arrived and Frank followed with the two Fischetti cousins. Only Al ran the brothels, with Ralph as his chief assistant. Among the girls he managed, Al was alleged to single out certain prostitutes who were not required to meet the same quotas as the girls he did not fancy. Some were as young as fifteen, and one in particular was his favorite. She was said to be dark and of Greek descent, and he allegedly made her dye her hair platinum blonde because he had indulged in several brief affairs before her, all of them with blondes. Mae found out, and in one of her most angry retaliations, she embarrassed him in front of his entire family; when he came home for Teresa's Sunday dinner, Mae met him in the dining room with her lovely brown hair dyed the same shade of blond as his new mistress. She kept it that color until she was old and it turned white, and his only comment, ever, was to say she looked lovely.

In most accounts that tell of this first known (and allegedly one of his longest-lasting) mistress, he was said to have taken the fifteen-year-old Greek girl out of the game and set her up in her own apartment, where he kept her for years until she found a man to marry her and moved away.

Most of the writers who have studied Al Capone's life and career hint at this liaison with the Greek girl, but none have provided any foundation for its veracity, so it continues to be another of the legends surrounding him. Most likely, he did consort with the girls he managed, keeping one (or more) in particular until he became bored, or the girl got too old, or something happened to make her quit the business. However, even though he made good money from the beginning, it was not enough in the early days to have kept even a single mistress in the manner the legends convey. And besides, he always kept his eye on the main prize, which in this instance was amassing enough money to bring his mother and the younger siblings to Chicago.

Despite his real or imagined appetites for prostitutes, Al Capone's managerial work was first-rate, and by 1921 he was promoted to work in Torrio's flagship, the Four Deuces, nicknamed for its address at 2222 South Wabash Avenue in the South Side Levee district. Here, he put his bookkeeping skills to work and began the first of the obfuscations designed to elude every government agency from tax collectors to law enforcement, this last group particularly active since the start of Prohibition. There was a brothel on a floor above the Four Deuces, but Capone wanted to distance himself from public connections with it; even though it was one of his most prosperous businesses and he had no qualms about frequenting brothels, he wanted to be known as a respectable businessman. At a fundamental level, he despised prostitution and was ashamed of his involvement with it. In later years, he flew into ferocious rages when anyone tried to question him about it, and reporters soon learned not to pursue that line of questioning.

Working in Torrio's headquarters marked the beginning of the financial creativity Capone employed for the rest of his business career. He needed a front to explain what he did for an occupation, so he had several different business cards printed up. One was for Al Brown, "Second Hand Furniture Dealer," and it covered the few shabby pieces he moved next door into the street-front store at 2220 South Wabash. He also had another printed for "A. Brown, M.D." with an address at 2146 South Michigan Avenue. He set up a waiting room and filled it with various medicinal bottles and supplies, but no one was ever there, and no office hours were ever held. Eventually, he had no use for these sham enterprises, and all that remained of them was the pseudonym he used from then on, Al Brown. When both buildings were raided several years later, confiscated materials revealed that they were the Torrio organization's financial headquarters.

———

Al Capone had risen quickly in his new profession, and now that he was earning good money, he was able to bring everyone to Chicago. Teresa came, leaving the only neighborhood she had ever known without fear or protest, for now that her husband was dead, the custom was that the eldest son became the new head of the family and the widowed mother had to bow to his every whim or will. In this case, however, succession passed to her fourth but most gifted son, whose duty it was to support her as hers was to obey him. So they all could live together, Al bought the large two-family house at 7244 South Prairie Avenue for the then-grand sum of $5,500 (approximately $77,000 in 2015). Each floor held a self-contained three-bedroom apartment with a full bath, kitchen, and living and dining rooms. The basement contained a multitude of rooms outfitted with beds that were used by men who worked for Capone as well as members of his extended family.

Because of the stairs, Teresa moved into the ground-floor unit, where she continued her role as the matriarch to whom all the other women in the family deferred. She (and later Mafalda when she was old enough) never hesitated to let Mae know that she might be Al's wife but they were in charge of the household. When Ralph brought his longtime mistress who became his second wife to the house, and Albert (Bites) brought his first wife, they, too, were ignored and never allowed to prepare any of the dishes served at the family's elaborate Sunday dinners. The first wives of Ralph and Albert were Italian, but they were quickly divorced, and subsequently not one of Teresa Capone's sons was married to an Italian girl. Even if they had been, she would have treated them as dismissively as she treated the "American" wives they brought to her home.

As for Mae, she became a great reader who sat with her novels and kept her mouth shut. For every criticism Teresa aimed her way, she sailed serenely past it. There was only one barb Teresa knew better than ever to level at her daughter-in-law, and that was about how she was raising Sonny. Mae made it clear that she was fully in charge of her son, and if anyone dared to challenge her, she could be instantly ferocious. Sonny was growing into a sweet child with a cheerful disposition, and Teresa did love him, so there was never a problem on this front. There was, however, a serious concern over Sonny's health. He was a sickly infant who grew into a school-age child felled for long periods of time by every childhood illness that struck him. Recovery was always so slow that he did not attend school until he was going into the seventh grade. Until then, Mae arranged for private tutors to teach him at home. Because they were together all the time, mother and son forged a bond that endured throughout their lives.

Of the brothers, Ralph and Frank did the most serious work for Al, while John did whatever chores he was assigned. John had no interest in school or in any profession and was content to do whatever did not bring notice or attention his way. Albert was the slow and steady one who eventually found a series of low-level quasi-legitimate jobs and stuck with them for most of his life. He was always a part of the family's ritual Sunday dinners and holiday celebrations but always on the sidelines, listening and saying little.

With the two youngest siblings, Al not only ordered Matthew and Mafalda to stay in school, he made sure they got good grades and behaved themselves. He, who quit school at the first opportunity, was unlike most Italians of his generation, for he believed in education as the way to succeed and he made it clear that he expected them to graduate from high school. Beyond that, he held no ambitions for Mafalda except marriage, but he was determined that Matty would be the first American Capone to go to college and graduate. Sonny was still a small child when they moved to Chicago, but Al was already envisioning the same educational path for him.

Al bought the house on Prairie Avenue before the Capone women had a chance to see it. He quickly had bars installed over all the windows that might have allowed easy access to potential assailants, and he had a sturdy garage built for the car he later had reinforced with steel plating. He was also alleged to have had an underground tunnel dug between the house and the garage so that he would not have to walk outside in rain or snow, but none has ever been found. Reporters who wrote those stories hinted (but never actually mentioned) that he had it dug to avoid the possibility of drive-by assassination attempts, for this was his home and his family, and they were always sacrosanct and separate from his business endeavors.

No one in the family had any interest in gardening or landscaping, so the exterior of the front of the property was barren except for one mid-sized tree, and there was never a single tomato or basil plant out back, let alone an actual garden. The house was simply there, existing in a curiously impersonal setting, giving no indication of the hobbies, interests, or occupations of those who lived inside it. It was sold shortly after Teresa died in

1952, but to this day the exterior looks the same as it did when the Capone family lived there.

In their several moves throughout Brooklyn, they always lived on the fringe of an Italian enclave, but in Chicago Al moved them into a quiet middle-class neighborhood in the heart of the city's South Side. They were the only Italians on a street where their neighbors were mostly upper-working-class families of Irish and German origin. Most of the residents owned their houses, and census records revealed that the street was home to a Scot who was a Presbyterian minister and quite a few policemen, which added a touch of irony to Al Capone's choice of where to place those he loved most.

As the years in Chicago passed, Al Capone became flamboyant in every other aspect of his life, but where housing was concerned, he remained low-key and discreet. He never thought of moving to the fashionable sections of the city or building a showy suburban estate; 7244 Prairie was his first and only home in Chicago. His family was safe and secure there, and he knew that no matter how long his business—for no matter how unsavory that was what he called it—kept him away from home, he could still telephone every day and be assured that some part of his life was under control and progressing in a smooth and orderly fashion.

Over the years, stories have circulated about the Capone family's neighborliness, of how Al played ball in the backyard with Sonny or how he invited neighbors in to eat the spaghetti doused in sauce that he cooked himself or to drink the good wines that he served all through the Prohibition years. There are even stories of how Teresa and Mae would borrow the proverbial cup of sugar from neighbors and how they socialized with many of them, or how Mafalda rode a bike (which she never had) up and down the street. These are all nice and warm stories, but they are not true. When it came to foodstuffs, the Capone pantry was always fully stocked; if anyone borrowed sugar, it might have been a neighbor who was curious to know what went on in the only house on the street that had bars on the windows and big black cars with tough-looking men lounging around them out front or in the back, where Al Capone always had one poised and ready to go in case he had to leave in a hurry. Any neighbors who rang that particular doorbell would have had to be very brave as well as very curious.

———

Whenever he was asked what he did for a living, Al insisted, "I am a property owner and a taxpayer in Chicago," and at least a part of his contention was true because he always took care to pay the property taxes on the house, and the annual real estate taxes in Cook County (the primary means of funding the public schools) have always been substantial. Prohibition brought violence and anarchy to the streets of Chicago, and from 1923 to 1925, as some of the most vicious gang wars and killings roiled the city, it was also engulfed in periodic cleanups by so-called reform administrations. These led the ever-astute Johnny Torrio, always the mediator, to make major changes to protect his interests when rival gangs ignored his philosophy that vice provided enough money for them all to profit. Ordinary citizens thought it a dull day if they did not wake up to news in their morning papers of violent killings, booze hijacks, and smashed stills, and in this climate Torrio decided to move his headquarters out of the city and into the suburb of Cicero, a factory town settled by immigrants from Bohemia. Residents were an upstanding mix of mostly Catholics and a sizable contingent of Protestants who kept two cemeteries (one for each religion). The locals did not tolerate prostitution until many years later, but many were already dedicated gamblers even before Torrio got there. Basically, it was wide-open and ready for corruption, and best of all it was a town where workers liked their beer and drank plenty of it.

Chicago's city government consisted of approximately three thousand voting precincts grouped into fifty wards, where committeemen worked for the elected politicians and dispensed patronage, and were thus the natural recipients of kickbacks and bribes. Gus Russo put it succinctly in *The Outfit*, his history of crime in Chicago: "For the gangsters, this translated as 'we'll get you elected, and we don't even want jobs. Just look the other way when we do our thing.'" And, Russo added, "that's just what the pols did."

Torrio did some traveling in these years, some of it for pleasure, but most of it to keep himself alive when other gangs started gunning for him. Gradually, he began to cede authority to two of the Capone brothers, Al and Frank. He put Al in charge of the day-to-day running of the operation in 1924, when he and his wife took his mother back to her native Italian village. She, who had left in penury and sailed in steerage, returned home on a luxury liner to live as the richest woman in the area when he installed her in a villa that took three dozen servants to staff. While Torrio was in Italy, Al took care of enforcing policies that kept rival gangs and possible miscreants in line; he put Ralph in charge of whatever physical enforcement was deemed necessary, and Frank became his front man for all things political.

Al had set up headquarters in Cicero's Hawthorne Hotel, and from there Frank handled payoffs and bribes to officials in Greater Chicago that ensured their cooperation in allowing the Outfit to function with impunity. "Vote early and vote often" was the phrase that suddenly came into widespread usage, and as Frank and his minions succeeded in rigging every election, the Capones were well on their way to securing control of all of Cicero for Johnny Torrio. As for Al himself, in the words of Phil D'Andrea, one of his faithful bodyguards, "he was a Republican when it fitted his clothes, I guess, and a Democrat otherwise." D'Andrea acknowledged that Al, his brothers, and all his men "played both sides of the street . . . whoever was in, that is where they . . ." He left the rest unsaid.

Johnny Torrio was much the same. He recognized that the solidly Bohemian population of Cicero was against every vice he offered but beer and gambling. He knew that once he installed a slate of public officials who would look the other way, the good citizens of Cicero could mount far less opposition than what he was up against in Chicago, where those with civic influence had the money and the media control to fight him. All went well for him and the Capones in Cicero until a young man who "burned with the reckless optimism of youth . . . set out to make a name for himself as a journalist." Robert St. John was a young writer twenty years old when he persuaded a business partner to provide modest financial backing for the weekly paper they started in 1922 and christened the *Cicero Tribune,* its name a nod toward the far richer and more powerful *Chicago Tribune.* From the start, St. John's intention was to reflect the population of "good, law-abiding citizens who simply wanted their beer" and were "very much against crime and prostitution and gambling and all the rest of it." St. John, as a crusading editor, thought it was the right time and the right place "for a newspaper that would be on the side of the people and against the Capones."

Al Capone, who was busy positioning himself as the businessman Al Brown, did not take any kind of criticism lightly, particularly when it was personally embarrassing. Every time St. John uncovered and printed a story about his bribes, threats, and intimidation, the editor could be sure that he or his reporter would suffer some consequence. If the story even mentioned that he was a brothel keeper, retaliation was swift and severe. There was so much harassment that the paper had "a big turnover of reporters," who nevertheless were successful in turning the population against Capone's machinations.

There was a primary election scheduled for April 1, 1924, and Al Capone and his cohorts had mounted a complete slate of candidates, all of whom they controlled and all under the aegis of the Republican Party. When it looked as if the townspeople, all solidly Democratic, were going to thwart his ambitions to take over city government, Al unleashed his famous temper against his brother Frank in front of his followers and some reporters. He launched a tirade of obscenities and thundered that Frank would be responsible if his slate was defeated.

Frank, who learned well from Torrio, always operated behind the scenes with mediation rather than force. He was the quiet and self-effacing brother who dressed like a prosperous businessman, content to get things done discreetly and away from public scrutiny. Now Al was screaming at Frank, telling him the only way they would gain complete control of Cicero was through political influence, and Frank was not doing enough to ensure it. He told Frank to get the streets cleaned up and paved, get other public works started, do civic good in every facet of community life, and, above all, to make sure it all got printed in the *Tribune*'s rival paper that was his mouthpiece, the *Cicero Life*. It was an extremely smart move that soon garnered public goodwill as various projects got under way, all of which Frank engineered with enough bribes to make sure the bidding was rigged and handsome kickbacks would come to the Outfit.

On the eve of the election, despite the *Cicero Tribune* writing about every crooked ploy Al Capone planned, it looked as if he would get away with it and his slate would be elected. The *Chicago Tribune,* following the lead of its tiny neighbor, exposed the happenings in Cicero for the larger metropolitan readership and concluded that the election would be dishonest and blood would run before Election Day was over. It did, indeed, as Democratic precinct workers were beaten up and some even kidnapped so that they could not do their jobs. The Capone henchmen stood by the ballot boxes to inspect ballots before they were deposited, and if the voter had not voted for the Capone slate, he was threatened with a beating until he changed the ballot or else left without casting a vote. Women, who were eager to use their newly won franchise, were either turned away if they went quietly or shoved aside and threatened if they did not. As the day went on, word of the Capone chicanery reached Chicago, where the mayor was urged to send police to restore an honest calm. Eventually, a contingent was dispatched, but not in uniform or official cars. Instead, they wore plain clothes and used the same black sedans driven by the Capone men and every other gang.

What happened next was both a comedy of unfocused behavior and a tragedy of confusion. Nearly everyone who wrote about Al's role in the shoot-out after it happened also wrote about Frank's death, and many different versions of so-called truth resulted. Most writers agree that between nine and a dozen plain black sedans just happened to drive down the street Frank Capone was attempting to cross. They were driving swiftly in single file, so when the first car screeched to a halt and all the others braked behind it, Frank—no doubt instinctively—reached for his revolver. Before he could get it out, he was hit by the gun blasts of so many plainclothes policemen that even though first one and then several others claimed to be the man who shot Frank Capone, his body was so bullet-ridden that any of them could have claimed the dubious honor. Herbert Asbury, an early historian of Chicago's crime, has Al, seeing that Frank is dead, racing down the street toward another group of policemen, "gun blazing in each hand," firing and fighting them off "until darkness came to his aid and he escaped." No other writer risks such drama in his writing, but there is no question that whatever response Al made, Frank's death was devastating for him.

Al Capone's slate won the election after a day of bloodshed in which, besides Frank, several of his other men were killed. Two ordinary citizens were also killed in the rain of bullets, but their deaths were mostly ignored; the only debate was the one that raged over Frank's death. He had been arrested some time earlier than the day of his death for carrying a concealed weapon, but a judge friendly to the Capones overruled the decision and permitted him to carry it for the euphemism of "his own protection." Legal inquiries were begun, leading to the first time Al Capone was summoned to testify about a shooting.

He identified himself as Al Brown, the used-furniture dealer whose brother Frank was a law-abiding businessman who did carry a gun, but only for his own protection, and who was in Cicero that day not to influence the voting but to see about a real estate transaction. When a coroner's jury was convened, the police insisted that Frank pulled his weapon while resisting arrest so they had no option but to shoot him. The final verdict was in their favor, as a justifiable homicide.

Al, always swift in retaliation against other gangs, bided his time after his brother's death. Now he was the sole Capone brother fully responsible for the many different facets of his daily life, from supervising his entire family to running the ever-enlarging Torrio empire. Cunning became his weapon of choice. One of the earliest observers of gangland Chicago, Edward Dean Sullivan, was correct in calling Al Capone "an unusual 'hood.' He has concentration and executive ability beyond the ordinary. He is utterly fearless except when it is sensible to be afraid."

———

Torrio, who despite the ruthless way he earned money, still managed to live a life of discreet dignity, had nevertheless run afoul of other criminal outfits. After the horrific effect of the turf wars that raged among rival gangs throughout the early teen years and culminated in the murder of Dean O'Banion on November 10, 1924, Torrio knew there would be retaliation attempts against him by the Moran, Weiss, and Drucci factions, so he wisely left for Hot Springs, Arkansas, a congenial place where the local populace looked the other way as mobsters hid out until the heat was off. When word filtered down to Torrio that he was a target, he kept moving, from Florida to Cuba and the Bahamas. While he was gone, just to let him know they were not easing up on targeting his gang, there was an assassination attempt, but at Al Capone as he was entering a Chicago restaurant for lunch on January 12, 1925. He fell to the floor and escaped the fusillade of bullets that riddled his car parked outside. It was the first time the Thompson submachine gun, colloquially known as the tommy gun, was used in gang warfare, and Al wasted no time acquiring what became his weapon of choice.

After the attempt on Al Capone's life, Torrio thought it meant the heat was off his and returned to Chicago several days later. On January 24, when he was coming home from a celebratory shopping expedition with his wife, their arms loaded with large and expensive packages, they did not pay attention to the big sedan that careened down the street in their direction. Hymie Weiss and Bugs Moran jumped out and wounded Torrio's driver before shooting Torrio in several places on his upper torso. Always courteous to women, the shooters ignored Ann Torrio who was lying on the ground, covering her head and screaming. Moran stood over Torrio, preparing to shoot him in the head with a .45, but it either jammed or— even worse in this comedy of errors—ran out of ammunition. There was enough other traffic on the street to distract the two frazzled would-be killers, so they drove off, expecting that Torrio's wounds were so severe he would die of them. But he did not die: he was rushed to a hospital where he spent a month recovering, all the time honoring the code of silence and not identifying the clumsy assassins.

This marked the second time Capone was called to testify before a committee convened to investigate a shooting. In an extremely sloppy and error-filled copy of his testimony, his name was recorded as Alphonse Caponi. When asked for his line of business, he said he sold antique furniture in a store that had no name, with a partner named Sol Van Praag, whose name was never heard again. Capone exaggerated when he said he had been in Chicago for five years, living before that at 18 Garfield Place in Brooklyn, where he had been a "paper and leather cutter." He perjured himself when he said he had only known Torrio "for three years," claiming they met "in Chicago at the race track" and did not see each other again until "the Bennie Leonard fight in East Chicago, about three years ago." The interviewer asked if he knew various other gangsters: Of the Costello brothers in New York, Capone said, "Only Frank," to whom he was introduced in a restaurant on Broadway; of Jake Guzik, who worked for Torrio and to whom he was close, he lied and said, "Not personally but I have seen him around." Asked if he knew the Genna brothers, Mike Merlo, Louie Weiss, Vincent Drucci, and a host of his other gangland opponents, Capone replied no to each name.

As for himself, he painted the picture of a business and family man, claiming he was at home for Sunday's midday family meal, and on Monday, when his furniture store was closed, he "went around the neighborhood and did some shopping." He "heard about" the Torrio shooting, which happened on "Tuesday," (he misspoke: it was a Saturday) when he was on his way to buy tickets for the movie *White Cargo*. He "just happened to pass" Al Bloom's cigar store, where "everyone was talking about it." He said he phoned the hospital and went to Torrio's room, where he found him "getting along nicely," but when the interviewer asked if they spoke in Italian, he contradicted himself and said no, because Torrio "was in no condition to talk." The interviewer pressed to see if Torrio had told Capone the names of his assailants, and he said no, adding that he had no idea who had done it.

The entire testimony from start to finish was a pack of lies except for the last exchange, when the interviewer asked, "Would you tell us if you did know?" "No," Al Capone replied. "I value my life too much to tell if I did know."

For the next month, Capone showed his muscle by stationing round-the-clock armed guards outside Torrio's hospital room and by sleeping there every night on a cot shielding Torrio's bed, facing the door with guns in full display. Hospital staff were terrified to enter the room but apparently too cowed to suggest the mobsters leave the weapons elsewhere or at least put them away. Capone was still in charge when the fully recovered Torrio left the hospital and was taken not to his home but to the courtroom. There, he was sentenced to spend the next nine months in the Lake County jail at Waukegan for an earlier arrest for operating a brewery. He passed the time in a cell his wife furnished with luxuries and came and went as he pleased to the sheriff's house, where he dined well and which he made his own while entertaining visitors. Capone took careful notice of Torrio's luxurious prison life and copied it fully when his own jail time came some years later.

He was there when Torrio was released at the end of 1925, first to escort him back to Chicago and then to see him on his way to a discreet and exceedingly comfortable retirement (so called) in the Westchester suburbs of New York. And then he took charge of the Outfit, as the Torrio organization was called. Al Capone was almost twenty-six when Torrio decided to step out of the limelight and put him in charge of a multimillion-dollar enterprise. It was not clear and easy sailing, for Capone had become a natural target, busily fending off everything from rumors of or actual assassination attempts on himself.

Al was still stunned by the senseless situation that led to Frank being gunned down in broad daylight and on turf he supposedly controlled. He was enraged with everyone who played a part in his brother's murder but could not help but blame himself for the circumstances that caused it: the clumsy attempts to take over Cicero's city government. After Frank's spectacular funeral, where all of gangland competed to send the most elaborate flower arrangements, Al took careful note of who paid homage and how visibly (and expensively) they displayed it, even as he was already bent on a revenge far greater than simple retaliation. His revenge would come in the form of absolute power, first in Cicero and then throughout much of Chicago, in everything from criminal activity to political authority. During the next six years, he would get that power and wield it, turning himself into the best-known and most flamboyant citizen of his adopted city. How he did it made him a legend far beyond his actual lifetime.

Chapter 5

——

THE OTHER CAPONES

There was already a family named Capone in Chicago several decades before Al and his clan arrived, and he, alone of all his brothers, became exceedingly close to them. These Capones came from the neighboring village of Acerra and were among the dozen or so young, single, and possibly indentured men who boarded the *Trojan Prince* in Naples in 1903. They gave "laborer" as their profession and said they were going to Chicago to live with a "cousin on Taylor Street." Subsequent generations joke that "every Italian who came to Chicago had the same cousin on Taylor Street," and no one really knows how they might all have conjured up the same fictitious address.

Two other men from Acerra who were related to that branch of Capones by marriage were directly responsible for how they came to choose Chicago as their final destination. Vincenzo Tufano was different from the others with whom he sailed: a single man who, like Gabriel Capone, could read and write and whose family was well enough off that he could book passage on the simple whim of wanting to see the New World; he had enough money that if he didn't like it, he could book return passage to go home at the earliest opportunity. It was different for his friend Vincenzo Piccolo, who arrived with him on March 11, 1903. Piccolo was also single and had no relatives in Chicago but was simply following his friend and fellow villagers in search of the glorious opportunities that earlier immigrants exaggerated in their letters to those they left behind. His initial reality soon became a life the same as theirs, of the same backbreaking day labor whenever he could find it, a series of exhausting days ending with miserable nights in a crowded boardinghouse in a dangerous part of town. One year later, his life had stabilized, and although the work was still hard, at least it was steady. Vincenzo was able to write truthfully when he urged his cousin Gennaro Capone to join him and to be assured that he would help him to find both work and a home.

Gennaro Capone arrived from Acerra on March 4, 1904, on the *Napolitan Prince*, was cleared at Ellis Island, and immediately boarded a train for Chicago. One year later, on May 8, 1905, his brother Raffaele sailed on the *Italia* and also made his way from Ellis Island to Chicago. Although they came from a large family and had numerous other brothers, they were the two oldest and the only two who immigrated. Eventually, they brought their widowed father to Chicago, but after that, except for an occasional sporadic letter, they soon lost touch with the family members who stayed behind. The other men who came from Acerra between the years 1903 and 1905 were all in search of steady work and a better life, but that was not Raffaele's reason, for, according to some family legends, he had the distinction of being the first Capone to settle in Chicago as a way to avoid going to jail.

Raffaele had the most dramatic immigration story of this branch of the Capone family. To begin with, it was unusual for him to be living in the same house as Vincenzo Tufano, for according to the traditions of the old country Raffaele had dishonored the Tufano family. Raffaele's father was Gennaro Capone, and his brother, the eldest son who preceded him, had the same name. The father Gennaro was a poor landless peasant who alternated working in the fields of others or doing odd jobs in the village. All his sons seemed destined for the same station in life, but Raffaele was ambitious on two separate fronts and wanted more. His descendants all agree that he had worked his way up in the world of that small village by sheer persistence and determination, but beyond that there is no agreement on why he had to leave.

Some insist he was an apprentice to the local police; others say he was learning to be a baker or pasta maker (as Gabriel Capone had been); still others are unsure of what he actually did but swear that whatever it was, it paid a steady income. It was not, however, enough money to convey sufficient social status for him to have looked once, let alone twice, at Adeline Clotilde Tufano, a beautiful young woman from a higher social class. That didn't stop him, for as soon as he saw her, he knew he wanted to marry her.

The story goes that she noticed him noticing her but never let on, for she was already betrothed to a young man whose station matched hers and far exceeded Raffaele's. Clotilde (as she was known) was the pampered daughter of a father who had "something to do with the legal professions," either as a courtroom lawyer or as a senior magistrate, perhaps even as a senior regional commander in the police. Here again, different family stories abound, and there are no Italian records to substantiate any of them. Her parents intended that Clotilde would enhance their status by making an excellent marriage, and they kept her in school beyond the elementary level. To ensure that she would become an ornament to her husband, she learned how to keep a fine home and had been trained in the arts of playing the piano and singing. She had a beautiful soprano voice, and all her life boasted that she took lessons from the famous opera singer Enrico Caruso's teacher, who encouraged her to make a career in the opera. She liked to tell her grandchildren that she met Caruso once and he encouraged her, too. These grandchildren, all elderly now, agree that she was indeed beautiful, particularly noted for the thick dark hair that became white in her old age, when her two daughters and several granddaughters competed for the privilege of brushing it every day. As she walked carefully chaperoned through the streets of Acerra, the graces of her upbringing were evident, and in such a closed society most men of Raffaele's background would never have tried to court her. But their attraction was mutual, and he and Clotilde were soon finding ways to meet. A secret courtship progressed until someone eventually tattled to her father, who forbade the lovers ever to meet again.

Family legend has it that when Clotilde's official suitor learned about Raffaele, he felt it necessary to defend her honor and challenged him to a duel. Here the legend is spotty: Raffaele either wounded the man severely or else beat him to death with his bare hands, so he had to flee Acerra and hide out in Naples until he could arrange passage to America. There is another legend as well, and his descendants tell this one with wonder in their eyes and voices, that Raffaele did indeed beat the suitor quite badly but had to flee for another reason: In this version, another man figures, an ordinary customer of the bakery who so enraged Raffaele by refusing to pay his bill that he picked the man up and threw him into the bakery oven, burning him alive. In that story, he left the village in darkest night and got on the first boat leaving Naples. His grandchildren like this version best because it fits so well with the personality they grew up hearing about, of a man who could turn thunderous and violent when provoked, whom everyone respected and no one dared to cross, not even Al Capone. But there is another, simpler story that the family laughingly shrugs off, probably because it is the one most likely true: there were no beatings or murders; Raffaele merely came with the other men from Acerra, lured by the dream of making a fortune so he could return home and claim Clotilde, who had promised to wait for him.

Meanwhile, Clotilde, bereft at his leaving and angry with her father for whatever part he played in Raffaele's departure, took to her room and refused all the ministrations designed to make her marry the proper suitor and rejoin the life of her family. Whether the man to whom she was officially betrothed had been involved in these attempts differs according to which version of the family history is being told, but what is verifiable is that less than a year after Raffaele's departure, on April 18, 1906, the ship *Prinz Oskar* arrived at Ellis Island from Naples and Clotilde Tufano was on board. She, too, traveled directly to Chicago, giving as her destination the mythical address on Taylor Street and the name of her real sponsor, Vincenzo Piccolo, in whose house her brother Vincenzo Tufano was now living. Raphael (as he was now spelling his name) was living there as well, and on December 18, 1906, she married him.

Several months after their marriage, Raphael and Clotilde Capone were living in their own house at 727 Morgan Street, where he had set himself up as a "storekeeper." The store, such as it was, consisted of a small collection of dusty olive oil cans on some shelves in the house's living room. His grandsons remember their fathers telling stories of how puzzled they were as small children whenever some men or an occasional woman wandered in, for there was nothing for them to buy. Nevertheless, this was Raphael's declared profession, and it was how he supported his growing family, and comfortably at that.

All Raphael's stores in Chicago were set up as legitimate businesses that had the requisite permits and paid the proper taxes, but they were also places where large sums of money could move swiftly and easily from one conduit to another. It was during the early months of 1920, just before the start of Prohibition, that he met Al Capone and began the association that forged a deep friendship and a bond that was perhaps based on something closer than sharing the same name or having mutual business interests, one that Al Capone honored and made use of for the next several decades. Men would arrive in Raphael's stores carrying heavy suitcases and packages and leave without them; others would arrive empty-handed and leave with them. When Prohibition went into effect, the store had a steady traffic in brown paper and cloth duffel bags, as well as a steady stream of Italian housewives who came to buy the increasing variety of so-called imported foods that were really supplies used to make illegal alcoholic beverages.

By the time of the 1920 census, both the business and the family had expanded, and they were living in a larger house at 1507 Flournoy Street. Their household included the five sons and two daughters to whom Clotilde gave birth in rapid succession. The eldest bore his grandfather's and uncle's name, Gennaro, which became Americanized to January or Jann. He was followed by Anthony (Tubby), Philomena (Phil), John, Annunziata (Nancy), Joseph (Pip), and James. The household was enlarged to nine children when Raphael and Clotilde took in another Philomena (called Fanny as a child and Phyllis as an adult) and another James (nicknamed Big Boy). Their father was Raphael's cousin and another Vincenzo Capone, a wife and child beater who had been deserted when his battered wife seized her third child, the infant daughter Annunziata (also called Nancy), and in fear for her life ran off to live with a man who took her to New York. She left behind the two older children, who never saw her again and never looked for her after they were told by their enraged father that she was dead.

This Vincenzo Capone treated his two children cruelly, sometimes locking them into a rat-infested cellar while he went off to work or to a bar to drink himself drunk. Raphael heard them crying one day when they were locked in the cellar. He was a man of exceptional kindness to all children, so he took them to his home and told their father never to try to see them and especially never to try to take them. He and Clotilde raised them with the warmth and love they showed their own children, and Fanny and Big Boy grew up amid cousins who were like siblings to them.

Soon after he took in the children, Raphael needed a bigger house and also, because of his ties to Al, a bigger store, so he made another move, to Flournoy and Laflin Streets. There were slightly more cans of olive oil on the shelves, and a few imported vinegars joined them, so Raphael could now claim the import business as his legitimate occupation. Soon, his acumen in evading Prohibition and serving the alcohol needs of the community made him a respected figure there and beyond. It brought him an exceedingly attractive job offer that the family believes did not come directly from Al, but when he learned of it, it came with his approval. It also came with some unwelcome attention.

The firm of Balaban and Katz, known as B&K, was famous for the extravagant and ornate movie theaters it built all over the greater Chicago area starting in 1916. For those they were building in the southern parts of the city, they needed someone who could speak the Italian language and keep the workers in line, and in the early 1920s Raphael was offered the plum manager's job. Here, the story takes on several interesting aspects.

It was well-known throughout the community that the Torrio organization was shaking down at least $1,000 per week from every one of the B&K theaters, a practice that continued for years after Al Capone took charge of the Outfit, and that both gang leaders always put their people on the inside to make sure the money was ready for the collector. Raphael was ready to accept the job when the first of the Black Hand letters arrived on his doorstep.

In the family lore, the letters were sent anonymously but were all of a kind; the usual demands for "protection" payments for the family grocery store now carried an additional warning: that Raphael should not work for Jews nor should he hire any. Also, that he should stay with his own people in his own little neighborhood and not hold a job that would take him above his station and away from it. The prejudice against Jews was real in the Italian-American community, but it was the latter part of the warning that was the strongest and most important.

Richard Gambino, in his authoritative study of Italian-Americans, quotes the proverb "*Chi lascia la via vecchia per la nuova, sa quel che perde e non sa quel che trova*—'Whoever forsakes the old way for the new knows what he is losing but not what he will find.'" It was an illustration of the Italian peasant's rigid adherence to *l'ordine della famiglia,* which Gambino translates as "the family system" and explains as "the unwritten but all-demanding and complex system of rules governing one's relations within, and responsibilities to, his own family, and his posture toward those outside the family." Loyalty to the family and the individual's responsibility for it always came first; toward all other aspects of society, be it ethnic identity, employer, or even the neighborhood where he lived, the American-Italian was expected to behave as if he were still in Italy, with his responses to outsiders filling "a spectrum of attitudes ranging from indifference to scorn and contempt."

Here again, as when Raphael persisted in courting and marrying Clotilde, he showed that by his willingness to contemplate a step outside tradition and take a job in the larger world, he was ready to adapt, to change, and to move beyond the age-old traditions of the family system. However, it was not an easy thing to do. Whether he paid this first (and comparatively small) attempt at extortion or not, he did decline the offer from B&K.

Al must have allowed him to do so, for shortly afterward he was offered another job, this one as the president of a new bank that was being funded by a local group of prosperous Italian-Americans. This offer came shrouded in secrecy and myth, which his descendants attribute to "something not on the up-and-up," adding that Al Capone was probably behind this offer. Raphael was no stranger to things that were not what they seemed, but in this case the unsavory aspects of the offer were more than he cared to entertain. Although there is no documentation to substantiate it, some of his descendants think these might have been his earliest business encounters with the Torrio organization, probably through Al, who had become Torrio's trusted spokesperson.

Once Raphael declined the bank offer, he moved his family again, a little farther west to Congress and California Streets, where he set up a store that was both "controversial and confusing," according to his grandsons. It was an actual business with real inventory, but "other things" went on there as well, and one day a fire of mysterious origin burned down and destroyed both house and store. "This was not the 'Cow Fire,'" his descendants like to say, but it was big enough that the family lost everything.

Still, even though they kept moving, Raphael was not entirely overthrowing the Italian traditions of the old country, for every move he made was a small one that kept him in the same environs: the move to nearby Flournoy and Laflin was only several blocks away from Taylor Street, and Congress and California was at best only double that distance. They were in this general area until 1927, when Clotilde became so sick with what her children and theirs called "stress" that Raphael, who adored his wife, gave in and moved the family out of the city, farther west to the town of Freeport, far from the centers of bootlegging Al Capone had by that time established in Cicero and Berwyn. There was never a store in the large Freeport house with its six bedrooms and multiple bathrooms, but Raphael still gave his profession as importer, and wherever his income came from, there was always enough money to support his family in gracious comfort.

The reason Raphael Capone completely bypassed Cicero and Berwyn first for Freeport and then to move even farther west to Rockford was that Clotilde's "stress" had its origin in his business dealings, and over the years a great part of what he did became tied up with Al Capone and the Outfit. By the time the family had its last store, the thirteen-year-old Philomena had left school and was working there as a clerk, while the boys who were old enough stocked shelves and delivered the occasional box of groceries. Mostly, however, they ran other mysterious errands that took them to different parts of the city, ferrying everything from bets on horse races to money collected from various extortions. Sometimes they even delivered booze-making supplies to families who were unable to come to the store for them.

None of this met with Clotilde's approval, but she was extremely fond of Al, and that made it difficult for her either to condemn or to condone how her family life was moving into a world beyond her comprehension or control. The move to Freeport was intended to calm her fears and worries, and for two short years it did, even though the friendship with Al Capone grew stronger and he and his men were frequently in her house. And then something happened that put her forever in his debt.

Anthony, called Tubby, was becoming an adolescent when he suddenly disappeared one day. He had been kidnapped, and no one knew by whom, although family lore credits the same small-time Black Hand gang that had been trying to extort Raphael for years, one composed of old Italian men who were permitted to operate because they posed no threat to the major gangs that were engaged in much larger criminal wars. Tubby was gone for almost a week when Raphael turned to Al for help. The next day, the boy walked back into the house as if he had never been away. Al came along a bit later and told them not to ask questions, so they never did.

The family's response was typical of Italian-American behavior in those years: if there was any kind of documentation pertaining to the kidnapping, such as a letter with the famous black ink handprint that gave this particular brand of extortion its name, it was not saved; a paper document was something that might be damaging to the family and therefore best destroyed, as it had always been in Italy. Also, there was a code of silence within these families: there were many things best not talked about, things better left unsaid. Tubby had come home safely, and that was all that mattered. From childhood on, he too maintained the code of silence. If he ever talked to his brothers about what happened, they did not pass the stories on to their sons, who are now the elders of the family. And so what happened to Tubby was known by everyone, but why he had been taken and what happened while he was gone were never discussed. What they did talk about was the heroic part Al Capone played in getting him back. In this branch of the family also named Capone, Al became larger than life, and Tubby's kidnapping was the first step toward the creation of their personal myth about him. There is always reverence when they tell this part of their family's history.

As the myth of the powerful and invincible Al Capone was building, there is another family story of reverence and respect, but this one is about Al's for Raphael. Al was often away from Mae for long periods of time when he was first in Chicago, and without her to keep him in line, he was not an attractive fellow. He dressed badly and behaved worse. Always boisterous and sometimes belligerent, he was a violent drunk and a frequenter of prostitutes. Raphael did not approve of Al's public and professional behavior, but he knew better than to criticize him directly about it. However, when it came to how he behaved in his personal life, it was another thing entirely. When Al treated people who respected Raphael like a boor and a bully, they complained to Raphael. He did not appreciate someone who shared his name exhibiting such gross behavior, and he issued several admonitions that Al ignored.

One day, when the big black sedan that bore Al and the men who now acted as his bodyguards pulled up in front of the house, Raphael was waiting for him, seated in the living room with a heavy cane in hand. Al entered, preceded by one bodyguard and followed by two more. He greeted Raphael respectfully, but Raphael did not reply. Wordlessly, he stood up and beat Al about the head and shoulders with the cane. The bodyguards moved in at once, but Al simply raised his hand to stop them, then bowed his head and stood there as Raphael struck several more blows. When he finished, he and Al sat in silence for a while before beginning to discuss whatever business had brought him to the house, as if nothing untoward had happened.

Most of the older children were there, not actually in the room where the beating took place, but close enough to hear it, and although this story has doubters among those who study Al Capone's life and crime in Chicago, Raphael's descendants swear that it happened. Unlike Tubby's kidnapping, they talked about this event for years, filled with wonder that their father had the nerve to strike Al Capone without being punished for it. First they told the tale among themselves, replaying every nuance as they argued, offered theories, and agreed or disagreed over what had happened. Not content to let it rest, they repeated the tale with all these ramifications for their children. Eventually, everyone in these two generations came to tell the story of the beating in the same way, with the same language, the same inflections, and the same gestures. And now the third generation coming into middle age also tells it that way. Most recite it as a factual text, a rote memory without the dramatic intensity of their fathers and grandfathers but with the exact version of the details, the highlight being that Raphael was the only man in Al Capone's life (or his legend) who ever laid a hand on him and lived to have his third-generation descendants tell about it. Here again, it was another example of behavior according to Italian tradition: Raphael never spoke of what provoked his outburst, so his family can only speculate about what caused it.

Al Capone was a frequent visitor throughout the time Raphael's family lived in Chicago and during their first several years after the move to the large Freeport house. They were always happy to see him because he brought baskets of good things for them to eat, including lots of candy, which Clotilde usually restricted unless Al took charge of dispensing it himself. The two smallest children, Fanny and Big Boy, were thrilled with the "dollar" Al always gave each of them, but it took several years before they understood why Clotilde always swooped in and took the money away the moment he left: Al always gave each child a $100 bill, telling them to "go buy some ice cream."

After Al greeted the family and they engaged in the ritualistic consumption of food and drink—usually coffee, pastries, and anisette, for his visits were often unannounced and took place in midday or after dinner—the children were always shooed upstairs and told to stay in their bedrooms until Al and his men were finished with business. They still remember the clump of heavy shoes as Al's men went up and down the stairs, from the dining room to the hallway closet that held the usual towels and sheets but also some mysterious business ledgers and brown paper packets that they now believe concealed money. Soon after that, the doors to the dining room closed, and if any of the children dared to risk their parents' wrath by going down to the kitchen on any pretense, they would see Al and the men bent over the books and talking intently. Raphael sat quietly and nodded from time to time, but the moment Clotilde and the teenage daughters Phil or Nancy (who were allowed to sit in the kitchen with their mother) spotted the younger children, they were sent running back upstairs. When they grew to adulthood, they all insisted that their house was where Al kept one of his several sets of "real" account books, and they like to speculate that their set was the one that was most truthful.

Raphael made frequent trips into Chicago on what his grandchildren remember their fathers calling "his weekly pickup." They don't know what this was, but in March 1929 it took a deadly turn. This is how the grandchildren tell what happened: "When he got as far as Elgin, he '*died*' [their emphasis, complete with air quotes]. The official death certificate said he was forty-seven years old, his occupation was 'none,' and the cause of death was 'heart failure, lung failure, kidney failure.'" But when his sons went to claim his body for the undertaker, they saw that it was riddled with bullets. "Yes, it's true," they told their own sons, "if you are shot like that, your heart, your lungs, and your kidneys do give out, and you do die from heart and lung and kidney failure."

It was around the time of Raphael's death that questions arose among his sons about why Al Capone was so devoted to their family. He still came to the house for the next several years, sometimes to hide out from the press and the law, but usually to bring baskets of food and candy and dispense $100 bills to the children. Even though the children were old enough to have left school, there were few jobs during the Depression, and Al Capone became the major support of Clotilde and her family. Their children explain it today by saying, "There were five grown men in this family, and none of them really worked. And the family always had enough to eat and the mortgage got paid, and no one ever wanted for anything."

That was when the other rumor surfaced that has since haunted this branch of the Capone family. Clotilde told her children, and they in turn told theirs, "You don't know how close you are to Al Capone, and you must never tell." Naturally, they wanted to know what she meant, but she never explained until she made them swear to "the Oath," as it has come to be known in that family. Several weeks after her husband was buried, she called her five sons, two daughters, and two wards together, so everyone crowded into the dining room where the doors that were usually open to the living room and the kitchen were tightly shut. On that day, the glass bowl filled with wax fruit on the crocheted doily that usually graced the extra-large table between meals was not there; instead, there was a Bible, strange to see for a Catholic family not much given to reading the holy book. In fact, some of them wondered where it came from because no one remembered who had brought it into the house or when.

The widow took an unaccustomed place at the head of the table, which, since her husband's unexpected demise, was always reserved for the eldest son, Gennaro (Jann). She told the others to gather around her, and they all shuffled somewhat uneasily into positions dictated by their age and station within the family. It was clear that something ceremonial, highly unusual, and therefore important was about to happen, even though there were no candles, no incense, nothing except the Bible.

Adeline Clotilde Tufano Capone spoke little English, so Jann got right to the point. "We are here today to take an oath," he said as he described what was about to happen. "What we say here today will never leave this room. None of us will ever speak of it again." He then put his hand on the Bible and instructed all the adults to do the same. His four brothers, two sisters, and the two puzzled wards all murmured some form of assent, but there was no other conversation. Everyone stood up and began the business of leaving, the dining room doors were opened, and the mid-afternoon business of the household resumed.

No one present that day really talked about what happened in that room even as the story of "the Oath" took on mythical—and mystical—importance over the years. It was not until eighty years later, in the first decade of the new century, that the youngest generation of this particular Capone family, having endured painful years of taunts, derision, and ridicule for bearing the name, demanded to know just what exactly "the Oath" was, why it had been sworn, and what it meant for those living three or four generations later. The relationship to the famous (or infamous) gangster still haunted them, and his name still carried such resonance that strangers often greeted them with hands formed into machine guns with accompanying ack-ack sounds or with snide comments about mobs, the Mafia, and hidden money. For the several generations who had prospered in legitimate businesses and professions, this was not a welcome association; rather, it was an ongoing embarrassment.

Only one person who was in the dining room in 1929 was still alive in 2015, and only she has revealed what was said there. Her relatives persuaded her to tell, and she insists that she has told them the truth, but the problem is that she has told several different "truths," all of them contradictory. In some versions, she said it was something that happened between Al's father, Gabriel, and Raphael in the old country that created a lasting bond their children were required to honor and respect in the new. In some versions, the closeness between Al and this family was because Teresa Raiola and Clotilde Tufano were related in some way, so their connection had to be honored by their children. But the last and most persistent family myth given as the real reason for "the Oath" was that one of Raphael and Clotilde's "sons" was actually the illegitimate son of Al Capone, brought into their family by him and raised by them on his behalf. The two younger sons in particular, Joseph (Pip) and James (Jimmy), were much more like Al and unlike their other brothers in physical appearance. When Pip, the middle son, lost his temper, he would tell his five sons "you don't know how close you are [to Al]," a maddening taunt that has haunted them all.

And yet, in all these rumors the only verifiable truth is that Al Capone continued to visit this family and use their house until he went to prison and after that his men continued to bring food and money until the end of Prohibition, clumping up and down the stairs between hallway and dining room as they went about his business.

Chapter 6

THE ROAD TO POWER

Al Capone's spectacular rise to leadership of the Outfit meant that he could not take one step in public without it being a hot topic for a world suddenly hungry for celebrity gossip. Communication was swift and easy in the 1920s, when everything desirable fell under the general rubric of the "modern." Even in the most isolated hamlets across America, people could listen to radio broadcasts that connected them to the larger world; small towns had one and sometimes two daily newspapers, and many major cities had at least half a dozen or more; it was the golden age of magazines, and most little towns had a public library. As for the many writers who earned their daily bread by writing for the "pulps" (or making up stories if the facts were too dull), what sold best was glorified grit and glamour, and that included criminals as well as movie stars. After Prohibition went into effect, booze runners, politicians, café society, and speakeasy habitués became grist for this mill. If the high living they portrayed was far removed from the daily struggle of most Americans, the media preferred to turn a blind eye to reality and concentrate on feeding them a steady diet of dreams, which was what most of the public wanted anyway.

Al Capone was tailor-made to fill newspaper column inches and radio minutes—no, actually much more—reams and hours of print and sound. Everyone knew his name, and it conveyed equal measures of envy and fear. By 1926, when he was twenty-seven and in control of the Outfit, the gross income taken in from rackets and vices was estimated at a conservative $105 million a year (approximately $1.377 billion in 2015). The Outfit had to meet a weekly payroll of approximately $300,000 (about $4 million in

2015) to cover salaries for a thousand or so men. It also had to factor in another steady stream of payments lumped together as "official graft disbursements" for public officials, elected or appointed. And Capone did not stint himself; by 1929, when he was thirty, his estimated personal net worth was over $40 million (approximately $550 million in 2015). Like so much else in his life that he compartmentalized, he threw his money around in public but spent much of it tastefully and thoughtfully in private.

He liked to make a huge splash at Matty's and Mafalda's schools at holidays and Christmas, lavishing baskets of gifts and goodies and arranging entertainments for faculty and students. Although both his siblings got decent marks, neither liked school and they did not make friends, but Al insisted that they had to graduate from high school, and they dared not disobey him, so they did. When Mafalda graduated from the Lucy Flower Vocational High School, there was no question of her going to college or getting a job; Italian women who were fortunate to have brothers or fathers to support them did not do such things. She stayed at home waiting for a husband to come along, all the while complaining bitterly that she never had a boyfriend and would never marry, because no one "would dare to go out with the sister of Al Capone."

Al was responsible for Matty's enrollment at Villanova, a Catholic institution outside Philadelphia, because he insisted that from then on, there would be educated (male) college graduates in the Capone family. Matty was uneasy in the strange new environment and unhappy to be away from his mother's ministrations; he enrolled in 1930 and lasted the better part of an academic year until he was arrested for driving without a license. It's not clear if he left or was asked to leave, but he went back to Chicago and the welcoming bosom of his family and the less-welcoming world of the Outfit. Al let it be known that he did not want his kid brother coming to harm, but Matty hung around, so Al gave him unimportant and relatively safe jobs to do, even as he made sure to keep the boy carefully on the fringes of whatever was happening in the increasingly violent gang wars.

Al bought a grand piano suitable for the concert stage and put it into the Prairie Avenue living room, even though no one in the family was interested in playing it. Matty and Mafalda had neither talent nor interest; Sonny had some lessons but used the hearing impairment that resulted from his ongoing ear infections as the reason it was too difficult and soon gave it up. Al loved music, particularly opera, and he tried to learn to play so he could sing arias along with it, but he, too, gave up the piano when he found he was more comfortable singing along with his mandolin. And besides, he was at home so seldom there was simply not enough time for learning through piano lessons.

Although there was not much change in his demeanor once the entire family was in Chicago, he did make a noticeable change in his dress, albeit exactly the opposite of Mae's. She kept her life intensely private, staying quietly at home except for weekly Mass and an occasional shopping foray. She made no friends in the community and depended for companionship on then-expensive telephone calls to her sisters in Brooklyn and their occasional visits, which she paid for. She and Sonny attended Sunday Mass regularly but in the early Chicago years almost never with Teresa, who always went to the earliest Mass while Mae chose a later one. Mae was easily recognized in the church, and some of the now-elderly children of parishioners remember their mothers saying she was a lovely and gracious lady who always kept to herself. She greeted everyone warmly, but other churchgoers were cautious with their responses. It was the same when Sonny was twelve after his homeschooling ended and he attended school; he made some friends, and when his mother came for events, everyone was courteous but distant, and no one attempted to befriend her. So Mae had to find pleasure in other things, and one of the most satisfying was shopping.

Mae engaged the personal shopper at Marshall Field's department store who specialized in helping rich women select the most prestigious lines of clothing, and soon she was wearing only designer dresses and the finest accessories. Usually, they were packed and sent to the house for her approval, but every once in a while she went to the store for private fashion shows, bundled in hat and veil and, in cold weather, wearing furs with collars that covered her face. She always had several fur coats at any given time, and unlike her husband, whose taste in jewelry was vulgar and flamboyant, hers was quietly exquisite. Everything she did, bought, or wore was designed to keep herself out of the public eye, while her husband's clothing was exactly the opposite.

He had a new nickname now, Snorky, which in the slang of the era translated loosely as a "swell" or "sharp" dresser. He would order a dozen custom-made suits at a time, costing a total of $5,000 or more (around $66,000 in current dollar value), but unlike Mae, who preferred soft colors and earth tones, he chose suits that were lime green, lemon yellow, and even lavender. He preferred them double-breasted because he thought they made him look taller and slimmer. His overcoats were a tad more discreet, usually dark-colored cashmere or camel's hair, while his favorite custom-made fedoras were pale pearl gray. The joke around Chicago was that no one else could wear that color for fear of being arrested because it was so closely associated with Al Capone. He always used a tailor at Marshall Field's department store, Oscar de Feo, who remembered filling orders for twenty suits and topcoats for Al, along with multiple suits for four or five of his best friends at the time. He wore a diamond pinkie ring, and depending on who told the tale, it ranged from 4.25 to 11 carats. He also sported huge diamonds in his tiepins, cuff links, and belt buckles, and he was fond of giving diamond-studded belt buckles to anyone who caught his fancy, particularly members of the media. His pockets were always filled with wads of money, big bills that he dispensed with brio, again to anyone who caught his fancy or told him a sob story.

It is often difficult to discern the truth in the sob stories that became embellished over the years with each retelling. One that was told so often it took on flourishes of mythological proportions was a tearjerker, but its details were basically true: Al Capone was indeed in a restaurant on a cold winter night when a shivering, soaking-wet newsboy asked him to buy a paper from his large unsold pile. Capone bought them all, paying the boy what amounted to several weeks of a workingman's salary, and told him to go home, get warm, and give the money to his mother. And, he concluded, the boy had to promise to go to school the next day and every day thereafter.

As Capone's power and influence grew, and concurrently his fame, there were many more stories like this one, many of them created by people who had not been there. There were witnesses for this one because it happened in a restaurant, but many other anecdotes grew from situations where the only witness was the person telling the tale. When stripped of their flourishes and exaggerations, most of them turn out to be true acts of kindness that passed into history because the recipient told anyone who would listen time and again about Al Capone's generosity.

As for Capone himself, he did such things for a number of reasons: First, they were the right thing to do within his culture. Certainly, he flashed wads of money in public and loved the adulation (and the positive publicity) it brought him, but there was also the upbringing he got from good and decent parents who taught him that the Italian (and Italian-American) way was to show quiet generosity to those who needed it. In his case, the generosity was often flamboyant and on a grand scale, but it was still sincerely given.

As the decade unfolded, the public violence in Chicago was like nothing the country had ever seen, but on Prairie Avenue things for the most part were progressing smoothly, at least on the surface. The Capone men were almost always absent, and the women had made accommodations among themselves so that the household was for the most part tranquil. They managed this by trying hard never to be in the same room together when the men were not around. Peace reigned because they stayed in separate parts of the house. Although she managed to hide her true feelings most of the time, Mae never really got along with any of the Capone siblings, nor they with her, and as the years progressed, she was skillful in managing various family dramas to make them end with no clear winners or losers and everyone saving face. Al was the revered patriarch and the major support of their family, and his word was law, so everyone took care to coexist as peacefully as possible.

The women hid the ongoing friction because the role each one played allowed her to assume a primary place within the familial structure. Mae was *Mrs.* Al Capone, and she expected that her status as Al's wife meant deference would be paid to her; Teresa was *Mama* Capone, and tradition dictated that she, as the Italian matriarch of the family, would be revered and her demands and desires within the home respected. Mafalda, who sided with her mother completely, played the role of the family's privileged princess who never hesitated to let Mae know she was an "American" (non-Italian) outsider. It was always two women pitted against one in an ongoing battle of wills.

As for the brothers, Mae was firm about what she wanted from them and was sophisticated enough to manipulate them into doing her bidding even as she kept what she thought of them to herself. She told no one within the family that she held them in contempt as hangers-on who were nothing without Al. It was not until years later that she confided in Al's doctors that she never got along with any of them and that there was "more or less constant friction" in all their interactions. How much of this Mae told her husband remains between them, but Al was shrewd, sharp, and insightful, so he probably knew most of what went on in the Prairie Avenue house, in part because Teresa usually told him everything, especially his wife's real or imagined sins.

No matter where he was, Al Capone made his daily telephone call to the women, either at noon, which was when he usually woke up when staying in one of his hotel hideouts after a long night of debauchery and drunkenness or secret Outfit strategy meetings. If he didn't telephone when he first woke, the women knew he would call around their dinnertime (which was early for him; he had probably just finished lunch). Mafalda usually grabbed the phone and passed it to Teresa, thus irritating Mae, to whom it was passed only when Teresa was good and ready to let her have it. Al knew their moods and could recognize Teresa's smugness and Mae's resentment just by listening to their voices, but he was a good Italian son and, in his way, a devoted husband, so he usually humored his mother and cajoled his wife back into good humor.

As for his siblings, Al's concern for their welfare had become ferociously protective, but when it came to his son, his love surpassed all that he felt for everyone other than Mae. She shielded the boy from learning about his father's profession for as long as she could, but that did not last long, for even very young children learned early how to taunt and bully a weaker playmate. Sonny was frail as a young boy, and his ongoing illnesses and hearing impairment made him an easy victim of teasing, which intensified over the years. By the time he was twelve, he had become physically robust enough for homeschooling to end, but attending a school presented new difficulties. Al was in despair over what the boy faced each day: "I can't tell you what it does to my twelve-year-old son when the other school children, cruel as they are, keep showing him newspaper stories that call me a killer or worse." There was nothing he would not do for Sonny, but there was little to be done in this situation.

All through these years, Sonny was his mama's boy, and for his own protection she seldom allowed him to be seen in his father's company. Keeping him out of the public eye was the deliberate strategy his parents hoped would protect him from ridicule or worse, because Mae had an almost irrational fear of kidnapping. She was determined to shelter Sonny and keep him as far away as possible from his father's profession; it was around this time that she began to use the sentences that became a mantra in later years: "Your father broke my heart. Don't you break my heart, too. Don't do anything like what he did."

Speculation was that Sonny stayed close to his mother because he was too puny to follow his father, that if he had been robust and healthy from childhood, Al would have played more of a role in his upbringing. However, the illnesses that began when he was a toddler became a steady stream of ear infections and mastoid problems from the ages of five to eight. In the days before antibiotics, surgery was often the only treatment option, but there was a very real fear that it could seriously damage his hearing, possibly resulting in deafness itself.

Here again, there are different stories about what Al decided to do about Sonny's medical treatment. In one, he feared that doctors in Chicago were not up to the job after most of them refused to treat the boy, saying his case was so severe that the only outcome would be total deafness and they did not want such an outcome to damage their reputations; in another, all the Chicago doctors Al contacted were so frightened of what he might do to them if the operations were a failure that they all painted the dire possibility of deafness as a way to ensure that they would not have to accept Sonny as their patient. No doubt both stories are partially true, leaving Al to seek treatment for his son elsewhere. He, who dealt on a daily basis with shootouts and assassination attempts, disregarded all the horror stories of what could happen to the Outfit if he went elsewhere to take charge of Sonny's treatment; he left Ralph and Jake Guzik in charge of business and with several bodyguards hulking in the background boarded a train for New York with Mae and Sonny, who was in the throes of a crippling ear infection so severe that neither parent could stand to see him in such pain.

They took him to New York in December 1925, where a Dr. Lloyd, who had an office on St. Nicholas Place in Harlem, agreed to do the necessary surgery. Rumor had it that Al was so distraught over the boy's condition that he offered the doctor $100,000 to save Sonny's life; the truth was that the boy's life was never in danger, only his hearing, and Al offered and the doctor was satisfied with his usual fee of $1,000. Sonny's children believe their grandfather offered the doctor "a generous bonus," but whether he did and whether the doctor accepted one remain in the realm of speculation. Sonny did lose most of the hearing in his left ear, but the surgery was successful enough that although he still had painful earaches from time to time, they were never as severe as the attack that had his father courting serious danger to his person in order to get the boy to New York.

Sonny grew into a healthy and cheerful young man but a shy one, which his daughters later attributed to his unease about his inability to hear clearly. For one who had been too sickly to attend elementary school, he thrived in high school, where he got good grades and became a good golfer and an excellent marksman. In his early adulthood, he took prizes for his shooting abilities, an irony that did not escape the press.

Al adored Sonny, hovering over him, fussing and worrying after the operation for many years to come. But suddenly Mae presented an even bigger worry. In 1925–26, she began to exhibit some alarming symptoms that led her to consult the family physician, Dr. David Omens, who recognized them as syphilis. It was advanced enough that he referred her to the Mayo Clinic. He had to frighten her into going there, for she was more worried about the publicity that could result if someone reported that Al Capone's wife had been diagnosed with neurosyphilis and was being treated in the hospital than she was about her health. She told Al she had syphilis, but as far as she knew then and later, he did not consent to be examined, let alone treated. When Dr. Joseph Moore, the physician who took care of Al at the end of his life, contacted Dr. Omens to see if Al had gone quietly for treatment in Chicago, he found no record that Al had ever been treated by anyone, neither Dr. Omens nor "any other private physician prior to his commitment to prison." This led Dr. Moore to conclude that "the date of [Al] Capone's infection is therefore unknown." The treatment Mae received at the Mayo Clinic relieved her symptoms but only for the time being. From then on and for many years afterward, she was treated periodically by Dr. Omens and other physicians.

———

There was a reason why Mae never knew whether Al sought treatment for his syphilis: it was not the sort of thing an Italian husband discussed with his wife, especially not on the telephone, which for months at a time was the only contact they had with each other. The gang wars were so violent that Al had to take extraordinary precautions to protect himself. There were times when he could not leave his fortified headquarters for days if not weeks on end. Al Capone was only in his mid-twenties when his life became an ongoing battle of wits just to survive. He had risen so far and so fast that he was every other gang's favorite target and they were all out to get him. Dealing with them took precedence over everything else, from his relationships to his health. The only thing that mattered was staying alive, and the next few years would find him inventing creative ways to do so.

Chapter 7

THE FORTUNES OF WAR

Al Capone's professional life had become one encounter after another with rival gangs who wanted to kill him, so he spent most of the last half of the 1920s either in one of the hotels he turned into armed-fortress headquarters or on the lam in a hideout, as the gang wars that raged throughout Chicago left him victorious and turned him into a folk hero to the rest of the world.

There have been many books—hundreds by some counts—written about Al Capone, from the contemporary accounts published during his earliest heyday in Chicago to the present, almost a century later. Every one of them is an attempt to sort out what *really* happened on many different fronts, from gangland rivalries to political chicanery. Sociologists and cultural historians have weighed in, and in the field of economics there is even a Harvard Business School (HBS) case study showing how Al ran the Outfit as if it were a major corporation. The HBS study examined the years 1920–33, when Al controlled literally hundreds of "brothels, speakeasies, and roadhouses, which served as venues for gang administered gambling, prostitution, and illegal alcohol sales." It qualified differences in the vast sums of money that the Outfit took in yearly by saying verifiable revenues were probably somewhat more than $100 million (almost $1.5 billion in 2015), while concluding there were probably millions more that were unaccounted for and undeclared. The study concluded that the Outfit was able to operate freely because of "political ties" and because "according to Capone himself . . . half of Chicago's police force [was] on his payroll."

When the case study gathered statistics about how Al Capone came to control all of Cicero and a large swath of Chicago, one of the most striking findings was that even though Prohibition was well under way in Cicero in 1921, there were still many saloons and beer gardens operating openly in the little town of sixty thousand people, but there was not a single brothel or gambling den. By 1924, along with 123 saloons, twenty-two brothels were operating openly alongside 161 gambling dens. To arrive at these astonishing numbers, the Torrio-Capone outfit had battled and bested gangs controlled by at least five different ethnic groups whose names have become synonymous with vicious killings, the most notable among them being the three brothers still alive of the six Sicilian Genna brothers; Dean O'Banion and his cohorts, Hymie Weiss and Bugs Moran; and the Irish O'Donnell brothers. Since 1921, there had been 349 murders, of which 215 were gang related. In 1925 alone, Greater Chicago was averaging one murder or more each day, with more than a hundred bombings in that year alone.

The conclusion of the Harvard case study was that there were roughly 700 gang-related deaths from 1920 to 1930, with Al Capone either "directly or indirectly responsible for over 200." The purported reasons why he ordered the killings ranged from attempts at hijacking beer (Joe Howard) to being in the wrong place at the wrong time (William H. McSwiggin), to double-crossers (Frankie Yale), to those who refused to support his slate in various elections (Diamond Joe Esposito). By the end of 1927, there were at least seven would-be assassins imported by other gangs, from New York, Cleveland, St. Louis, and other cities, all of whom Capone and his men dispatched before they could dispatch him. When all the killings were added up, "the brutality, efficiency, and wealth of Capone's organization demonstrated the destructive forms of American entrepreneurship in the early 20th century."

When Torrio turned the Outfit over to Capone in 1925, he said he had to do it because "I am getting too prominent for my own good." He certainly was, for once he was gone, there was no one in his organization more powerful than Al Capone, and he became everyone's new target. The closest anyone came had been the drive-by shooting of Weiss and Moran in January 1925. Capone went briefly into hiding until things cooled off, only to find when he emerged that his bodyguard-chauffeur had been tortured and dumped at the bottom of a well by O'Banion's men for refusing to tell them where he had gone. This sort of retaliation was typical: if they could not get Al Capone, they got someone else, such as happened on the night of November 28, 1926, when he was dining with his friend Theodore "Tony the Greek" Anton, the owner of his favorite restaurant, conveniently located on the ground floor of Capone's Hawthorne Hotel headquarters in Cicero. They were the only diners late that night when Anton went to answer the doorbell and never returned. There are rumors here, too, that men from the Outfit carried out Anton's murder on their boss's orders after he did something that displeased Al Capone. To this day, however, the accepted story is that he was kidnapped and murdered by an unidentified rival gang.

Capone made his headquarters at the Hawthorne Hotel until 1926. He had bulletproof shutters installed on the windows and stationed armed guards all over the lobby. Everyone who worked on the hotel's staff knew they were also working for Al Capone: few ordinary citizens dared walk in for a drink or a meal for fear of what they might encounter, and no one booked a room because they were all taken by men from the Outfit. Tour bus conductors called it "Capone's Castle" and pointed it out to sightseers eager for a harmless fright.

Torrio had bought the building shortly before Al arrived in Chicago. It housed a gambling den in a space called the Hawthorne Smoke Shop, and there was also a bar frequented only by members of the organization, clearly off-limits to the local populace, where prostitutes who worked from rooms on an upper floor could be hired openly. After Capone took over and created his redoubt, he found that he had no secrecy or privacy at the Hawthorne Hotel because everyone knew when he was in the building. He needed another place, somewhere private where he could carry out his escapades so discreetly that only those members of his entourage that he chose to accompany him would know where he was and what he was doing.

At the end of 1926, Capone bought a small apartment building on a quiet residential street some distance from the Hawthorne, where he became the only resident. He had the front door reinforced with steel plating, built an eight-foot-high brick wall that surrounded the garage and the backyard, and had a tunnel dug between the house and the garage so he could enter and exit the property without being seen. He was now driving a seven-ton, bulletproof, armored Cadillac sedan, custom fitted at a cost of $20,000 (more than $250,000 in today's money). The windows were bulletproof glass, with the rear one designed to be lowered so that a machine gun could be aimed out. The body was covered with specially made steel, and the fenders were designed to be "non-dentable."

Those who were permitted to see inside the building saw rooms furnished like any typical middle-class home, except for the bedroom, which was an over-the-top bordello, complete with a mirrored ceiling. This was where he entertained his mistresses and, according to one of his many biographers, where he inhaled so much cocaine that it resulted in a deviated nasal septum. Although the Outfit did deal in drugs, no evidence has ever verified that Capone used them, but women, one after the other, did indeed pass through the bedroom as if through a revolving door, and liquor flowed through the rest of the building in body-punishing quantities. There is nothing in Capone's voluminous medical history to support the contention that he used drugs, so this charge remains in the realm of conjecture. Furthermore, he also knew that if he took drugs, there was the very real possibility that he would be vulnerable to danger to his person as well as physical damage to his surroundings. Drugs could well render him helpless to call the shots; drugs meant losing control, and that he would never risk.

Capone might have imbibed liquor to the point of such stupefaction that it deranged him enough to destroy his surroundings and beat or kill anyone who dared to thwart him, but he did so while still exerting a kind of self-control: he only drank with abandon when he was in one or another of his headquarters or hideouts, surrounded by devoted attendants and most particularly his brother Ralph, who could always be counted on to keep him safe. He was known for giving parties for outsiders that could last as long as a week, such as the one he threw at the Metropole Hotel for Jack Dempsey after he lost the heavyweight championship of the world to Gene Tunney in 1927. The famous New York madam Polly Adler, who was a guest, said the party lasted "a solid week, during all of which time the champagne and every other kind of liquor flowed like Niagara . . . and his guests, among whom were legal lights, politicians, and mobsters from all over the country, made the most of his lavish hospitality."

He began to hold these parties shortly after Torrio retired and left him fully in charge of the Outfit. With gang wars roiling, he needed his wits about him more than ever, and entertaining lavishly was another way to announce his ascendency. The first thing he did was to let all Chicago see that he was now the boss by moving his headquarters from Cicero to the Metropole Hotel on South Michigan Avenue, in what was then a busy hub of the city's commerce and culture. He could not afford to commandeer the entire seven-story building, but he took enough space that his daily rental bill was around $1,500 (over $20,000 in today's money). It was often more if the booze bill was high or his men did damage to the premises. Capone created a private five-room suite for himself on the fourth floor, with the room he used as an office opening into a turret-like structure with circular windows and an impressive view of the streetscape below. He kept two so-called guest rooms on each of the fifth and sixth floors, where his full-time bodyguards took turns sleeping after their shifts. He also had a gym installed where he insisted that the men work out on a regular basis, although he himself was never seen there. Eight bodyguards traveled with him on a rotating basis, some in his bulletproof car, others in cars that flanked it front and back. The bodyguards were so formidable that they actually became the focus of an article about him in *The New Yorker,* where they were described as offering the protection of a "double-walled fortress of meat."

There was one other aspect of the hotel's structure that particularly appealed to Capone. A network of basement tunnels had been constructed to connect the hotel with other buildings on Michigan Avenue and the nearby streets, created to ease deliveries of supplies in winter, everything from coal for heat and food for the restaurants. In the Outfit's line of work, Al Capone recognized that the tunnels would provide handy escape routes if they were needed.

There were even more connecting delivery tunnels under the Lexington Hotel, one block up the street and where he moved his headquarters in 1928. Long after his death, a 1986 television special was hosted by Geraldo Rivera, who claimed that when a particular underground vault beneath the hotel was opened, it would reveal that Al Capone had stashed his fortune there, the hypothetical vast amount of missing money that had been rumored to exist since the day of his death. The NBC network went overboard on hype and publicity to create an audience riveted to their sets for the two hours it took for Rivera to find nothing at all in an empty vault.

The Lexington was a far grander address, and Capone rented a far more ostentatious space. He took a ten-room suite on the top floor, where, from his office, he had a panoramic view of Chicago's South Side, all of which his Outfit controlled. His decorating choices received startled attention from those who were ushered into his most sacred inner sanctum. There, he sat in a chair with a bulletproof back, a gift from Dominic Roberto, one of the cohorts who helped him rule the Chicago Heights area. On the wall behind him were three framed portraits: two reporters who saw them agreed that two of the three were steel engravings, of George Washington and Abraham Lincoln, but they disagreed on the third and most prominent that hung between them. One said it was a drawing of Big Bill Thompson, the crooked mayor of Chicago; another wrote that it was a portrait of Al Capone himself, "wearing knickerbockers and holding a golf club."

If all his earlier headquarters could be compared to fortified medieval castles surrounded by moats, the Lexington was as impervious to the possibility of hostile attack as Fort Knox. There were "all kinds of traps and escape routes . . . alarms, hidden panels, moving walls, everything a security-conscious gangster required." Capone always entered and exited his private floor via the freight elevator, and he always rode it flanked by the gun-toting "wall of meat" bodyguards. He also carried a holstered pistol under each armpit. There were so many obstacles an intruder would have had to overcome before ever reaching his bedroom that even if one managed to do so, he would find bodyguards who always slept on a cot outside Capone's door. And if the would-be assassin should manage to kill the guards, he would still have to make it through a steel-plated locked door in order to get to Al Capone. Nothing was left to chance: Capone's meals were prepared in his private kitchen, where every move the chef made was supervised by men Capone trusted. And he did not stop there: when the food was served, he watched as the chef tasted it first.

All these precautions were necessary because of the carnage of the past several years. So, too, were the periodic escapes he took to places where no one would think to look for him. As the violence went on and on, and the arson, mayhem, and murders became increasingly grisly and grim, no matter who had actually committed the outrage, the authorities looked first for Al Capone. He quipped that they held him "responsible for everything but the Chicago fire."

By the start of 1928, he insisted that he was "tired of gang murders and gang shootings. It's a tough life to lead. You fear death at every moment, and worse than death, you fear the rats of the game who'd run around and tell the police if you don't constantly satisfy them with money and favors."

During a fourteen-month period from 1926 to 1928, he lived mostly in hiding at the Hawthorne Hotel because he was too afraid of what might happen if he slept in his own bed on Prairie Avenue, where he was "afraid to sit near a window or an open door." He told reporters that he wanted to stop the killing so he could go home at night like any other businessman: "Why not treat our business like any other man treats his, as something to work at in the daytime and forget when he goes home at night?" He said he couldn't stand listening to Sonny's plaintive plea as he asked his father "why didn't I stay home."

Not everyone was sympathetic to Al Capone's self-created plight. Alva Johnston, the Pulitzer Prize–winning journalist whose story about him in *The New Yorker* described his phalanx of bodyguards, was coldly appraising when he described Al's "soft, fat, sentimental features, large red lips with exaggerated curves of sympathy, large eyes with active tear ducts, black eyebrows which contract rather fiercely when certain ideas strike him." Johnston's physical description might have been exaggerated, but he took Al Capone's measure correctly: in August 1928, he was the first writer to anoint him "the greatest gang leader in history." Capone was nothing if not canny, a man of shrewd intelligence who was pleased to accept a title that conferred supremacy in his field, but he did not let it go to his head. Instead, he appraised his situation realistically: "I've been in this racket long enough to realize that a man in my game must take the breaks, the fortunes of war. I haven't had any peace of mind in years. Every minute I'm in danger of death . . . I don't want to end up in the gutter punctuated by machine gun slugs."

That being the case, hiding in plain sight, whether in downtown Chicago or in fortress Cicero, was becoming too dangerous. It was time to leave town and not tell anyone where he was going.

Chapter 8

IN HIDING

As early as 1926, it was apparent to Al that he would need to secure a place where no one could find him. Ralph had bought property in northern Wisconsin's Hayward area that he named after himself by abbreviating his two names: RaCap. Al followed Ralph's example when he heard about a property twenty-three miles down the road in the hamlet of Couderay: four hundred acres in a pine and hardwood forest with numerous existing buildings on top of a hill that had commanding views down to the private Cranberry Lake. Although Ralph was the official owner (and not Al, as legend often had it), he did not buy the property in his name but put the deed of sale in the name of the mob's lawyer, Edward J. "Artful Eddie" O'Hare.

The Capone brothers were initially drawn to the area because Joe Saltis, with whom the Outfit was then on cautious (and temporary) good terms, had bought property in the area to use as a way station for contraband booze trundled in from Canada. The possibility of doing the same was always uppermost in Al Capone's mind, but there were other things about the property that made it so attractive to a man in an always-threatened position. It was well-nigh impossible for a rival gang to stage a surprise attack, because the only way to the house was down a gated and heavily guarded dirt road; situated high atop a hill, it had a clear view across the lake, so no boat could arrive undetected.

It was O'Hare who arranged for the original house to be enlarged and fortified and for the other buildings to be constructed according to the needs of a mobster primarily looking for a hideout and a quick getaway. All this cost upwards of $250,000 (in 2015, more than $3.25 million). The main house was old and small until he turned it into a ten-room, six-bedroom lodge with eighteen-inch-thick stone walls. Windows were small and sparse in the main room, whose most dramatic features were a native-stone fireplace that rose to the vaulted ceiling and a huge custom-made mahogany spiral staircase that led to the second-floor bedrooms.

Around two hundred local men were hired to upgrade the property, many of them skilled stonecutters who worked on the main house and the numerous outbuildings where the men from the Outfit were lodged. Because the property was far from the nearest towns, the workers bunked there during the week, and to the present day their descendants can describe in detail the gargantuan meals Capone's cooks fed them. The locals always had company, for anyone in the Outfit who needed a break from the Chicago gang wars could find one in Couderay; all they had to do was board the train on the Chicago and North Western Railroad, where a local resident (not in the Outfit's pay) was the conductor and would let them ride for free.

Residents of the little town knew something unusual was happening when furniture vans with Chicago addresses printed on their sides roared down the little main street. Sixty years later in the 1980s, when the property had been turned into a hotel and resort called the Hideout, visitors could still sit on some of the original sofas and chairs, walk on the expensive Oriental rugs, and look at the stuffed owls and zebra skins that Al Capone had transported from the city.

Capone had the land's natural defenses supplemented during construction, and by the time the work was done, there were eight other buildings surrounding the main house. Everything was easily kept under surveillance from a gun tower adjacent to the main lodge, where armed guards were always on duty and spotlights shone across the lake at night. He loved to swim and enjoyed fishing and boating, so there was also a boathouse with several kinds of boats and places within and around the structure where guards could be securely stationed. There was a bunkhouse where the rotating shifts of guards slept, ate, and amused themselves in their off-hours and an eight-car garage in which the big black limousines were carefully stashed, always facing outward and ready for quick getaways. It, too, had thick stone walls into which little portholes had been carved so that machine guns could be fitted and fired with ease. There was even a jail cell just in case someone was foolish enough to try to invade the premises, but no one ever did, and eventually it was used for storage.

From the beginning of the Capone tenancy, rumors flew. As late as the 1980s, the most persistent one was of underground tunnels that connected all the buildings, none of which were ever found. There were also tales of seaplanes taking off and landing in the depths of night to unload contraband booze and weapons. These stories were connected more to Saltis than to Capone, although unmarked trucks did make frequent stops at the property. Another legend had Al worrying that the kerosene lanterns used to light the property did not offer enough protection, and because electric utilities had not yet come to that part of Wisconsin, he had his own power station built. That was not true either, and if he or Ralph did have some form of primitive generator installed, traces of it have not survived.

The stories that are true show Ralph as a shadowy, background figure whom most local people tried to avoid. Although he lived in that general area of the state from middle age until he died, elderly townspeople are reluctant to tell stories about him, even as they tell many about his famous brother. Many men and boys who live around Hayward, Wisconsin, helped to build Al Capone's hideaway, and the various stories they tell flourish to this day. The travel editor of the local paper, writing tongue in cheek in the 1980s, said, "Al must have never gotten anywhere because [his car] was always in a ditch or getting a flat tire fixed, according to the tales of those who 'helped' Scarface Al in the old days."

Many old-timers tell how, when they were children, their parents gave them strict instructions about what to do if they ever saw the fleet of big black sedans driving through the streets of town: they were to run into the nearest store and duck down behind the counters and away from the windows. A vivid memory for two of those children, now elderly, is of running into the penny candy store after they saw a big black sedan stop outside. They were hiding behind the counter with some of their friends when a big man came in and asked the clerk to fill the biggest bags available, all of which he paid for and then gave to each of the children. They said their parents never got over the danger they had been in as they told and retold the tale of their children's encounter with Al Capone. Actually, it was probably Ralph, who was fond of making such gestures all his life.

The daughter of the town barber remembered how she went into her father's shop one day to ask him for a nickel when the big man in the chair facing the door yelled at the barber to get his daughter out of there because it was too dangerous. She remembered that in both the front and the back of the shop there were "big black cars, with the motors running." She, too, insists it was Al, but more likely it was Ralph.

It is not clear if Al was in residence when the incident for which he is most fondly remembered happened. There was a Catholic mission to the Native American Chippewa tribe located about six miles from his property on the Lac Courte Oreilles Reservation. Everything on the reservation was in serious disrepair, and there was no actual church building. The priest, Father Ignatius Kinney, was a mild-mannered man whose pleas for aid to the local bishop went unanswered. As his relatives tell the tale, one night the bright lights across the lake that he saw when the Outfit was in residence looked brighter than usual, as if they were calling to him. Here the tale takes on the qualities of a miracle: Father Kinney knew he was taking his life in his hands to go out on the lake, but something made him get into a boat, row across it, and not only walk up to the house but walk straight into "a room where the gang lords were playing poker." No guards stopped him, and no cardplayers seemed surprised when Father Kinney spoke eloquently about the mission's many needs; all they wanted was to get rid of him so they could get on with the game. They scooped up all the money on the table, about $700 (almost $10,000 in 2015), and told him to "get out of there." Father Kinney used the money to build a church, which was named St. Ignatius Loyola with a nod to the saint but with grateful thanks to Al Capone.

———

The Hideout, as it came to be called, was the perfect retreat in every sense of what Al needed and wanted in 1926, but in its way it was as visible as the house on Prairie Avenue or his hotel headquarters. It was a long drive from Chicago, and there were many places along the road that made him a target for anyone looking to bump him off. "He is the most-shot-at man in America," wrote Fred Pasley in 1930. "There have been more attempts upon his life than upon that of any other gangster." There had been at least a dozen attempts to kill him after the drive-by shooting in 1925 when he was in a restaurant; by conservative estimates, thirty-five cars and numerous buildings were riddled with more than a thousand bullets and slugs from machine guns, automatic pistols, and shotguns—incredibly, all of them missing Capone. In other attempts more reminiscent of the medieval Borgias than modern America, a restaurant cook was offered a bribe to poison his food (which he declined), and a $50,000 reward was offered to anyone who could deliver his dead body. The accidental assassination of the up-and-coming assistant district attorney William H. McSwiggin in April 1926 proved the crucial turning point when Northern Wisconsin no longer served as sufficient sanctuary. Al needed another place to hide, one where none of his enemies could get to him.

"Of all Chicago's gangland killings, the death of Billy McSwiggin remains one of its most complex and intriguing mysteries," wrote one of Capone's many biographers. McSwiggin was a young prosecutor who boasted that he was going to get Capone for the earlier murder of the small-time gangster Joe Howard, but he liked to consort with gangsters and was sometimes seen in Al Capone's company, drinking, joking, and laughing. Capone was heard to boast publicly that McSwiggin was on his payroll. However, if it was a true boast, McSwiggin was paid in cash and off the books, for none of the many investigations of how the Outfit operated have turned up information to verify this claim.

Interestingly, although they were approximately the same age, McSwiggin was always described as a mere boy, whereas Al was always portrayed as older, slower, and darkly brooding. In all the media coverage, McSwiggin was the blond *ingénu* defending the law, and Capone was the heavy, swarthy villain who always broke it.

McSwiggin had the misfortune to go carousing on a drunken spree through Capone-controlled Cicero in a big black limousine that was easily identified as belonging to the rival O'Donnell gang. That they would venture into territory he controlled was a slight Al Capone could not ignore; he and his men formed a five-car cavalcade that eventually caught up with the O'Donnells' car and poured bullets into it and its passengers, wounding several but killing McSwiggin. One of the most important of the still-unanswered questions is what McSwiggin was doing in the company of known gangsters, the O'Donnells. Nevertheless, his death was a major event sure to attract unwanted attention. The heat was on, and Al the Big Guy was sweating.

Herbert Asbury, who was among the earliest (and most florid) writers to chronicle crime in Chicago, flat out blamed Capone for firing the actual shots that killed McSwiggin. The even more florid Fred Pasley went further, quoting newspaper accounts saying Capone handled the machine gun himself "in order to set an example of fearlessness to his less eager companions." Pasley did add, however, that in Chicago "murder cases are tried in the newspapers long before they reach the courtroom." But here again, the truth is elusive: How was anyone to tell where the hundreds of rounds that had been fired came from? Unquestionably, Al Capone had a weapon, and if he was there, he was probably responsible for wounding or killing some of the car's passengers; however, to assign blame specifically to him, one person out of the thirty or so occupants of the five-car cavalcade, would be difficult if not impossible.

He was used to being the primary suspect in every murder investigation. "It's a waste of time to arrest him," said one of the Chicago police chiefs who spoke for them all during the investigation into the murder of Hymie Weiss. Still, the authorities spent the next four months trying and failing to indict him for McSwiggin's murder, with a large part of the failure stemming from the fact that they could not find him long enough to question or charge him.

First they raided Ralph's apartment, where they found a cache of weapons they could not connect to McSwiggin's murder and no Al; then they raided the Prairie Avenue house, finding nothing but a hysterical Teresa, a grim and silent Mae, and a belligerent John (Mimi), whom they arrested and released shortly after. The authorities looked everywhere, but from May to October Al Capone was not to be found. Or so it seemed.

———

Meanwhile, the gang turf wars raged that, as Asbury put it, "spread Chicago's evil renown to the far corners of the earth." He wrote of how "territorial claims were ignored, trucks were hi-jacked, breweries and distilleries robbed, and Chicago's streets echoed to the roar of shotguns, the crack of automatic pistols, and the rattle of machine-guns." Al left Ralph to deal with most of the carnage and went into hiding at the Chicago Heights home of Dominic Roberto, a lieutenant in the Outfit. Al trusted him enough to give him one of the diamond-studded belt buckles similar to the one he now sported and that he had begun to give to anyone who did him a favor or merely caught his fancy. In this case, it was for Roberto's hospitality and in exchange for the earlier gift of the bulletproof chair. Capone had retreated there before, but this time he "holed up" for eight days and never once went outside to walk the spacious grounds.

Roberto was compulsive about everything connected to his property and did not allow his wife to have any choice about the furnishings or the hired help. She was his ornament, and he even vetted her maid. Al was very fond of Roberto's wife, a Kentucky girl born Ray Rucker, who started out in Chicago singing in Big Jim Colosimo's nightclub and eventually became the chanteuse and elderly character-around-town known as Rio Burke. Many years later in one of the more than a hundred interviews she gave about Al Capone, she said he liked her mostly because she knew her place: "Gangsters don't tell their wives anything. Nothing! The wife is for the nursery, the kitchen and the bed. The mistresses, they knew what was going on." In Al's case, she was only partly correct, for even though he told Mae as little as possible because he did not want to upset her, she always knew exactly what he was doing. Rio knew her place and "stayed in the background," for her only job was to "look pretty" and leave the conversation to the men. She was allowed to speak to Capone long enough to ask if he wanted something to eat or drink, but that was all. As for him, "he was a perfect gentleman at all times."

Being in Roberto's highly controlled environment made him restless, and so after eight days when no one seemed to be looking for him, he left in the dark of night for Freeport and Raphael Capone's house and the occasion when he allowed himself to be beaten with the cane. He stayed only long enough for some of his men to go over the ledgers because this house did not offer the privacy of the Roberto house, so here again he was always inside, cooped up. He twitched with restlessness, but having no alternative to release pent-up frustrations, he bided his time.

Freeport was a good place to lie low, mainly because so few people in Chicago knew of this particular Capone family's existence, but even though it was a big house, it was crowded with the large family, and there was scant room for Al Capone and the contingent of men he needed to protect him. He had to go somewhere else. One possibility was to a house along the Indiana dunes on the shore of Lake Michigan, but that idea was quickly discarded. Even though the setting was isolated, there were enough year-round residents who might decide to court danger by telling authorities about the big black cars and ferocious-looking strangers in their midst.

He decided to go to Lansing, Michigan, where he mostly stayed from late May until the end of July. Occasionally, he made forays to Benton Harbor, where his friend and right-hand man, Tony Lombardo, had a large house on spacious grounds. The difference in lifestyle in each place was pronounced: in Benton Harbor, the Lombardo house and grounds were patrolled by bodyguards day and night, whereas in Lansing Al Capone moved about the town like an ordinary citizen.

Lombardo held a high-level position in the mob, while the patriarch of the Lansing family had been one of the lowly workers who had been in the Outfit but who knew so little about its activities that he was allowed to leave it and "go straight." In later years, when Capone had been long gone from Lansing, his descendants honored his directive never to talk about Al Capone. Unlike so many others who encountered him at various times in their lives, this family, whose surname remains deeply private, is now in its third and fourth generations and has been careful about what stories they chose to tell. Lombardo's descendants are also in their third and fourth generations, but they never hesitate to tell stories about their patriarch's exploits, real or alleged.

When the Lansing patriarch worked for the Outfit, he was a lowly "soldier," a laborer who sometimes loaded and unloaded cases of contraband booze and was sometimes promoted to drive a truck; fortunately for him, he only made short-distance deliveries and was seldom in real danger. His job meant that he knew little or nothing about how the Outfit operated, so no other gang was going to torture him for information because everyone knew he had none. When he asked to leave Chicago, he went with Al Capone's approval, and after he settled in Lansing, he started a business that was so small and insignificant that with the exception of one or two "small jobs" he was never asked to handle money, numbers, or any other vice.

He told the Outfit's boss repeatedly that if he ever needed a favor, he had only to ask, and when Capone did, it must have seemed that no one could provide a more secure and anonymous hideout than this honest man and his family. How strange, then, that Al Capone, the man whom Chicago authorities were actively seeking and whose face was in every newspaper in the country—never mind the rest of the world—could have stayed in one place for several months without anyone turning him in. And yet he did, hiding in plain sight, in the capital of the state of Michigan. Or so it seemed.

One of the first things he did was put out feelers to an officer in the Lansing Police Department, John O'Brien, who was rumored to be open to being put on the Outfit's payroll in exchange for his silence. O'Brien has been credited for keeping the lid on Capone's whereabouts, which is credit he does not deserve, because he was not highly enough placed in the department to have wielded the kind of clout many Lansing residents claimed for him in later years. O'Brien alone could not have guaranteed that Capone's hideout was never leaked to the Chicago authorities. Another spurious contention comes from today's residents of Lansing, many of them the patriarch's descendants, who claim that O'Brien's graft was uncovered as early as 1930 and that he ended his life in disgrace. In the official history of the Lansing Police Department, the record shows that O'Brien began his career as a lowly patrolman in 1917 and throughout the 1920s, especially during Capone's time in Lansing, was a low-level officer in the detective bureau; in 1937, when Capone was long gone from Lansing, he became the city's chief of police and, by all existing accounts, a popular and respected one who retired to a quiet life with a good pension.

And yet there was Al Capone, seeming fearlessly unconcerned about his privacy and safety as he walked freely up and down the streets of Lansing, where he was easily recognized. He enjoyed waving and chatting with people who shouted, "How ya doin', Al?" No one snubbed him or scurried off in fear when his big car drove by, and no one teased him by making what had become the familiar gesture of shaping their arms to hold a tommy gun, pointing their fingers, and grunting an "ack-ack" in greeting. People seemed unconcerned that he was Al Capone, the reputed murdering mobster; they liked him because he was generous with money, so the story goes, dropping a fiver on a child and telling him to buy ice cream for his friends, paying a poor widow's food or coal bill, or offering to buy a new car for the family that sheltered him (the patriarch declined this offer). Stories abound of how he guaranteed to pay for college educations and expensive medical treatments. Some of them may be true, but because very few people in those ethnic and social classes kept records or documents, and because Capone always paid in cash, none of this extraordinary generosity can be proven. There is no question, however, that he liked to play Lord Bountiful because he enjoyed the adulation it brought, so if stories proliferated and if they were all positive, so much the better. Indeed, on the Fourth of July, he was a highly visible participant in the annual fireworks display and was written up in the local papers. No one tried to stop the stories from being printed because Al Capone did not mind the publicity at all.

Capone needed more room than his patron's house provided, so he often convened his men for meetings at one of Lansing's most visible and popular hotels, the same one where members of the state legislature often gathered. His men drove up from Chicago in their usual long black sedans, and their dress and deportment ensured that anyone who saw them would know what line of business they were in. Local newspaper reporters hung out in the general area around the hotel, usually on the hunt for a political story but always on the lookout for anything interesting, especially a big scoop they could put on the wire services.

Surprisingly, little of Al Capone's professional activity found its way into the local press, most likely because money was flashing everywhere when he and his men were out and about in Lansing; perhaps some of it was flashy enough to blind the members of the fourth estate. Curious, too, is the fact that Chicago police, who tailed gang members as a routine matter, never seemed to follow any of Capone's men as they left for Lansing and never asked any of their stoolie sources where they had been after the men returned. Comparatively speaking, things were quiet in Chicago now that Al Capone was gone, and the authorities liked it that way.

And then he moved on, this time to a resort area a slight distance from Lansing known as Round Lake, where other Chicago mobsters, among them Frank Nitti, had bought land and property both for summer homes and for hideouts. Capone brought in his bodyguard Frankie Rio and his chief terminator, "Machine Gun" Jack McGurn, and set them up in beach cottages surrounding the one he took for himself. It was a quiet area on a little lake, where he indulged in two of his favorite pastimes, swimming and fishing. When he tired of the bucolic life, there was a speakeasy roadhouse just down the road, and there he found the female companionship he had been without since he left Chicago.

Like all his other mistresses, this one was young and blond, and as pretty as his wife, who remained quietly at home in Chicago. Rio Burke was right: the mistresses were on the spot and therefore knew everything that was happening; the wives—Mae among them—stayed at home and, whether or not they knew anything, kept their mouths shut.

———

By mid-July, Capone had had enough of loafing, glad-handing, and adulation and was itching to get back into the swing of things. He was constantly alert to what was going on in Chicago, thanks to the men who made the trek back and forth from the city. He knew that the police were frustrated in their attempts to pin McSwiggin's murder on anyone, let alone him, and he knew that other gangs were in disarray now that so many of their leaders were dead and gone. His own Outfit was running smoothly, and his place at the head of it was secure, and so it was time to return and claim the spoils of victory.

At the end of July, Al Capone let it be known that he was planning to turn himself in and that on the morning of July 28, 1926, the police could find him standing on 106th Street, the Indiana-Illinois border, where they were welcome to meet and escort him into the city. He is alleged to have feigned innocence as he said something like "I understand you boys are looking for me," a remark the press had great fun inserting into stories of his surrender.

Federal agents took him directly to the Chicago Criminal Courts Building, where he staunchly denied having had anything to do with the O'Donnell killings and particularly that of McSwiggin, whom he claimed as a friend and whose reputation he clouded forever with a single remark: "I paid McSwiggin ... plenty and I got what I was paying for." Capone expected that because no charges could be filed against him, he would be released. But the judge had other ideas and sentenced him to spend the night in an ordinary jail cell. At the next day's hearing, the prosecutors sheepishly admitted they had no evidence to tie him to the killings, and the judge had no recourse but to dismiss all charges. Capone was a free man and could go anywhere in Chicago he chose.

Instead of going home to Prairie Avenue and the wife and child he had not seen for several months, he chose to go directly to Cicero and the Hawthorne Hotel. The first order of business for the undisputed victor was to receive the homage that would solidify his rightful place as the supreme head of Chicago's underworld.

Fred Pasley exaggerated when he wrote what is generally considered the first biography, describing Al's domain as "supreme on the west, from the Loop to Cicero, and on the south from the world's busiest corner to the Indiana boundary line at the lake and 106th Street, and on down to Chicago Heights." However, it was not an exaggeration when he described Al Capone as "the John D. Rockefeller of some 20,000 anti-Volstead filling stations. He was sitting on top of the bootleg world." He was indeed, and it was time to let the rest of the world know it.

Chapter 9

———

THE GLORY YEARS

A ll over Chicago, gang murders proliferated as one bunch killed off its foes and the others retaliated to avenge them; there was so much vicious creativity in how they carried out the violence and gore that a jaded public greeted the front-page stories of the daily papers with a yawn, a ho hum, and a cursory glance at the headlines before dismissing one more story that was more of the same. John Stege, the chief of detectives in the Chicago Police Department, was so distressed by public complacency that in January 1927 he wrote a series of articles for the *Chicago Herald and Examiner* entreating readers not to take the attitude that the murders didn't matter because it was only one gangster killing another. Stege raged against the "czar-like power" wielded by gang leaders and begged the public to shed its indifference and rise up in protest. He ranted and raved, but no one seemed to listen, especially not Al Capone.

On the few occasions when he managed to go home to Prairie Avenue, Teresa alternately cried, cooked, and berated him (but gently) for the worry and heartache he caused her. Mae neither cried nor cooked, but she did make her usual plea for him to retire, citing the strain it put on her and the increasingly bewildered Sonny, who heard enough household chatter to ask for explanations about the nasty things newspapers and radio were saying about his father. Al let Sonny know how much he loved him and reassured the women of his invincibility, but he also told them firmly that retirement was impossible.

"I'm the boss [and] I'm going to continue to run things," he told a reporter as he described how many times other crooks had tried to "put the roscoe" on him. "Don't let anybody kid you into thinking I can be run out of town. I haven't run yet and I'm not going to."

All the while, Capone was positioning the Outfit to take the lead in what William J. Helmer, one of the most consistent observers of the Chicago crime scene, called his "own form of venture capitalism." Georgette Winkeler, a smart and savvy woman whose husband, Gus, was one of Capone's most trusted gunmen, had ample opportunity to analyze how he operated. She thought it unfair to call him a gangster when in reality he was only "a racketeer," which she considered a cut above the usual thug: "This definition may seem like splitting hairs, but as a matter of fact, the entire Capone enterprise was based on illegitimate business, and not the cruder forms of crime." Capone was turning the Outfit into such a smoothly running criminal organization that the Harvard Business School case study explicitly examined its structure with an organizational chart.

The name "Alphonse Capone (alias Al Brown)" was all alone in a box at the top of the chart with the title "President of the Syndicate." Slightly below Capone's box and linked to it on the left was another box, with a partial listing of the many "personal attendants" a man in his position required, among them valets, chefs, chauffeurs, trainers, waiters, barbers, secretaries, doctors, and an unspecified "etc." To the right was another link to a separate box for his "personal bodyguards," who numbered "several dozen men, but they all [also] had important other duties," here again left unspecified. "His body guards were legion," according to one of the many histories of Prohibition. Some of the most colorful were Phil D'Andrea, who could slice a quarter in midair with a single rifle shot; Antonio Leonardo Accardo (alias Joe Batters); "Machine Gun" Jack McGurn; and "the most loyal of all," Frankie Rio.

The box for the twelve "Board of Directors" was just below these three and included Ralph, the only brother who held such a position and whose job title was "general assistant in the liquor, vice, and gambling rackets"; Frank Nitti, the "enforcer" who provided Capone's link with the Unione Siciliana and later took over the entire operation, was then only "chairman of the board and vice president of the Syndicate." Jake (sometimes "Jack," sometimes "Greasy Thumb" but never to his face) Guzik was "business manager and chief statistician," leaving out his assignments in money laundering, bribery, extortion, and other rackets. Edward J. O'Hare (misspelled on the chart as O'Hara) was another director, but his task was "big dog track and race track manager, etc.," with no reference to his legal duties as the Outfit's lawyer. In two equal-sized boxes just below the board of directors were the departments of "Income" and "Protection," and below them, stretching across the bottom of the chart, was a box describing "mostly gunmen but many were in the bootleg liquor business, vice, gambling, and labor rackets and other undertakings with Al Capone."

All told, there were several hundred names on the Harvard Business School chart. Some of the most notorious were Charlie Fischetti and Lawrence "Dago" Mangano, who distributed liquor; Frank Pope and Peter Penovich [Jr.], who controlled gambling houses and who were later called by the prosecution to give testimony against Capone; and Mike "de Pike" Heitler and Harry Guzik, who controlled the brothels. Hymie "Loud Mouth" Levine was the Outfit's "chief collector," and Louis Cowen, a newsagent, posted bail for anyone arrested, having been given control by Al Capone of various real estate parcels to post as security (he, too, would be named during Capone's trial). And because someone had to be put in charge of bombings, the former Black Hand extortionist James Belcastro held that position.

These several hundred workers toiled in the office of the phony "Dr. Brown" several blocks from the Metropole Hotel. Fred Pasley described it as "a supertrust operating with the efficiency of a great corporation." Jake Guzik was the "brains" of the corporation, and under his direction between twenty and thirty people made up the clerical staff that kept records of everything from the names of police officers and Prohibition agents on the payroll to ledgers detailing the cost system used in the brothels. There was also a special ledger for the names of well-known Chicagoans who patronized the Outfit's various holdings, from the speakeasies to the gambling dens and brothels. Special records were kept for the various channels through which liquor was brought into the country via cities that included New York, Miami, New Orleans, and Detroit. The Outfit controlled four large breweries in Chicago that produced beer, and they, too, needed separate bookkeeping records. At its most robust, the Outfit had at least five hundred "gorillas" on the payroll, all of whom made sure the beer was delivered where intended.

Jake Guzik knew to the penny what the Outfit brought in annually, because it was all in his books. However, he was neither "inconvenienced [nor] dismayed" when the records were seized by police on the mayor's orders to clean up the city. The policeman in charge ostentatiously refused a bribe of $5,000 to "forget" he found them, which did not matter at all, because the municipal judge in charge of the hearing that followed the raid simply returned them to the Outfit, and everyone it employed went quietly back to work.

By the end of 1928, the Outfit controlled a large percentage of the rackets in Chicago, but depending on the source, estimates can range from a high of 70 percent to a low of something around 30–40 percent. The estimates vary, but the usually accepted number of annual gross profits is $105 million (almost $1.5 billion in 2015), and all of it in cash. When Al moved the headquarters from the Metropole Hotel to the Lexington, the cash was stored in padlocked canvas bags until it could be deposited in many different bank accounts under a variety of fictitious names. To guard the loot, it is estimated that he employed "between seven hundred and a thousand men, machine gunners or sluggers, or bombers."

"You know what will happen if you put me out of business?" Capone asked a reporter who questioned his enterprises. "I have 185 men on my personal payroll and I pay them [each] from $300 to $400 a week. They're all ex-convicts and gunmen, but they are respectable businessmen now, just as respectable as the people who buy my stuff and gamble in my places . . . If you put me out of business, I'll turn every one of those 185 respectable old convicts loose on Chicago." The boast was so dangerous to public safety that no one dared put him in a position to fulfill it.

He could make such threats now because no one seemed able to stop him from doing whatever he wanted. A. P. "Art" Madden, the IRS agent who had been sent to meet Capone when he returned from Lansing and who would play a significant role several years later in his downfall, wrote a report for the agency that was scathing in its appraisal of his character. With a nod to Capone's intelligence and business acumen, Madden wrote, "He's the boss, make no mistake about that, but he listens to advice, particularly from lawyers." Madden also noted cryptically and without further comment that Al Capone had "many friends in the police force."

As for the man personally, Madden had far less respect: "He is one mobster who doesn't care about money. He wants to be the Big Guy, and if he can take the bows he doesn't care much who gets the cash; just so long as he can bet on horses, buy the horrible junk he calls clothes, and collect jewelry. He likes women, but . . . he is sensitive about that source of income." Madden was not the first observer to note how prickly Capone became whenever the subject of brothels and prostitutes was raised. It was wise to be cautious, for he had beaten lesser men to a pulp for even the most casual remarks that might have only hinted about him as pimp and procurer.

Al Capone did indeed want to be the "Big Guy," and until the end of the decade he was, as the most colorful stories about him proliferated. He was allegedly spotted riding merrily through the streets of the city tossing silver dollars out of his car windows to pedestrians and passersby. If true, he must have kept a stash of the heavy coins in the car for just such encounters, because no one ever wrote of his pockets jingling with change. Other stories have him tossing $1,000 bills when he was enjoying the role of padrone at Italian weddings, baptisms, and other celebrations. No doubt he was generous with money, but more likely he peeled it off the roll of $100 bills he carried routinely. Tales of his extravagant gambling, of how he could drop $100,000 on a single throw of the dice, were common gossip and probably contained a modicum of truth. Money was no object when it came to betting, especially on the horses, but even if the games or races were fixed, he still found ways to lose.

His betting was even more out of hand with his new passion, golf, where he had no talent but almost always won because the other players feared his terrible temper if they didn't let him win. Golf was an excuse for heavy drinking and betting, made particularly dangerous because he and his cohorts carried loaded weapons onto the course and did not hesitate to take them out and at least brandish if not fire them. An accident was bound to happen, and eventually one did, when he slammed down his golf bag in a fit of temper and his gun went off. Some accounts say the bullet hit the flesh of his right leg and plowed through to the left, while others said he merely shot himself in the foot and became "a terrible sight . . . hopping around on the other foot, bellowing like a bull." Official government medical records taken later say the bullet never touched his leg at all but penetrated his scrotum and made a large hole there. He did spend close to a week in the hospital, enduring the pain and the even more excruciating tongue-lashings Mae gave during her visits.

Mae was nobody's fool, and even though she stayed at home and kept herself aloof from Al's involvements with other women, she was well aware that his public embarrassment over the golfing incident was compounded by the private affair he had launched with the sister of his caddy. Mae heard the gossip that he was so besotted with Babe Sullivan, the crafty girl who only dispensed her favors in exchange for gifts and money, and that he was supposedly swearing to divorce his wife if she would marry him. Ida Mae Sullivan was smart enough to know that would never happen, and she didn't care; she was content with fancy dinners, diamond bracelets, and loads of cash she brought home to help her parents feed her many siblings. She was young and fearless and got her thrills from being in the company of all the big shots and flashy entertainers she met at Capone's parties.

The parties were legendary, particularly after he took over most of the rooms at the Metropole (and later did the same when he moved to the Lexington). He was not the only one to install a mistress (and sometimes more than one at the same time); his men were given suites for their ladies of the moment as well. Everywhere he made his headquarters, it became known as Caponeville, a name shouted out by the guides on tourist buses, but one always uttered with a mixture of resentment by those who felt they had to prostrate themselves to his power. In both, there was grudging respect for the homage they had to pay to the one man who could grant what they wanted.

Under Al Capone's direction, the Metropole became "a covert annex to the mayoral campaign of Big Bill Thompson," or as Pasley put it, "Mayor Thompson, [who] was for America First, and Capone, [who] was for America's Thirst. They weren't so far apart at that." After Thompson's election, there was a constant traffic jam between the hotel, city hall, and police headquarters as men formed lines and waited their turn to plead their cases or pledge their fealty. From city hall, there was "a steady stream of purchasable magistrates, administrators, and politicians," while from the police building came "officers to collect their reward for such services as escorting consignments of liquor to their destination, warning of raids about to be staged ... furnishing Capone's triggermen with officially stamped cards, reading: 'to the Police Department: you will extend the courtesies of this department to the bearer.'" Pasley called this last period of Thompson's mayoralty "so weird that the world sat back and gasped, incredulous." As for Capone, it was "coincident with the apotheosis . . . of the gangster, when the shadow of Al Capone was cast across City Hall and County Building as the Frankenstein monster of politics."

Thompson further rewarded Capone for his political support by inviting him to be on the welcoming committee for the Italian airman Francesco de Pinedo, Mussolini's goodwill ambassador for Fascism who, on May 15, 1927, landed his hydroplane on Lake Michigan during a round-the-world flight. Actually, there was another and more important reason for Capone's invitation: the committee was a prestigious one that included the Italian consul and other prominent Italian-Americans; Capone was invited mainly because Thompson feared an anti-Fascist riot and knew he was the one person who could guarantee that it would not happen. Capone made sure it didn't, and the event was peaceful.

Still, he had not "arrived" in the social circles where he wanted to be, and he was intelligent and sensitive enough to know when he was being mocked or snubbed. Despite the reverence, adulation, and homage the public gave him, despite the deference and respect—grudging to be sure—paid by some elected officials, despite the power he held over the famous entertainers in his speakeasies and cabarets who feared what would happen to them if they did not comply with his every whim and wish, in the eyes of the political and social leaders he most wanted to impress, he was still an ill-mannered, semiliterate outsider. He could throw bushels of cash at schools, churches, and hospitals, he could stand up at sporting events and wave his hat to the spectators who cheered his mere presence, and he could guarantee public officials that events would take place without incident because his men would see to it, but he was still a lower-class Italian, a "dago" and a "wop."

He could make the joke that "when I sell liquor, they call it bootlegging. When my patrons serve it on silver trays on Lake Shore Drive, they call it hospitality." He left unsaid the fact that the residents of Lake Shore Drive were perfectly happy to accept gifts of his booze by the case while he was never invited to help them drink it at their parties. When they went slumming in speakeasies, they could give themselves a cheap thrill by hobnobbing with dangerous criminals because they were old money, and they could thumb their noses with impunity at the social class they inhabited simply because they were born into it. Al Capone was new (and openly dirty) money, and he could use it to try to wedge his way into their environment by acting, dressing, and living in a manner he thought mirrored theirs, but he could never be a part of it. They might have enjoyed toying with what was sometimes called "gangster chic" to describe the middle class's attraction to the underside of society that began during Prohibition and particularly to the larger-than-life figures who inhabited the criminal world. However, there was an unbridgeable difference between the residents of Lake Shore Drive and Al Capone of Prairie Avenue: when they tired of their pet crooks, they always had the option of dropping them and going home; there was never any chance that they would let Al Capone go with them.

———

Al Capone might have quit school in the sixth grade, but he had never stopped learning about things that interested him. He had acquired a genuine appreciation of culture, particularly of music and the theater. He loved opera, especially the works of Verdi, and amassed a large collection of recordings by Caruso. He learned enough about the genre that he could discuss how various singers approached their roles and what special talents they brought to them. As he listened to recordings, he read scores and followed them carefully whenever he attended a performance, usually surrounded by strategically positioned bodyguards who studied the audience and not the stage. In one season alone, he required seats for thirty-eight men who were carefully positioned around him, including the two gun-toting thugs who stood backstage on either side of the curtain.

Where he was welcomed, and where he felt most secure and comfortable, was in the company of entertainers, many of whom got their start in his nightclubs and cabarets before going on to great fame. Stories of his interaction with many have been expanded and exaggerated into legends of great friendships, most of them originating within the memoirs and biographies of the entertainers themselves. Sophie Tucker's biographers claim she played cards with Al Capone every night for a year, but he was still in Brooklyn and not yet in Chicago when this was supposed to have happened; perhaps they played together in other, later years, but with all his other activities and hers, surely only occasionally.

Joe E. Lewis ran afoul of Capone's prime assassinator, Jack McGurn, and his thugs, who disfigured him horribly, bashing his skull with rifle butts, slitting his throat and peeling back his facial skin, crushing his jaw, and otherwise beating him senseless. There is disagreement over the reason for the beating, with most sources saying he wanted to leave an Outfit-controlled club to perform at one owned by the North Side gangster Ted Newberry, while others merely cite a host of Lewis's alleged insults and bad behavior. The basic conclusion of every account is that no one could insult the Outfit and get away with it. Some say that Lewis miraculously returned to performing, swathed in bandages, within weeks; others claim he was hospitalized for over a year. Stories abound about how Capone found ways to provide the alcoholic Lewis with the cash he was always in need of, with everything from tips on rigged horse races where Lewis was sure to win to allegedly playing the Good Samaritan and proclaiming to the public that he paid all Lewis's medical expenses. He also put out a more sinister story to reporters when he let it be known that if Lewis had come to him in the first place, he would have persuaded the performer to stay, thus making the beating unnecessary. He left unspoken what form the persuasion would have taken, and no reporter was brave enough to ask.

Al Capone played the role of Lewis's caring friend while he was entirely responsible for the beating. McGurn took all his orders from Capone and would never have dared to make such a heinous attack on his own volition. It made Al Capone look good before a public curiously indifferent to his complicity and allowed him, in this and every other atrocity to date, to stand aloof and above the violence. After Lewis recovered, and whenever he worked in Chicago, it was only in Outfit-controlled clubs, where Capone made sure his access to the bar was always open and his gambling bills always paid.

There were many examples of the dual behaviors, double standards, and even the double life that Al Capone had forged for himself, and his relationships with entertainers provided many of the clearest illustrations. For a man of the historically segregated time in which he lived, he was mostly color-blind when it came to hiring and promoting African-Americans. Although no blacks worked directly on the Outfit's payroll, some of Capone's descendants are convinced that the main reason for the Outfit's success as a business entity was that there were always men of many different origins and nationalities on the payroll. Although they were mostly white, they were not all Italian and therefore not bound by the customs, superstitions, and rules of honor that had to be respected in the old country. Managing Slovaks and Germans was much easier than overseeing Sicilians, who were suspicious of Neapolitans, or Calabrians, who were wary of them both. The divisions between northern and southern Italians were enormous, because those from the North despised those from the South, whose cultural cringe in the face of northern claims of superiority often led to irrational vendettas.

In Chicago's Outfit-controlled territories, whites and blacks mingled freely in the rough area around Thirty-Fifth and State, where the two most popular cabarets, the Plantation and the Sunset, catered to an African-American clientele. Their buskers guided white voyeurs safely to bars and brothels, and despite an article in the original *Vanity Fair* magazine that warned against the dangers of mixed socializing, on New Year's Eve 1926 five hundred "white and colored" celebrants could be found there drinking heavily and dancing with each other.

In the segregated club world, Capone's reputation for treating African-American musicians fairly was supreme. The jazz bass player Milt Hinton called him "more or less a Robin Hood in the black community." Hinton and Cab Calloway were not on the Outfit's payroll, but they both had uncles who worked for it. Hinton recalled how Al Capone "had all the black guys, he'd sit down and talk to them. I'm the boss, I'm running it, but you're going to run the south side. You're going to make money as long as you buy your alcohol from me."

Capone also had Louis Armstrong playing at the Sunset in what one of Satchmo's biographers surmised was his "first exposure to gangsters and their ways, a world he would remain connected to for years to come." Armstrong quickly became a pet of Capone's and for a time enjoyed his special protection whenever he played in Chicago. To him, Capone was "a nice little cute fat boy, young, like some professor who had just come out of college to teach or something." He was a gentleman with Armstrong, but not so with the clarinetist Johnny Dodds, a man of great dignity who had the misfortune of not knowing how to play a song Capone wanted to hear. The story goes that Capone whipped out a $100 bill, ripped it in half, and put half into each of their pockets with the warning "Nigger, you better learn it for next time." Earl "Fatha" Hines, who also played at the Sunset, told how most musicians overlooked such crudity because of Capone's other good deeds toward them, such as when he made two bodyguards accompany Hines on a road trip to clubs where whites did not welcome blacks. Hines knew he and the other musicians were only protected "because we kept their clubs open," but he was also astute enough to know that he and the others "belonged" to a ruthless man who would do anything to ensure that these possessions were secure.

A terrified Fats Waller found out just how much of a possession he was when four of Capone's henchmen kidnapped him with guns drawn, shoved him into a big black gangster car, and took him to the Hawthorne Hotel, where he was plunked down in front of a piano and ordered to play. It was Capone's birthday party, and it lasted for three days, during which Waller played whenever and whatever the Big Guy commanded. The kidnapping had a happy ending, because the same men took him home, again with their guns at the ready to protect him, for Capone had stuffed Waller's pockets with $1,000 bills.

One "possession" he could not buy was the boxer Jack Dempsey. Capone loved the fights and wagered heavily on them, here again losing more often than he won. Dempsey had become a friend some time before the famous September 22, 1927, "Battle of the Long Count," which he lost to Gene Tunney, but Capone did not, as so many legends have it, know Dempsey or visit him at his Benton Harbor, Michigan, training camp before his 1920 fight there, simply because he was not yet an important presence in Chicago's

gangland. Capone's spending on boxing was not confined to betting. Boxing had not only become big business, as exemplified by the "gate" (gross
ticket sales) for the Dempsey-Tunney fight at $2.75 million; it was also a
society sport frequented by high rollers from the upper echelons of society
who sat at ringside in black tie beside elegant women in furs and jewels and
by celebrities from Hollywood to Wall Street. Dempsey's wife at the time
was the silent film star Estelle Taylor, who was seated for the Chicago fight
at ringside near Alfred Sloan of General Motors and Charles Schwab of
Bethlehem Steel. Also sitting near them was Al Capone, who made sure he
and his retinue occupied some of the best seats. He also let journalists from
every venue know that he threw the biggest and best parties, and of course
they were all invited to the one he was hosting after the fight. Everyone
knew that he had bet $50,000 on Dempsey to win and that the party was
in his honor and would cost the same or more. Everyone came to it, from
the madam Polly Adler to the gossip columnist Louella Parsons and the
sportswriter Ring Lardner.

Capone wanted to ensure that the party was a victory celebration, so
he offered to fix the fight in Dempsey's favor. He could make such a casual
offer because he had the clout to ensure it happened. Dempsey, who according to one of his biographers was embarrassed that he "remained Capone's
great hero," sent a letter written in his painstaking longhand, asking him
to "lay off" and keep the fight a fair one. He signed it "your friend . . . Jack
Dempsey." Capone had the good grace to do as Dempsey asked, but the
next day a huge floral delivery arrived at his training camp, unsigned and
bearing the message "to the Dempseys, in the name of sportsmanship."
Everyone knew who sent it.

———

By 1927, Al Capone had become the most feared leader in the second-largest
city in the country, not only of its acknowledged criminal element, but
also as the de facto director of how it functioned politically. Even Charles
G. Dawes, the vice president of the United States under Calvin Coolidge
from 1925 to 1929, was forced to admit that the government of the city of
Chicago and all of Cook County was powerless to stop him. All forms of
governance, legal or otherwise, had broken down and were helpless when
pitted against Al Capone.

His name was becoming increasingly famous throughout the world
despite his infamous deeds, which brought admiration more than oppro-

brium, but it was still galling when he was made the butt of jokes and turned into a laughingstock by posturing public officials and low-level policemen. He knew how to quell this, which he did during the quiet period in which 1926 was ending, mainly because enough gang leaders had been killed that the ones still alive felt they had no other option but to agree once again to the territorial truce Capone constructed, which simply reasserted the boundaries established by Torrio in 1920. He proposed minor changes when he convened all the still-living gang leaders at the Morrison Hotel to divide up the city into bootlegging fiefdoms, a solution they grudgingly accepted.

"I told them we are making a shooting gallery out of a great business and nobody is going to profit by it," Capone said after the cease-fire, bragging that for the first time in several years he was able to ride to Prairie Avenue all alone in his bulletproof car. Before the truce, he said, he needed the protective cavalcade of flotilla before and behind his so that every journey looked like a funeral procession, which it "had to . . . so it wouldn't be one."

But there were different kinds of funeral processions: some took place after a sudden and unexpected death, and they were shocking and difficult to accept; others were slow and steady declines that brought great relief to those left behind. To those who lived in Chicago during the years of his domination, Al Capone's eventual downfall encompassed both and a bit more: a shock that it could happen, a relief when it was over, and then an enduring and unending drive to stand over the metaphorical grave site and ponder what had happened. The most amazing thing about it was how quickly it occurred.

Chapter 10

INVENTING AL CAPONE

The first time Al Capone tried directly to influence public opinion happened in January 1927, just after Theodore "Tony the Greek" Anton's body was found: tortured, frozen, and dumped in such a way as to serve a warning that the killers could get away with murder whenever they wanted. Several days later and without reference to Anton, Al called a very different kind of press conference. What made it extraordinary was that he did not summon reporters to his hotel headquarters but instead invited them to his house on Prairie Avenue. There, he met them in house slippers and a pink apron (!), waving the large wooden spoon with which he had been stirring his mother's spaghetti sauce (not his, for he liked to eat but didn't cook). He treated them to a sit-down dinner in the dining room, with platter after platter of Teresa's cooking, washed down with good red wine (which of course they did not mention when they wrote stories about what a good, kind, and happy family man he was). Temporarily, the press conference had the moderating effect he wanted: in their stories of gang warfare, reporters inserted references to how Al Capone deplored the violence.

Capone was kept busy as 1927 unfolded, settling scores, masterminding takeovers, and fending off investigations into his business practices, so when he did talk to the press, it was usually as a spur-of-the-moment response to something that had happened, with remarks that were generally impromptu and off-the-cuff. He was a master of "spin" long before the term was coined, a shrewd manipulator who could think on his feet and was usually in command of every comment he uttered. The occasional problem arose when some of the reporters, as adept at turning a phrase as he was, managed to turn what he said against him. He knew he could not afford to be depicted as a foolish and ridiculous buffoon, which meant that he had to do more than react and respond whenever he found himself in an awkward situation. He realized that he had to conduct and control the outcome of every encounter with the press.

One way to do it was to put reporters on his payroll, as he was alleged to have done with Jake Lingle of the *Chicago Tribune,* but there were too many other honest journalists he could not bribe. Robert St. John in Cicero was most notable among them, seeing Al's machinations for what they were and refusing to be part of them. Others, like Harry Read, a city editor at the *Chicago Herald and Examiner,* recognized the extent of Capone's control and sought a quid pro quo; Read did not cut a deal that involved taking money but agreed to one that was guaranteed to give each man what he wanted: Capone would supply tips for exclusive stories and interviews for Read to assign to reporters who he thought (and hoped) were honest and independent, and Read would in turn give Capone tips on how to comport himself so that the resulting articles would be flattering and positive.

Anthony "Tony" Berardi Sr., the photographer most often assigned to cover Capone, credited Read with having "educated the guy in this respect." He quotes Read as telling Al Capone that he was now too prominent a figure to "act like a hoodlum" and that he had to learn how to "quit hiding [and] be nice to people." Berardi's photographs became one of the most complete archives of Capone's Chicago years, and he photographed Capone objectively even as he despised him for the harm he did to the reputation of every Italian-American. Berardi thought they all suffered guilt by association simply for bearing a name that ended with a vowel: "I knew what he was and what he did . . . He hurt the Italian people." Berardi took his photographs as he saw each situation unfolding, no matter how Capone was behaving: if they flattered him, fine; if not, they showed the reality of what was happening. They remain one of the most useful and accurate archives of Al Capone's multifaceted public life.

––––

There was a territorial truce as 1927 began, a fragile truce that should have given Capone time to concentrate on his family, but because of his stature throughout Chicago that proved impossible. He had been absent from Prairie Avenue for such long periods of time that an overt jousting for position had developed among the women. Mae wanted her husband around to mitigate the constant bickering in the house, particularly now that Mafalda was at an age where she felt she had the right to sass and argue with her as much as Teresa did. Mae was also getting antsy about being so confined during the winter months and wanted to get away from the household conflict and the never-ending snowstorms. She wanted Al to take her on a vacation as far away from Prairie Avenue as she could get, and Los Angeles seemed like a good bet for warmth and sunshine. Al liked the idea of California and thought it might be a good place to look for a second home, especially because life in Chicago had taken on another dimension that was quite literally overwhelming.

In today's parlance, Al Capone had become a celebrity whose every doing was a feast for the newspaper paparazzi of the time. Everything he said or did was fed into the endlessly grinding publicity mill, and within the small world of Chicago journalism he had camp followers and hangers-on who were always on the lookout for a scoop. He could not appear anywhere without a slew of reporters and photographers waiting to capture every word he said and every move he made, in the hope that one day they could shout the magic phrase that was more myth than reality in the news business: "Stop the presses!" Because his every move was followed, Al Capone had no privacy, and that in itself was dangerous, for who knew what enemies were lurking in wait to do him harm.

Despite the temporary truce, rival gang leaders were still looking for ways to kill him as soon as an opportunity presented itself. Then there were the crazies who seemed to crawl out of the woodwork, and on that front there were those who would be delighted to have Al Capone do a little harm for them. There was the woman in London who invited him to come to England and kill a neighbor with whom she was feuding. There was the man who somehow managed to get past Capone's massive security measures and onto the floor of the Metropole where he had his well-guarded office. The man promised to take out an insurance policy for $15,000 in Capone's name; his only condition was that Capone first had to loan him $3,000, after which he could then kill the man and recoup his money by collecting the insurance! It took several bodyguards to subdue the poor fellow and toss him out onto the street.

Capone was never alone, and he had no time for anything personal. When Tony Berardi invited him one afternoon to go to the gym for a few rounds of boxing, he refused, saying there were so many men waiting outside his office door to see him "on business" that he simply could not take the time for pleasure. Nor could he take time for his family either, because even going home for Teresa's Sunday dinner was fraught with complications and dangers. It seemed that if he wanted to spend time with Mae and Sonny, a good way to do it would be to take them to Los Angeles. It would also be a good way to combine business with pleasure, for the Outfit had begun to make inroads into organizing and extorting unions, and those in the movie industry were ripe for the picking.

———

Here, the accounts differ. Some newspaper articles and the biographies based on them claim he left his wife and son at home and only took Ralph and several bodyguards, telling Mae it was to be a scouting expedition and if everything worked out, he would take her and Sonny a short time later. Other accounts have him taking everyone: Ralph, the bodyguards, and also Mae and Sonny. His descendants claim the latter is true, as in later years Mae Capone often spoke of this trip as the first time she saw the West Coast and how she wished she could have stayed longer.

The entourage departed from Chicago's Union Station on December 6, 1927, unbothered because members of the press had all been told at an earlier press conference that Capone was on his way to St. Petersburg, Florida. He had to resort to such ruses for self-protection, for the gang leaders' truce was breaking down, Joe Aiello in particular was still gunning for him, and he feared who might board the train if his true destination was known.

Capone had deliberately called the press conference just before he left, where, as one of his earliest biographers put it, he "allowed his imagination to take over." He wanted to control the focus by initiating questions where he could give self-serving answers that would, in today's parlance, make excellent sound bites. He began by asking what he had done "to deserve such persecution." He told his audience that his hands were spotlessly clean, he had never killed anyone, and certainly he would never have anything to do with "a vice resort." His mission had always been to rehabilitate hoodlums, burglars, and robbers, to turn them into responsible citizens and return them to an upright, God-fearing, and law-abiding society. And what did all that public-spirited good behavior get him? Nothing but "constant public abuse." It was all so unfair, he said plaintively. His mother and family were hurt by unjust tales of his terrible criminality; it was "getting too much for them and I'm sick of it all myself."

He insisted that all he had done since coming to Chicago was to give the public "what the public wants." Yes, he admitted, he did break the laws of Prohibition, but so, too, did the people who bought his booze. What, he asked, was the difference between his selling it and the customer who bought and drank it? Weren't the legal and moral issues blurred here, and didn't both parties share equal responsibility for breaking the law? "I've been spending the best years of my life as a public benefactor," he concluded, and most of the people who read newspapers agreed with him. In their eyes, Al Capone was a hero.

Nevertheless, he was leaving Chicago and going just before Christmas, implying that it would be a permanent move, which was alarming to all those on his various payrolls who worried they would not be getting their holiday handout. Before he went, he said he wanted to thank the friends "who have stood by me through this unjust ordeal." He offered "forgiveness" to his enemies and said the "coppers" would have to "find a new gangland chief" to persecute.

"Maybe they'll find a new hero for the headlines," he mused, but that was wishful thinking indeed, for his notoriety was only just beginning.

———

The trip to California was not the long and leisurely vacation Mae wanted. Instead, it was a short one of eight days, with six of them spent on trains to and from Los Angeles. A host of reporters and photographers was waiting when the train arrived at the city's Union Station, eager to watch the chief of police and his deputies, who had assembled to tell Al Capone that he and his party were not welcome. The Capone group was allowed to keep the reservation at the Biltmore Hotel, where rooms had been reserved in the name of Al Brown (that mysterious fellow who owned the used-furniture store in Chicago), but when the hotel people learned who he really was, Al Capone and his party were permitted to stay only for one night—two at the very most—just long enough to make return train reservations. The same public officials who met them upon arrival would be at the station to make sure they departed.

Capone tried to put a good front on the unceremonious booting he got in Los Angeles, telling reporters afterward that he had been treated "just fine," and "by prominent people, too." Although he never left the hotel grounds in the less than two days he was there, he claimed to have visited the homes of movie stars and toured a film studio before going to elaborate lunches and dinners at the homes of various dignitaries. He was also said to have told reporters that he went to Tijuana, Mexico, for the horse races at Agua Caliente; it was a mythical claim because his only visit to the West Coast was in December 1927 and the racetrack did not open until June 1928, but one that has been magnified over the years to insist that he used the visit to become a kingpin in Baja crime circles.

There are those who swear that he was personally responsible for persuading the Mexican government to build a hotel-casino called the Rosarito Beach Hotel. He was said to be the driving force behind marinas built to shelter his booze-running boats at a place called Los Coronados and that he also had tunnels constructed in which to hide the stuff. None of this was true: liquor was legal in Mexico, and there were never any tunnels built into the sandy beaches. There was a marina, but it had been built by the government to lure people to the hotel and casino, both of which were already in severe disrepair in 1927 and totally unusable by 1930. As they have with so many other urban legends, guides have made a good living ever since escorting gullible tourists to see the ruins of things Al Capone never ordered to be built because he was never there.

———

And so the little band of travelers left the Biltmore, returned sheepishly to Union Station, and got back on the eastbound train, only to learn that Chicago didn't want Al Capone either. The police chief had called in reporters to proclaim that Capone had only gone to Los Angeles because his force had driven him out of town and would certainly not permit him to return. Capone was not cowed and responded with a brief statement of his legal rights: "I'm a property owner and tax payer in Chicago. I can certainly return to my own home."

On the return trip, everywhere the train stopped, crowds held back by cordons of armed policemen thronged to catch a glimpse of the notorious criminal. The cheering hordes hoped he would at least appear on the platform for a breath of fresh air so they could see him, while the local police proclaimed themselves ready to shoot him if he tried to step down even for a moment. At several stops along the way, enterprising reporters found a way to board the train but were kept away from Capone by his bodyguards. When the train entered southern Illinois, only Jake Lingle succeeded in getting a story, but only because Al Capone wanted him to have it.

Lingle was the chief crime reporter for the *Chicago Tribune* and was most likely deeply embedded in the Outfit's payroll shortly after Capone took over the organization. Naturally, he painted Capone as a much-maligned public benefactor. There were dangers in getting too close to Capone that often outnumbered the rewards, and Lingle made a very convincing example of what could happen to those who did. He was one of Capone's favorites at the time but several years later was also most likely assassinated on his command, when he overstepped the bounds of what Al Capone wanted to be known about himself and the Outfit.

In this instance, Lingle was still a Capone favorite and happy to write what Al told him to say, that he was "a citizen with an unblemished record ... hounded from his home by the very policemen whose salaries are paid, at least in part, from the victim's pocket." Capone pretended to be dismayed when Lingle quoted him as saying everything that happened since he left for Los Angeles had left him "feeling very bad, very bad." In a plea for public sympathy, he painted himself as a sad victim of unfortunate circumstances who had no idea why he was of such interest to the public or "what all this fuss is about." It was Capone's blatant pitch to sway public opinion and get the better of the authorities, but he was also crafty enough to be plotting strategy as the train rolled on toward Chicago. He decided not to be on it when it arrived.

Al left Mae and Sonny on board to detrain in the city, but he got off in Joliet on December 14, where six shotgun-carrying local policemen were waiting and where he was promptly arrested for carrying a concealed weapon. He was the only one with a sense of humor as he reached into his pocket to offer the ammunition as well, saying, "You'd think I was Jesse James and the Youngers, all in one." The unsmiling officers led him to the police station, where he was booked and locked into a small cell with two smelly derelicts. He promptly paid their fines to get rid of them and had the cell to himself for an overnight stay.

Early the next day, his lawyers arrived to oversee him as he peeled off bills from his large wad of cash and paid the steep fines and court costs of almost $3,000. A cheering throng was there to see him off in the cortege of big black sedans driven by his men who had come to bring their leader and his lawyers home. They went directly to Chicago Heights, where Jake Guzik and the others on the Outfit's "Board of Directors" threw a welcome-home bash to celebrate his return. After the party, Capone disappeared until just before Christmas, to reunite with his family when he thought it was finally safe to return to Prairie Avenue and the holiday celebrations.

Once he was in Prairie Avenue, still more rumors flew about where he had been, most of them assigning him to the house of one of the many underlings who lived in the Chicago Heights area, but he had not stayed with them after the party; instead, he had gone to Freeport and the home of Raphael and Clotilde Capone, where he spent long hours closeted in conversation with him before letting her pamper him with her excellent meals. Al did a lot of thinking as he and Raphael talked, mostly about the indignities he had just been through and how to ensure they never happened again.

Here he was, the best-known and most feared figure in Chicago's criminal world, as well as the de facto director of how it functioned politically. His name was known internationally by 1925, and until the end of 1927 he was more admired than reviled throughout the world. Thus, it was galling to be turned away from Los Angeles, made into the butt of jokes, and turned into a laughingstock by posturing public officials and low-level policemen. It was especially embarrassing to find that the statements he gave to reporters he counted on to do his bidding sometimes received an entirely different response from the public. Granted, the statements were self-serving and self-aggrandizing, but the public had always been sympathetic before. After the Los Angeles debacle, he realized that the public was snickering more than admiring him. Clearly, he needed to do something other than what he had been doing.

When he finally returned to Prairie Avenue after the Los Angeles fiasco, he found the house surrounded by police who had orders to arrest him every time he tried to leave it. He was the No. 1 target of the authorities, who decided that since they could not force the criminal element to leave the city unless they actually witnessed them committing a crime, they would instead shadow their every move, hoping it might make them uncomfortable enough to pull up stakes and move away. It had an effect on the press, as reporters began to emphasize the negative whenever the opportunity presented itself. It began when Mae became so upset by the constant surveillance that she actually broke her vow never to speak to the press and called Jake Lingle to ask him to write a story begging everyone camped outside to go away, if only for Sonny's sake. Like everything else that was now printed about any of the Capone family, this story also had the opposite effect from what she (and Al) had intended.

"Capone's Son Finds Sins of Father Heavy," read the headline with the subhead "Mother Pleads for Lad, Victim of Schoolmates' Torment." It was an interesting but untrue headline, for Sonny Capone did not attend school;

he was still being taught at home by his mother and private tutors. In the article, Lingle was partially kind to Mae as he let her explain in her own words how hurt she was to see her little boy suffer. She explained that she wanted all the negative publicity to stop and for all those camped outside her house to leave them alone and stop writing about them. Mae was naive enough to think it would be that simple, that all she had to do was appeal to people's better natures and they would go away, freeing her and her family from living in a public fishbowl. Al, being more sophisticated, thought he could control other, larger issues if he kept a few malleable reporters on the payroll and got them to print his version of whatever that day's story was.

Neither Mae nor Al understood that they had become celebrities who would be forever hounded, and even if they did nothing newsworthy, stories would still be written about them. Both would eventually realize that events were spiraling beyond their control and they had no chance to maintain any semblance of privacy in the public circus their lives had become. There was no going back, and a new way had to be found to move forward.

———

Al Capone thought he had found a way to manage the press when he let reporters know (truthfully) in January 1928 that he was setting out for Florida with the intention of spending the winter months in Miami. To ensure that every big-city and small-town official knew he was coming, he told reporters exactly what he wanted them to print: that he intended to buy a house somewhere in the state but was concentrating on Miami. Then he indulged in a bit of embellishment designed to placate the populace, saying he would live the life of an honest and law-abiding citizen who would plant himself firmly in the community by opening a restaurant and joining the Rotary Club. That did more to inflame than soothe public apprehension and outrage; it also encouraged reporters to ask the chief of police in Miami what he intended to do when the most prominent gangster in the country detrained in his city. What else could the chief say but "if he's just here to have a good time and doesn't start any rough stuff, I won't bother him"? And that was exactly what Al Capone wanted to know.

The press conference was a preemptive strike, for Capone knew there could be the same sort of resistance in Miami that he had encountered in Los Angeles, particularly after he announced that he wanted to buy property. There were a lot of rich people in the area, and none of them wanted him for a neighbor, so it seemed prudent to let everyone see him doing exactly what he said he would do, live the quiet life of an exemplary citizen. It also seemed prudent to rent until he could get the lay of the land, but there again he was canny enough to know that no homeowner would entrust valuable property to him if he used his real name. His lawyers used a false one to rent a house on a posh Miami Beach street for six months, which might have gone unnoticed if they had not also rented the penthouse of the swank Hotel Ponce de León in downtown Miami for his headquarters by using a straw man there as well.

Actually, both actions bordered on the silly, for reporters had been covering his every move since he left Chicago and were staking out both the house and the hotel before he even got there. He could promote himself all he wanted as an unfortunate businessman who was just looking for a refuge, but nobody was buying that story. The reporters and Capone's bodyguards took turns teasing and taunting each other outside the house, thus ensuring a constant supply of unflattering anecdotes for news stories. And when the menacing miens of the bruisers who protected him were on display in the hotel lobby, they were enough to frighten the tourists away, never mind the good citizens. Groups like the chamber of commerce and the local Women's Club were in high dander as they besieged the mayor, John Newton Lummus Jr., to get rid of Al Capone. His Honor dutifully obeyed, summoning Capone to his office in January 1928 and asking him to leave because "a majority of the citizens do not want him here."

Capone went to the office as commanded and promptly proceeded to charm not only the mayor but also the city manager and the police chief, who flanked him on either side. He won them all over without offering a single bribe or the hint of a threat by suavely playing the poor picked-upon good guy who couldn't get a break or a square deal wherever he went. He told Mayor Lummus that he would never stay where he was not wanted, but he liked Florida and hoped he would not have to leave Miami, as he had not had time to think about where he would take his sweet wife and innocent son if they had to go. Some of Al's descendants chuckle when they tell this story, saying he already knew Miami was his last hope for finding a haven. He had earlier been told he would be run out of St. Petersburg after some of his lawyers made discreet inquiries about several properties there, and Ralph and Albert had been thrown unceremoniously in jail overnight when they tried to buy real estate for him in New Orleans. When asked why he would not consider Cuba, Al turned that idea down flat because of the language difference; he simply did not like Puerto Rico (too poor for his taste), and when the Bahamas (which he did like) heard he was interested, an ordinance was passed to ban him from owning property there.

Capone so charmed the Miami mayor that after the meeting ended, Lummus repeated Capone's own words to reporters, saying Al was a fair and reasonable man who only wanted to be left in peace to enjoy the sunshine with his wife and son, whose health was fragile. After that, it was smooth sailing, even though the couple who owned the rental house quaked at the thought of the damage Chicago gangsters might do to the property when they learned the real name of their tenant.

Mae was thrilled to be in Miami, first, because Teresa and Mafalda were not there and, second, because it was the first time in her marriage that she had ever lived apart from them in a house of her own. Even though it was a rental and the furnishings were of fine quality, she quickly set out on shopping sprees to buy all sorts of extra comforts for the house. She endeared herself to the local shopkeepers who could not overpraise the charming, modest, cultured, polite, and elegant Mrs. Capone (the adjectives abounded), the smartly dressed and chic wife of the notorious and dangerous criminal in their midst. They waxed eloquent in public but privately derided her taste in interior decor, which her grandchildren admit was often that of someone who grew up poor and was suddenly able to spend vast sums of money on household objects and furnishings that were of excellent quality but also sometimes quite over the top.

Unfortunately for Mae, there was one major irritant that came with the house: it also came with Al's brothers, their wives and girlfriends, and many of the men from the Outfit, who all thought nothing of dropping in unannounced and staying for hours. Al expected Mae to offer hospitality to everyone, no matter who they were or what time they arrived, and she was gracious enough to do it. He also needed her to arrange parties that were extravagant in their food and drink and at the same time passed for good taste in an often flamboyant community, for he knew that if he wanted to buy his own house and ensure that the deal would proceed smoothly, he needed to woo prominent locals to help him acquire it.

He was always careful in his business dealings, never signing his name to any document, never establishing banking accounts in his own name, always working through intermediaries who did the deeds that made things happen the way he wanted. Tony Berardi put it best: "He was no dummy. He was one hell of an organizer. He knew how to pick people for certain positions in certain categories."

Even though he had used phony names for rentals, he knew better than to risk doing so in the purchase of a real estate property transaction, and because there was still enough residual resentment of his being in Miami, he knew it would be best to have an outsider make the deal for real property. He needed someone both malleable and gullible to do his bidding, and he found just such a wide-eyed sycophant in the manager of the Ponce de León, a young man called Parker A. Henderson Jr., who also happened to be the well-connected son of a former mayor. Henderson was only too eager to befriend the local celebrity-in-residence, as he found it both thrilling and chilling to hang out with the tough guys who surrounded him.

"Mr. A. Costa" had taken the lease on the hotel suite, and whenever he needed someone to pick up a money order that had come from Chicago or to send one off, Henderson didn't mind disguising his handwriting and signing Mr. Costa's name for him. Eventually, Henderson was only too happy to represent Mr. Costa when he was "too busy to expend his energy" inspecting real estate in person. Henderson worked directly with agents who scrambled to gather a selection of suitable properties that could be presented for the rich, mysterious, and fictitious Mr. Costa's approval. Very soon that ruse became unnecessary, once newspaper headlines splashed the news of the search.

"Capone Hunted," blared the *Chicago Tribune;* "But by Realty Men," read the subhead in smaller type. As it turned out, working with real estate agents was just another ruse, for Mayor Lummus was also in the real estate business, a part of a family concern that had been involved in developing Miami tourism for several generations, and it was he who conveniently became the buyer's agent of record when Al Capone finally bought his house on March 27, 1928.

He had received enough sound legal advice to know that besides not using a fictitious name on the deed of sale, he should not give the necessary cash directly or have it pass through channels in his real name. Cash wired from Chicago was passed surreptitiously to Henderson to secure the purchase in his name until he could transfer the property quietly and easily to Mrs. Mae Capone. In all, Henderson signed for cash and money orders totaling $31,000 that Al used for his lavish living and business expenses, plus another $10,000 that was filtered for Henderson to use as the down payment on a property costing $40,000. Lummus secured a mortgage for the remaining $30,000, and all was well until Henderson went to transfer the property to Mae. By law at the time, all mortgages had to be insured, so when the application was made in Mae's name, every insurance company recoiled in horror, and none would sell a policy to the gangster Capone or any member of his family. Thus no mortgage could be secured, so Al simply paid the rest of the money owed in "other ways," which meant that he filtered cash to Henderson in names other than his own.

Unfortunately, the pleasure, indeed the joy, he took in acquiring the house turned out to have serious consequences that were not foreseen by him or his lawyers. In 1927, the U.S. Supreme Court upheld a vague and ill-defined law that said even illegal income was subject to taxation, which was the first time the federal government had a concrete issue to pursue against Al Capone. Federal officials were aware that he had been living lavishly in Florida, even gifting Henderson with one of his trademark diamond belt buckles, and that he was now the owner of an expensive property that was being thoroughly and expensively renovated and expanded. Tax law at that time required that anyone earning more than $5,000 in *legitimate* income had to pay income taxes, which Al Capone had never paid, because he did not earn that amount legitimately. And as everything he did earn was carefully shielded and sheltered by the financial wizards who worked for the Outfit, he ostensibly had no *illegitimate* income either. But deeds of sale for expensive property did not float down like feathers to land on the heads of lucky buyers, and so the IRS had every right to raise its collective bureaucratic eyebrows as it looked on Al Capone long enough to wonder: Where did all the money come from?

———

The address was 93 Palm Avenue on Palm Island, a strip of land on Biscayne Bay that was part of Miami Beach and not in Miami proper, just slightly out of reach and thus offering a respite from the angry citizens of the city. It was built in 1922 by Clarence M. Busch of the Anheuser-Busch dynasty. Ironically, Prohibition, which was the basis of Al's fortune, meant hard times for the legitimate brewing industry, so Busch had sold the house several years earlier to another buyer, who then sold it to the Capones in 1928. By area standards, it was pleasant but not palatial. The house itself was white stucco with a separate three-room gatehouse next to the public road that guarded access. The lot was relatively small, but it had a hundred feet of water frontage where Al docked the speedboat and thirty-two-foot cabin cruiser he bought as soon as the property was legally his. He was so proud of the cabin cruiser that he named it the *Sonny and Ralphie,* after his and Ralph's sons, who had become as close as brothers while being raised together mainly by Mae in the Prairie Avenue house. They were close friends as children and remained so as adults. There was no pool, so Al had one built with a double-filtration system for both salt and fresh water; at thirty by sixty feet, it was then the largest private swimming pool in all of Florida. There were never any fish in this pool, although stories persist to this day that there were. Al had a two-story cabana house built next to it and also another separate two-story guesthouse. He loved spiral staircases, so some of the buildings had at least one. By the time he was finished remodeling, there were seven bedrooms, five full baths, and two powder rooms in the main house. There was also a rock pool, which gave him a tranquil setting he enjoyed, but contrary to some of the fables told about the property, members of the Capone family never met there for daily group prayers that included saying the rosary.

Al had the entire property enclosed by tall privacy walls of concrete blocks that were screened from view by expensive shrubbery; the heavy iron gates were further fortified by massive oak doors inside them that barred outsiders from seeing down the driveway. An exterior telephone allowed visitors to call the main house, and bodyguards could screen them through a peephole before they were admitted. Iron bars were installed on the windows of the guardhouse, and the entire lot was turned into an impregnable fortress. All this cost well over an additional $100,000 (almost $1.5 million in contemporary dollars).

And then there was the interior, on which Mae lavished untold and never-totaled sums of money. With a few exceptions, like the gold-plated faucets on the black fixtures in the downstairs powder room, she had fairly good taste despite a penchant for ornate (but excellent) reproductions of furniture in the French Louis XIV style, most of which she had painted white with gold gilt and upholstered in a vibrant chartreuse because it was *the* fashionable color of the moment. Al insisted on a life-sized oil painting of himself and Sonny that dominated the living room, and she decorated contentedly around it. The master bedroom featured a king-sized four-poster bed, which she had covered in subdued fabrics that did little to divert attention from the massive wooden trunk at the foot of it. It was supposedly filled with cash, with Al allegedly boasting that it was safer to keep it there than to put it in a bank, where robbers could steal it. Al and Mae's descendants claim this is another myth, for the chest was where she stored extra bedding.

Mae set an elegant table, as she was fond of silver and bought lavishly in flatware and serving pieces; she liked fine china and lots of it, so there were many complete sets of dishes. Otherwise, she chose things that were similar to and would have been suitable for any upscale dwelling in the area. She did give parties that were huge and extravagant, but the people who attended knew they were expected to behave; if guests wanted to be invited back, there would be no raucous behavior, spilled drinks, or unfortunate stains on any of Mae Capone's pale upholstery and expensive rugs. The only sour note to her entertaining came when some of the guests decided they needed to have a souvenir of their visit and walked off with something that could fit into pockets or purses. Over the years, everything from silver salvers to spoons and ashtrays found their way to various auction blocks claiming provenance from the "Capone mansion."

Two of her parties were so elaborate and so different from the usual manner in which Miami socialites celebrated that they became staples of local dinner party chatter before becoming legends about the Capone family's life in Miami. To calm the outrage (real or feigned) of the Miami business community over the purchase of the Palm Island property, Al invited around seventy-five of the most influential men in town to dinner. Mae had her cooking staff prepare an elaborate Italian feast that featured pasta—an item hitherto not offered at fancy dinner parties—while Al provided a bar that featured soft drinks, mineral waters, juices, and no booze. After a musicale, one of the guests saluted him as "the new businessman of the community" and gifted him with a fountain pen.

Sonny's twelfth birthday party was held on December 18, 1930, and was another event that brought the children of some of Miami's elite to Palm Island. Mae had no intention of going back to Chicago when winter came, so she had enrolled Sonny in the prestigious and private Catholic school St. Patrick's, where the nuns tried to screen the students from any unpleasant and unsavory news of the outside world. For his party, she had invited fifty classmates. However, before they could enter the property, all of the young guests had to provide, along with their presents, a letter signed by their parents saying they were allowed to be there, for Mae had carefully included such a document along with the engraved invitations. Whether out of "curiosity, dare-deviltry, or inverted snobbishness," all the parents agreed to let their children eat cake and ice cream and frolic on the Capone family's property.

Sonny was about to become a teenager, and Mae was still doing everything she could to shield him from the reality of his father's life. He had a good idea of what that entailed, having seen the tough guys always hanging around and having assimilated details of his father's doings from snatches of overheard conversation and seeing the occasional headline when Mae was not quick enough to hide the papers. He also had Ralphie as a source of information, for his father, Ralph "Bottles," was an uncouth man who did nothing to mitigate his vulgarity and shot off his mouth in front of everyone, even his sensitive young son. Nevertheless, Sonny loved his mother—and his father, too—and as he grew up, he went along with the facade of respectability Mae built around Al, and the loving and compliant Sonny was willing to let her think that he believed it.

Eventually, Teresa and Mafalda came to Palm Island, but Mae made it very clear that this was her house and she was in complete charge of it. She had daily but never live-in help, which is a matter of some disagreement within the later generations of Capones, some of whom believe this was her choice as a precaution against what they might reveal about the family's private life, others who think it was because she could find no one willing to live in a dangerous gangster's house. However, she did have a daily staff that included a cook, a manservant who acted as butler and general overseer of the property, and several maids and cleaning people. When Teresa visited, she immediately bustled to take over the kitchen but only after she secured Mae's blessing. And if Mafalda had any criticisms, she was smart enough to keep quiet and keep them to herself.

Mae took to the role of chatelaine of a grand property as if she had been born to it and had done it all her life. Just by her discreet participation in public events, she did much to soothe any reservations townspeople might have had about Al Capone and to placate most of the ill feelings his overwhelming presence in the Ponce de León aroused. She was known for her generous contributions to philanthropic and charitable events, but what really secured the affection of the community was a private matter that very quickly became a staple of local lore.

After the lease expired on the rental house and the owners returned, they were surprised to find the place in better condition than they had left it and to find that Mae had left many of her little touches behind as gifts, among them some of the fine china and silver flatware she had bought for her large parties. She had also left an unpaid telephone bill of more than $700, which the upset owners believed she had done deliberately. Before they even had a chance to spread the news of the deadbeat Capones as town gossip, their doorbell rang, and they answered it to find an attractive blond woman standing there.

It was Mae, who told them she had just realized that one last phone bill must have come after they departed and she was there to pay it. She extracted a $1,000 bill from her purse and told the owners to keep it all because there might be some other minor damage that would need repairing. She made a gracious farewell and they never saw her again, but they lost no time in telling all of Miami about what had happened. Over the years, the tale has been embellished in a number of legends, both favorable and not about the Capones, but the truth is that no one could ever say Al and Mae did not pay their way, and usually more than what was due.

———

Al Capone was thrilled to own Palm Island, as the house came to be called in the family's private shorthand. He envisioned himself spending the late winter and early spring overseeing the initial changes and additions to the property, swimming in his pool and fishing from his boat, and in general ingratiating himself with everyone in Miami who mattered. And if Outfit business was done there (as it surely was), that would only add to his pleasure. It was such a relief to be warm, in balmy breezes and sunshine, and away from the misery of a Chicago winter and nonstop violence. If there was any time in his life when he hoped to have the opportunity to develop what might loosely be called an inner life, it was during the early months of 1928. But as always, "business" interfered.

Local newspapers learned the details of how he purchased Palm Island through Henderson, and the stories caused an outburst of public indignation. Calls for the mayor to resign went unheeded, but the city council ordered a standing police detail of three to five men to follow Capone wherever he went. Things eventually quieted down because it was an election year and he had many allies in the local Republican Party who benefited from his "donations" to their campaigns. And yet tranquillity still eluded him.

The flurry of outrage over the house purchase was brief, but as it was dying down, there was another one in Chicago that had more serious repercussions. The primary election of April 1928 was nicknamed the Pineapple Primary because of the shape of the bombs that were set off seemingly nonstop, and even though Al Capone was not there, the Outfit was closely involved. The election for state and local offices did major damage to the homes of four supporters of Mayor Big Bill Thompson, who was not up for reelection that year but whose slate was facing another of the numerous so-called reform opponents he faced periodically. Diamond Joe Esposito, a rival to Al and the Outfit who was supporting the rival reform faction, had been warned by Al's men to withdraw, but he felt honor-bound to keep his word and thus sealed his death sentence. He was gunned down in front of his home by a barrage of bullets from a speeding car, his death witnessed by his bodyguards and his wife and children. As was usual in such events, none of the witnesses identified his killers. His death would have been ignored as just another gang-related assassination, but shortly after his funeral two more bombs went off at the homes of other anti-Thompson candidates.

Thompson and his cohorts also knew how to spin a story, so they accused their opponents of planting the bombs themselves in order to diminish voter support for the mayor's slate. Naturally, the opposition fought back, rightly claiming the bombings were the work of Capone's Outfit on Thompson's behalf to instill enough fear and chaos to ensure that he was victorious. As the accusations flew and the violence continued, the Chicago primary became national and international news, and reporters from all parts of the world flocked to the city. Things were so bad that shortly after Capone returned to Chicago for a brief spell, Judge Frank Loesch, the president of the Chicago Crime Commission (CCC), gritted his teeth and went, hat in hand, to ask for his help in controlling the situation.

Loesch knew that what the press had written was indisputable: the "Caponites" (as one of Al Capone's many biographers called his henchmen and their willing workers) were in control. With threats, bribes, murders, and beatings added to the continuing bombings, the only choice for the honest voters who braved the gun-carrying thugs on patrol at the polling stations seemed to be a ballot box rigged for the Thompsonites. Everyone expected his slate to coast to easy victory because the police had largely absented themselves, leaving Capone's men free to make sure every dishonest ruse or ploy prevailed.

Perhaps if Mayor Thompson had not been so cavalier, the election might have settled into history without consequences after the usual low voter turnout and the desultory shrugs that crime and Chicago politics were synonymous. Unfortunately for Thompson, he enraged the electorate when he had the bad taste to boast to reporters that Chicago was no different from any other major city, where "you can get a man's arm broken for so much, a leg for so much, or beaten up for so much." The only difference between Chicago and New York, he concluded, was that "we print [news stories about] our crime and they don't."

To the astonishment of pundits, pollsters, and political reporters, there was a huge voter turnout; approximately 400,000 voters were expected to cast ballots on primary day, April 10, 1928, but the actual number was more than double, well into 800,000. Thompson's slate was rousingly defeated, and as the *Chicago Tribune* reported, "an outraged citizenship resolved to end corruption, the machine gunning, the pineappling, and the plundering which have made the state and the city a reproach throughout the civilized world." For Al Capone, this meant that he was in a decidedly uncomfortable spotlight. Bombs continued to burst and vitriol to flourish; someone had to be blamed, and he was an easy target.

———

Damon Runyon, the newspaperman who chronicled Broadway and the seamier side of New York, became Capone's Miami Beach neighbor when he bought an expensive house just across the bay on Hibiscus Island. He lost no time in contributing to the general blame and mockery that intensified against Capone after the Pineapple Primary in 1928, and he kept it up for years afterward, such as in a biting 1931 satire titled "Gentlemen, the King!" Runyon acted as the narrator who listens in as a mobster answers a child's question about Al Capone's "pineapples" and has the mobster produce one for the child to see. The narrator immediately recognizes it "as a bomb such as these Guineas chuck at people they do not like, especially Guineas from Chicago." It is interesting that Runyon resorted to ethnic slurs, for his fascination with "gangster chic" and his friendships with gangsters were well-known. He hung out with Arnold Rothstein at Lindy's in New York and when in Miami was a regular at Al Capone's lavish parties. In all his writings, he was stridently against establishment wealth and privilege and on the side of the poor, the picked upon, and the dispossessed, all of whom Capone claimed to represent. Runyon wrote with gusto about gangsters who flouted their ill-gained wealth in the face of "old money" and excused how they got it by blaming Prohibition for forcing them into lives of crime. Al Capone often said the same about his own career.

Runyon was well-known as a "womanizing narcissist," and his tastes were so similar to Capone's that some said he deliberately copied them: he also liked high living, flashy expensive clothes, gambling, and playing the horses. He made no secret of his closeness to Capone and hinted that he used many of his attributes as models for his characters. And yet from their very first encounter, he joined the general clamor deriding, ridiculing, and denouncing his so-called friend.

Capone had a lot of these fair-weather friends among the famous and the talented, and their impressions, true or not, have helped to form the opinion posterity has created of Al the man, as opposed to Capone the ruthless killer. Many, among them entertainers like Louis Armstrong and Harry Richman, claimed they accepted his hospitality because they were afraid to refuse it, while others, including the early film star Bebe Daniels, said they accepted it because curiosity got the best of them. Very few were like Polly Adler and Sophie Tucker, who excused his profession and had only had good things to say about the polite gentleman with whom they occasionally played cards and partied.

Some of Al's detractors were like Runyon, who had access to immediate publication in newspaper columns and books, where they had ready outlets for snide commentary that elided their own unseemly and quite possibly unethical behavior. Biographers of his contemporary detractors have influenced subsequent cultural histories, which repeat many of their opinions and observations as the truth. Reporters on the major daily papers in the biggest cities also contributed to the creation of Al Capone as a cultural phenomenon. Prominent among them was the *Chicago Daily News* columnist Ben Hecht, who wrote the screenplay for *Scarface*, the 1932 gangster movie that became one of Hollywood's most successful films ever made. Newsmen covering the crime beat were expected to convey the facts about the nefarious activities of the Outfit's henchmen, which they usually did, but many found it almost impossible to write about murder, mayhem, and carnage without using a vocabulary that was colorful in the extreme; thus, the truth became enveloped in bloody bombast used to sell papers. Myths were created that became accepted as fact, but the metamorphosis of Al the man into Capone the cultural phenomenon was neither simple nor direct.

Contradictory versions also endure in books. Here are but two examples of how he was portrayed: Fred Pasley, who published in 1930 what he claimed was objective biography, titled it *Al Capone: The Biography of a Self-Made Man* and asked the reader to think about how Capone was able to create so many different personae, all of them true to a certain degree. An even more popular book appeared shortly after Pasley's, but the author Richard T. Enright's title tells the reader what he is expected to think before he turns a single page: *Al Capone on the Spot: The Inside Story of the Mas-*

ter Criminal and His Bloody Career. These two were just the beginning; depending on who was counting, between five and seven books appeared from 1929 to 1931 purporting to give "the real truth."

"Journalists took the leading role in inventing Al Capone," wrote the cultural historian David E. Ruth in a book entitled *Inventing the Public Enemy.* He credited Al's contemporaries with "sifting known facts, conjuring up others, and, perhaps most important, choosing the defining metaphors." Certainly Ruth is correct, but only by half, for Al Capone was a smart man, smart enough to know how to manipulate the media, and with varying degrees of success he became adept at doing so.

He seldom said anything uncomplimentary about anyone, and he left few personal documents or letters to tell what he really thought of events or people. He might have been "Sunny Jim" to the press, but he knew when to keep his political opinions to himself or when friendship was genuine and when it was not. He knew when he was being used, but he also knew how to use others, and he did it suavely and smoothly. He gave the impression that everyone in the world was his friend—until such time as they were not. With some of those former friends, he had the wherewithal to deal with them, and usually he did. But for those whom he could not have his minions kill or intimidate into silence, and for those he could not manage or manipulate, he had to find other ways to get his message out.

Capone read all the daily papers and kept up to date on current affairs, especially with the newest methods of doing corporate business. He was always on the lookout for anything that could further the operations of the Outfit, and he knew he needed help to counter the mostly negative publicity he had attracted since the trip to Los Angeles. As was usual for him, he tried to find the best man for the important job of changing his public image. That seemed to be Ivy Lee, the public relations genius who had succeeded in defusing the outrage over John D. Rockefeller's Standard Oil Company by turning him into an admirable, civic-minded philanthropist. Although the novelist Upton Sinclair dubbed Lee "Poison Ivy" for his ability to manipulate public opinion, Lee had created a stellar reputation for himself through the careful acceptance of clients that included corporations such as Bethlehem Steel and individuals such as Charles Lindbergh and Walter Chrysler. Among his many honors, Lee had been appointed to the Council on Foreign Relations and had the ear of President Herbert Hoover. He was certainly not interested in sullying his reputation by representing Al Capone, so Capone had to look elsewhere.

Once again, Capone turned to Harry Read, the Chicago editor who had hitherto managed to provide him with positive stories while maintaining the carefully distanced relationship that allowed him to claim that his actions were ethical. Read advised Capone to talk as often as he could to the press but to steer clear of saying anything about Chicago politics. He took Read's advice, so he stayed mainly in Miami and said little about the Pineapple Primary while he concentrated instead on becoming, as the investigative reporter Gus Russo put it, "the toast of Chicago—at least among the city's downtrodden blue-collar segments." On his occasional forays back to the city, Al could count on ovations lasting as long as five minutes whenever he watched the Cubs play baseball; crowds cheered him at prizefights and yelled to ask for betting tips when he went to the races. Little guys, the ordinary working classes, loved him because "he gave writers and perfect strangers tips on fixed fights and horse races."

John Kobler, who conducted extensive interviews throughout the 1960s with elderly people who had known Al Capone in his heyday, wrote in his 1971 biography of an aged waitress who told him she thought he was "a wonderful person." Her reason: "He took from the rich and gave to the poor, didn't he?" Kobler quoted a "former Negro doorman" who still lived near the site of the Four Deuces as saying, "These folks 'round here never knowed who paid the rent, but it was Al . . . They was all fine boys and they was real good to me." The waitress and the doorman were typical of most Chicagoans, who did not fathom the connection between Capone and the corrupt political establishment.

"It is a curious fact that Capone is the object of a sort of hero worship," wrote Pasley, the on-the-spot observer. "Time had, indeed, wrought vast changes in our fellow townsman. Few now would recognize in the political Big Shot the roughneck bouncer of the Four Deuces, or in the tailored and chauffeured man about town the vulgar hoodlum." Pasley's beat was gangland, and he saw the gore and the mayhem firsthand, often on a daily basis. He was a skeptic who marveled at the preferential treatment Capone received everywhere he went. To illustrate his contention, Pasley quoted the columnist and sportswriter Westbrook Pegler when he covered the Stribling-Sharkey prizefight on February 27, 1929, in Miami Beach.

Pegler called Capone "the doyen of the racketeers" as he described the deference Jack Dempsey paid when he escorted Capone to a prime seat in the press box. He waxed sarcastic when he acknowledged that the "Gangland King" was "not there in an official capacity, but the public impression is such that persons are on official business at all times, wherever they may be." Capone probably did have a heavy bet riding on the fight, so perhaps Pegler should not be criticized for interpreting Dempsey's welcome as "an exchange of amenities between two professions having much in common," that is, boxers in fixed fights and those who fixed them. Like Runyon, Pegler never turned down Capone's hospitality but always made sure to cover himself with a snide remark about his reason for having accepted it.

Al Capone had learned well from Harry Read and wanted to reward him. Read did tell the truth to his superiors at the *Chicago American* when he said that he wanted to recover from pneumonia in a warm climate and in April 1929 would go to Miami to do so. He neglected to mention that he intended to combine his recovery with picking up some good stories about Capone's latest doings. Read gave his editors the Ritz Hotel as his contact address, but he never stayed there; Ralph was waiting in the lobby to whisk him to Palm Island, where Al insisted he stay. To cover such blatantly unethical behavior, Read scheduled a series of photo shoots that showed Al fishing or swimming and claiming to be "in retirement from the booze business," as he insisted on portraying himself to any reporter who wrote about him. That might have gotten past editorial scrutiny, albeit grudgingly, but Read made the fatal mistake that cost him his job when he allowed Al, Ralph, and their bodyguards to load him onto a private plane bound for a jaunt in Cuba.

When his bosses grilled him, Read insisted he was in his Havana hotel bedroom by 8:00 p.m. and had not participated in the carousing that brought the secret police to the hotel the next morning. Everyone in the Capone party, Read included, was taken to headquarters and questioned about the allegation that the Outfit intended to bomb a public building (or buildings) on May 1 in order to disrupt labor union celebrations. By becoming part of his story, Read had crossed the line, and when the *American* published an article giving the barest details of why he was fired, it still included the carefully constructed quotation from Al Capone that he was only in Cuba "to spend some money and drink some wine." They also quoted the chief of the secret police, who said the government was glad to have him as a guest and hoped his stay would be pleasant. It seemed that once again he had managed to keep the public squarely on his side, but with Read gone, one of his major resources for getting his version out was lost.

More and more, try as he might to woo and win the press, he was not succeeding, mainly because there were too many other burgeoning venues he could not control. Radio had become a popular pastime in even the most remote and isolated homes where there was electricity, and news programs and serials drew entire families who listened avidly. The movies were taking him up as a feature subject, and most moviegoers were taking these representations for the gospel truth of Al Capone's life. And now there was the spate of books devoted entirely or in large part to his life and career, all purporting to be objective biographies and most of them painting him in a decidedly bad light. As books about him began to appear steadily in the United States and England and in French and German translations, it seemed the entire world had succumbed to what Damon Runyon portrayed as "gangster chic" and could not get enough of him; publications ranging from sleazy pulps to respected magazines and journals dedicated enormous amounts of print to the phenomenon he had become. There was no question that he was good for business when even the highly respected *Time* put him on its cover on March 24, 1930, because his face sold magazines.

Some of these books and articles took many of their cues from what Capone managed to float into the public forum, but only a few fully accepted the positive self-portraits he created. He liked to call himself a businessman, so some authors obliged him even as they omitted what his business activities entailed; he described himself as the loving patriarch of a large extended family (which he actually was), and because this resonated nicely and positively with many ordinary working-class Americans, feature writers of every persuasion from respected columnists to sob sisters went along with it. Still there were the pulps, which sold more copies when they portrayed him as the ultimate big spender, lousy gambler, and womanizing playboy (which he also was). There were many American men who lived vicariously through his excesses and bought copies to celebrate behavior they would never be able to emulate or afford.

Al Capone read the books about him as soon as they were published. He tended to disregard most of them, but Pasley's really bothered him. He claimed that he could not recognize himself in any part of it, that it was not about him but "about somebody else." The Pasley book stuck in his craw, and he decided that his only recourse was to commission an authorized biography that would paint him in the colors he wanted the public to see. He liked the stories that Howard Vincent O'Brien wrote for the *Chicago Daily News,* so he contacted him.

O'Brien told the story of how he came to be involved with Capone in a curiously convoluted essay. In 1933, when Capone was gone from the Chicago scene, O'Brien wrote about the experience in a memoir replete with so many factual errors that it is difficult to sort out where his authentic memories of Capone drifted into fictional re-creations. The basic story begins with O'Brien's claim that he became involved in the project when a detective he identified only as "Dudley" contacted him. This Dudley was allegedly employed by the Secret Six, a group of wealthy Chicago men who had formed a committee to try to end Capone's domination of the city. That might have been why Dudley had investigated Capone so thoroughly, but it does not explain why he was charged by Capone to contact O'Brien and bring him to the Lexington Hotel for a serious look over. Unless, of course, Dudley was like so many others in Chicago and on the Outfit's payroll as well as the Secret Six's. O'Brien never addresses such possible double-dipping.

The story becomes even more curious, for Capone specifically wanted O'Brien not to write an authorized biography, which might have guaranteed him some semblance of independence and objectivity, but to ghostwrite his "autobiography." Whether Capone intended to pass it off as his own writing or whether he would have allowed O'Brien's name to appear on it in an "as told to" form is not known, for O'Brien never published anything but the account he gave in the memoir that he did not publish until 1948, a year after Capone's death.

O'Brien described his first meeting with Capone in his private and heavily guarded headquarters on the twenty-third floor of the Lexington Hotel. He was particularly struck by the three portraits behind the desk, of Washington and Lincoln and, in his memory, of Al Capone between them wearing knickerbockers and holding a golf club (thus disputing that it was Big Bill Thompson between the two presidents). O'Brien noted that Capone greeted him "as starched and pressed as a fashion plate ... heavily built with an obvious tendency to fat. His manner was suave, his voice gently modulated."

The conversation began with small talk about golf, but Capone wasted little time before getting down to business. He was a busy man, O'Brien wrote, letting his readers know the reach of the Outfit's tentacles when he described Capone pausing in their conversation to take a call from an unnamed senator in Washington who needed a favor. Then it was back to the proposed "autobiography."

Capone said Pasley had written "cruel and unkind things" that were "definitely libelous" about him, and he wanted O'Brien's advice on taking legal action. They disagreed about how many copies Pasley had sold; Al insisted it was seventy thousand, and O'Brien said it was far fewer. Capone's estimate was nearer the truth, which was why he was so upset; Pasley was a respected *Tribune* reporter, and many people believed that what he wrote was true. O'Brien managed to dissuade him from legal action, telling him that proving libel was so difficult it would be "easier to get blood out of a turnip than money out of an author." Capone agreed to drop his pursuit of Pasley and concentrate on his own book.

O'Brien described being excited by the prospect of writing it: "It seemed to me that if this book were what I thought it might be made into, it would be perhaps the most significant contribution to current history that could possibly be written." He was entirely correct about such a book's importance, but almost immediately as he began to conduct interviews with Al Capone, he began "to feel doubt about the outcome." O'Brien asked everything, from soft questions such as the correct spelling of his name (Al didn't know if *i* or *e* was the correct ending and said he preferred "Capone") to hard ones such as if he really gave a banquet for Albert Anselmi and John Scalise before he beat them to death with a baseball bat. No matter what he asked, Capone's answer was always the same: "I can't tell you that. It wouldn't be fair to my people."

Al Capone had constructed his version of his life, and he expected O'Brien to write it. He wanted O'Brien to find a publisher who would pay him (Capone) a $1 million advance, and when O'Brien discussed it with an editor in New York, he agreed that the story would merit such an amount but only if it were "true and unadorned" because it would probably be "the most startling story of modern times." However, no publishing contract was ever signed because O'Brien knew early on what the project would become, that Capone would insist on "not a revelation but a monument." He wanted a book that would focus on his good deeds, charitable gifts, and devotion to his mother. Nobody was going to pay $1 million for such recycled pap and O'Brien knew it. The problem was how to extricate himself from a tricky situation.

"More and more I wanted to write the true and complete story of Al Capone and his world but more and more it became clear that it never could be done," he concluded. He was growing increasingly nervous when Outfit men began to give him an eye that clearly indicated they suspected him of knowing too much, which was not the healthiest of circumstances. His trepidation was magnified one day during a casual conversation when Capone told O'Brien how carefully he had to speak to his men; sometimes when he lost his temper, he would say without thinking something like "gee, I wish somebody would bump that guy off." He did not really mean it, but the problem was that "one of these young punks who wants to make a name for himself goes ahead and does it." "Poor Al," Capone said about himself as he continued to try to enlist sympathy, his hit men did the dastardly deed and then left him to clean up the mess and pick up the pieces. That was enough for O'Brien, who bided his time until he could drop the project, when Capone suddenly had a rash of far more "serious matters" to take care of, all of which began and ended in courtrooms. By that time, it was too late for publicity and public relations.

Chapter 11

LEGAL WOES

Everything in Al Capone's criminal empire began to fall apart as early as 1929 and from then until the teen years of the new millennium, hindsight has been a convenient tool with which to make pronouncements about what caused its disintegration and his downfall. Some say it started with the death of Frankie Yale in July 1928, calling it a totally unnecessary killing that Capone should not have ordered because it only focused unwanted attention on his penchant for irrational cruelty. Others said the same thing about the assassination two years later, in June 1930, of the reporter Jake Lingle, who allegedly knew too much and was ready to tell it to the world. It was one thing to knock off another mobster but quite another to silence a public figure whose articles were eagerly awaited by a large audience who received vicarious thrills from Lingle's insider status with the mob.

Others say no, the collapse of the Capone Empire really began with an event at which he was not even present, when twenty-seven men of Sicilian origin—criminals all—met in Cleveland in December 1928 to turn crime in the United States into a business both organized and national. Neither Capone nor Johnny Torrio (who kept his hand in from his suburban New York outpost) had been invited. The ostensible reason was that they were not Sicilian, but a more accurate interpretation was that unlike Capone, who courted publicity and basked in it, the Sicilians operated outside the limelight and wanted to stay quietly in the dark.

Capone and Torrio might not have been in Cleveland in person, but their influence was huge, and their ideas were clearly the foundation for the corporate structure that the other gang bosses voted to adopt and implement. Historians of crime generally agree that this meeting was the first attempt to divide the country up into the criminal fiefdoms that eventually resulted in regional control by "families," as the organizations came to be called. It was also the first time that Al Capone's primacy in the criminal world was disregarded by his fellow gang leaders; his absence was a snub and a marginalization. Whatever he thought about such a meeting taking place without him is not known, for despite the attendees who came from many parts of the nation, it was so low-key that the few reporters who filed stories never asked anyone why Al Capone was not there.

———

Al was busy enjoying life in Florida during the holiday season of 1928, but shortly after it ended, he had other concerns to worry about. Sonny had another of his recurring bouts of mastoiditis, this one so severe that he needed a second operation. Dr. Kenneth Phillips, the young Miami physician who had become the Capone family's primary doctor and who continued to serve them into his own old age long after Al's death, took care of the boy. Once the operation was successfully completed, he recommended that "Albert" (as he called the boy in his medical records) be tested for syphilis along with Mae, who was about to undergo another of her periodic examinations. Dr. Phillips did not say whether his recommendation for Sonny's testing was prompted by an examination of Al, but his suggestion that everyone have immediate tests came shortly after he learned from Al's Chicago physician that he was treating one of Al's mistresses for the genital sores that were manifestations of the early stages of the disease.

Dr. Phillips used discreet language when he wrote about the disease in his medical histories of the principals, which leads to the assumption that he learned about the girl from someone other than Al, for despite his treatment of Mae and their open conversations about her condition and Sonny's the doctor never described having any direct discussion with Al.

Besides the Chicago physician, Dr. Phillips's sources about Al or his mistresses might also have been one or more of the brothers, who had begun to consult him when they were in Miami. Ralph was almost always there when Al was, and so too was Mimi (now calling himself John Martin); Albert ("Bites," who was now using a variant of Teresa's maiden name, Rayola) was there less frequently, particularly after he deliberately tried (unsuccessfully) to distance himself from both the family and the Outfit.

Mae probably never knew that Al's mistress's symptoms were what prompted Dr. Phillips to insist that she and Sonny have the tests, but they took them and were both found disease-free. Al allegedly refused even to let the doctor examine, let alone treat, him, which gave rise to the rumor that has since evolved into an accepted fact: that he refused to be tested or treated because he was pathologically afraid of needles. The doctors who took care of him in his heyday were the same ones who took care of him until he died, and they make no mention of such a fear in the extensive medical records and voluminous correspondence they exchanged. None of the government's physicians who treated him in prison refer to a fear of needles either. Such allegations only come from the reporters and the writers whose books were based on newspaper accounts and were written after his death, when the cause became public knowledge and speculation swirled that Al Capone had a needle phobia and refused to be treated until it was too late to do him any good.

As for the young blond prostitute in Chicago who exhibited symptoms of the disease, perhaps "mistress" is too strong a term, as she was just another in the series of ongoing sexual liaisons he had there. Who she was or what became of her has never been verified except to say that she quietly disappeared and was never heard from again in connection with Al Capone, most likely because (as several of his brothers' now-elderly grandchildren put it) he "paid for her to get out of the game." They all insist, however, that whether or not Al enjoyed the pleasures of the many prostitutes who worked for him, he was known for his kindness to those who became infected with disease, and he always saw that they received the best medical treatment available at the time before he sent them on their way. But there was another far more important reason why this particular girl and all the others like her faded into obscurity: he had become so infatuated with a woman he met in Miami that from that time on, with the exception of the occasional one-night stand when he was in Cuba or the Bahamas, he had little interest in taking any other mistresses.

Mae continued to play her part as the docile wife who stayed obediently at home; she kept her mouth shut, but her eyes and ears were always open, and she knew everything that was happening in her husband's life, no matter where he was or with whom. The men who lounged around the gatehouse, the guardhouse, and her kitchen talked quietly among themselves, but her hearing was acute, and she heard everything they said. She knew about Al's new infatuation, the young brunette he met at the racetrack whose hair was soon dyed the same blond shade as hers because Al wanted it that way, but she was not worried. She was his legal wife whose marriage had been sanctified in the Catholic Church, and she was the mother of his only child and beloved son; as such, her status was both permanent and privileged.

Al did love Mae deeply, but she was the Madonna of his house, and he looked for his whores elsewhere. All his life, he treated her with the utmost respect, consideration, and discretion; he was never photographed with any of his female playmates, and although everyone who covered his activities during his lifetime knew of his mistresses, no one dared to write about them directly, first because the times were different and it was not seemly to put such information in print, and second because no one had the nerve to inspire Al Capone's wrath by embarrassing his wife (and by extension, his mother and sister).

Al elevated Mae to sainthood, and she stood upon her pedestal with dignity and grace. She might have stayed contentedly at home, but she kept attuned to every one of her husband's peccadilloes. She played her role well, always perfectly groomed and ready to be the gracious hostess at the ever-more-elaborate parties Al gave nonstop, frenziedly inventing reasons to hold them when he had none. A local prizefight or a visiting celebrity he had not yet met was all he needed to fill Palm Island with everyone from the staid WASP pillars of the local community to the seedier element who had moved into the area and were suspected of being his newest cohorts in rum-running and other rackets. Invitations to his parties were command performances, and no one dared refuse them.

When not at home, Al socialized frenetically and was seen everywhere from racetracks to nightclubs, fishing off his boat or chartering planes to fly off to the Bahamas. He threw vast sums of money around as he had some of the best times of his life, and more and more this included the young woman (now blond) whom he met at Hialeah, the one who was never seen at Palm Island but who frequented many of the other parties and places that he did, and always with her protective brother along as chaperone. Her name was Jeanette DeMarco, and her brother was Vincent, called Vinny. Interestingly, none of the Capone descendants were aware of her presence in Al's life, particularly of the assertion that he took such good care of her financially during his lifetime that she never had to worry about money until she died at a very old age in the new millennium.

Also, none of the people who knew and took care of Jeanette in her old age know anything about what she and Vinny did for a living before they met Al, but they all insist that neither she nor her brother ever worked a day in their lives from that time on. They do agree that she liked to play the horses and that she always excused her penchant for the ponies by saying that she only frequented the track because her brother "worked there." Whatever the work was, she never specified; she was often quite happy to brag about how she "made a killing" on a modest bet as she showed off new and expensive pieces of jewelry that she always insisted she bought for herself. However, there was one exception, a necklace she wore all the time and that she allowed others to think was one that Al had given her (a claim she hinted at but never made directly). She was a mystery woman during Al's last few years of freedom, a role she parlayed into exoticism for the rest of her life.

Mae was supposed to have known all about Jeanette, and there have been numerous versions of how she reacted to her in the different stories others tell about the two women. Mae's descendants state emphatically that she never mentioned this mistress. Some people who knew Mae in Florida, either friends or people who worked for her at Palm Island, think that she tolerated Jeanette because she had no other option; some of Al's brothers' descendants offer the unlikely opinion that she might have been too frightened of her husband to do anything but accept his mistress (or mistresses). The group of people unrelated to the Capones who recall hearing their elders talk about this triangle of husband, wife, and mistress offer a totally different view: they are convinced Mae was relieved that Al had other outlets for his sexuality so that her health and well-being were not further compromised by another outbreak of disease. They all insist that even though they continued to sleep in the same bed when Al was at home, Mae "put herself [sexually] out of bounds" as soon as they moved to Florida and both were content with the situation.

Whichever of these versions might have been true, entirely or in part, Mae kept her own counsel and said nothing to anyone. If she did confide in someone, it was most likely her brother and sisters, who were spending more and more time with her in Florida before settling there themselves, but neither they nor their descendants who so loved and revered Mae ever revealed anything about the personal life of their beloved sister and aunt. At some point during their years together, Al and Mae must have talked about "that other thing," for during his darkest years in prison Al told Mae, "I love you alone and have forgotten all about the other party." He told her that it was "all over," that she was the only one he loved, and that he would be true to her for the rest of his life.

Al Capone was genuinely ill in the first weeks of January, felled by the flu that Sonny brought home from school and that swiftly infected many of the others who lived in the house or worked on the grounds. The flu was epidemic in the winter of 1928–29; Mae caught it first, but she and Sonny recovered quickly, whereas Al seemed unable to shake it. When he took so much longer than the others to get better, Mae asked Dr. Phillips to phone the family's Chicago physician to confer about treatment. Dr. Phillips knew that Al's general health was robust enough that he would eventually recover, but to ease Mae's worrying, he made the courtesy call.

Although she seemed happy enough with the life she led, Dr. Phillips saw how worrying about her husband kept Mae thin, jittery, nervous, and often unable to eat or hold down her food. He admired her courage to be married to such a man whom she knew for what he was and still loved deeply, but he also felt sorry for her. His sympathetic ear allowed him to gain her confidence, so she entrusted him with information about the family dynamic, for she made no secret of her dislike of all of the Capones and especially Ralph.

This was exceedingly helpful to Dr. Phillips, who was afraid of Ralph, the braggart and blowhard who knew nothing about medicine but still never hesitated to second-guess everything about Al's treatment, his hand running threateningly over the bulge under his armpit where the gun he toted was always at the ready. One of the reasons Dr. Phillips was not happy when Al anointed him the family's physician was that he was afraid of Ralph's trigger temper, so he found it helpful to capitalize on Mae's dislike of all the brothers to keep him reliably apprised of the shifting moods and relationships among them.

Al did recover, and by the third week of January 1929 was well enough to start visiting his usual haunts, attending Hialeah races, hitting the night-spots, and dining at the best restaurants, where he threw big bills to all and sundry. In early February, he chartered a boat to take him, his brother Albert, and several bodyguards to Bimini in the Bahamas. He also took Dr. Phillips, who was reluctant to go, but Al insisted that the doctor needed a little holiday. Even though Dr. Phillips never got over his uneasiness around Al and his brothers, the physician went because he knew better than to cross his patient.

The trip was a brief weekend jaunt, and Al Capone returned to Miami in time for two major events; the first was a party he planned to host at Palm Island on February 14, allegedly for no special reason, perhaps to celebrate

St. Valentine's Day, but most likely (as he and his brothers told everyone) he just wanted to have a party. Several weeks later, he planned to throw another, much larger one after the Stribling-Sharkey boxing match, where he had ringside seats and upon which he had let it be known that he was betting heavily.

He was in robust good health by February 14, and it showed when he kept his appointment earlier that day to meet an assistant district attorney who was coming down from Brooklyn to question him—so he was told—about his possible role in the killing of Frankie Yale in New York on July 1, 1928. The guns that had been used to mow him down during a car chase were traced to Capone's great pal Parker Henderson, who had bought them as surreptitiously as he had bought the Palm Island property. But because Al was nowhere near Brooklyn on the day of Yale's murder, he was cavalier enough about the meeting to visit the office of the Dade County prosecutor alone, without any of the several lawyers who always accompanied him to anything that even hinted at a legal encounter. It was an act of hubris on his part and one that was later used against him with great effect.

He thought it would be a brief and fairly routine exchange, and to demonstrate that he was showing respect for the law, if not for the Brooklyn lawyer himself, he arrived exactly on time. As usual, he was impeccably dressed, and if there is accuracy in the contemporary newspaper accounts (which vary about what actually happened during the meeting), Capone sauntered from his car and took his time chatting with well-wishers who greeted him outside the building, making sure to pose long enough for photographers to get their best shots. Once inside, he was surprised to find that the Brooklyn prosecutor was not alone but flanked by the Dade County prosecutor and the county sheriff, as well as by a court stenographer, who was there to record everything he said. Grim visages and serious questioning were not at all what he'd expected.

None of the questions were about Yale's murder; every single one was about Capone's financial dealings, and he had the same dismissive answer for them all. To questions about where Parker Henderson got the money to buy the property for "A. Costa," or who sent money from Chicago and how it made its way to him, he replied, "I don't remember." And when questions were posed in such a way that he could not say he did not remember, he simply lied. Asked if he was a bootlegger, he said no, he had never been a bootlegger. When asked what Jake Guzik did for a living, Capone replied, "He fights." When the questioners grew so annoyed with his evasions that they asked specifically if it was his cousin Charlie Fischetti who sent him large sums of money, a nonplussed Capone could only ask in return, "What has money got to do with it?" Capone was a smart man, but if he had any intimation that money would have everything to do with his life from then on, he gave no sign of it. This meeting was arguably the beginning of the serious investigation into his financial dealings that led to his downfall, but it did not gather strength until after a galvanizing event that happened on that very same day, back in Chicago.

———

While Al Capone was being questioned in Miami, six of Bugs Moran's men were gunned down in a garage on Chicago's North Clark Street, in a bloody crime that transfixed the world press and all its readers. Occurring on February 14, the date when love is celebrated, the event naturally became immortalized as the St. Valentine's Day Massacre. Capone had made sure he was nowhere near Chicago when it happened, and everyone from law enforcers to newspaper reporters had different opinions of his role in it. Some accounts slightingly dismissed him as a "Cicero mobster in the public's mind and not instantly suspected in the crime," but most painted him as a suspect from the very beginning, with every accusatory finger firmly pointed in his direction as the criminal mastermind. The outgoing police commissioner, William Russell, whose tenure had been ineffectual in curbing crime or controlling the Outfit, suspected Capone from the beginning and made a comment that (coming from him) was laughed at. Russell called the massacre "the death knell of gangdom" and declared "a war to the finish" on Al Capone. His prediction was off on the former but correct on the latter.

There had been so many other violent and vicious killings before the massacre, none of which could be directly tied to Capone, even though "everyone knows" became the most frequently heard comment that he was behind them all. Usually it was followed by a dismissive shrug because "everyone" also knew that nothing could be done about it. The statement was particularly rife after the ill-advised murder of Frankie Yale in New York. Even the esteemed *Literary Digest* got into the blame game with an editorial cartoon showing a gigantic gun-toting gangster whose body arched all the way from Chicago to Manhattan and who was meant to be a caricature of Capone. Yet while the brutal killings of gangsters by other gangsters filled the papers on an almost daily basis, as long as all these killings did not touch the lives of law-abiding citizens, there was a certain amount of silent rejoicing among the good people over the daily demise of yet another of society's outcasts, and there was no outcry for an organized effort to stop them.

Then the St. Valentine's Day Massacre happened, and there was an abrupt change in public opinion. General indifference came to a swift and stunned end with the nonstop barrage of horrific photographs of the dead bodies and the bathetic stories about the only survivor, a dog belonging to one of the victims. Despite Chicago's reputation for criminal brutality, the public expressed far greater outrage at these killings than they had at previous gangland mass murders. This one was considered so heinous that if all the years of previous bloodshed were added up, they still could not compare with the magnitude of its effect on public consciousness. When that lone event was single-handedly being blamed for harming every aspect of local society from culture to commerce, the city's moneymakers and movers and shakers were finally galvanized into taking serious action to stop the killings. It seemed there was no better way to start than to go after the kingpin who dominated so much of the fabric of the city's life. Al Capone became firmly fixed in the legal sights of different government agencies and the several groups that sprang up around them. And yet he still thought he could thumb his nose at the law.

Accusations flew as multiple inquiries limped along. At least four and possibly five (depending on how they are counted) independent investigations looked into the St. Valentine's Day Massacre. Among them were those of the district police, the detective bureau, the State's Attorney's Office, and the coroner. These initial attempts to sort out what had happened, and when, and who was responsible, turned into a fiasco resembling the incompetent and bumbling policemen in Mack Sennett's Keystone Kops silent films, when high-ranking officials in several departments were either fired or assigned elsewhere. All sorts of evidence was either stolen, destroyed, or buried in unmarked files, so most of what actually happened is to this day considered lost and probably gone forever. With all these bureaus working at cross-purposes, and "each agency [having] its own agenda and turf to protect," even Commissioner Russell, who should have been directing the central clearinghouse, was "sometimes so overloaded with theories or dead-end leads that no centralized operation could be mounted."

Rewards proliferated: The Chicago Association of Commerce offered $50,000 for the arrest and conviction of the killers. Independent citizens banded together and raised $10,000. The city council and the state's attorney each put up $20,000. And still, nothing could be pinned on Al Capone. Allegations of guilt abounded, but none proved provable, and no arrests were made.

There was need for a scapegoat, and local bootlegging, "so commonplace that it certainly didn't merit a massacre," provided a good place to begin. It offered a convenient focus for all the stymied agencies because there were so many speakeasies in the city (ten thousand or more by most counts) and Al Capone's Outfit controlled so many of them. And yet, now that he was spending so much time in Florida and expending great effort to present himself as an upright and law-abiding local citizen, there was speculation throughout Chicago that he had indeed lived up to his public declaration to give up his life of crime. Assigning blame and then prosecuting him seemed an impossible task.

Capone appeared to be a law unto himself, and no one who worked with him or for him dared to suggest directly that he watch his step until things cooled down. Instead, he floated seemingly above the fray, truly "untouchable" in a very different sense from what that word later came to stand for. However, the Chicago grand jury had no such qualms about his imperviousness, and three days after the massacre, February 17, he received a subpoena to appear before it in Chicago on a bootlegging charge. Capone laughed at the summons, since it was something the law had been unable to pin on him for almost a decade, and set out to ignore it—but in his own inimitable fashion.

—

The February 17 subpoena from a U.S. marshal in Chicago instructed him to return from Miami for a March 12 appearance before a federal grand jury that was investigating what was commonly known as "bootlegging." When Fred Pasley wrote about it a year later, he described Al's summons sarcastically as "a Volsteadian paradox that the Government in one role should stalk as criminals the class [that] Prohibition has enriched and in another should seek to share in its gains. There is an element of comedy in it." Capone thought much the same and decided to ignore the subpoena.

He persuaded the hesitant Dr. Phillips to provide him with an affidavit saying that he was still suffering from "broncho-pneumonia pleurisy with extreme chest congestion" and that he had been confined to bed for the previous six weeks—an outright lie and risky for the doctor to swear to, because his presence on the jaunt to the Bahamas was well-known on account of the newspaper publicity it garnered. The fact that he would risk professional censure with a sworn statement shows just how frightened he was of his most famous client and his entourage.

Capone's lawyers used the affidavit to ask for a forty-day postponement, but the judge denied it and instructed him to show up one week after the original date, March 19, 1929. At the same time, the U.S. marshal used the publicity about how the allegedly bedridden Capone had been cavorting all over Miami and the Caribbean to charge him with contempt of court and set a $5,000 bond he would have to post if he wanted to remain at liberty after his Chicago appearance.

Capone took his time and arrived in Chicago one day late, on March 20, apparently unaware of the ruckus he had kicked up among the many different government entities that now had him firmly in their targets for differing reasons. The press kept up the pressure by printing Bugs Moran's alleged comment about the massacre that "only Capone kills like that." It was an embarrassment for the legal enforcers, who were made to seem ineffectual and powerless because they were unable to pin it or any other crime on him.

J. Edgar Hoover, who was named director of the Justice Department's Bureau of Investigation (as the FBI was then known) in 1924, had been curiously lax about pursuing bootleggers throughout Prohibition because he rightly recognized that putting them out of business was a battle he could not win. He suddenly became interested in Al Capone when he saw how the Treasury Department under Andrew Mellon (a hypocrite who thought the Volstead Act a stupidity and routinely flouted it) was looking into Capone's tax evasions. That was something else entirely, and J. Edgar, described by a friend as akin to "an electric wire, with almost trigger response," was perceptive enough to realize that it might be the quickest route to prosecute Capone and at the same time ensure glory for himself. Here, too, another turf war was at stake, because Hoover could not bear to think Mellon's Treasury Department could succeed where his own bureau could not. This was a fight he thought he could win, and he geared up for it.

Hoover was only twenty-nine when he was appointed to the position he held for the rest of his career, and one of the people who recommended him highly was his great good friend Mabel Walker Willebrandt, the woman who described him as an electric wire. Willebrandt was an unusual woman for her time: she served in both the Harding and the Hoover administrations as an assistant attorney general from 1921 to 1929, a moral crusader charged with enforcing Prohibition and widely known as the "Prohibition Portia." She was often called the most powerful woman in the federal government and "possessor of one of the keenest legal minds" in the entire country. "If Mabel had worn trousers, she could have been president" was a remark often attributed to her lifelong friend Judge John J. Sirica (later of Watergate fame). Her original interest in Al Capone was certainly because of the beer wars in Chicago, but she turned her sights on him seriously in 1929 because she was so incensed by what she believed was Dr. Phillips's false and flippant affidavit. She was determined to punish both the doctor and his patient with contempt citations.

Her source for most of the complaints against Capone was the U.S. attorney in Chicago, George Emerson Q. Johnson, who like Willebrandt was an incorruptible public servant. Together the two of them set Capone's eventual downfall in motion. Johnson sent Willebrandt a copy of the affidavit Dr. Phillips swore, saying he had "the honor" of sending it on after A. P. "Art" Madden of the Chicago Intelligence Unit declined to investigate because it was "not within his authority to do so." In Chicago, there was the usual speculation about why Madden would not go after Capone, but that did not stop Mabel Willebrandt. She was famous for hinting obliquely about the agents in her own department by saying that within the entire population of the United States, "it is impossible to find four thousand men . . . who cannot be bought."

Willebrandt was a housewife who had abandoned an unhappy marriage and taught in public schools to put herself through USC Law School at night. She made her early reputation as a public defender representing battered women and prostitutes in the Los Angeles courts, and because she saw so much misery in her position, it was another reason she reviled Al Capone. As an assistant attorney general in President Harding's administration, she was put in charge of enforcing Prohibition, a job she probably got because she was a woman so recently graduated from law school that no one expected her to succeed where so many self-important men before her had not. Daniel Okrent, in his history of Prohibition, *Last Call*, described what happened after she was appointed as "something devotees of dime novels, fairy tales, or other ritualized clichés could have predicted: she became a terror."

To dismantle the illegal sale of liquor, Willebrandt looked beyond the destruction caused by its production and distribution to focus on what is today a simple and effective idea: Why was it that criminals involved in Prohibition flaunted such great wealth even as they never paid taxes? Now such prosecutions are a commonplace of law enforcement, but at the time it was an idea no one had thought of, one that was "brilliantly original . . . completely, stunningly out of left field," but that most judicial authorities thought was "completely insane." Johnson was one of the few who took her idea seriously.

Both were rarities in law enforcement, as was the cooperation they gave each other. Willebrandt was a dowdy middle-aged woman who dressed in business suits without style or grace and whose usual facial expression was so serious that it sometimes inspired fear as well as respect. It was exactly how the few women in professional life at that time were expected to look, dress, and act, and George E. Q. Johnson could be described as her male counterpart. Newspapers of his day described him as "mild, middle-aged . . . and of ministerial mien." Reports by United Press called him "the most dangerous foe Chicago gangsters ever encountered."

After Willebrandt heard what newspapers were writing about Johnson, she wrote an impassioned memorandum to J. Edgar Hoover, telling him it was "a personal matter of great importance" to her that he punish both Dr. Phillips and Capone, "secretly and soon." At almost the same time, President Herbert Hoover was receiving Colonel Robert McCormick, the influential owner and publisher of the *Chicago Tribune* and one of the six (or more) civic leaders who had united to crack down on crime. President Hoover's way of dealing with problematic situations was not by drafting legislation to solve them; instead, he liked to set up commissions or hold conferences, and one of his favorite ways to try to effect social change was to create fact-finding groups of prominent people who would fund them through their personal fortunes and private philanthropy, especially when Congress was unlikely to authorize legal government participation.

Like J. Edgar Hoover, President Herbert Hoover was reluctant to enforce Prohibition because he acknowledged that hard liquor was "a vehicle of joy [that] could not be generally suppressed by Federal law." The president had been aware of the out-of-control situation in Chicago since 1926, when his predecessor Calvin Coolidge's vice president, the Chicago banker Charles G. Dawes, described the city's "reign of lawlessness and terror" to the U.S. Senate. Coolidge did nothing to stem it, and neither did Hoover until March 1929, shortly after McCormick's initial visit, when he and another contingent of prominent Chicago citizens went to the White House to implore him to do something. Among them was Judge Frank Loesch, the president of the Chicago Crime Commission, who was still smarting from having had to ask Capone to help control the violence in the 1928 Pineapple Primary.

As President Hoover later wrote in his memoirs, Loesch told him that the city was "in the hands of gangsters, that the police and magistrates were completely under their control, that the governor of the state was futile, that the Federal government was the only force by which the city's ability to govern itself could be restored." The suggestion was made that troops be recalled from Nicaragua and sent to Chicago to restore order. When the president heard how bad things had become, he directed all federal agencies to "concentrate upon Mr. Capone and his allies." He agreed with Willebrandt and Johnson that the federal government's authority would not extend to cover the Outfit's criminal activity, so he asked them to concentrate on Capone's nonpayment of federal taxes and bootlegging. To be in charge of the entire investigation, Hoover appointed his good friend the Prohibition-flouting secretary of the Treasury, Andrew Mellon, who never hesitated to take a drink. Hoover's daily question later became his catchphrase: Did Mellon "get Capone" yet? The president thought it ironic "that a man guilty of inciting hundreds of murders, in some of which he took a personal hand, had to be punished merely for failure to pay taxes on the money he had made by murder."

When President Hoover wrote his memoirs some years after he left office, he described how it took two years to assemble the evidence against Al Capone and conduct the trials that sent him to prison but how it was worth it in the end because "we restored the freedom of Chicago." From the day he sent Capone to jail, in light of the city's subsequent history, his statement has been eminently debatable.

———

As required by the subpoena, Capone returned to Chicago on March 20, 1929, to face Johnson's questioning. The media were on high alert, covering the railroads and highways leading into the city from every direction and even staking out the Prairie Avenue house. But there was no sign of Capone, causing Johnson, who never showed emotion in public, to lose control and shriek at reporters that when he showed himself, he would be treated "like the hoodlum he is." The hoodlum evaded the media until he arrived at Johnson's office, exactly on time and prepared to face the grand jury and Judge James H. Wilkerson, who presided that day and would later become the canny adversary who eventually presided over Capone's trial and conviction.

Law enforcement officials wanted important answers, but all the press wanted was a good story, and Al Capone gave them one. He did his usual posturing and performing, even inviting the reporters to follow him into Johnson's office for interviews, at which point Johnson lost control again and shouted at them to leave. The main questions for which reporters wanted answers were, where had Al Capone been, and how had he sneaked into Chicago without anyone noticing? It was simple, he told them: he drove from Florida, in a car with his brother Ralph. All the reporters accepted this story, and none asked follow-up questions about the route he took or where he stayed along the way, and neither Al nor Ralph bothered to enlighten them. All the Chicago stories that were printed gave incorrect information, saying that he had arrived, as he had done earlier, via the Indiana border. Only two suburban newspapers filed correct versions, the *Belvidere Daily Republican* and the *Rockford Daily Republic*. They knew that he came to Chicago via Rockford and that he had been there for the better part of a week, but even knowing he was in their midst, no reporter had seen him, and none knew where he had stayed.

Actually, he was with the other Capones, Raphael and Clotilde and their now-grown children. No one knew of his relationship with this family, and the seclusion of their home offered a way to hide in plain sight, to regroup and plot strategy. It was probably the last time he was ever there, and the last time he saw Raphael Capone alive, just weeks before he was gunned down on his way to do Outfit business.

Rockford was an especially good setting for the partial anonymity and seclusion it afforded, for he had kept his closeness to this couple so deeply private that the only people who knew about it were the bookkeepers who went there regularly to work on the duplicate books or deliver everything from cash to food baskets for the family. Even though Capone made daily use of the house's telephone to keep in touch with his wife and mother, none of his brothers ever went to the home of the Rockford Capones. And when he sneaked in and eluded all but the local press as he had done this time, he could summon the men from the Outfit he wanted to see, and they could come undetected to bring him up to date on everything from finances to gang-world happenings. The latter was one of the primary reasons Capone wanted to hide out in Rockford before appearing publicly in Chicago, for threats against his life were coming at him from all the gangs engaged in the ongoing turf wars who had been emboldened by his absence.

He was a very busy man in March 1929 as all the government agencies were uniting to begin the case against him. He had to work on damage control via the press, fend off assassination attempts from rival gangs, and work on plans to dispatch members of the Outfit he believed had betrayed him. There was much to do, and most of it had to do with cleaning up various gangland messes that arose while he was in Florida, when he was concentrating more on enjoying himself than taking care of Outfit business. He plotted strategy and then went into battle.

Chapter 12

ATLANTIC CITY AND AFTER

The photographer Tony Berardi followed Al Capone closely and had seen many atrocities committed in his name, but when he saw the bodies at the site of the St. Valentine's Day Massacre, he said it was "a crime so hideous that even gangsters turned against him." Most English-language newspapers said the same, while the Italian-language newspapers considered the massacre such an embarrassing black mark on the nationality that Al Capone's very name was anathema: they refused to print it or even mention that the massacre happened because of Chicago's increasingly violent beer wars.

The federal government was not the only entity out to "get Capone"; his fellow mobsters were intent to do the same. Capone needed to make a dramatic move to let his enemies know he was still in charge and capable of serious retaliatory damage, but that would take time, and he had other things to take care of first. Before he left Rockford, he summoned some of his accountants to explain the Outfit's financial situation through the extra set of record books he kept there. After Raphael was murdered while making his weekly pickup for the Outfit's burgeoning slot machine business, he gave instructions from Chicago about the stipend he would pay to Clotilde and her children for their upkeep.

Al had invested heavily in slot machines several years previously, buying a number of factories where they were manufactured throughout other midwestern states. The machines had to be transported to the greater Chicago area and hidden in secure locations before they were delivered to their final destinations in venues the Outfit controlled. Once they were installed, only trusted workers could empty each machine of its money and then take it to a central location where it could be sorted, counted, and sent on its shady way to the Outfit's coffers, and Raphael was one of the men who made what his now-elderly grandchildren still remember as a "weekly pickup." They were not told how or why he was murdered, but the assumption was that another gang was involved. Because his bullet-ridden body was released quickly and quietly for burial, his family was certain that whoever prepared the official death certificate was in the Outfit's employ and no one connected with it wanted any publicity.

From then until Al Capone relinquished control of the Outfit's money to others, he made sure the widow and her children were provided with what they needed. Capone was good to this family who bore the same surname; throughout the 1930s while the country staggered under poverty and unemployment, they were comfortable. Raphael's grandchildren remember hearing their fathers express their gratitude for Al Capone's generosity; the five grown men in that house could not find a good day's work, but there was always enough money, and food was always on the table. They acknowledge that their family owed its security during tough times to Al Capone.

———

Frankie Rio, Capone's personal bodyguard and most faithful retainer, was far less sanguine than his boss about the return to Chicago in March 1929. He recognized how dangerous it could be once the government began to ask questions about undeclared income and unpaid taxes, and he urged Capone to treat it seriously. Rio's impassioned warnings tended to anger Capone, so he took to couching them as jokes. Rio told his boss that every time he ordered a new suit, he should make sure it was one with stripes because that was what he would be wearing in jail if he didn't pay attention to the charges and do something to get the government off his back. Capone ignored him: there was another, far more pressing matter, and he couldn't concentrate on anything else until he took care of it. Rio was the only person he trusted to help him resolve it.

"Slippery Frank," as Rio was called, was a ruthless killer and a reckless robber who once got away with $500,000 in bonds heisted in broad daylight from Chicago's Union Station. Whenever it seemed there was enough evidence against him that he would have to stand trial, he terrified potential witnesses into refusing to testify, and when he needed a little extra insurance to make sure he would walk away a free man, he simply bribed the judges. His fearlessness and street smarts made him one of Al's favorites, and his loyalty earned him the prize job of chief confidant. It also earned him a permanent guest room in the Miami house, which Mae didn't like but knew better than to complain about. When she hinted to Al that perhaps Frankie could stay in the gatehouse with the other men, he told her not to be "jealous" of "Faithful Frankie's" constantly hovering presence because he was "trusted like a brother." And that was why Frankie Rio became the only person Al Capone chose to help him dispatch John Scalise, Albert Anselmi, and Joseph "Hop Toad" Giunta. It took careful playacting and planning to bring off their brutal murders.

Of the many threats against Capone's life, the most serious came from his old adversaries in the Unione Siciliana, one of the few remaining gangland entities with enough nerve and clout to take him on. Hop Toad Giunta was the newly elected president, and he had thrown his allegiance to Joe Aiello, Capone's loudmouthed and long-standing rival who had previously boasted of assassination threats against him that Capone had not dared to carry out. This time Aiello was serious, letting it be known that he had $50,000 for the man who would kill Al Capone. Capone learned of the bounty on his life through Rio, who heard the stunning news on the gangland grapevine that Scalise and Anselmi, the prime assassins on the Outfit's payroll, had accepted Aiello's offer. The rumor shocked even other jaded gangsters, for Scalise and Anselmi made a very good living as Al Capone's most trusted killers. The two men had no grudge against him; they simply took the offer because they were greedy for money and always ready to kill for the highest bidder. This time it just happened to be Aiello. Capone knew he had to get them before they got him and that it would take (as one wag put it) a combination of "political showmanship, Sicilian hospitality, Renaissance statesmanship, and medieval torture." He was ready for the challenge.

Their elimination was supposed to be carried out like any other gangland murders, a straightforward rubout in response to a rival faction's threat, designed to let all the other gangs know they had better not get ideas because Al Capone was still the untouchable kingpin of crime. And of course the traitors had to be dealt with in a way that would keep him clean and clear of involvement. Instead, the turncoats were beaten and battered beyond recognition before they were riddled with bullets, "taken for a ride" (as the expression came to be coined), and left in their own burned-out car on a street in Hammond, Indiana. That much of the incident has been verified and is truthful, but over the years the details of what happened have accreted so many additional layers that nothing else is certain, starting with who actually committed the murders and where they were carried out.

The original account begins in late March or early April 1929, just after Capone left Rockford and returned to Chicago, when he and Rio began their counterattack by staging a mock disagreement in a restaurant where Scalise and Anselmi were also eating. They pretended to argue loudly until Rio ended it by slapping Capone's face and rushing out of the restaurant. Scalise and Anselmi were impressed enough by Rio's fearlessness to invite him to join them in the assassination plot and to share the loot in a three-way split. Rio was the key to their getting close to Capone, so they allowed him to lay out a plan in which he would offer a pretend apology to get back into his boss's good graces. He did and told them afterward that Capone wanted to hold a reconciliation dinner to show there were no hard feelings. Rio told them that because they were witnesses to the altercation, he would see that they were invited to the reconciliation. It is here that the story diverges.

Some accounts say it was a banquet dinner in the Hawthorne Hotel; others say it was held at a restaurant (or roadhouse, or speakeasy) just over the Indiana line in Hammond. While other biographers and historians provide vague descriptions of the diners invited to a private room in various unnamed places, John Kobler is the only one who named the sources for what he called "the account generally accepted," all of whom told him that the Hawthorne Hotel was the venue. Among his sources, Kobler listed everyone from "the [general] underworld" to "[unidentified] stool pigeons" to "knowledgeable old cops like John Stege and . . . Chicago's top crime reporters like Ray Brennan and Clem Lane." Interestingly, his description does not provide the gory details that almost every other chronicler of the incident gives; Kobler is content to say merely that the three Sicilians were murdered in an "execution following a banquet at the Hawthorne Inn on May 7," after which "their bodies were loaded into the back of their own car, which the driver abandoned near Hammond, Indiana." Kobler concludes his restrained account by saying the coroner who examined the bodies "found hardly a bone unbroken, hardly an area of flesh without bruises."

A far more florid and garish tale is repeated by other writers who all base their versions on the one that originated in 1931, when Walter Noble Burns published a book titled *The One-Way Ride*. Contemporary readers must bear in mind that the years from 1926–27 to around 1933 were the heyday of the public's fascination with Al Capone and that these years coincided with the rampant proliferation of media. The movies became America's favorite pastime, and everyone who could get to a theater went to see the films and newsreels that covered his every move. The appetite for print was burgeoning beyond the capacity of writers to file enough copy to satisfy it, which is probably how truth and fiction became inextricably mixed.

No doubt a great deal of what was printed as fact was highly embellished, if not actually fiction created out of whole cloth. And this is probably why Burns, who wrote a long and otherwise mostly accurate book based largely on Al's run-ins with the law, got so carried away when he wrote about the Scalise-Anselmi murders (and Giunta's as well, he who usually gets the short shrift and is sometimes absent from the various retellings). It is also why Burns's account has carried the day in many later versions.

Burns invites his reader to imagine a private dining room somewhere other than the Hawthorne Hotel, in which the three guests of honor *might* have been drinking drugged wine, when suddenly guns *might* have been pulled and bullets *might* have flown, even though in the end the three men do indeed die. Over the years, Burns's tale became the one embellished by others, who describe how the turncoats gorged themselves on food and drink to the point of stupefaction, after which they were so drunk they allowed themselves to be tied up in their chairs by Capone's men. How three trained killers could sit quietly and let this happen is one of the several mind-bogglers in the various fables, all of which end with Capone supposedly standing behind them while all this is happening, roaring curses as he became so enraged that he battered them to death with a baseball bat. Where the baseball bat was stashed throughout the evening and why he settled on it as his weapon of choice are never explained, only that Al Capone used it. His men, hardened killers all, were nevertheless struck dumb, according to Burns, horrified by their out-of-control leader but too frightened to do anything to stop him. Once he exhausted himself with the alleged bashings, his men loaded the three bloodied bodies into their own car and drove to Hammond, where the car was abandoned on a side street and burned with them in it. They were then riddled with bullets just to make sure they were well and truly dead.

But this is the legend that grew, directly implicating Al Capone by word of mouth or in the occasional article that hinted at it in the years immediately after his death in 1947. Each time it was told, it acquired such a veneer of veracity that by the time George Murray presented it in his 1975 book, *The Legacy of Al Capone*, it had become the point of departure for all other depictions. It was re-created in Brian De Palma's 1987 movie, *The Untouchables*, where one of the most riveting scenes had Robert De Niro as Capone, swinging a baseball bat repeatedly against the splattering head of an enemy, spewing blood and gore all over the pristine white tablecloth that fills the screen and horrifies even the hardened henchmen who watch him in stunned silence.

So many questions could be asked about the actual incident, starting with whether or not Al Capone was really there. There is no record of the actual date he left Rockford for Chicago or where he went after he got there. He had sneaked around so quietly that once his court appearance in Chicago was over, it took the reporters who had been there several days to track him down. The children of his own brothers who either were living in the Prairie Avenue house or were frequent visitors to it say they have no way of knowing when (or even if) Al eventually showed up there, or how long he remained in Chicago before he went to the gangland convocation in Atlantic City that began on May 13, 1929. However, it does seem suspect that he, who took such pains to stage-manage the St. Valentine's Day Massacre from the safe distance of his Florida home, would risk the possibility of detection and subsequent conviction by participating in such a visible crime while he was most likely sequestered in his headquarters at the Hawthorne Hotel.

And yet so many of his contemporaries placed him at that grisly scene, each providing a detail here, an observation there, a random speculation that, when added up, allowed others to morph all the speculation into hardened fact. In one sense, the story became a simple one: that in his own way, Al Capone was as reckless and fearless as Frankie Rio and that he had no qualms about killing three men in cold blood so soon after the unfathomable massacre in the garage on North Clark Street. General agreement came to be that there had to be truth somewhere in the stories about Al's participation.

When the most recent (and the strongest and longest-lasting) trend of mythologizing Al Capone as the character Scarface was picking up steam in the 1980s, the writer Sean Dennis Cashman referred to the spate of 1930s movies that portrayed gangsters as fallen heroes and good guys who had gone wrong. He compared Capone's life to a whodunit written for stage or screen, saying it would not matter if the audience came late to the performance, for "they will certainly discover who did it, but they will not know what it is that he did." Indeed.

Even though none of the heinous deeds could be pinned firmly or directly onto Capone, his high visibility meant that whatever his antics, he was fast becoming a worrisome problem for his fellow crime bosses. At least this is what reporters in Chicago wrote as they scurried to find him, staking out his hotel headquarters and the house on Prairie Avenue, eventually knocking on the door and trying to bribe Ralphie (who answered and slammed it in their faces). Why no one thought to look for him in Miami remains unknown, but Capone was back there in April 1929, conferring in secret with selected allies before they went to the mob boss convention in Atlantic City. Home movies taken at Palm Island show a happy Capone cavorting at his swimming pool with a smiling Lucky Luciano and other members of the New York crime families shortly before they convened on May 13–16. The movie showed much jollity and many high jinks, but there is no way to determine if the participants were genuinely friendly or just pretending to be for the camera. Nevertheless, they did gather at Al Capone's mansion before their official meetings, where the discussions would once again be about defining territories and delineating illicit spoils.

Enoch "Nucky" Johnson, the political boss of Atlantic City and its racketeer in chief, made all the arrangements, booking them into posh hotels where no one would dare to bother them. The mob domination by men of Sicilian origin that had been centered primarily in the East had finally been broken after a reign of murderous terror similar to Chicago's, but theirs was carried out by men who eschewed Capone's flashy high-profile visibility. These new lords of crime were a diverse group of relatively young men, similar in age to Capone (who was then thirty) and of Jewish, Irish, and Slav origins, as well as Italians who were natives of other regions and who complemented the remaining Sicilians. Capone's rivals from Chicago Frank McErlane and Joe Saltis were there; Dutch Schultz, Frank Costello, and Lucky Luciano represented New York; Max Hoff, Sam Lazar, and Charles Schwartz drove down from Philadelphia. The only major Chicago crime figure who was not there was Bugs Moran, but one other Chicagoan did attend who was, in his way, as powerful as Al Capone, who knew that he could not afford to ignore or offend him.

Moses Annenberg was well on his way to building the publishing empire that started with the *Daily Racing Form* and ended with *TV Digest* and the *Philadelphia Inquirer*. His rise was meteoric, and by 1929 he was feared by many as the most dangerous and powerful non-Italian racketeer in the country. The distrust and dislike between the two men was mutual, but Capone knew better than to ignore or offend Annenberg. Both men were careful to hide their private mutual distrust behind a public show of cordiality.

The criminal group that met in Atlantic City brought new and different approaches to conducting gangland business, many of which had originated with John Torrio and were further implemented by Al Capone. They were still largely separate criminal entities; they were cooperating simply to make as much money as possible while avoiding bloodshed. All the newspapers sent reporters to cover the event, from the *New York Times* to every newspaper in Philadelphia and Chicago. They all contributed to wire services, so every paper throughout the country had swift access to everything that happened in the Atlantic City meetings. Because reporters were barred from most access, they resorted to creativity in what they wrote. In many accounts, Capone was quoted at length, not only because he provided the most colorful copy, but also because the other gang bosses took care to avoid publicity.

Capone said the same thing to everyone. He gave the impression that he was speaking with all due sincerity when he said there was enough business in crime to make everyone rich, so it was time for the rulers of all the fiefdoms to stop killing each other and treat their daily doings as just another business. He said they should all learn to go about their murder and mayhem as simply another job, one to be put aside for another day when they went home at night to have dinner with their wives and families. He also claimed that much of the three-day convocation had been devoted to drawing up a written agreement that they all consented to sign.

Much speculation has surrounded what actually went on in the meetings, but all the rumors end in a consensus that the attendees did agree to form a loosely allied—but still separate—confederation of crime that would let them create and rule over mutually agreed-upon areas in different parts of the country. In Capone's case, it meant that the feuding gangs throughout Chicago were to stick to their own territories and try to avoid bloodshed. Each gang controlled its own fiefdom, but if the statutes that were released to a reporter from the United Press wire service were true, the power in Chicago would mostly be shared by Torrio and Aiello, which was a definite insult to Capone. Although long gone from Chicago and no longer in charge of the Outfit's day-to-day functioning, Torrio was still considered the gray eminence who had the final say. If such a plan as the

Atlantic City statutes had gone into effect, Torrio would have been the big winner, reaping most of the money for the Outfit; Joe Aiello would have shared it, but, more important to Aiello, he would have held most of the power, and that was what he really wanted.

Capone knew better than to stage a public protest while at the meetings, for he knew that none of these larger-than-life personalities would consent to any diminution of their empires. He knew they would never agree to put aside their guns and stop the killings and nothing would really change. By his reasoning, things would eventually calm down, and in the meantime all he had to do was to get himself safely out of harm's way and wait. However, with the likes of Bugs Moran and Joe Aiello gunning for him, he knew there was plenty to worry about right now.

He knew how much he was envied and hated and how many "hits" had been put out on him in Chicago. Moran was determined to avenge the St. Valentine's Day Massacre; Aiello was still offering $50,000 to whoever managed to murder him; the Unione Siciliana was not going to surrender its sovereignty to any Neapolitan, least of all him; and there was a growing number of smaller Sicilian cohorts who wanted revenge for the killings of Scalise, Giunta, and Anselmi. Also, the New York contingent was still simmering over his audacity in killing Frankie Yale, on their turf and without their permission. So many groups were determined to kill Al Capone that there was a very good chance that if he went back to Chicago directly from Atlantic City, he might not live another day.

Nevertheless, Capone was determined to operate from a position of strength, which he demonstrated by going to Atlantic City unlike all the others, who took their usual flotillas of goons and gorillas. He took only the three people he trusted most: Frankie Rio as his only bodyguard and, to protect the Outfit's business interests, the treasurer, Frank Nitti, and the business manager, Jake Guzik.

Although the agreement to divvy up the spoils geographically was created in dead seriousness, the newspapers provided much humor about how it came together. Bugged rooms were a serious concern, so the mob leaders held many of their meetings on the famed Boardwalk, taking walks in small groups of two or three or riding in the wicker carriages that carried them past the parade of tourists who gaped in starstruck awe at the unusual sight before them. They were all well and fashionably dressed, most of them in fairly discreet fabrics and colors. Everyone, that is, with the exception of Capone, who sported his usual shiny materials, flashy colors, and pale pearl gray fedora. Not surprisingly, he became more than an item of conversation among reporters who covered the gathering; he became a major item of business on the mobsters' agenda.

He was just too much of a publicity hound to suit the others, and because of him more than the usual contingent of reporters who followed the mob were there, eager to snatch up every scrap of information and, if there was none, to make up what they did not actually see or hear. After all, there were reams of daily copy to file, and Al always provided excellent material. When he said he would rather the newspapers didn't print a line about him, no one paid attention.

They issued banner headlines speculating on whether he was retiring or being pushed out after he gave his canned reason for asking reporters not to write about him: "No more brass bands for me. There's a lot of grief attached to the limelight." Through reporters, he posed rhetorical questions to his fellow mobsters, asking what they were aiming for, to "get yourself killed before you are thirty?" He had some good advice for them all: "You'd better get some sense while a few of us are left alive."

He knew what he had to do to stay alive, and once again it was to follow Johnny Torrio's example. Capone decided to do what Torrio had done in 1925, when he allowed himself to be sentenced to nine months in the Waukegan, Illinois, jail, but this time nowhere near Chicago. He heard there was a pretty good prison in Philadelphia, far enough away from imminent danger and in a city where officials were known to be easily persuaded to look the other way by some of the very people who were with him in Atlantic City. One or two months there would be just the ticket. Mae could be counted on to provide his jail cell with every luxury he wanted, and the faithful Frankie Rio was ready to join his boss in getting himself arrested so that he would have full-time protection even in jail. Al Capone could rest, relax, and recoup; what more could an exhausted gangster want?

Unfortunately, it didn't work out exactly as he planned.

Chapter 13

———

IN PRISON

Mae was in Miami and sheltered from most of Al's travails, but in all of their daily telephone conversations she implored him to settle his problems and come to live quietly on Palm Island. As for Sonny, the fear of kidnapping was always uppermost in Mae's mind, but even though Sonny was at the age where a father's presence was important, and much as Al loved him, they both knew what a difficult time the boy would have if he was seen in public with his father, or the damage that could be done to Sonny if they were together when an assassin came gunning for Al. If there was no other way for Al to ensure their well-being than by staying far away from them, then that is what he would do.

He did not tell Mae until he was ready to put his plan to keep himself safe into effect, but he knew what he was going to do even before he went to Atlantic City. When the conference ended, he would pretend to be returning to Chicago via Philadelphia but instead would follow Johnny Torrio's lead and make sure that he went to jail. He probably talked it over with Ralph, Jake Guzik, and Frank Nitti (who was becoming increasingly important to the Outfit), and the night before he took action, he told Mae but instructed her not to tell his mother.

Mae had become a full-time resident of Florida now that Sonny was happily enrolled in school and wanted to spend vacations there playing with his new friends. Two of her sisters and a brother were also living nearby, so she had pleasant company. Unfortunately for her, Teresa liked Florida too and was often a long-term houseguest who no longer asked permission to take over the kitchen and express strong opinions about how the entire household should be run. Mae generally ignored her, for the mostly secluded life she led on Palm Island suited her much better than Chicago, where not only Teresa but also Mafalda watched her every move as closely as did the reporters and photographers who followed Al. Despite the constant stream of people in and out, the guards at the gates, Al's bodyguards in the house, his mother, his brothers, and their retinues all being there, Palm Island was Mae's refuge, and she reveled in being there.

Teresa and most of the rest of the family were in Chicago, however, when Mae called to tell them that Al had been arrested. Once the newspapers began their breathless reports of what had happened, the family agreed that they needed to do something to counteract all the negativity, so they invited reporters into the Prairie Avenue house to present their side of Al's story. When one looks at the barrage of press coverage the occasion generated, the kindest way to describe the family's efforts is to say that everything they tried to do backfired. Teresa was almost sixty, relatively young looking and in good health, but at that cultural moment sixty was considered old age, and that was how she was portrayed, as a doddering old woman. Of Ralph they said nothing, for he was noticeably absent. Albert was now using a variant of Teresa's maiden name, Rayola, and although he held low-level jobs within the Outfit off and on throughout his life, he was such a cipher that the press mostly ignored him. Apparently, he said nothing quotable, nor did John, who was lackadaisically shuffling through daily life and hoping to follow Al and Ralph. Matty was still enrolled at Villanova— technically, for he paid no attention to his classes and was determined to quit.

Some reporters described the interior of the house as a setting filled with expensive knickknacks and other gewgaws: overstuffed, overblown, and in general bad taste. Some wrote of how Teresa tried to impress them in her best black dress, while others said she received them in an ordinary "house dress" (as a woman's daily garb was called then). Some said her mixture of Italian dialect and "broken English" was charming; others claimed she was dour and sour as she loaded her table with Italian dishes. They wrote disdainfully about her food, neglecting to write about how much they relished eating it.

Mafalda got the worst of the press coverage. She was seventeen and had just graduated from high school, and like all good Italian girls of a certain class and upbringing she was living at home and waiting to marry the first suitable man who came calling. She had been in bed, recovering from a bad cold or flu, and she got up to greet reporters in a bathrobe. In various accounts, it became a sheer and slinky green negligee that showed her adult body to great advantage, especially after she was said to drape it "coyly" to show off one bare shoulder. The hints, if not the outright statements, were that she was showing off her body to announce that she was now ready for matrimony. In reality, Mafalda had grown to become a heavy-set woman, short and squat, with unruly black hair and thick eyebrows. There was nothing pretty about her, but that did not stop reporters from describing her as "radiant" and "eloquent" or calling her a gracious hostess who invited them into her "boudoir." Nothing like that would ever have happened in Teresa Capone's house, especially with Mafalda's big brothers there to make sure she was properly chaperoned.

What both women labored to do was to try to soften the public perception of their beloved Al. Mafalda came across in some accounts as arrogant when her intention was to defend loyally her brother's reason for carrying a gun: "Would anybody expect him to walk the streets anywhere without protection?" Teresa insisted that if people could only know her son as she did, they would not write such terrible things about him. She was over-wrought when she told them that Al was her "life," and she adored him: "He's so very good, so kind to us." She pleaded with them to persuade read-ers who only knew him from newspaper stories to change their opinions; otherwise they would "never realize the real man he is." Everything the two women said about the loving son and brother they knew at home was true, but of course it was not at all true of the man who conducted his grim busi-ness before the eyes of the world. Naturally, the reporters focused on that side of Al "Snorky" "Scarface" Capone, the one who was in the public eye. That was what their jobs required, so that was what they did.

———

Capone made sure he went to jail in Philadelphia as planned, and the basic gist of the stories that were written about what happened there was true, that he and the ever-faithful Frankie Rio were arrested for carrying guns when they left a very public downtown movie theater. Later, most of the newspaper "gangsterologists" learned that Capone had carefully arranged for the policeman James "Shooey" Malone to be there when they left the theater and to go through the sham of finding concealed weapons. Capone had met and befriended Malone a year earlier at Hialeah racetrack in Flor-ida, where he had also met John Creedon, the colleague Malone brought along to assist with the arrest. Both men had attended parties at the Palm Island house, and rumor (unproven but possibly true) has always had it that Capone paid each of them $10,000 to arrest him.

Capone, who never carried a gun if he could help it, and Rio, who usually carried for them both, made sure the bulges under their coats were conspicuous. It was a carefully stage-managed arrest, in broad daylight at one of the largest and most popular theaters on Market Street, one of the city's main thoroughfares, and it did not take long for the press to pounce.

Before leaving Atlantic City, Capone and Rio made sure they had a few thousand dollars in their wallets, a rather small amount that they would need for fines, spontaneous handouts, and, if necessary, bribes. They did not anticipate needing the larger amounts they usually carried because they expected to be sentenced at their arraignment to a fairly comfortable week or two, perhaps a month, in jail. To their surprise, bail for each was set at $35,000, so they had to spend the night in the city's Moyamensing prison while their high-profile lawyers argued that they were being treated unfairly. The lawyers were strident and vociferous, as was Rio, who really didn't want to go to prison. Capone signaled for Rio to shut up, while he, relieved just to be in the relatively safe hands of the law, was polite and deferential. However, as soon as he heard how high the bail was set, he was deflated, knowing he would be imprisoned longer than he expected.

Capone appeared before a judge again in May 1929 and thought that his sentence would probably be for several months at the most, ideally giving him enough time to rest, recoup, and decide what to do next. It was another shock when the uncompromised and uncompromising judge sentenced both him and Rio to a one-year term ending in May 1930 in the notorious Holmesburg prison, where conditions were so punitive that prisoners had recently rioted by setting fire to their mattresses. Capone let it be known that any lawyer—anywhere—who could spring him from Holmesburg would receive a $50,000 bonus on top of his normal fees, but none were able to do so. He and Rio remained there during Philadelphia's hot and humid summer until August, when enough strings were pulled that they were transferred to Philadelphia's Eastern State Penitentiary.

Al Capone got the rest he needed at Eastern Pen because the warden gave him full run of the facility, allowing him to live there as if he were vacationing at a fine resort hotel. After his family's public relations fiasco in Chicago, he told Mae to stay put and stay quiet in Florida and to tell Sonny that he was away in Europe traveling on unspecified business. Sonny was of the age where children overhear conversations at home, and he knew where his father was, and to make sure that he did, his classmates at school let him hear it from them. Enterprising reporters who had no real news to write invented the story that Al told them every time "his little son" saw a picture of a ship, he asked his mother if his father was on it and if it was bringing him home. Sonny was far too old and intelligent to have said such a thing, and even if he did, Al was far too protective of the boy to have told it to reporters. But at home, Mae did keep up the facade that Al was away traveling, and Sonny pretended to accept it, even though he knew she made her frequent trips to Philadelphia in order to turn Al's cell into a downright posh apartment.

She had his own mattress and bedding shipped in, and she bought the latest, best, and biggest radio, one that cost the then-astronomical sum of $500. He kept the volume loud enough for other inmates to hear it, while he himself sat in his easy chair, reading under the lamp she thoughtfully provided, or at his desk, where he wrote his many loving letters to her. His feet were never cold, because she put thick and expensive rugs on the floor, and he was always warm and comfortable because he wore his own fine silk underclothes (which he kept in the capacious chest of drawers she provided). His hand-tailored wardrobe of suits and casual wear hung in a wardrobe she also sent. Mae saw that Frankie, whose cell was next to Al's, enjoyed many of the same perks as his boss. Both men held court as they passed out favors to other inmates by adjudicating internal rivalries and dispensing gifts of money for their struggling families. They were highly popular among those who vied for their favors, and, more important, it provided excellent insurance, because their devoted following protected them from anyone who might have wanted to do them harm.

The only event that upset the daily equilibrium occurred in early September 1929, when Capone's tonsils became severely inflamed and had to be removed. Dr. Herbert Goddard, a surgeon from the State Board of Prisons and a member of the prison's board of trustees, performed the successful operation and afterward found a contingent of reporters eager to hear the results. He had nothing but praise for his famous patient, painting him as an ideal prisoner who was the picture of kindness, goodness, and cooperation. Dr. Goddard acknowledged that yes, indeed, Al Capone was in the rackets, before going on to praise him for his "brains [and] a high degree of intelligence." He was one of Capone's staunchest boosters at the time as he argued with reporters who thought otherwise: "You can't tell me he's all bad after I've seen him many times a week for ten months." Dr. Goddard had come to his conclusion freely and independently, for despite Capone's trying, he never accepted a single gift or gratuity.

That was the thing about Al Capone: he made friends wherever he went because he was sincere in how he related to people. He genuinely liked to meet people whose lives were far removed from his own closed and encapsulated criminal world. He was curious about their families and their daily lives, their education, expertise, and interests. He liked to hear their stories; that is, until they angered or disappointed him. Then he could turn on a dime to become a vicious and relentless dispenser of justice and punishment.

Visitors to Eastern Pen were supposed to be restricted, but the warden and the guards did not enforce the rule for Capone, whose constant stream of trusted lieutenants came and went with a wink and a money-filled handshake whenever he wished to see them. Family members also came and went much as they pleased. Mae usually came to Philadelphia in a private train compartment, so discreet in her travel arrangements that she was never photographed or written about. The distances were too great for Teresa and Mafalda to get there routinely from Chicago, but they also traveled by train in private compartments on the few occasions when they did visit. Al didn't want to eat prison food, and as Philadelphia was famed for its Italian community, Mae quickly found restaurants that were only too happy to prepare and deliver his daily meals. He ate well and left prison heavier than he went in, with one headline blaring that he had gained eleven pounds.

Capone was a frequent visitor to the warden's office, where he sat at the desk to conduct his business and used the phone as if it were his own private line. He still made his daily calls to Mae in Florida and his mother in Chicago, but mostly he kept abreast of the Outfit's business through frequent calls to Ralph and Jake Guzik. He became a good friend to the warden, who often sent his private car to drive the erstwhile prisoner to dinner at his house.

Capone's work assignment was supposed to be in the prison library, but the "work" consisted of his occasionally browsing for books and magazines to take back to his cell. He liked to read magazines, especially those that kept him abreast of current events, financial affairs, and world politics. Reporters were often surprised by the knowledgeable and insightful comments he made. John Kobler had the good fortune to conduct most of his research during the 1960s, when many people who were present during Al's incarceration were still alive. Kobler wrote that Capone was happy to invite reporters into his cell because their conversations broke up what might otherwise have been long and—after a while—boring days. Kobler cast a doubtful eye on many of the stories that quoted him effusively, correctly noting that Capone's life was one of such routine that there was hardly anything new, leaving them to fill "column after column with the minutiae of his daily existence." Some reporters translated his expressions of boredom into supreme discontent, with several headlines standing for them all: "Capone in Sixth Legal Move to Get Out of Jail" and "Scarface Al's Lawyers File New Petition." The lawyers certainly did file multiple petitions because this was what he paid them to do, but they all knew he was hoist on his own petard and would have to serve his full term. After a while, the headlines changed and in doing so correctly expressed the monotony of his days: "Capone Picks Cubs to Win 1930 Flag," "Capone Doesn't Go to Church on Sundays." More intriguing was the breathless headline for the story written by one imaginative reporter who learned of his library forays: "Capone Reads Life of Napoleon."

Capone allegedly told the reporter that Napoleon was "the world's greatest racketeer" and that he could have "wised [him] up" about how to run his "business," that is, the country of France: "The trouble with that guy was he got the swelled head. He overplayed his hand and they made a bum out of him." He was probably thinking of himself when he said that Napoleon "was just like the rest of us. He didn't know when to quit [and he made it] too easy for the other gangs to take him." He sensed a kinship between himself and Napoleon when he added that Napoleon should have had "sense enough . . . to kiss himself out of the game."

His insight into Napoleon's failings eerily corresponded to a conversation he had with Frank Loesch at their secret 1928 meeting in Chicago before the Pineapple Primary. Loesch had asked Capone how he expected to "beat the law"; he replied that he would always beat it but would most likely "die at the business end of a shotgun." In prison, he told reporters that the same thing would have happened to Napoleon if he had lived in Chicago, but in his case he believed in a very different outcome: "They'll only get me when I'm not looking." And there was no chance of this happening while he was in Eastern Pen.

———

All in all, it was not an unpleasant life. Visitors today can see it for themselves as the prison has been turned into a museum that is one of Philadelphia's primary tourist attractions, with Al Capone's cell much as he left it. However, all vacations must come to an end, and his peaceful respite ended when he and Rio were released two months early for good behavior, on St. Patrick's Day, March 17, 1930. Here, too, Capone used "pull" to make his exit, with the warden as his willing accomplice.

He knew, as did the warden, local elected officials, and members of various police boards, that his release was going to be a media event unlike any the staid City of Brotherly Love had ever seen. Capone knew that reporters were ready to form caravans that would choke highways as they followed him wherever he went, but even more troubling was the fear that other gangs might be lying in wait and gunning for him. It was more to ensure his safety than to divert the press that he proposed a secret plan that everyone quickly agreed made sense. It was put into effect on March 16, the day before the release was to become official. Capone and Rio were sneaked into the warden's private car and taken to another prison in nearby Graterford. They were hustled into a part of the facility far removed from other prisoners, to stay overnight and wait until the legal hour for their release in the late afternoon on the seventeenth. At that time, a large car driven from Chicago by some of Al's men pulled inside the gates, loaded the two ex-prisoners, and roared away toward Chicago and home. Depending on who wrote the story, it was either a Cadillac, a Packard, or a Lincoln. It might have been all three, because Al's men took the precaution of using multiple vehicles as decoys. The ruse worked, and they were long gone when the warden stepped out the front doors of Eastern Pen and told the waiting crowds, "We stuck one in your eye. The big guy's gone."

Chapter 14

"THE ELUSIVE 'SCARFACE' AL"

There were howls of outrage from the Chicago reporters when none could track him down. Because they had no real news to write, it became a contest to see who could pen the most embellished take, and their articles became exercises in shrillness, frustration, and hyperbole. In one, Capone was "the grand mogul of Chicago's gangland," and he and "a select crew of men at arms" were said to have boarded a "Chicago Express" at the North Philadelphia Station. In another, he was "the elusive 'Scarface' Al" who vanished into "a new cloud" when the "Broadway Limited" arrived in Chicago without "the notorious passenger who had been reported on it."

The Philadelphia papers did their share to contribute to the general hysteria. They were as furious with the warden as they were with Capone when they wrote how he was "aided by perfect cooperation from his former enemies—the police." Of his secret departure, they could only complain that he "disappeared more mysteriously today than at any of the many times when authorities of the law have searched the continent for him."

If the major metropolitan dailies had cared to look beyond their own private fiefdoms, they might have noticed how they were being partially scooped by two suburban papers that got his whereabouts not entirely but at least half-right. "Capone Here?" the *Rockford Daily Republic*'s headline queried. The lead paragraph outdid all other papers combined: "'Scarface Al' Capone, Chicago's notorious gangland king often painted as the world's most sinister racketeer, was reported to be on his way to Rockford today with a gang of personal bodyguards traveling in several high powered automobiles." Not content with that, the story had them "fully armed and traveling in automobiles with bullet-proof windshields." Unfortunately for this paper, its reporter was forced to admit that after all the hotels and the homes of his (unnamed) "relatives" had been searched, there was no trace of "Capone and his satellites."

The nearby *Belvidere Daily Republican* offered another possible scenario: that he had taken the train as far as Champaign before sneaking off and getting into one of several Packard limousines, his going directly to Rockford while the others took alternate routes and served as decoys. The story reported that he was driven to the home of an alleged cousin named Phillip Vella for the express purpose of meeting with Mrs. Tony Lombardo, the widow of one of his Outfit associates slain in a gangland shoot-out.

Several things were wrong with this story: So many reporters had boarded the Broadway Limited, starting at Philadelphia and then at every stop along the way, that it would have been inconceivable for Capone to have been on it, let alone to have gotten off anywhere along the way. As for Mrs. Lombardo, at some point he would certainly have paid a sympathy call on the widow of the man described as his "left bower," the slang expression of the time for a right-hand man. However, as Lombardo had died in 1928, it was unlikely that seeing her in 1930 was his first priority after ten months in prison.

There was a repeat version of his earlier return to Chicago from Florida as reporters who had boarded the train at Philadelphia and every city along the way detrained between Champaign and Rockford to scour every location between there and Chicago for Capone. By the time they gave up on trying to find him in Rockford, they rushed off to Chicago, all of them knowing that he had to appear before a federal grand jury on March 20 on charges of tax evasion. They were frustrated there, too, because he did keep the appointment, but not on that day. He learned that the city's deputy police commissioner, John Stege, was still smarting over the slayings of Moran's men on St. Valentine's Day the previous year and wanted to nab him for questioning before the Feds could place him in their jurisdiction and out of the city's reach. Stege had not only assigned every policeman and detective in the city to be on the lookout for Capone but also assigned a rotating group to watch the Prairie Avenue house and arrest him the minute he showed up there. Ralph was there and, when his brother phoned, told him not to go there or to Jake Guzik's, because Stege had staked out his house as well.

Capone was willing to be questioned by federal officials, but he was adamant about avoiding any legal entity connected to the city. Newspapers later quoted him as saying he was perfectly willing to subject himself to something along the lines of a "Federal Inquisition" but not to a "grilling by 'them ignorant coppers,' as he scornfully terms them." Most of the reporters decided to join the police stakeout at the Prairie Avenue house, where Ralph, who usually answered the telephone, said truthfully that he had no idea where Al could be. Because he had chosen the car and its drivers, he knew they were taking a circuitous and zigzagging route that would leave them undetected.

This trip was only one of the many road trips Al Capone supposedly took that have given rise to legends very much in the manner of the old saw "George Washington slept here." If even half of those stories were true, it would have taken the Capone entourage at least a month to reach Chicago because hotels in every small town between there and Philadelphia claimed he slept there. Reporters did know about some of the booze hideouts where gunmen on the run holed up in Indiana, southern Michigan, and Illinois, and they had their sources and stooges in those localities primed to report any sightings of Capone. But if he did use any of them on this trip, he was careful to get in and get out before they were alerted to his presence. The journey might have seemed haphazard, but the route had been carefully planned beforehand, and Al Capone eluded them all.

Eventually, he did go to Rockford, just long enough to arrange for secret transportation to his hotel headquarters in Cicero. The last surviving member of the generation who knew him described him during interactions with the family as his usual gentlemanly self but also uncharacteristically quiet and removed, spending most of his time when not on the phone seated at the dining room table looking over "the books" they kept for him in the upstairs closet. He was gone early the next morning before the household awoke to face the day, and according to the stories told by their descendants, they continued to store his books until some of his men took them away during one of the regular deliveries of food and money they brought throughout the Depression. But they never saw Al Capone again.

Enough time had passed for Capone to have reached Chicago, so reporters were reduced to congregating at Prairie Avenue, desperate to find him and to write something other than how he had outsmarted them all by disappearing in plain sight. Family members had been burned so badly from their one brief foray into trying to manipulate press sentiment that they did not answer the phone, so those reporters who had various kinds of clout among the staked-out police were able to cross barriers and pound on the door. It was only opened once, by Ralphie, who gave them a smart answer about what kind of pasta his grandmother might cook for Uncle Al's homecoming before he slammed the door in their faces. He was only twelve, but he learned quickly about how the family responded to outsiders.

Reporters eventually learned of Capone's whereabouts through a legal ruse, when a wiretap was placed on the family's phone and news of a conversation got around. The name of the Treasury agent Eliot Ness meant little then, but it was he who ordered wiretaps on the house as well as on Ralph's suite at the Western Hotel (as the Hawthorne had recently been renamed). Ralph used the hotel as his headquarters and had carelessly and stupidly resumed the direct management of his bootlegging activities. Ness also placed wiretaps on the several speakeasies where Ralph routinely made phone calls, and here again he was careless about what he said. Because of his brother's success in averting every conviction for each criminal act he was ever accused of, Ralph thought the same invincibility would extend to him. Unfortunately, he was so shortsighted that he made an easy target for the Feds.

Ness got permission for wiretaps after Ralph was indicted in October 1929, on seven separate counts of attempting to defraud the government of tax revenues, the same charges that would later be leveled against Al. The first six charges against Ralph were based on his flashy displays of wealth, starting with his large and vulgar diamond ring, his several expensive automobiles, his suite at the Western Hotel, and his flagrant and public spending on women, elaborate parties, and heavy betting. Still, he brazenly told the IRS that he had no income and therefore owed no taxes. Even more foolishly, he cried poverty and refused to pay the less than $5,000 the government originally fined him; by the time of the seventh indictment, he had incited an investigation that revealed he had more than $25,000 in one of his bank accounts. That finding led to the most serious charge against him, of attempting to defraud the U.S. government.

Here again, he proved his obtuseness: instead of settling the tax bills, he demanded a trial and got it. It was to take place in May 1930, two months after Al was released from prison, and by that time it would be too late for Al to try to use his connections and intercede in a wiser and more cautious manner. The only intelligent thing Ralph did throughout the government's investigation was to hire an excellent lawyer, but even that was futile, because the presiding judge was the incorruptible James H. Wilkerson, whom the Capone brothers would come to know well and who would make short shrift of both their legal representations.

The wiretaps on Ralph had a beneficial side effect for law enforcement officials and the newspaper reporters who curried their favor: they provided up-to-date information about Al's whereabouts and activities. He had been a model prisoner at Eastern Pen, quietly self-effacing, always with a smile and a readiness to cooperate on anything he was asked to do. He was the same with the Rockford family, still handing out $100 bills to the now-grown children. He had been the perfect gentleman for almost a year, and now it was time to release the pent-up emotions he had kept under stringent control throughout that time.

He needed to release all the seething energy of having to sit on the sidelines and watch as Torrio, who ran the Outfit in his absence, gave long-distance orders about how to govern the Outfit and Nitti assumed more and more authority. He had to think about what could be done to heed the warnings Jake Guzik was raising about how revenues on every front had declined now that the Depression had gripped the entire country. For the next several days, Capone huddled at the Western with Guzik, who told him how sales of beer and whiskey were steadily dropping so that if projections were correct, by the end of the year they would be two-thirds less than what they had been in the heyday of the 1920s. The bad news continued, because gambling and prostitution were down as well.

Occasionally, they conferred with trusted associates who kept the accounts or brought in reports from the various enterprises. The Outfit was still making money, but economic uncertainty ruled the land, and the little guys they had counted on to buy their booze, visit their brothels, and gamble their paychecks were either suffering hard times or, worried that they were coming, were holding tightly to the little they still had.

For Al Capone, there were troubles on every front. The Prairie Avenue house was still surrounded by police, so he was unable to go there to see his mother and the family. Unable to appear anywhere in public without being hounded, he stewed at the Western, drinking himself into an incoherent drunken rage. The wiretappers learned he was there when one of Ralph's foot soldiers phoned and begged him to come get Al before he could do any more destructive damage.

"You're the only one who can handle him when he gets like this," Ralph's caller told him, adding that Al had drunk himself into such a stupor that they were sending "for a lot of towels" to clean up his messes. While he was throwing furniture and destroying the premises, he managed somehow to burn his hand quite badly. When reporters asked about it, he invented the excuse that he had put his hand on a hot pan while cooking roast beef. They all knew he never cooked, but they still reported the incident with his tongue-in-cheek explanation as if it were true.

Once he sobered up, Al sent for Mae. She managed to elude the press as she slipped into town and was spirited to Cicero. He took a private suite for her at the Western, and whether or not either of them invited Mafalda to share it, she was there as well. He trotted both women out briefly when he began another public relations campaign in March 1930 to counter all the negative publicity that his release from prison had generated. The first interview he granted was to the *Tribune*'s Genevieve Forbes Herrick, one of the few female reporters on staff with the then-enviable reputation as a "front-page girl" for her ability to land interviews with elusive subjects. In the words of John Kobler, what he told her was a "tirade of self-justification." He claimed Mae was only twenty-eight when in reality she was thirty-two, and he urged the reporter to look at her hair, nicely colored blond to cover her original brown but which he claimed had turned gray because she was so worried about "things in Chicago." Painting himself once again as "poor picked-upon Al," he concluded his protestations of innocence with the usual excuse he offered time and again: that no matter what happened in Chicago, he was unjustly blamed for every terrible thing, starting with the Chicago fire.

Later the same day, he continued his saga of self-justification when he gave a second interview, this time to a reporter from the *Chicago American*. Here, he repeated his oft-made contention that he was only providing a service to the American public and that no one was being forced to take a drink or enter a gambling establishment. He used a euphemism to disguise the brothels he was ashamed of running when he said no one was being forced "to go to a place to have some fun." All very true, but nonetheless all very illegal.

The Capone women did not see much of Al over the next several days as he sobered up and prepared to appear in the office of Chicago's deputy chief of police, the loudmouthed braggart John Stege, who had been boasting that he would arrest Al Capone the minute he appeared in the city. Because he had no grounds on which to make such an arrest, Capone called his bluff by leaving the Western in Cicero and moving very publicly into his suite at the Lexington in the heart of downtown Chicago. When Stege did nothing about such a blatant challenge, Capone decided to further capitalize on publicity by taunting him with a personal visit on March 21, 1930.

First, he got in touch with his favorite photographer, Tony Berardi, asking him to come along and take pictures, and to make sure nothing untoward happened, he also took his lawyer Thomas Nash. They went first to police headquarters, where Capone strode up to the desk to ask if the chief of police, the state's attorney, the U.S. attorney, or any other official—anywhere—wanted to see him. He was told no one did, so, still determined to stage an event and surrounded by a phalanx of policemen, he and his entourage went on to the federal building, where they found Stege. An exchange ensued between him and Capone in which they traded taunts that quickly degenerated into a foolish non sequitur.

Stege asked if Capone had played a role in gangland hits, giving the examples of the St. Valentine's Day Massacre and Frankie Yale's murder; Capone proclaimed his innocence with his usual retort, that he was blamed for every heinous killing that happened no matter where. He indulged in a bit of gloating when he said no legal accusation against him had ever resulted in a conviction and that his only reason for calling on Stege was that he knew there were no grounds to arrest him. He wanted the deputy chief to be aware of his real reason for being there—the very fact that he could stroll in and demand a meeting showed how ineffectual the Chicago police were—but he was careful to say this in softer language, merely stating that he wanted to make sure he was neither harassed nor arrested whenever he moved about the city.

Stege must have been frustrated by his powerlessness, but he still tried to exert authority. He knew that the Miami police were trying to invent some reason to arrest Capone whenever he showed up at Palm Island, so Stege shouted that his luck had run out and asked when he would leave the city. He knew that the day before Capone bearded him in Chicago, Miami police had raided the Palm Island house and confiscated a cache of liquor before arresting a group of men that included his brothers John and Albert. Undaunted, Capone told Stege he planned to go to Florida as soon as he could get away. Stege told him he was free to go before once again making the unenforceable threat that the next time he was in Chicago, he would be put in jail. In an attempt to defuse the increasingly testy exchange, Al's diplomatic lawyer, Thomas Nash, who had a great deal of earlier experience representing mobsters like Dean O'Banion and Bugs Moran, responded by saying arrests without cause could not happen in America and even in Russia, Lenin and Trotsky had rebelled against them. Stege must have been semi-hysterical when he shouted, "I hope Capone goes to Russia." Al Capone left his office on that high note and prepared to go to Florida for the tranquillity and privacy he sorely needed.

———

Even though arrest without cause was not supposed to happen in America, the governor of Florida still decided to try. On March 19, Governor Doyle E. Carlton sent telegrams to every sheriff in the state telling them to arrest Al Capone on sight the moment he crossed the state line. Capone's attorneys in Miami demanded that the governor explain how he could keep a taxpaying American citizen and property owner who was not accused of any crime out of his own home. When the case was presented to the federal judge Halsted L. Ritter, he agreed with the lawyers, albeit reluctantly in the gangster's case, that the United States was a country of laws, enforced "without reference to popular opinion or consequences." He must have been dismayed when the headline for the story about his ruling ran in the *Miami Daily News:* "Federal Judge Weeps for Abused Al Capone."

The Miami paper's headline was typical of the response that the police harassment there and in Chicago generated in Capone's favor. Throughout the United States, civic groups, private citizens, even chambers of commerce, all vied to tell him he was welcome to visit them at any time. In Monticello, Iowa, voters went beyond asking him to visit; in a mayoral election, more than fifty citizens cast write-in ballots for Al Capone. Chicago newspapers reported that as far away as Java, Burma, and the Philippines "the [name of] the Scarface is as well known in the Orient as it is here." He was that popular and that much of a folk hero.

———

Ralph's trial began three weeks after Al was released from prison, with the Honorable James H. Wilkerson presiding in the U.S. District Court for the Northern District of Illinois. Ralph feinted and parried, lied and evaded, but the prosecuting attorneys were clever. They made scant mention of his illegal activities to concentrate instead on his nonpayment of federal income taxes. It was fairly easy to prove that Ralph had a lot of money because he had opened multiple accounts under fictitious names in the Pinkert State Bank in Cicero that were quickly traced back to him. By the time of his trial, the government had amassed so many records of his misdeeds that a truckload of supporting documents had to be wheeled into court. Ralph still tried to wheedle out of the charges by claiming that his occupation was gambling and his banking practices were how all gamblers dealt with their winnings. As his defense, he argued that because the law allowed for gambling losses to be deductible against winnings and because his losses were far greater than his winnings, he had not violated any laws. The trial lasted for two weeks, but the jury was not convinced by Ralph's defense and took only two hours to find him guilty on all counts. His lawyers immediately began appeals. Judge Wilkerson sentenced Ralph to three years in Leavenworth prison and fined him $10,000. When Ralph heard the verdict, he was reputed to have said, "I don't understand this at all." He was not the only one.

Ralph's incomprehension was similar to Frank Nitti's a year later, after he was also tried, convicted, and sent to Leavenworth. Nitti's defense was that he didn't pay income taxes because the laws were not clear, and he had a point. Confusion originated after the 1926 ruling by the Fourth Circuit Court of Appeals, that income from illegal sources could not be taxed, was reversed in 1927 by the Supreme Court in what came to be known as the *Sullivan* decision. It held that gains from illicit traffic in liquor are subject to income tax, and the Fifth Amendment does not protect the recipient of such income from prosecution for failure to file a tax return on such income. *United States v. Sullivan* took its name from the trial of Manley Sullivan, a small-time criminal whose defense was that if he declared illegal income, it was tantamount to waiving the Fifth Amendment rights that protected individuals from self-incrimination. In the decades since the *Sullivan* ruling, when bar associations and law schools around the country have reenacted Al Capone's trial, the lawyers on both sides usually arrive at the same conclusion: that almost ninety years after the *Sullivan* decision, there were aspects of the ruling that were still unclear and questionable. Nevertheless, *United States v. Sullivan* was used in relentless pursuit against Frank Nitti and Jake Guzik, who were both convicted and sent to Leavenworth.

As soon as he was charged, Nitti went into hiding and managed to elude federal agents for almost six months until someone decided to shadow his wife, for she, if anyone, would know where he was. Agents followed her as she drove a car with stolen license plates to his latest in a string of hideouts, where he was captured in October 1930 and sent to prison. Guzik was indicted in November 1930, after informers told the Feds that he was trying to sabotage the case against him by exerting the pressure of (as the agent Frank J. Wilson summarized it) "political influence or otherwise." Fearing that Guzik's attempts to coerce or threaten witnesses who would testify against him would succeed, Wilson exerted so much effort that the trial took one month from indictment to conviction before Guzik was also on his way to Leavenworth for the next five years.

Federal agents were emboldened by the success of tracking Nitti down and convicting Guzik, and they did not hesitate to let it be known that those convictions were only the warm-up for Al Capone, their biggest target and the one their sights were set on from the beginning. And in Chicago, it would appear that some of the city's leading citizens had had their fill of him. They were equally determined to bring down Al Capone, and they were ready to start the process of doing so.

Chapter 15

A NEW DAY FOR CHICAGO

.

T he elite group of private citizens known as the Secret Six were well aware that Capone's admirers dubbed him the unofficial mayor of Chicago. Even though loath to admit it, they had to agree that if he wanted to run for the office, he would probably be elected, and honestly at that—no ballot box stuffing would be needed. By 1930, he was boasting to any reporter who wanted to write about him of everything he did to boost the city's economic welfare, particularly of the six to seven thousand citizens on his payroll. He was more discreet about the fact that this number consisted mainly of civil servants, including more than 60 percent of the entire police force. The horrified Secret Six decided that this could not be allowed to continue. In retrospect, they were so fixated on destroying Al Capone that they gave little thought of what would happen to the unfortunate citizens who would be unemployed once he was gone. All they cared about was making Al Capone go away.

The Secret Six came from the class of wealthy men who had been well educated, were well traveled on the contemporary version of the European grand tour, and were all brought up to believe they should contribute to public philanthropy. Some were first generation, self-created millionaires; others were the descendants of men who had created enormous fortunes. They led sophisticated lives, no doubt most among them representing the Lake Shore Drive socialites whom Al derided for drinking his bootleg liquor in private while denouncing him in public. They had access to political power far beyond Chicago's city limits that he could never hope to match, and once they set their minds to battling him, they could pose a tremendous threat.

Of the Six themselves, to this day it remains difficult to identify them precisely, for various names have been floated over the years, thus making the "Six" a possible misnomer. Scholars of the Capone era and of crime in Chicago have disagreed about who were the actual members and who were their sympathizers and financial benefactors. As with many historical investigations of this era and of the people who were important in it, there is so much conflicting evidence and so little reliable documentation that, for the time being, no stronger conclusions can be drawn than informed speculation.

What can be verified about the Secret Six is that they originally banded together as a committee of equals because their wealth and social position placed them on the same footing. And, as usually happens when such groups form, some members assumed a more commanding role than others in the movement to destroy Al Capone. The names of the most likely members have always been drawn from the best known among Chicago's glittering elite, starting with Charles G. Dawes.

If Al Capone was Chicago's "best known citizen," Dawes most certainly qualified as its "best." He was a banker who had served in the McKinley administration as comptroller of the currency and, under President Warren G. Harding, was the first director of the U.S. Bureau of the Budget. In 1925, he became Calvin Coolidge's vice president and in that same year was a co-winner of the Nobel Peace Prize for what was known as the Dawes Plan for World War I reparations. When he focused his attention on Al Capone, he was serving as President Hoover's ambassador to Great Britain. He had access to the highest seats of power in government and finance, but his protean intelligence also brought him success in fields far beyond them; he was a self-taught pianist and composer whose 1912 "Melody in A Major" was given words in 1951 to become the popular song titled "It's All in the Game." Recorded by countless artists who ranged from Nat King Cole to Donny and Marie Osmond, it made Dawes the only vice-president and Nobel Peace Prize winner with a No. 1 pop hit in both Britain and America.

Another probable member, Colonel Robert Rutherford McCormick, was Dawes's peer in every sense. As the owner, editor, and publisher of Chicago's most powerful and influential newspaper, the *Chicago Tribune,* he was a prime example of what *Time* magazine called "one of the last anachronistic citadels of muscular personal journalism." Scholars and critics have long debated his various influences, but all agree that he evoked mixed emotions and was feared and hated even as he was admired and respected. He was a man "bitterly attacked . . . and warmly defended," and everyone "realized his power." McCormick was a curious dichotomy: a staunchly conservative Republican who derided President Hoover as ineffectual and who was at the same time a social drinker who flouted Prohibition publicly and was an outspoken advocate for its repeal. And even as he ridiculed Hoover, he would come to despise Roosevelt and the New Deal.

The events McCormick chose to focus on in his tightly controlled newspaper domain seemed arbitrary and capricious to some of his critics. For example, when all Chicago was shocked and enthralled by the St. Valentine's Day Massacre, which pushed other reformers into action, McCormick did not concentrate his newspaper's accounts on Capone's possible involvement; he only became focused on the gang boss after another outrage, the brutal assassination on June 9, 1930, of Jake Lingle, the reporter who was his chief "gangsterologist." Furious that one of his own had been targeted, McCormick conveniently forgot to tell the public that Lingle was also a friend of Capone's and on his payroll, which was how he became the source of inside information for the many gangland "scoops" the *Tribune* scored.

Lingle's murder was certainly a primary reason for McCormick's focus on Capone, but an alternate and equally important reason might have been the attempted murder of Philip Meagher, a construction supervisor who refused to accede to mob demands. Harrison Barnard, the contractor who employed him and who declared himself a member of the Secret Six, claimed credit for galvanizing them and various other citizen groups into taking action after he spent an entire lunchtime conversation persuading Colonel McCormick that something had to be done about the Outfit's incursion into every aspect of business in Chicago.

Another committee member name, cited and disputed in equal measure, was Burt A. Massee, who was reportedly the one spurring the others into concentrated action. He had been a member of the coroner's jury that investigated Lingle's murder, and that led him to recommend the formation of the first independent crime lab in the United States, the Scientific Crime Detection Laboratory, which opened on the Northwestern University campus in 1930. Massee was responsible for bringing in Calvin Goddard, M.D., also a possible Secret Six member, who became the lab's first director. Goddard was an expert on ballistics whose research furthered the creation of one of the most important tools in crime fighting: the comparison microscope that could determine whether bullets were fired from particular weapons. That technology initially put only a mild sort of fear into some gangsters because most did not realize its importance in solving crimes until it became a routine tool that resulted in many gangland convictions.

This small group of reformers chose its members carefully for what they could contribute to bringing down Al Capone, and two other names are usually cited as completing the membership. Like the first four, the last two were selected for their particular skills. Robert Isham Randolph was an engineer widely praised for his organizational abilities; he is believed by some factions to have been the executive director of the Secret Six, the one who planned daily strategies and put them into effect. Last but certainly not least, they needed someone who could manipulate public opinion through publicity and public relations, and for that they chose Henry Barrett Chamberlin, who was as skilled in manipulating the media and public opinion as Capone. He was trained as a lawyer but spent most of his career as a newspaper reporter and magazine editor and was also instrumental in promoting the founding in 1919 of the Chicago Crime Commission (CCC), which had been largely ineffectual for most of the following decade.

Chamberlin knew the value of molding public sentiment. Long before he set his sights on Capone, he was one of the first to recognize that a reinvigorated CCC could make a powerful public statement, even though he also knew that its ability to effect change would be minimal. Chamberlin viewed organized crime as a business (albeit an illegal one) and, as such, one that had to be fought with business methods. He was the committee member who had the legal background and public relations skills to do it, and he did not hesitate to use them on Capone.

These were all wealthy men, but they knew it was not going to be cheap to bring down Al Capone. They would need to enlist others to donate large infusions of cash to support their endeavors. Samuel Insull was a magnate in public utilities who gave readily whenever he was asked, thereby gaining the reputation of a not-so-secret bankroller. He would be instrumental in Al's conviction, but shortly afterward he was hauled into court for his own very public trial on charges of embezzlement, violation of federal bankruptcy acts, and mail fraud. Not surprisingly, the jury acquitted this pillar of Chicago society of every charge against him. Julius Rosenwald, who began his career running a department store in Springfield and went on to hold a high-level position in which he was largely responsible for taking Sears, Roebuck to national prominence, was Insull's equal in providing money. Rosenwald was more discreet in all his dealings, and even though he had been investigated for illegalities in 1915, the charges against him were also dismissed.

As these men trained their sights on Capone, he continued his machinations and peregrinations, seemingly oblivious to their increasing determination to bring him to justice. In March 1929, Colonel McCormick went to Washington to meet with President Hoover, primarily to discuss the rampant crime in Chicago. The two men agreed that most of it stemmed from Prohibition and that the law was ineffectual and should be abolished, but they also agreed that the criminals who had amassed great wealth from flouting the law had to be punished. Hoover assigned Andrew Mellon, then the secretary of the Treasury, to head a task force that concentrated on illegal income and nonpayment of taxes.

Mellon was a curious choice because he was an avowed enemy of the Volstead Act and made no secret of his social drinking. Described by his son, Paul, the great philanthropist, as a man with an "ice water smile," Andrew Mellon was also the co-owner of the Old Overholt rye distillery, one of the chief employers in western Pennsylvania's exceedingly poor Westmoreland County, and was thus just another criminal flouting the law of the land. Mellon named a man with a reputation as icy as his own, Elmer Irey of the Internal Revenue Service, to be in charge of bringing down Al Capone.

In Chicago, the Secret Six selected their own man to end Al Capone's "dictatorship in politics." Frank Loesch was a seventy-six-year-old corporate lawyer in 1928 who postponed his retirement when the Six persuaded him to take on the dubious honor of serving as president of the Chicago Crime Commission. After the city's chief of police was quoted as saying that "sixty percent of my police [force] is in the bootleg business," civic leaders had awakened at last to the fact that Capone's de facto rule was causing so much damage to the city's reputation and economy and, by extension, damage to their personal fortunes.

Loesch had been one of the original organizers of the CCC in 1919 and had been a committee member since 1922. Until he took charge in 1928, the commission was best known for compiling excellent records of what the crooks had been up to and creating highly readable reports about their colorful activities—and nothing more. After Big Bill Thompson's slate was defeated in 1928, Loesch placed a newspaper ad proclaiming that "Chicago has shown it means to clean house" and that "every self-respecting citizen" would soon be proud of his or her city because "a new day for Chicago has dawned." However, when it actually came to curbing crime, the CCC had neither power nor authority to stop the relentless murdering of gangsters by other gangsters, the epidemic bribery of public servants, or any of the many different kinds of extortion.

When Loesch accepted the call to mend the commission's ineffectual ways, most of his contemporaries thought he was one of three things: "a crazy man, a crank reformer, or a publicity seeker." Actually, he was none of the above, but a Bible-teaching elder of the Presbyterian Church who believed in "Samaritanism," the idea that a good Christian had the obligation to help everyone, from the lowest individual to the wealthiest and most influential. Like George E. Q. Johnson and Mabel Willebrandt, Loesch was incorruptible and fearless and accepted the premise that going after criminals by trying to end crime would not work. Other, more sophisticated and creative ways had to be found to stop them.

Loesch found a willing colleague in the new state's attorney, John Swanson, who was elected in the landslide that swept Big Bill Thompson's men out of office. Swanson was determined to rid all of Cook County of crime, and not just the city of Chicago, thus giving the criminal element nowhere to move operations when the city's heat became too hot. One of his first acts was to name Frank Loesch as his first assistant state's attorney, a position Loesch held in conjunction with his appointment to the CCC. Loesch's directive was to investigate the connections between criminal acts and their influence on political decisions; to ensure that he could successfully continue on this course in his new appointments, he brought most of his staff with him to the State's Attorney's Office.

Swanson's strategy was the one Loesch, Willebrandt, and the other early investigators had put forth, that the best way to cripple the influence of organized crime was to cut off its sources of income. In his remarks to the newspapers, he made what had become the fairly usual speech by political crusaders, saying that he would shut down speakeasies, gambling dens, and brothels so that "the 'rackets' which have pestered and pillaged legitimate business shall be stopped and ended." With Loesch, the CCC, and the Secret Six fully poised to give Swanson the cooperation he needed, the apparatus intent on bringing down Al Capone was securely in place.

But in the face of this well-organized, well-financed effort to unseat him, Capone appeared oblivious, leading many contemporaries and subsequent biographers to wonder how a smart and savvy fellow like Al Capone failed to realize that his fight with these crusading reformers would be an entirely different kind of battle from those he had fought in the past. When even Frankie Rio was perceptive enough to warn him that any new suits would have to be tailored from striped prison material, why couldn't he see for himself that these opponents were formidable, and why didn't he react accordingly? Did he think he was invincible because of the CCC's hapless conclusion after its 1929 investigation into his liquor, vice, and gambling activities that because they had "no other record of conviction," all they could do was dismiss him as "notorious in these activities"? In 1930, when he was well aware of the foes allied against him, a reporter for the *Chicago Tribune* who wrote about the dire situation he faced seemed puzzled by his lackadaisical attitude, describing Capone as "intelligent and affable . . . happy-go-lucky [and] harmless as a Saint Bernard puppy dog." How could Al Capone have been so cavalier?

Many reasons have been offered for the passive approach his high-powered and exceedingly well-paid lawyers took to gear up for criminal proceedings. The most likely one was that because he had been totally untouched by all the criminal charges that had been leveled against him over the years, he believed he could make these new ones go away before a trial, one way or another. If payoffs and bribes didn't work, people could always be taken for euphemistic one-way rides; assassinations and murders were last resorts, but threats of them were certainly enough to put the fear in just about everyone. Capone probably thought these newest do-gooders might eventually tire of their pursuit and go away as well.

As a former bookkeeper who knew how to manipulate numbers, he should have been wary, but he had no respect for government bureaucrats and considered them little more than paper pushers who could always be bought off. Even though the federal government estimated his share of illegal profits from 1925 to 1929 to be in the neighborhood of $6 million (at the very least), and the *New York Times* agreed that he was indeed a multimillionaire, how could he possibly be charged with tax evasion if he never showed any income? And so, in the beginning, as the case against him started to build, he scoffed. He thought public opinion was on his side even after the CCC released a list of "Public Enemies" in April 1930 with Al Capone leading as No. 1.

Loesch released two separate numerical lists with twenty-eight different names on each. He called them all Chicago's "most prominent and well-known and notorious gangsters," and Al Capone led as "Public Enemy Number One." In a perverse way, being at the top of such a highly publicized list gave Capone and his cohorts something to brag about. He thought it was nothing to take seriously when even the respected *New York Times* ridiculed Loesch as a bombastic blowhard and publicity seeker. Capone considered himself untouchable after that newspaper rightly acknowledged that the "Capones and Morans" were not operating within the law but also that there was little proof to tie them directly to illegal operations: "They dwell in a twilight zone where the courts cannot function but where the police department may [only] harry them and keep them moving."

That Loesch called all his public enemies "prominent" was an interesting word choice. It certainly described Al Capone, by now a firmly established worldwide legend whose flamboyance made him deserving of first place, while Ralph's rank of No. 2 was only because of his relationship to his younger brother. Jake Guzik made the list at No. 10 with one of the more colorful descriptions: "vice monger, business manager in the Capone Syndicate, paymaster in the bribery of politicians and public officials."

The CCC huffed and puffed as it put out a call for police officers to arrest every one of the criminals who made the list on the trumped-up charge of vagrancy, saying for every one rounded up, each police officer would be commended and given "creditable mention and special consideration." No one took this directive seriously, first because "vagrancy" was such a vague, ill-defined, and unenforceable charge and second because so many police officers (by the commission's own admission) were being paid off by Guzik.

The phrase "Public Enemy" only helped to solidify the positive perception of gangsters identified with it in the public's eye. The FBI adopted the phrase for the ubiquitous posters that hung in every post office across the land, and it became such an ingrained cultural byword that it was even the title of the Hollywood movie that made James Cagney a star. All these gangster glorifications made Al Capone even more famous and more of a target for the increasingly furious and frustrated entities of law enforcement.

He was already larger than life, and his name had become a synonym for power both admired and feared, and like all such publicity there were two sides to his renown. There is a popular expression in Australia that tall poppies make for highly visible targets easily chopped down. Al Capone, the relentless publicity seeker, should have realized that he was the tallest poppy and therefore the most visible and that a modicum of discretion might have been advisable.

How such a street-smart man could have disregarded all the warning

, signs once so many different organizations composed of outraged civic leaders banded together is puzzling. The men of the Secret Six were well aware of how Capone was idolized far more than he was vilified, and he knew that their political influence and financial clout reached to the highest levels of government and that they controlled the media outlets that would allow them to manipulate public opinion. They had more than enough of both money and method to turn the public against him, a public that, despite its better collective judgment, still mostly admired and adored him.

But Al thought the Secret Six could never turn his fans against him, especially after the grudging admiration in the *New York Times,* which wrote that "the free advertising that has accompanied [his celebrity status] ought to be worth literally millions of dollars." The paper even noted his transfiguration when he toned down (temporarily, as it turned out) some of his bilious green and sleazy yellow silk suits for custom-made "soft blues," "modest grays," and the other trappings of a "successful businessman." The term "businessman" was one Capone had long insisted described him best, and it seemed he had been widely successful in planting that image when Fred Pasley's 1930 biography was reviewed in the *Saturday Review of Literature.* The reviewer concluded that all Capone could be accused of was "supplying a huge public demand" for liquor and that his business acumen should place him on a par with other titans of industry and commerce, such as "Mr. Ford, Mr. Hearst, and Procter and Gamble."

Capone also counted on public-spirited generosity to keep the public firmly on his side, particularly after the Great Depression began: he established a soup kitchen that on any given day fed as many as two to three thousand out-of-work people. It was an altruistic stance, and it did keep the public more or less on his side; that is, until the rumors mounted that he paid for little of it himself but rather used bribery and extortion to get other businesses to stock his pantries. Rumors like this started the rumblings that encouraged many attacks against him, such as the one in *Harper's Magazine* that called him "an ambidextrous giant who kills with one hand and feeds with the other."

These attempts to retain the public's goodwill were certainly interesting, but they never seemed the result of a concerted effort on Al's part, and they did nothing to curb his opponents. Capone's descendants attribute his relative indifference to sheer exhaustion; it had been a stunning gravity-defying spree during the six or so years when he rose to become one of the richest and most powerful men in America. Getting to the top and then staying there took so much energy that he had few long respites aside from his stay in the Philadelphia prison. The occasional disappearances to Rockford or the few fishing trips on which he sneaked away with Ralph to the wilds of Michigan or Wisconsin served the same purpose, but they were few, far between, and of short duration.

All his relatives insist that he was not ill but simply exhausted during the years 1929–31 and that there were no symptoms of the mental deterioration that later contributed to his death. The medical records kept by his physicians support their contention. Mae Capone's pleas for him to retire and let someone else take over intensified during this period, and family members say he was so tired he actually paid attention to her and promised to try.

One sign of his exhaustion can be found in how the remarks he had made earlier about wanting to retire proliferated during this time, especially statements about wanting to be able to stay at home without fear of attack, to be able to dine with his family and spend time with the son who (thanks to his mother) was growing into a fine young man. As his problems intensified throughout 1930, Capone admitted, "I'm no angel. I'm not posing as a model for youth. I've had to do a lot of things I don't like to do. But I'm not as black as I'm painted. I'm human. I've got a heart in me."

"Yes," wrote Dale Carnegie, author of the vastly influential *How to Win Friends and Influence People.* "That's Al Capone speaking: the most sinister gang leader who ever shot up Chicago. Capone doesn't condemn himself. He actually regards himself as a public benefactor, an unappreciated and misunderstood public benefactor." Capone, according to Carnegie, defended himself by avoiding the reality of his criminal activity and insisting that he had spent the best years of his life "giving people the lighter pleasures, helping them have a good time." Carnegie quotes a version of the remark Capone said many times previously: "All I get is abuse, the existence of a hunted man."

However, he was wise enough to know that retirement was not possible. "Once in the racket, you're in it for life. Your past holds you in it. The gang won't let you out. Murder, murder, that's all this racket means. I'm sick of it." He insisted he would be "the happiest man alive" if he could only go to Florida and live quietly for the rest of his days. Even as he said it, he knew it was a fantasy.

————

Swanson's directive to go after the money was paying off as first Ralph, then Jake Guzik and other members of the Outfit were being sentenced to prison for nonpayment of federal income taxes. As one after the other was convicted, there was no one Al Capone could depend on to run the Outfit, so it was up to him to stay in charge of operations. And yet, even though he knew that because of the convictions the others were facing, the CCC and the Secret Six would have their sights trained on him, he seemed passively indifferent as he sat back and depended on his lawyers to keep him out of jail.

Throughout his career in crime, Capone had never been in awe of wealth and power, legitimate or otherwise, so if he had wanted to intimidate his wealthy and well-connected enemies through reprisals, he would probably have tried to do so. He seems to have done nothing to try to harm them, and to date no documentation has been found to show that he authorized any of his usual methods against these particular adversaries or the large staff they had assembled to assist them. There is no evidence either in legal documents, in public accounts, or within the memories of his family that he took the Secret Six seriously enough even to make any comment or express concern about them.

Physical intimidation aside, there were any number of levers Capone could have pulled in the media to counter the Secret Six. He had many reporters and editors on his payroll, so he had his own press outlets and could easily have responded to the Six's negative stories. He could have used his people to organize a campaign painting himself as a philanthropic and highly public do-gooder whom the rich and powerful were harassing for selfish reasons of their own; he could have used class warfare to paint them as men who thought themselves above the law, waging a vendetta against ethnic citizens for no valid legal reasons. And yet he did nothing.

All the activity against Al Capone that began in the spring of 1929 was coalescing throughout 1930. On the side of law enforcement, President Hoover was getting regular reports from Mellon, Irey, and others who reported to him. On the gangland side, Capone knew that within Chicago his rivals were well informed about the government's fixation on his and his cohorts' undeclared income. He knew they were counting on this distraction and lack of focus on running the various businesses to create opportunities for inroads (or worse).

Still, Al Capone kept to his low-key, defensive media campaign about wanting to retire to the quiet life, and the many interviews he gave to that effect seemed to be working well enough with the public. Loesch was aware of how Capone was playing his "poor picked-upon Al" role for the press and got busy mounting a barrage of his own to counteract it. He told the

Chicago Daily News, "If Al Capone is not murdered, the law will get him, or he will die in poverty." It was an ominous prediction that became true in both parts, but Al Capone's response was to appear indifferent, detached, and oblivious. In retrospect, he should have paid closer attention and taken a stronger stand.

Chapter 16

ON THE ROAD TO JAIL

A new player entered the game to get Al Capone in March 1930 when Agent Frank J. Wilson began to focus on sending Ralph Capone, Jake Guzik and his brother Harry, and Frank Nitti all to federal prison. He boasted to his Washington superiors that they were only the warm-up for his "most strenuous efforts . . . making real headway" in building the case against Capone. Wilson bragged about being so effective that he had foiled Capone's most "sensational method, to prevent further molestation of [Capone] and his gang." Wilson claimed he had "reliable informers" who told him that Capone ordered his henchmen to murder him and the three other agents working with him: the U.S. attorney George E. Q. Johnson, Special Agent in Charge A. P. "Art" Madden, and the Cook County state's investigator, Pat Roche. To support his contention, Wilson cited "imported gunmen" who had been spotted in Chicago "cruising around in a blue sedan bearing a New York license tag."

This astonishing claim takes on aspects of a silent movie shoot-'em-up in Wilson's explanation, in which he said that the "tip" was "partly corroborated through information furnished voluntarily to the Chicago *Tribune* from a source considered dependable by them which was entirely unrelated to the original source which furnished us the above report regarding the plot to murder us." It was a breathtakingly roundabout and convoluted defense for a highly dubious assertion, but Wilson and the other agents were still frightened enough to go into hiding while police searched for Capone so they could bring him in for questioning. They were frustrated when he could not be found because Cook County detectives on the Outfit's payroll tipped him off, which allowed Capone to keep several steps ahead of his pursuers, moving between a variety of alleged hideouts in Cicero and elsewhere. Wilson claimed that these same detectives supposedly told Al that the Feds were wise to his planned assassination, which was the only reason he called it off and gave in long enough to show up and face his accusers.

Wilson never offered any specifics about this alleged hit, so it must remain in the realm of unsubstantiated, undated fact. However, what makes it unlikely that Capone ever conceived such a plan stems from the three incidents that led the combined wrath of government and law enforcement to bear down on him: the firestorm that followed the murder of McSwiggin, the St. Valentine's Day Massacre, and Lingle's assassination. All three turned what had been overwhelming public approval solidly against him, so it is unlikely that he would have risked losing even more support by taking such a glaringly visible action. Al Capone was a smart man who made the decisions about what would happen to his enemies—real or merely suspected—and who controlled whatever actions transpired, but he always did so from behind the scenes.

Because of the trials and convictions of his Outfit cohorts and his own tax problems, frenzied publicity accompanied Capone wherever he went, so that was another reason why it was unlikely he would have ordered such public "hits" as the one on Wilson and his colleagues. For Wilson's inflamed dramatization of this unproven allegation to be true, Capone would have had to be more than dumb, actually stupid. And he was neither.

Nothing had yet been pinned on him, but research into every aspect of his public and private life was ramping up. A top secret report prepared at the start of 1931 by the Treasury Department's Intelligence Unit gives an indication of the ferocious digging that was well under way. The report began by describing Capone as "without a doubt, the best advertised and most talked of gangster in the United States today." That contention should have included the rest of the world, for long before he was tried, members of the foreign press were gathering in Chicago to devote "reams and reams of newsprint and magazine paper" to the "Big Shot," another of the many names now tagging him. However, despite all the copy he generated, the writers of the intelligence report had to concede that "possibly some of the stories are true, but no doubt a great deal of the stuff printed originated in the fartile [sic: fertile] brow of some newspaper reporter or magazine writer." The "punk hoodlum" who first arrived in Chicago had become "Capone, the immune; Capone, the idol of the hoodlum element; the dictator, free from arrest and prosecution." He was indeed still free because every criminal case against him had to be dismissed "for the reason that no policemen could be found in Chicago who knew Al Capone!"

"That Al Capone is shrewd, there is no doubt," wrote the intelligence agent before using an ethnic slur to make his point. "Together with his native Italian secretiveness, [it] has made this case a most difficult one to handle."

———

From his so-called retirement in New York, John Torrio had been quietly masterminding Capone's situation, just as he had done since the Atlantic City mob boss gathering and Capone's subsequent imprisonment. Now that Guzik was in prison, Torrio was once again directing the day-to-day running of the Outfit, flying from New York to Chicago on the average of once a month to receive reports and issue orders. He oversaw the alliance holding the North Siders and the Outfit peacefully together, and now he had the urgent task of devising a strategy to spare Capone from a second prison sentence. Torrio told Capone to start a defense by hiring his own personal tax lawyer, Lawrence P. Mattingly, who had a respected practice in Washington, D.C. Capone did as directed, even as he continued to remain aloof and passively indifferent to his plight. In retrospect and with the perfect hindsight that goes with it, he allowed his lawyer to make decisions that did not serve him well.

Capone had always been careful about distancing himself from all records of the Outfit's profits, and he made sure that none were kept for how he spent his personal income. There were no bank accounts in his name; he used intermediaries to transfer money through telegrams and checks that were often written to third parties who used fictitious names and took care to disguise their handwriting. He carried huge wads of money and paid cash for everything; the house in Chicago was in his mother's and Mae's names, and Palm Island was in Mae's. The Outfit's books were kept in duplicate—some even in triplicate—and they were not kept in one place. The bookkeepers were trained to make references to Capone in an abbreviated, coded shorthand, and those ledgers were separate from the Outfit's. Now the dilemma was whether to admit that he had made money in years past, even though illegal, and, if so, how much.

The issue became whether or not he should offer to pay the Bureau of Internal Revenue on the chance that Mattingly could structure a deal that would allow him to admit to a certain income, pay the taxes and any fines, and then walk away from the threat of prosecution. The general thinking at that particular time was that the bureau simply wanted to collect money owed and did not want to expend the time or face the expense of taking tax dodgers and delinquents to court, and Mattingly decided to pursue this course. Hindsight provides serious flaws to the lawyer's initial thinking: the bureau's philosophy might have applied to other tax delinquents, but Al Capone was a different matter entirely.

Al Capone came out of hiding and began to move around Chicago in March 1930. The bureau requested that Mattingly come in person to the office—and to bring his client with him. Because he was in court for a trial, he asked for and was granted a continuance until April 17, but he did agree to bring his client. It was a decision that led most lawyers who re-created Al Capone's trial in the years since to reach the same conclusion: a wise counselor would never have agreed to put his client in such a precarious situation by complying. But that was exactly what Mattingly did.

On the morning of April 17, as directed, he and Capone appeared in the bureau's office before several agents and a stenographer. The recorded remarks showed that Agent C. W. Herrick of the Chicago bureau began the interview with an early version of what would become the law known as the *Miranda* ruling. Herrick told Capone that any statement he made would be subject to scrutiny in order to verify it, and anything he said in the meeting not only could be used against him but "would probably be used." Contemporary legal scholars believe this is where Mattingly should have ended the interview and removed his client from the premises. Instead, he said Capone was there to comply with the request for a meeting but at no time would he admit either guilt or liability and that everything he said would be off the record. Obviously, the bureau's agents did not agree to Mattingly's demand, because they did not refrain from combing the text of Capone's remarks to find even the scintilla of a lead they could use for further investigation.

The client did all the talking, and his lawyer seldom interrupted to counsel or caution him or to object to his questioners. Capone was asked questions about his income, property purchases, banking and brokerage accounts. The agents wanted him to state his net worth and asked if he had safe-deposit boxes, owned horses, or had stock in dog racing. His answers were either "no" or "I would rather let my lawyer answer that question." The transcript does not show that Mattingly answered anything that Capone deferred to him. Only after the Treasury agents concluded the interview did he try to strike a bargain by offering to provide an estimate of his client's income so that payment for a settlement could be arranged. They accepted his offer to have the document in their hands in three weeks, but for whatever the reason it took almost seven months before Mattingly handed it over the following November.

The transcript of the April interview has been evaluated by many writers and lawyers who all agree that what was recorded is an accurate account of the interview, but only as far as it went because Agent Herrick—and perhaps others—continued to ask probing questions long after the record ended. In the transcribed account, there is a passing reference to some others who were not involved in the questioning but who came and went during Capone's interview. They ranged from agents actively involved in the case, to curious people who worked in the building, to passersby who simply wanted to see the arch-villain under scrutiny. In later years when some of these spectators wrote their own memoirs or talked to journalists, they claimed to have been present after the transcript ended, so several versions of what followed have come to be accepted as truth.

The lead investigator, Treasury agent Frank J. Wilson, wrote about it in a highly embellished memoir many years later. Throughout his investigations, Wilson sent written reports to Irey, who kept President Hoover up to date on the events as Wilson reported them. Wilson seemed to have the most recent garish mob hits on his mind when he wrote his memoir, because he insisted that he had been in the room during and after the transcript ended, even though his name was not among those the stenographer recorded. In one of his most dramatic assertions, he wrote that as Capone was leaving, he asked about Wilson's wife's health in a tone of voice that could only be described as a not-so-veiled threat. That anecdote has been repeated as often as the one about the "hit" on Wilson's life and the lives of the other three agents. Depending on who tells that tale, payment was either $25,000 or $50,000.

Because all subsequent writings about this event take Wilson's memoir as their source, it is best to take these alleged threats as two more of the legends that surrounded Al Capone during the events leading up to his trial, but it is true that Wilson and his wife did move secretly from one hotel to another and that they were given full-time protection by guards stationed strategically throughout the new one.

———

By the time of the April meeting, one month had elapsed since Al Capone was released from the Philadelphia prison, and he finally got his wish to go to Palm Island. In late April, he boarded a train for Miami, only to arrive and find himself hounded worse than he had been in Chicago. The injunction signed by Judge Ritter that forbade Governor Carlton to "seize, arrest, kidnap, or otherwise abuse a property owner" who had not been convicted of any crime did not stop the Miami police from a continuing pattern of harassment.

A city ordinance had been passed, saying that vagrancy could be charged against anyone whose income was gained by "unlawful or illegal means or methods" and anyone known or suspected of being "crooks [or] gangsters" would be considered "dangerous to public safety or peace of the city" and could be arrested on sight. And, the ordinance further stated, if any part was found to be unconstitutional, the other parts could still be applied. The police were waiting for Capone every time he stepped off his property, and in May alone he was arrested four separate times on the vagrancy charge. The harassment only ended after his two local lawyers fought aggressively for the second time on his behalf and decided to let the courts work in his favor once again.

After taking on the governor the first time, the lawyers J. F. Gordon and Vincent C. Giblin accused S. D. McCreary, the director of public safety for the city of Miami, of false arrest, and when the case was heard, they called Capone to appear as a witness on his own behalf. He was sworn in and asked to describe his version of what had happened to him since he returned to Palm Island. In his sworn testimony, he said that during one of the vagrancy arrests, the police did not permit him to call his lawyers before he was thrown into a cell so hot and stifling that he had trouble breathing. Guards were told not to give Capone food or water and, when night came, not to provide blankets either. When he was relieved of his possessions, McCreary threw his money (reputed to be $1,000), his expensive watch, and all his other personal items into a toilet, which he then flushed. All these "facts" were regarded as the truth because Al Capone stated them under oath, but as he had done in the past, he was not reluctant to bend the facts to suit the needs of the moment.

The case was heard before Warren L. Newcomb, a justice of the peace who conducted a bench trial. Most observers considered him an honorable man, but after the case was heard, there were also those who claimed he was on Capone's payroll. Early in the proceedings, Newcomb declared that city officials could not continue to harass and arrest a citizen without proper cause, and if they were to do so again, they would have to have a specific warrant issued. Newcomb further cautioned that just because the newspapers had picked up the sobriquet of "Public Enemy #1" for every inflammatory article that appeared in Miami, it did not allow vigilante justice to flourish. Things seemed to be going well for Al Capone.

The prosecution called several witnesses to ask about their knowledge of Capone, which was really a way of inquiring into his character and personality. The city commissioner, John C. Knight, proved Judge Newcomb's point about inflammatory journalism when he said he had based his view of Capone as "a menace to the community" on those very same newspaper accounts. Newcomb then asked Knight if that meant he believed that "mob rule" functioned in Miami. Knight said no, and when the judge asked if he believed in allowing the law to take due course, Knight said yes. Newcomb ended his questioning by saying that if Knight did indeed believe in the rule of law, then he must also believe "that Capone should [not] be arrested and placed in jail incommunicado at any time without a specific charge against him." If Knight replied, the *Miami Herald* did not record his statement. Justice Newcomb then ruled that the order to arrest Capone on sight should be discharged and that anyone who attempted to arrest him without cause would have to answer to the court.

However, the ruling applied only to law enforcement in the city of Miami, so the state of Florida remained on the warpath. Several days later, the gates before the house on Palm Island were sealed and padlocked because, according to the state, the mere presence of the house made it a public nuisance. Judge Paul D. Barns ruled against the state because the only possible "cause of annoyance" was that the property owner was inside his own home. Even then, the harassment did not end; S. D. McCreary struck again several hours later, this time charging that Capone had perjured himself in his statements about what had happened to him in jail because everything he said was a lie.

When the hearing was held, Capone took the stand again, hedging, feinting, and obfuscating: to some questions, he wanted to "correct" his testimony; to others, his memory was either "to the best" or "not to the best" of his knowledge; and in one instance, he could not "swear to it." The ploy to qualify—if not actually to retract—his earlier testimony worked; in his second questioning, he had not actually lied and therefore had not perjured himself. The judge ruled that the case had to be dismissed. With the legal entanglements settled, it appeared that Capone would get the Miami vacation he wanted, but it was not to be for as long as he wished.

By now, reporters were growing tired of having to invent yet another way to write about this kind of nuisance hazing; such stories are only fresh and new up to a point, after which they become routine and boring and don't sell newspapers. No one paid much attention to McCreary, other city and state officials retreated in embarrassment to lick their wounds, and the public rallied around Al Capone. The press needed dirt, and they found it in Jake Lingle's murder on June 9, 1930, in Chicago. Lingle was on his way to the races shortly after noon, when he was gunned down in a tunnel leading to the train track. The gunman shot him in the midst of the midday crowd before walking sedately away, uncaught.

Lingle's murder set off a firestorm of speculation about Al Capone's financial circumstances after Lingle's records showed there was no way he could have lived so extravagantly on the salary of a newspaper reporter. There was a very short moment after the revelations about his opulent lifestyle when other papers turned spotlights onto their own staffs and a "newspaper war" was briefly under way. Even though there had been many gangland slayings that year (up to a hundred by some counts), it took "the cowardly murder" of Lingle, the eleventh slaying in ten days, to galvanize the publishers of the Chicago papers into signing a resolution in which they pledged to concentrate their resources on cleaning up the city. The manifesto gave a straightforward list of names of all the high-level gangsters who were slain over the years, from Big Jim Colosimo to the victims of the St. Valentine's Day Massacre, but it was only when Lingle's murder was added that their ire was apparent, for his was "the name . . . of a man whose business was to expose the work of killers." Such a murder could not be allowed to happen, but even so the agreement to cooperate did not last long, because all the papers vied to see which one would scoop all the others.

Reporters from cities other than Chicago smelled a good story and homed in on the ensuing squabbles. Things heated up when two St. Louis papers started looking into the activities of those who worked in Chicago. Harry T. Brundidge, who was then with the *St. Louis Star,* wrote a two-part series, July 18 and 19, 1930, in which he named all the reporters who were on the take, employed either by gangs or by politicians. One of his most inflammatory contentions was to quote a reporter who told him, "Only the dumb wits in the newspaper game in Chicago are without a racket." Brundidge named all those who were connected in some way, including two he called the "unofficial mayor" and the "unofficial police chief." Colonel McCormick, in a grim and vindictive mood, reprinted Brundidge's entire series in the *Tribune.*

Brundidge decided to capitalize on his newfound notoriety by getting a story from "the Big Guy" himself, so he went to Miami in early July and staked out the Palm Island house. He wrote that it was night, and Capone was out for the evening and returned after 10:00 p.m. When Capone saw his unexpected visitor, he chuckled over the "merry hell" he had raised in Chicago and invited him into the house. Brundidge claimed that he spent the next four hours with Capone, most of the time talking, walking on the grounds, and then being given a tour of the house. His ostensible reason for being there was to gain information about the Lingle murder, but in reality he was there because no other reporter had created the opportunity to interview Capone since before he went to prison in Philadelphia, and Brundidge wanted to scoop them all.

Brundidge was nobody's fool, and he knew from the start that everything he wrote would be subject to interpretation, pro and con. He took care to address this by inserting into the story an exchange he claimed to have had with Capone, in which he said all quotations would be Capone's exact words. He then wrote that Capone allegedly responded, "If you do, I'll deny it." Thus, both the reporter and his subject managed to cover themselves.

The story was printed in several parts in Brundidge's paper, the *St. Louis Star,* and also in the *Chicago Tribune.* As he had threatened, Capone said every remark attributed to him was a lie, a fabrication created by Brundidge that had no basis in reality. Whether true or not, the story carried the version of reality Capone wanted to portray, his oft-repeated insistence that he had made enough money and now wanted only to retire and enjoy life with his family. He must have taken Brundidge on a tour, for the reporter wrote accurately about the expensive and elaborate furnishings in the house and the well-tended grounds. What Brundidge described screamed of money, as did Capone's response to his question about the expensive diamond belt buckle that he had given as a gift to Jake Lingle.

All the fuss over newspaper articles stirred up the Missouri state's attorney, who called for an investigation into whether or not they were true. Newspaper articles are not sworn testimony, but nevertheless a grand jury was convened in the fall, and a host of reporters, editors, and publishers (including Colonel McCormick) were called to testify whether or not Brundidge had forged the interview. Brundidge was called, and of course he defended himself. Eventually, the grand jury decided that none of those who testified could give concrete evidence and nothing Brundidge said could be substantiated. They ruled that everything connected with the story was therefore speculation or invention.

Capone felt he had no option but to return to Chicago at the end of July for a few days to take care of the business that had been piling up since he arrived in Miami and to see what could be done to quiet the press coverage of the Lingle murder, which was as lurid as that of the St. Valentine's Day Massacre. Even though he had the same alibi for both, that he was nowhere near the city when either one happened, reporters came a-calling once again. And once again, his gregariousness did not serve him well; it served only to enhance the government's fixation on his illegal businesses, criminal activities, and tax evasion and to increase the determination to see him in jail.

———

The mess in Chicago aside, the summer of 1930 offered many pleasures. Once they were assembled at Palm Island, the Capones were in a frenzy of joy as Al took delight in everything connected with the household. After more than a year away from his family, he could not get enough of them. This was the period in which he forged his deepest bond with his son, who was eleven going on twelve. Al lavished love and attention on the boy, taking him fishing, spending long afternoons swimming in the pool, and lazing around afterward, just the two of them talking. In the evenings, both in robes and slippers, they played board games and listened to music while Mae sat and smiled upon them. The Capones hosted another of their lavish parties for Sonny, when his teachers at St. Patrick's school asked if other students could come to swim in the pool. Once again, Mae was careful with the invitations she sent to the fifty (or more) parents, telling them they had to sign it and their children had to bring it with them if they wanted to be admitted to the house. All the stops were pulled out as every sort of food children liked to eat was set up and served on tables next to the pool. Everything written about the occasion relates what an unqualified success it was, further evidence that Sonny Capone was well liked by his classmates despite what his father did for a living.

Sonny was old enough to know why Al was being harassed by various authorities. Perhaps another boy would have resented the scrutiny and opprobrium having such a father brought to his life, but if this were true, Sonny never said so to any of his friends or his cousins. The descendants of Al's brothers who are old enough to have known Sonny agree that the love and affection between him and his father was something quite beautiful and often quite touching. Sonny's daughters insist that all their father ever got from his father was unqualified love and affection, and he in turn gave the same to his four daughters.

Al threw himself into party giving, and Mae proved herself his equal partner. If they were to entertain large crowds, there were things she needed for Palm Island, and there were also things Teresa wanted for the house on Prairie Avenue. Al and Mae both behaved as if they did not have a care in the world and there were no investigations into their finances. Both dwellings received serious makeovers, and money flowed out. Trucks wended their way to Palm Island, loaded with new furniture, sets of china, silver flatware, and other articles of table decor. The house on Prairie Avenue received everything from buffets and beds to ornamental ceramic elephants.

Al and Mae gave so many elaborate parties during the summer of 1930 that several new myths about how he threw money to the winds came into being. During a cocktail party in which the house overflowed with guests, a Miami society matron looking for someplace to sit claimed that she sat on what she thought was a closed trunk but which turned out to be a repository of rifles, machine guns, and other weapons, all covered by a heavy cloth. If such a weapons cache existed, neither Mae nor Al would have permitted it to be stashed just outside their living room, especially in the midst of a lavish party attended by sympathetic members of the press and public officials, who denigrated Al in public but enjoyed his hospitality in private.

The lawyer Vincent Giblin was the source of another myth, eagerly picked up by all the newspapers and accepted as fact thereafter. He claimed that Al reneged on a $50,000 fee for legal representation, so he went to the house, where he boldly grabbed Al by his necktie (or his shirt collar, or his jacket lapels, as the various accounts had it). Giblin claimed that he forced Al to go up to his bedroom and open the trunk at the foot of the bed, where he allegedly stashed wads of cash. Al did keep large amounts of cash in the house but not in the bedroom trunk, where Mae kept extra bed linens. In reality, Al paid Giblin $10,000, which was far more than he was entitled to according to pay standards of the time, and then only after he agreed to represent all members of the Capone family afterward, free of charge, and in perpetuity.

These myths were added to the others that accrued during Al's stay in Miami, but there were also true stories about his lavish entertainment that were given during his 1931 tax evasion trial, in testimony by witnesses under oath. Mostly they showed that no matter how the Capones tried to fit into the community, they were never going to be accepted. Business moguls, society leaders, and politicians were happy to accept the hospitality at Palm Island, even if only to be able to say they had been there. However, it was a different matter altogether when it came to returning hospitality, for they never offered it.

Mae did take part in parental activities at Sonny's school, where she had cordial relationships but no friendships. Her closest friends remained her siblings, so hers was a limited social circle. Al received a reserved, qualified, and distanced welcome in the legitimate business world when he invited many prominent business leaders to his parties. His main motive was to enlist them firmly on his side as he enlarged the many rackets already under the Outfit's control and as he moved to acquire new ones. At that time, the Outfit controlled all the gambling in Dade County, the casino in the Floridian Hotel, the Palm Island Club, and the South Beach Dog Track, where there were slot machines and table games as well as dog racing. In one of his ongoing parties, more than thirty men accepted the invitation of their fellow business leader (as he liked to present himself), even welcoming him by saluting him as a new member of Miami's business community and gifting him with an engraved fountain pen. It was all for show, and even though Al continued to expand his business interests (as he always called them), everything within polite society that he wanted was greeted with polite rebuffs, marginalization, or outright denials.

Nevertheless, buoyed by this welcome into the business community, Al followed it by donating $1,000 to the chairman of the Community Chest (precursor of the United Way), who was also the president of the local country club. As a prelude to applying for membership, he asked the president to arrange a meeting wherein he could meet other members who would look favorably upon his application. The man said he would try, knowing full well he had no intention of doing so, for "Mr. Capone . . . just does not fit into what I call society . . . he just would not mix."

———

Despite his being snubbed by the upper echelons of Miami society, most everything else was going Al Capone's way there, and despite the ongoing investigations into the Lingle murder things were going his way in Chicago as well. He returned in early August 1930 and was so unconcerned by the activities of the federal and state agencies that were busily gathering evidence against him that he moved about the city with impunity. There were no further spurious attempts to arrest him, so taking care of the Outfit's business became his primary focus.

The consensus was that Prohibition was on its last legs and would be repealed in a short time. Like a great beast of prey, the Depression had sunk its teeth firmly into the country by early fall 1930, and revenues from bootlegging, gambling, and prostitution were in serious decline. Forward-thinking businessman that he was, Capone recognized that he would have to find other ways to meet his large payroll, and labor racketeering seemed the most lucrative way to start. By 1930, the Outfit controlled the street cleaners, plumbers, and garbage handlers, and as John Binder noted, "an assault on the Pie Handlers' Union was underway." In all, thirty-three union locals related to transportation were controlled by the Outfit, and new takeovers were occurring almost daily. In business rackets, everything from cleaners and textile dyers to miniature golf courses and ice cream shops were either already under the Outfit's control or about to come under it. Transportation unions like the Teamsters, the building trades, plumbers, and steam fitters—all were about to be brought into the Outfit.

At the same time, he concentrated on politicians, starting with municipal workers' unions. In a calculated ploy, state legislators like Dan Serritella and Roland Libonati were the most prominent among those whose names began to be associated with Capone's. He was well aware of the increasing fixation on his tax status, and to have so many high-level politicians in his direct employ or his debt might allow him to evade, if not prosecution, then certainly conviction.

The several months between August and November 1930 were important for shoring up his situation. At the end of November, Mattingly sent the long-delayed letter he had promised the previous April to the Chicago Bureau of Internal Revenue, and it was a masterwork of vagueness and equivocation. He began by saying that no part of it was an admission of any form of guilt that could be used against his client. The entire content was to be considered "without prejudice to the above-mentioned tax payer in any proceedings that may be instituted against him." Mattingly said the facts he was stating were based "upon [his] information and belief only." After a paragraph in which he outlined Capone's responsibilities as the sole support of his entire extended family, Mattingly claimed that until late 1926 his only income was a salary that was never greater than $75 per week. How Capone could have managed to provide for six (or more) people in two households on that amount required a willing suspension of disbelief, which Mattingly tried to dispel with a vague and convoluted description of how Al earned his money between 1926 and 1929.

He had indeed received "considerable sums" but only "by right of possession" because they merely passed through his hands on their way to others. He admitted that Capone had become a principal "with three associates" in an unnamed business but had never invested capital in it. Thus, Capone was never "the banker for the organization, nor did he, ever, actively participate in the conduct of its individual enterprises." Determined to prove that Capone had not made large amounts of money and to prove that he did not employ anyone directly, Mattingly named four lawyers and "so-called bodyguards" who were all on the payroll of "the organization" and who "participated in its profits." To prove that the "large force of bodyguards did not continually surround him," he added that only Frankie Rio had gone with him to jail.

Mattingly turned next to real estate as he discussed the Florida house and its contents. He wrote that he had not sought financial information from "the associates of the tax payer" (his name throughout for Capone), but he could still verify that his taxable income for 1925 and 1926 did not exceed "$26,000 and $40,000 respectively" and for 1928 and 1929 did not "exceed $100,000." He did not describe how he was able to ascertain Capone's income without doing any research into how he got it. How the lawyer could have thought such a letter would benefit his client has boggled the minds of many other lawyers who have studied Al Capone's legal woes.

In 1933, two years after the trial of Al Capone had been concluded, Special Agent Frank J. Wilson wrote its chronological history in a report for the government. In it, he described how Mattingly's letter worked against his client's best interests and how he should have known that, just as in his earlier personal interview, the stipulation that nothing in it be held against his client was not legally binding and could indeed be used against him. Wilson wrote that between May 19 and September 20, 1930, Mattingly met several times in the bureau's office with another agent surnamed Wilson and the revenue agent W. C. Hodgins. On each occasion, Mattingly expressed the strong desire to settle the case of nonpayment of taxes promptly and expeditiously. And each time, the agents told him that anything he wrote "would be used if necessary or advisable by the government in a criminal prosecution against the [non] taxpayer."

The letter had the exact opposite effect of what Mattingly intended. It verified that Capone was at the very least a "member" of an illegal organization and more likely a "principal" and that he received a large share of the organization's profits. Wilson went on to list the many ways in which Mattingly's letter helped to convict rather than clear his client and how it became one of "the most definite evidences of the tax payer's income." Still, it was not easy for Wilson and his colleagues to find definite proof of income, legal or otherwise, to connect him to "big gambling places, horse parlors, brothels, or bootleg joints," and there was no written evidence that he received payment from any of them. If he found people who might provide testimony, they were either so hostile to the government that they were ready to perjure themselves or were so afraid of Capone and the Outfit that "they evaded, lied, or left town."

In retrospect, and keeping everything that subsequently happened in mind, Al Capone's swift downfall is astonishing, for despite all the obstacles in the government's path and the still puzzling and unexplained conduct of his lawyer it took less than a year to convict him, and by June 18, 1931, the road to jail was inevitable.

Chapter 17

———

LAW ENFORCEMENT BY STIGMA

Al Capone didn't stay on in Chicago after he attended to business, because he had several reasons to make himself scarce. There was yet another murder, but it was of mobster Joe Aiello and not a newspaperman, so it did not garner the same amount of outraged media coverage as Lingle's had. The Unione Siciliana had always been the proverbial thorn in the Outfit's side, as was Aiello, especially after he took over as president. The underworld grapevine was swift and accurate, and word soon reached Capone that Aiello thought it would be a good time to go after him again while he was distracted by his legal imbroglio. A short time later, in October 1930, Aiello was murdered, felled by what all agreed was a classic Capone hit.

The investigation that followed also came to a classic Capone conclusion: although several people said they saw the gunmen who fled the scene, they claimed they could not identify the shooters, the police made no arrests, and the investigation was closed. Even though it was just another gangland hit, every group investigating Al Capone was enraged by another instance of his allegedly getting away with murder, this time literally as well as figuratively. On top of his tax evasion, it was too much for law-abiding reformers to accept without wanting justice.

When Frank Loesch first issued his public enemies list, he said they were "not to be treated as citizens entitled to a fair administration of justice," and he vowed to "keep the light of publicity" and "constant observation of law enforcing authorities" on them. The *New York Times* was one of the few papers to note how empty such statements were; in a story titled "Law Enforcement by Stigma," it was rightly noted that Chicago authorities were exchanging all attempts at valid prosecution for one of simple harassment.

It just so happened that at the same time as the Aiello murder a munici-pal court judge in Chicago decided to go after every public enemy by send-ing them all to jail on an 1871 statute of vagrancy, seldom used then or since. Naturally, he intended to start with No. 1. In the words of Robert J. Schoen-berg, Al's most engagingly readable biographer, Judge John H. Lyle was "a lean, long-faced grump" as well as "a publicity hound." He was most likely put up to using the 1871 statute by reporters or other crime-fighting groups, for no one thought him clever enough to conceive the idea on his own.

Lyle based his reasoning on a section of the statute that read "persons who neglect all lawful business and who habitually misspend their time by frequenting houses of ill fame, gaming houses, or tippling shops, are vaga-bonds" who, if found guilty, could be sentenced to hard labor for anything from ten days to six months. He argued that criminals belonged in this category, for they lived lavishly expensive lives, even though they did not have a visibly declared income or occupation to support them. Further-more, if they were arrested and charged with vagrancy, they would need to pay exorbitant fines for bail, and if they paid the fines, the court could ask where they got the money. If they refused to explain or gave an untrue answer, they could be indicted by a grand jury, charged with perjury, and made to stand trial. There were so many flaws in Lyle's line of reasoning that skillful lawyers knew they could clear their clients before they were arrested. However, Capone's case was a special one and fraught with all sorts of danger after Mattingly's disastrous decisions to let him appear before Bureau of Internal Revenue agents and voluntarily submit the state-ment of his income. Both these actions left him particularly exposed, pos-sibly to legal moves not yet envisioned.

Meanwhile, Judge Lyle "bombinated from the bench," declaiming that Capone should be put to death in the electric chair, never mind that he had not been proven guilty of anything. "Capone has no right to live," the judge fulminated as he explained why he thought Al should die: "Capone has become almost a mythical being in Chicago . . . He is more than a con-centrated crime wave. He is a real and powerful political force." Indeed, Al Capone was everything the judge said he was, but the law required much more than a judge's personal bombast for a conviction, let alone a sentence of death.

On four different occasions, Lyle was so out of control with his pub-lic comments that his superiors had him transferred from criminal to civil cases, where he could "torture propriety a little less." Unfortunately for Capone, the public adored Lyle because the CCC sang his praises and newspapers touted him as a heroic defender of the public good, so he was returned to criminal cases. Every time Capone's case was transferred out of criminal court, the CCC succeeded in having it sent back, cheering Lyle to go after him and every other of the public enemies. When a reporter for the *Tribune* asked Lyle what he hoped to accomplish with vagrancy warrants, he said they would keep the criminals so busy in court that they would not have time for their lives of crime. It was a simplistic and highly unrealistic line of reasoning, laughable because the first (and only) criminal he ever arrested was Danny Stanton, a low-level felon who went to jail on a charge of gun possession. His lawyer paid the bail, and he was out the same day as he was arrested.

Once again, Lyle "bombinated" after Stanton's release, excusing himself for being unable to enforce the vagrancy statute indicting criminals because they all bought lawyers "who feed, fatten, and thrive on large fees from these despicable characters." Heretofore, said lawyers had won their cases on "legal technicalities," but Judge Lyle bragged that he was now ready for them in his courtroom, where the "weapons will be law books instead of machine guns."

While all this was going on, Ralph, Jake Guzik, and Jake's brother Harry were appearing before Judge Lyle on the vagrancy charge. Already convicted and sentenced to Leavenworth, Ralph was waiting for the appellate court to decide if he would have to serve his sentence. Lyle made so many intemperate remarks in their separate appearances before him that all three men asked for and received changes of venue. Still undaunted, Lyle boasted that with all the newspapers lining up to back him, his movement to rid Chicago of the "Capone men" could not be stopped. Temporarily it was, however, when the Illinois Supreme Court became involved in a case totally unrelated to them but directly related to the judge.

The unreasonable amounts Lyle had set for bail in previous cases were what brought him to the court's attention. It ruled that such amounts were punitive and harmful to everyone from ordinary citizens to public enemies and thus could not be enforced. Nor could vagrancy be invoked simply because a judge made the vague and unspecified claim that the rule of law had broken down. The Illinois Supreme Court declared the vagrancy act unconstitutional because it wanted to enforce punishment not for what a person actually did but only for what he was accused of being.

The CCC rushed to Lyle's defense with a statement for the newspapers that said there were certain historical times when "expediency, necessity, and public peace" trumped the rule of law. In "abnormal crime situation[s]," the normal application of the law would just not work. In other words, the CCC thought the law should be disregarded because "there is no other way to deal with a certain class of criminals than to break them to pieces or they will break you." The general public, so used to the law being disregarded or bought out, seemed to agree.

Lyle's fixation on Al Capone went back several years to 1928, when he ran against Big Bill Thompson in the mayoralty race and Capone let it be known that Lyle would get no support from him at the polls. Even though the judge claimed to be incorruptible, he knew he would have a difficult time without the Outfit's money and the fear its goons instilled in voters. Indeed, he did have a difficult time because he lost the election, but he gained the energy and initiative to concentrate on Al Capone. In 1930, Lyle faced the difficulty of making a vagrancy charge stick, for police officials (no doubt those in the Outfit's pay) continued to insist that Capone had stayed in Chicago for only five days, and then only long enough to cooperate with police in their investigation of Lingle's murder. With straight faces, the police said they thought he was back in Miami, even though they and everyone else knew he was still in town.

While he was in residence at his Lexington Hotel headquarters, Capone did think briefly of calling Judge Lyle's bluff by turning himself in. He assumed that Lyle would set an unrealistically high bail that he could count on being reversed, and even if he had to spend a night in jail, he'd be out the next day, free and clear because the vagrancy charge would not have been enforceable. He dismissed this plan after his lawyers sent an emissary from the Teamsters' union, Michael J. Galvin, to Chief Justice John P. McGoorty of the criminal court to try to make a deal on behalf of "Al Brown" (his alias). In exchange for the vagrancy charge being dropped, Capone offered to end his attempts to control the labor unions not yet under his sway, but only if there would not be any more raids or other kinds of interference with his liquor business. He said if they accepted his proposal, he would leave Chicago for good and oversee all his interests from somewhere else, meaning Miami.

The judge called his offer "cool effrontery" and soundly rejected it. When McGoorty testified later before a grand jury, he said it would have been "unthinkable" to allow Capone to get away with dictating such terms. Because he had always "ruthlessly exterminated" anyone who opposed him, and because the only thing still in his way was the legal system, the judge warned that "the time has come when the public must choose between the rule of the gangster and the rule of law."

And so, still under Judge Lyle's threat of arrest, Capone hid in plain sight, with the police turning such a blind eye to his presence that the CCC had to hire special investigators to track him down. Despite all his hideouts being known, it took several days before they found him enjoying a high school football game in Cicero, surrounded by bodyguards while police officers in full uniform stood there looking everywhere but at him and his entourage. He eluded arrest this time as well, for the warrant had been issued by Judge Lyle in Chicago and the game was being played in Cicero: Chicago police welcomed the excuse not to be able to make an arrest outside city limits, and Cicero police were not about to arrest Al Capone and hand him over to them. He had frustrated Judge Lyle once again, but he was smart enough to realize that discretion would be the better part of valor, so he left town, taking a circuitous route back to Miami via New York, after a strategy meeting with Johnny Torrio.

––––

Al had intended to stay in Chicago long enough to give Mafalda away at her December 14, 1930, wedding to John J. Maritote, but that honor fell to Ralph when Al decided to stay alone (except for bodyguards) in Miami. He was the only family member who did not attend. Mae claimed the title of the official matron of honor, which in reality she shared with Ralph's second wife, Valma Pheasant. There were only three bridesmaids, for the bride had few girlfriends and never a boyfriend until the sudden announcement of her engagement. "Who would dare to risk dating Al Capone's little sister?" Mafalda had always moaned bitterly to anyone who cared to listen, so when the betrothal was announced, rumors abounded that it was a marriage arranged to unite two gangland factions. The bride was eighteen and the only female in the Capone clan, and the groom, John J. Maritote, was the twenty-three-year-old younger brother of Frank "Frankie Diamond" Maritote, a mid-level member of the Outfit. John was allegedly in love with another woman and unhappy about having to give her up, while Mafalda told the press she was blissfully happy to be marrying her childhood sweetheart. It seemed to escape her (and everyone else, from the family to the media) that she could not complain of never having had a date if she was marrying the man she had supposedly loved all her life.

Al pulled out all the stops for his baby sister's wedding. Despite the heavy snowstorm on that day, more than four thousand invited guests showed up at St. Mary's Church in Cicero, and at least another thousand rubberneckers stood outside to see the bride. Mafalda was already a hefty girl on her way to becoming a stocky, overweight woman. Her size made her strong enough to bear the heavyweight ivory satin gown, balance the twenty-five-foot train, and carry a bouquet that boasted more than four hundred flowers. It was a colorful procession that entered the church on that gray day, with all her attendants in deep pink taffeta, large hats of the same color, and bright blue shoes. The men, most of them large and tough, were nervous and uncomfortable in tuxedos. Sonny and Ralphie smiled and looked happy as awkward young ushers, unsure of what they were supposed to be doing. Teresa, as the bride's mother, was resplendent in an enormous fur coat (probably mink) that made her look like a rotund brown ball. Some newspapers reported that police officers and detectives tried to move inconspicuously among the guests as they took half a dozen or so outside the church to confiscate their weapons.

After the ceremony, the family, the wedding party, and selected invited guests (between three and four hundred) went on to a private reception, while Ralph's Cotton Club in Cicero hosted all others who managed to fit themselves in. The wedding cake cost well over $2,000 and was colossal: at least ten feet long, four feet high, shaped like a yacht, and decorated in a tropical theme. Family photographs showed the bride standing to the right of it, looking at the camera with a tentative smile on her face, while the groom stood well away from her on its left, not looking at his new wife but frowning at the monstrously huge concoction.

Hawaii was supposed to be where they honeymooned, but some newspapers had them returning to Chicago from Cuba, and to this day family members do not know if they went to one or both places. Rumor had it that Al gifted them with either $50,000 or $75,000 and a new house, but once the honeymoon was over, the glum couple moved in with Teresa on Prairie Avenue. John gave his profession as "movie projector operator," although he was more often seen in his brother's company in various gang hangouts than in any theater.

The couple welcomed their only child, Dolores Teresa, on April 10, 1932. After that, with the exception of ceremonial occasions, they were seldom seen out together in public, even though they owned various mom-and-pop delis and pizza parlors in Chicago in which they worked side by side.

They lived to very old ages and stayed married until the end of their lives, for the most part out of the public eye except for an incident in January 1933. They were nearly gunned down after a visit to John's parents' home as they walked to their car with Mafalda carrying her nine-month-old daughter. Every newspaper in the country picked up the story, giving much the same account as the paper that scooped the others, the *Chicago Herald and Examiner,* of how four gunmen jumped out of a fast-moving car and began to fire at Al Capone's little sister. None noted correctly that the intended target was Frankie Diamond Maritote, who was not there. All the stories reprinted most of what the *Herald and Examiner* wrote, that when Mafalda heard the first shots, she screamed, fell to the ground, and promptly fainted. John and unnamed others hid behind their cars to fire back until the would-be assassins got back into theirs and sped away. Both Maritotes were unharmed, Mafalda was revived, and they went home to Prairie Avenue.

After that, their only public notice came whenever a reporter desperate for a story wrote something loosely described as human interest. These stories usually focused on how the little sister of the jailed mobster was now reduced to ruling a greatly diminished domain from behind the counter of a convenience store and how she never hesitated to unleash her wicked tongue on any customer who displeased her.

———

Al Capone had no choice about returning to Chicago when his trial on the 1929 contempt of court charge was finally and firmly set to start on February 25, 1931. Judge Lyle's warrant for his arrest on vagrancy was still active, but it was no longer a threat, because he had been soundly trounced in the Republican primary by Capone's firm ally Big Bill Thompson, who was seeking reelection in the forthcoming general election. Although everything connected with politics in Chicago during the Prohibition era was colorfully outsized, this mayoral primary had been over the top, with the two candidates exchanging one hilarious insult after another. Judge Lyle found another sobriquet added to his list when Thompson called him "the nutty judge." He responded by calling Thompson a "blubbering jungle hippopotamus." All Chicago roared with laughter, and Al Capone was amused, thinking that his problems with Lyle were over now that Thompson was on his way to being firmly back in power. But like many other Chicagoans, he was surprised when the even more corrupt Democrat Anton Cermak defeated Thompson to take office in 1931 by the largest margin ever recorded. Capone was surprised but not dismayed, for he knew Cermak was a smart man with whom he could do business.

Al Capone showed up in court that cold February day in 1931 in "a sumptuous blue suit, accented by white silk hankie, pearl gray spats, and diamond studded platinum watch chain." The suit's material was "soft as cat's fur." The next day, he sported "a misty-morning gray ensemble," and on subsequent court appearances most papers wrote that he wore a different custom-tailored suit every day, but their accounts differed as to whether it was brown, blue, gray, or other colors described as "bilious Sulphur" and "Shrieking banana." In most stories, he sported "the inevitable pearl-gray fedora and a gold watch chain studded with countless diamonds stretching across his vest." Usually, it is only women who garner so much media attention for their clothing, but with Al Capone the press paid as much attention to what he wore as to what was happening in the courtroom. Although he was discreet enough not to hold actual press conferences, he welcomed the reporters who followed his every movement, especially those gathered outside the courtroom to report what he said off the cuff, even if they occasionally had to invent it.

The case was heard before Judge James H. Wilkerson in the first of Capone's two courtroom encounters with him, this one without a jury. Capone was in court to explain why he ignored a subpoena from the grand jury by claiming he was allegedly too sick in bed in Miami to appear in Chicago. If true, the prosecution asked, how then could he explain being seen in the winter of 1929 enjoying himself at restaurants and racetracks in Miami and flying to the Bahamas for more sun and fun?

During the lunch recess for this trial, Capone had to appear in another courtroom to face the still-pending vagrancy charge. Another judge (not Judge Lyle) set his bail at $10,000 before "continuing" that case for another week. To secure the bail, Capone's lawyers put up property they claimed he owned, valued at $80,000. When some courtroom observers asked his profession, he joked that he was in "real estate." Nice work for a man who was supposedly without income and in court to answer the accusation of vagrancy.

He went back that afternoon to federal court and the first trial, where Capone's Miami physician, Dr. Kenneth Phillips, was asked by the prosecution to explain how someone so ill could have been such a healthy and active man-about-town. The doctor was visibly uncomfortable under questioning, finally admitting that the affidavit to which he had sworn was not his work but that of the Miami lawyer who prepared it under Capone's direction. Dr. Phillips said all he did was sign it when it was presented to him. He did not say it in court, but in later correspondence with Dr. Joseph Moore, the other physician who treated Capone, Dr. Phillips admitted how afraid he was of Al and his brothers, especially of Ralph, and of how he usually did what they asked.

Accurate testimony by the two nurses who took care of Al during his January 1929 flu followed. In those two weeks at least, Al was too sick to get out of bed, let alone gallivant all over Dade County. However, everything hinged on the date the subpoena was issued, in early March, when Al was surely recovered well enough to honor it. Based on the fact that he did not, Judge Wilkerson found him guilty and imposed a sentence of six months in the county jail. Capone's lawyers posted bond and filed an appeal. This time he only had to come up with $5,000, but the press reported it, and the various agencies who had him under surveillance took careful note of it.

There was still the matter of the vagrancy charge, but as with so much associated with the politically toxic Judge Lyle, it became yet another fiasco. After several continuances, the case was not heard until late April and then with a different judge presiding. When the policeman who signed the vagrancy complaint was called to testify, he said he only did so as a favor to another policeman. Claiming innocence, he testified that he had no reason to arrest Al Capone, for he did not know the man, nor did he know much about him. The frustrated prosecutor reluctantly admitted that he could not find a single witness, policeman or otherwise, who knew anything about Al Capone, and the judge had no option but to dismiss the entire case.

And so Al Capone beat the vagrancy rap and was out indefinitely pending appeal of his conviction for ignoring the grand jury summons. He wasn't worried, and he fully expected that with his various "connections" he would win the appeal as well. At the end of April, he was ready to resume business as usual, but the respite did not last long. On June 5, 1931, a federal grand jury indicted him on twenty-four counts of nonpayment of income taxes. This indictment he would have to take far more seriously.

Chapter 18

JAIL IS A BAD PLACE UNDER ANY
CIRCUMSTANCES

The fall, when it came, was swift. Even as Al was winning one law-suit and trying to delay the other, his adversaries were busy lining up their evidence and preparing to strike. The criminal grapevine, populated as it was by politicians, civil appointees, and policemen on Al's payroll, lost no time in letting him know what was going on. But for whatever reason, he did not give the investigation the serious atten-tion it deserved.

Agents from the Bureau of Internal Revenue were putting pressure on men who had been bookkeepers and general overseers in the Outfit's vari-ous establishments with threats that they either testify before a grand jury or face serious jail time. Some of them were so terrified of Outfit repri-sal that several had to be kept in witness protection until they could give their testimony in secret sessions. Frank Wilson and his colleagues were also pressuring other gangsters as well as those who worked directly for the Outfit to tell what they knew. Wiretapping was widespread, and the records of calls made to and from Capone's phones in the Lexington Hotel were added to the burgeoning files.

There were other acts of chicanery designed to put pressure on reluc-tant witnesses who had no mob connections but who had either openly or inadvertently helped Al Capone to hide money; if they refused to testify, they were also threatened with indictment for perjury. An agent who was a skillful spy was sent to infiltrate the Outfit's domain, and he and other stool pigeons collected incriminating information that was duly reported to Wilson. Ralph's headquarters, the Cotton Club in Cicero, was raided dra-matically in a scene that could have been filmed for a movie: customers screamed and tried to hide, liquor was seized and bottles smashed, workers were arrested, and the safe was opened with acetylene torches in the hunt for evidence. By the spring of 1931 as the investigation was coming to a close, the documentation collected by the prosecution was literally mountainous. Wilson sent impassioned requests to Elmer Irey for permission to relocate to a bigger office because his present space could no longer hold the almost two thousand documents collected by George E. Q. Johnson, on top of the several thousand more his own agents had gathered. Irey eventually granted the request, and the unending flow of new and incriminating documents soon filled the larger space as well.

Agents Johnson and Wilson had both worked as secretively as possible, but not the publicity-seeking federal agent Eliot Ness, who sought the limelight as much as Al Capone did. He reveled in being called a gangbuster as he and his men raided breweries and stills in and around Chicago, each time making sure the press was there to take his photograph as he struck heroic poses over gallons of illegal booze being smashed to pieces and going down the drains and into the sewers. Ness did do serious damage to the Outfit's income and profit, but the real work toward conviction happened behind the scenes in the offices of Johnson and Wilson, who were painstakingly putting together a paper trail that led to conviction on charges of tax evasion and defrauding the federal government.

The file, designated (Special Investigation) "SI-7085-F, In re: Alphonse Capone," whose official address was given as the Lexington Hotel, was started much earlier, on October 15, 1928, by the special agent then in charge of the Chicago bureau, A. P. "Art" Madden. Wilson did not become involved until May 19, 1930, when Elmer Irey sent him to Chicago to take charge. Starting on May 23 and continuing to October 20, 1931, Wilson and his team gathered documents and testimony in Chicago, Miami, St. Louis, New York, and Washington and also in "other points" such as testimony taken from convicts in Leavenworth prison.

One of the first big breaks in the case against Capone came about because of an unrelated 1926 raid on the Hawthorne Hotel's Smoke Shop, when it was searched for evidence connected to the McSwiggin murder. Among the papers confiscated by the Illinois State's Attorney's Office were several ledgers that no one then deemed important and that were among the several thousand documents turned over to Wilson's office after his probe began. Wilson described how he stumbled upon them in the self-aggrandizing memoir he published years later in 1965. Wilson wrote of his frustration when he "prowled the crummy streets of Cicero, where a twitch of Al's little finger had the force of an edict, but there was no clue that a dollar from the big gambling places, the horse parlors, the brothels, or the bootleg joints ever reached his coffers." When he did find potential witnesses, some were so hostile that if compelled to testify, they would prefer to lie rather than betray Al Capone; others were so afraid of him and the Outfit that they either "evaded . . . or left town."

Wilson wrote of how he found the ledgers late at night after an exhausting day of reading documents, when he accidentally stumbled on a brown paper packet in an unlocked file cabinet drawer. He was curious about what was in the packet, and when he opened it, he realized it contained ledgers kept by the bookkeepers at the Ship gambling house for the years 1924–26 that gave detailed accounts of money taken in from gambling and paid out to principals in the Outfit.

No longer bleary-eyed, Wilson snapped to attention as he realized that the initials and abbreviations of names stood for Al, Ralph, Jake Guzik, and several other mid-level operatives who were entitled to differing shares of the profits. On other pages, he found the takes and totals of every gambling activity, from roulette and craps to bets on horses. Adding them up, Wilson estimated that net profits over eighteen months—for just gambling and only for that single location—totaled more than $500,000. All of it had been neatly divided and doled out to the three principals, their underlings, and an entry listed only as "Town," which he surmised was the code name for payola to police and other Cicero officials.

And so the ledgers provided the federal agents with proof that Al made plenty of money that he did not declare as income, but they needed more than just the books to proceed before a grand jury; they needed the verbal sworn testimony of those who kept them to buffer the written evidence. As Wilson told reporters almost three decades after the trial, "Hanging an income tax rap on Al Capone would be as easy as hanging a foreclosure sign on the moon . . . Evidence of lavish living wasn't enough. The courts had to see income."

The agents started with the ledger entries, where they found three different and distinct handwritings. They needed to find these unnamed and unidentified writers and make them testify before the grand jury that what they wrote was true. Wilson claimed with bravado that he and the other agents found the writers in a remarkably short time, saying they were ferreted out by comparing handwriting samples in the ledgers with those collected from every possible agency, from bail bondsmen and criminal court forms, to signatures on driver's licenses in the Department of Motor Vehicles. No doubt they did do all this, but still, having seized records from the Ship, they had to have known the names of the employees who were arrested during the raid, so the hunt for the culprits was probably easier and far more direct than the version Wilson gave.

Curiosity also rises about how the federal agents were able to gain such easy access to the private banking records of Leslie "Lou" Shumway, one of the ledger keepers, for to this day there is no documentation pertaining to a subpoena or search warrant, which was the law at that time. They never explained (nor were they ever asked in court or on the record) how they were able to see canceled checks that allowed them to compare signatures without first obtaining legal authorization. The supposition is that the checks were traced back to a 1928 incident wherein one Miami bank reportedly asked another to cash a $1,500 check in large bills that had been endorsed by Capone and a fictional J. C. Dunbar (actually Fred Ries), whose name appeared with slight changes in several other instances. The second bank told the first to "wash their own dirty linen" and reported it to the local IRS office. Although the memo to Irey was forwarded to Chicago and other offices, and although it became connected to other witnesses who helped Capone launder money, there was nothing to tie it to Shumway. It was not until they gained access to his bank records that they got lucky.

Besides Ries, there were several occasional small notations in the ledgers that were eventually traced to Peter Penovich Jr. (who had a small share in the profits) and Ben Pope (who worked at the Ship briefly), but the first real break came when a bank deposit slip Shumway submitted matched the signature on a canceled check. Because the agents could not have asked for the records of every depositor in every bank in Chicago, they must have learned (or else already knew) that Shumway had been the Ship's cashier and that he had been succeeded in the job by Fred Ries. The natural surmise was that one of the handwritings was Shumway's and the other was Ries's, and two out of three was a good start toward making the ledgers stand up before a grand jury. Even though both men were well-known to everyone involved in the case, the task became how to find them, for neither was in Chicago. They found Ries fairly quickly in St. Louis, but it took them four months to locate Shumway in Miami.

Ries had testified before, when he gave important testimony against Guzik in his 1930 tax evasion trial. He admitted that he had worked since

1927 as a cashier-bookkeeper in four different gambling houses, including the Ship, and that among the owners were Ralph and Al "Brown," the alias the Capone brothers used. Ries provided comic relief when he also told how Guzik "took him to task because the gambling places were not making money."

Capone had his grapevine into the legal system, but Wilson also had one for the Outfit, thanks to the snitches who infiltrated it. While the Guzik trial was under way, they told Wilson two helpful facts about Ries: that on Guzik's orders he had fled to St. Louis, where he was being paid to hide out until he could make his way to Mexico, and that he was phobic about insects, especially cockroaches and bedbugs. Wilson sent men to arrest Ries but told them not to take him to a Chicago jail; instead, he told them to put him in a vermin-infested cell in the small town of Danville. Wilson wrote gleefully of how the "cocky, beady eyed, cop-hating" Ries held out for four days until he could no longer stand living in a cell where "cockroaches and other wild life were virtually holding a convention." He became one of the most important and convincing witnesses in both Guzik's and Nitti's trials, where he named them, Al, and Ralph as the owners of various illegal businesses and recipients of their profits. That was in 1930, and the problem in 1931 was how to keep Ries alive to testify against Al Capone when (no longer "if") his trial began. At this point, the Secret Six took over, raising enough money for Ries to be taken to an unnamed destination in South America, where he remained under guard until the trial began.

———

They found Leslie Shumway, the exact opposite of Ries and "a perfect little gentleman," in Miami, thanks to information provided by Edward J. O'Hare, an informant who was directly connected to Capone through a partnership in the Hawthorne Kennel Club. Dubbed Artful, Fast, or Easy Eddie, O'Hare has gone down in history as the turncoat who informed on Al Capone for a high and noble cause, the love of a father for his son. He is supposed to have volunteered to snitch because his beloved son, called Butch and also named Edward, wanted to go to the U.S. Naval Academy and, despite the danger of mob retaliation, Easy Eddie willingly traded information in the hope that Wilson would use his influence to help his son. It is a tender story and probably does have a grain of truth in it, but it was far from the only reason O'Hare turned on his partner in the lucrative business of dog racing.

Edward "Butch" O'Hare did go to Annapolis and became an aviator-hero who lost his life when his plane was shot down during a World War II raid on Japanese ships. Today, Butch's name is kept alive and honored through Chicago's chief airport, O'Hare Field. Easy Eddie, however, is known not so much for being his father as for the dishonorable way he died. The Outfit bided its time until November 1939, when O'Hare was murdered by shotgun fire while driving his car, with his own gun in full view beside him on the passenger seat. Whether his death was directly connected in any way to Al Capone has never been proven, for by 1939 he was totally removed from authority within the Outfit. What is known is that Capone's successor, Frank Nitti, was married one month later to the woman who had been O'Hare's mistress for the better part of a decade.

Easy Eddie's career had been a shady one that began in St. Louis, where he had been the lawyer who represented Owen P. Smith, the man who was the real inventor of the mechanical rabbit that greyhounds chase around a track. O'Hare was not averse to letting people believe it was he whose invention revolutionized dog racing, but he only gained control of it when Smith died and he allegedly "bought" the patent from Smith's widow. The sale has always been clouded by the rumor that she was a reluctant seller whom O'Hare paid a mere pittance, while he used it as the basis for making a fortune. O'Hare was nobody's fool, and when local gang pressure became too uncomfortable in St. Louis, he moved his dog track operations to Cicero. Rather than trying to best Al Capone, he was smart enough to ask for a partnership instead. He was the front man, while Capone stayed behind the scenes, collecting hefty profits that O'Hare helped him move from place to place through third parties.

Wilson always praised O'Hare as being "inside the gang . . . one of the best undercover men I have ever known," yet the story of who contacted whom first is much like that of the proverbial chicken and egg. Wilson takes the credit for decoding the ledgers, while O'Hare claims it was he who did so; Wilson claims his agents found Shumway, while O'Hare claims he told Wilson where to find him; Wilson does not name the source(s) who told him Capone allegedly placed a hit on him and the three other agents, while O'Hare claims it was he who gave the warning. It is probably best to say that all these things did indeed occur without choosing one man over the other as the one who made them possible.

———

Whoever tracked down Lou Shumway, it was Wilson who went to Miami in February 1931 and found him working behind one of the betting windows at a dog track. Wilson had begun his search the night before at Hialeah, but the only person of interest he saw there was Capone. His shrill distaste was still palpable several decades later when he described how he saw "Scarface Al, [sitting] with a jeweled moll on either side of him, smoking a long cigar . . . greeting a parade of fawning sycophants who came to shake his hand." Al took care never to dishonor Mae while he was out and about and especially where he could be photographed, so the "molls" were most likely there with other men whom Wilson conveniently forgot to include. He could not resist overindulging in the hyperbole that Al Capone inspired: "I looked upon his pudgy face, his thick pursed lips, the rolls of fat descending from his chin—and the scar, like a heavy pencil line across his cheek." Because no other descriptions of Capone at this time matched Wilson's portrayal, clearly he was a man obsessed with his job.

He was skilled enough to know not to accost Shumway in public, where any of the Outfit's men might see them talking. Wilson "tailed him home" and waited until early the next morning to ring the bell. He does not describe their conversation but jumps to what happened next, when they were in his car on their way to the federal building; he has Shumway "turning a real green," even though he had not been told "what the case was about." It seems strange that a man who had been around the rackets for as long as Shumway had, and who was well aware of all the tricks gangsters and their lawyers used, would have gotten into a car so easily without first asking Wilson why he was wanted or whether there was a warrant for his arrest. But if Wilson's account is correct, Shumway went willingly and without protest. With glee he could not restrain, Wilson wrote that when he told Shumway he was investigating Al Capone, the poor man did not "merely shake . . . He rattled."

Wilson told him he had two choices: either agree to testify in private or else face being arrested at his job, where all Capone's men could see him, which would surely guarantee that he would be disposed of before he could ever squeal in court. Shumway chose the former, and once again the Secret Six were enlisted to help. They paid for him to tell his wife he had to make an emergency visit to a sick relative in Oklahoma, while they actually hid him in California.

Wilson tracked down one other witness whose hostility was assured and whose testimony was bound to be suspect. Louis LaCava, a gambler and low-level Outfit worker, had been banished from Chicago by Capone in 1927 because he was a loose cannon, unpredictable and uncontrollable.

Wilson's agents found LaCava in Pittsburgh and brought him to Chicago, where, as expected, his hatred of Capone was so obvious that his testimony carried far less weight than that of Shumway or Ries.

While Wilson was busily pursuing possible witnesses against Capone, Special Agent James N. Sullivan was cultivating another source who has all but disappeared from the story. Brought from New York to assist Wilson, Sullivan was assigned to find connections between the Outfit and income from its brothels. He spent his Saturday nights hanging around the courtrooms in the federal courthouse where prostitutes were arraigned, and when he spied a pathetic-looking "bedraggled veteran in her fifties, at the end of her professional career," he signed her up as an informant. She called herself Reigh Count, after the horse that won the Kentucky Derby in 1928, and for $50 a week, far more than she ever earned through her usual employment, she went to work for him. There is no record that she ever contributed any information of any importance to them, but the federal government (and/or the Secret Six) contributed nicely to her retirement account.

———

Gradually but steadily, as the case against Capone was building, those pursuing him thought it important to have someone inside the Outfit who could watch him on a daily basis and report his every deed. After the Secret Six told Elmer Irey they would meet all the expenses for the undercover operation, he agreed to transfer the special agent Michael F. Malone to Wilson's team. Malone was to leave his posting in Washington and arrive undercover in Chicago as a small-time drifter and grifter on the lam. He was to take his time to build this image by stopping first in Philadelphia and then in Brooklyn, where he was to hang about on the fringes of local gangs. When he arrived in Chicago, he was to position himself in the lobby of the Lexington and wait to be noticed. When Al's foot soldiers engaged him in conversation, he was to hint that he had done something irregular and had to hide out in a place where another gang was unlikely to start trouble on a rival's turf.

He went by the name of Michael Lepito, an Italian-American on the run. It helped that he was a swarthy and stocky Irishman originally from Jersey City who had the accent and could talk the talk he picked up on the city's roughest streets. He knew how mobsters dressed, so one of his first stops was the famed John Wanamaker's department store in Philadelphia, where he bought the appropriate clothing and sent the bill to the bureau's Chicago office, where it was in turn sent to the Secret Six, who paid it without question.

Malone's role as Lepito in helping to bring down Al Capone was painted in dramatic, self-aggrandizing strokes when Wilson and his boss, Elmer Irey, penned their separate memoirs. Both vied to present themselves, along with Malone, as fearless and brave in the face of constant danger. They describe Malone's undercover career as one perilous adventure after another that kept them fraught with tension and in constant fear that they would be responsible for his death if the deception were unmasked. Wilson called Malone "the greatest undercover agent in the history of law enforcement," a statement echoed many years later by another IRS agent who called it "the riskiest assignment you could ever think of. People were dying left and right, witnesses were dying left and right. Nobody wanted to be with these guys." Well, perhaps. The biographer Robert J. Schoenberg, who accepts the view that neither Wilson nor Irey actually lied about Malone's undercover activity, thinks they "merely exaggerated the danger beyond recognition." One could say the same for the agent quoted above.

Schoenberg tells a different and far more realistic story about what would have happened to Malone if he had been outed as a federal agent. Murdering him was highly unlikely, for no gang would risk bringing such attention and wrath upon themselves, and "besides," Schoenberg writes, "why kill him? He sat at no inner councils, could have seen and heard nothing Capone didn't want him to learn." Schoenberg posits that Al's top counselors were well aware of Malone's duplicity, so they fed him whatever information they wanted him to know. As the top secret "Operative Number One" in the bureau's parlance, he told whatever he found out to O'Hare, who in turn sent it on to Wilson. High-level gamesmanship existed on both sides, but the real evidence against Al Capone was amassed as Wilson and his agents continued with the "very painstaking, and very boring, checkup on all the recorded money transactions." Cloak-and-dagger stories make for exciting reading, but as with so much else surrounding the eventual trial, they have to be put into proper perspective.

―――――

Chapter 19

"WHO WOULDN'T BE WORRIED?"

While all Wilson's machinations were going on and Capone's lawyers were busily trying to make deals on his behalf, he himself stayed uncharacteristically subdued and out of the public eye. For the first half of 1931, he was mostly at his headquarters in the Lexington, only leaving there long enough to go to his mother's for as many meals as he could manage. Mae was in Miami because Sonny was still in school there, and he stayed in touch with her through daily phone conversations. Despite being surrounded by his men, and with a floor full of kept women should he have wanted them, he was relatively lonely without the companionship offered by Ralph, Nitti, and the Guzik brothers, all of whom were serving their prison terms in Leavenworth.

It is difficult to assess Al Capone's behavior during the six months when so much concrete legal evidence was building the case against him. His passivity continued, and he seemed indifferent each time a new brick was laid. He had given Mattingly his power of attorney and knew that the lawyer was using it as he made overtures to both Wilson and Johnson after he had submitted the letter listing Capone's purported income. He had already used the letter as the basis of several conferences with Wilson and Agent W. C. Hodgins, in which he tried to persuade the government to settle the case. Each time, they warned Mattingly that the letter would not be granted any degree of immunity, either full, qualified, or transactional, and that they would use it to fortify their case.

Wilson and Hodgins knew what ammunition they had with the letter, "an admission of large taxable income for the four years 1925 to 1928," and they were determined to introduce it at trial. Mattingly was equally determined that it should not be entered into evidence, but by that time he had removed himself as counsel with the declaration that he was a tax and not a trial lawyer and therefore of no further use to his client. Even Al Capone had to admit Mattingly's incompetence when the first indictment against him was issued. He dismissed Mattingly and turned again to the two lawyers who had represented him in earlier encounters with the law, Thomas Nash and Michael Ahern. They worked as a team, both highly skilled in the ins and outs of Chicago politics and known for their ability to make favorable deals for often-unsavory clients as well as actual gang members. Ahern was "the backroom brief writing partner," and Nash "the courtroom wizard half." They were later joined by the "recruit" lawyer Albert Fink, who ended up playing a major role in Capone's defense. Capone probably settled so cavalierly on them because they had represented the Outfit, usually with favorable outcomes, on other matters.

Capone gave the impression that he was unconcerned about the matter of counsel, and several reasons have been suggested for his apparent acceptance of their methods. Some of his descendants wonder if his brain damage from the syphilis that eventually killed him might have already begun. He still preened and postured in public, wearing his colorful clothing and trading quips with onlookers and reporters, but not nearly as much as he had done in the past. For the flamboyant fellow the public was used to seeing, he was noticeably subdued. His behavior led other observers to believe he was unconcerned about his legal team because he thought there was nothing to worry about: if the case was not dismissed for lack of evidence and went to trial, he thought he could always bribe the jury and anyone else who might be needed to "fix things." If worse came to worst and a trial began, he planned to plead guilty to nonpayment of taxes and accept the minimum jail term. At the same time, there were those who could not understand how he could continue to believe himself invincible after he had been marginalized at the 1929 gangland meetings in Atlantic City; they thought he should have been aware of how the protective gangland wall around him was crumbling. Nevertheless, even though his behavior was uncharacteristically muted and the ripostes and repartees with reporters and interviewers did not have the wit and bite he usually exhibited, he kept up the appearance that there was no need for him to be concerned.

———

By the time Capone's lawyers paid their first visit to Johnson's office in May 1931, they and he knew everything that had happened in the grand jury's chambers since Leslie Shumway's supposedly secret testimony back in February. They knew that what Shumway told the jurors contributed to the issuance of the indictment for the 1924 tax year and that others for subsequent years were soon to follow. Their task had moved beyond trying to quash the case to one of trying to settle it in their client's favor.

Wilson was still busily amassing evidence for the U.S. attorney Johnson, who would be the chief prosecutor when the case went to trial. Ahern and Nash made a preemptive strike in May, when they went to Johnson's office and stunned him by recounting everything that had happened within the grand jury's chambers. They argued that because of it there was no possibility that Al Capone could receive a fair trial in any court in his jurisdiction. It would be far better for both sides to settle the case and have it over and done with. They told Johnson they were there to plea-bargain on Capone's behalf, pointing out the ways in which Johnson's case would be difficult to prove, and even if he won, how they could drag out appeals for years after the trial concluded. A plea bargain would allow everyone to bring the matter to a swift conclusion.

Even though the newspapers and wire services praised Johnson's track record for convictions, by nature he was cautious and a worrier. Johnson knew there were many risks associated with taking the case to trial. Capone was famed for bribing juries, "convincing" witnesses to change their stories, and, when all else failed, making them die or disappear. Johnson was a circumspect man who looked for the sure win before he entered a courtroom, so he hesitated to make the decision on his own. Instead of committing to the lawyers' request, he told them he had to discuss it with his superiors in the Department of Justice in Washington. The lawyers found this approach encouraging, and they left thinking that negotiations were still ongoing, fairly confident that Johnson would return with a deal that allowed everyone to save face. However, he surprised them when he returned from Washington without a definite answer, for his superiors had decided to wait and see what the forthcoming indictments would bring.

The rebuff was worrisome, and Ahern and Nash knew there were multiple indictments for 1925–29 in preparation, so it would be in Capone's best interests to settle before they were served. In their original proposal, the lawyers said Capone would agree to pay taxes for 1924 and accept a prison term of eighteen months. Johnson refused it because he thought eighteen months was an insultingly brief sentence and said it should be at least two and a half years. Capone's lawyers were still not ready to give up, so they asked Johnson to offer a counterproposal. He declined and instead consulted Judge James H. Wilkerson to ask his advice.

Judge Wilkerson had already proven himself a formidable adversary in Capone's earlier trial, a by-the-books jurist who had long railed against little guys in his courtroom taking the rap for the big ones who called all the shots: bar owners and speakeasy operators were the ones who appeared before him while the higher-ups who shipped the booze and kept all the profits were left unscathed. Johnson explained his qualms about taking Capone into a courtroom where almost everything the government had against him was circumstantial. The witnesses Ries and Shumway were, if not actual criminals themselves, certainly involved in suspect activity; there was a possibility that tax evasion might be judged a misdemeanor and not a felony; and although they had invoices of everything from silverware to tailored suits that were shipped to the Capone households, it could be argued that that evidence was also circumstantial. Johnson told all this to Wilkerson, but if he was asking straight-out for the judge's advice or consent, he got neither.

Johnson left that meeting as he had done the earlier one in Washington, without any sort of resolution and thus no direction. He was on his own. Eventually, he and Capone's lawyers agreed on a guilty plea and the prison sentence of two and a half years. In record time, the newspapers and wire services, which obviously had sources inside both camps, knew of the agreement and reported every last detail to a mesmerized public. The Associated Press competed with the *Chicago Tribune* to give the minute particulars of what happened every day. And as the news of Capone's deal filled front pages all across the country, Judge Wilkerson seethed with a quiet and well-hidden rage. To think that a criminal of Al Capone's magnitude could waltz into a government office and not only bargain but also actually dictate the terms of the penalty he was willing to pay, and not for his most heinous crimes of murder—it made Judge Wilkerson livid. Certainly, Capone's lawyers were acting on their client's behalf with the attempt to plea-bargain; clearly, the judge did not want Al Capone to benefit from it.

Judge Wilkerson knew Capone well, for he had presided over the earlier contempt trial, and if there was to be one for tax evasion, he would preside over it as well. What he told Johnson was short and to the point: he said that the chief prosecutor should never have engaged in plea bargain discussions with Nash and Ahern; he should have told them from the start that Al Capone was going to trial for failing to pay income tax for the years

1924–29. He never told Johnson explicitly that if the case was heard in his courtroom, there would be no deal, so Johnson left that meeting thinking the judge had accepted the two-and-a-half-year prison bargain.

Johnson and his associates busied themselves preparing an indictment that was served to Al Capone on June 5, 1931. It listed twenty-two counts based on an income of $1,038,654.84, for which he owed taxes in the amount of $215,080.48. Newspapers everywhere followed the lead of the *New York Times* and scoffed at these estimations as being far too small. Johnson countered that even if the amount was only partial, it was still enough for a jury to be able to render a verdict. Theoretically, if convicted on these amounts, Al could have received a maximum prison sentence as long as thirty-two years, with fines amounting to something between $80,000 and $90,000 and court costs to be determined separately and added to the fines. However, the longest prison term that had been given to that date was Jake Guzik's for five years, so if Capone were found guilty, his lawyers were banking on something between two and five years, per their discussions with Johnson.

Ahern and Johnson agreed that Al Capone would plead guilty to non-payment of taxes and go to prison for two and a half years. Ahern relayed the terms to Capone: he must agree to plead guilty and go to prison for two years on the tax charge and an additional six months for the violation of Prohibition laws. Also, he must agree not to appeal the sentence but should go to prison directly after he left the courtroom. Ahern thought it was as good a deal as Capone was likely to get, but first he wanted Johnson to submit written approval from his superiors in Washington that they would accept it. If such a document was prepared, it has not been found among Johnson's records.

There is no evidence that Ahern ever received such a communication, which legal scholars consider another black mark against his haphazard representation. There is, however, an unofficial letter to Johnson from the attorney general in Washington that said almost casually that it was okay to proceed. It appeared that both sides accepted the informal and unwritten agreement as binding and that all Al Capone had to do was appear in court on June 16, plead guilty, and go directly to prison.

Capone was ready to accept it, for he was only thirty-two and would still be a young man when he got out. There was an attitude of resignation in his response to all the dickering and bargaining, but also an air of simple fatigue. Everything since the two previous trials had taken a toll, from the tension attached to the back-and-forth negotiations of the present indictments, the ongoing nuisance suits in Miami, the constant hounding by the press and the public crowds that left him without a moment of privacy; it made it difficult for him to focus on business and family. He was tired and could do with a rest, and if he had to take it in prison (as he had done in Philadelphia), then so be it. He expected to be sentenced to Leavenworth, where Ralph and Jake were comfortably ensconced, so he wanted his case to be over and done.

But the indictments kept coming, with the next centered on his violation of Prohibition laws. Capone's lawyers were disappointed when Johnson decided to include it but not to emphasize it, for if he were convicted on this charge rather than on tax evasion, the sentence carried penalties of two years or less in prison and only $10,000 in fines. They thought that pursuing it would be a surefire way to guarantee a short sentence.

The battle of wits and jousting for primacy in a settlement continued. Nash had been joined on Capone's courtroom team by the novice criminal defense lawyer Albert Fink, who did not have the stature of Ahern and Nash. The majority of legal analysts who have since dissected Capone's trial agree that having two lawyers who specialized in criminal defense and none skilled in the practice of tax law was unwise. But here again, Capone agreed to the decision of the two senior lawyers and accepted Fink without question. Johnson also accepted the additional lawyer without comment or concern, even though he was still hesitant about going to trial. And he had every right to be.

There were many gray areas in the laws pertaining to the relatively new income tax. Since the Sixteenth Amendment was passed in 1913, tax laws were so unsettled that they were being rewritten all the time, as both criminals and ordinary citizens were crowding appeals court dockets throughout the country. In Capone's case, the government's evidence was heavily dependent on the testimony of highly suspect criminal witnesses who were likely to change it on a personal whim or a perceived threat of retaliation. There were also statutes of limitations, and in this case many had already expired, and Capone's lawyers should have known it. If they did know, they did nothing to have the charges invalidated. Also, if Capone himself had been paying attention to the trials of Ralph, Nitti, and Guzik, he should have been aware of the various expirations and advised his lawyers accordingly. The lawyers, who should have been informed, were either sloppy or simply indifferent; if the latter, they were mirroring their client, who was now unconcerned because he knew a fix was in and if necessary he would take one for the team by serving the prison time.

Meanwhile, Johnson feared the statutes of limitations would have a serious negative effect on his case, especially the first (and main) indictment, which he had rushed to prepare and serve on March 13, 1931, two days before the charges expired on the fifteenth. Income tax throughout the 1920s was far from being as regulated, all-inclusive, and bureaucratically organized as it is today. There was nothing like a standard 1040 form, and only 10 percent of the population paid the tax; many were often unaware of what level of income required filing. In the cases of those who did pay, it was akin to an honor system because it was up to the payee to declare income and apply for the necessary documentation in order to make the payment. It was a gray area subject to many different interpretations, and the ever-cautious Johnson was well aware of the loopholes. There were so many areas open to differing interpretations in Capone's case that, careful as he was, he made the decision on his own to compromise with Ahern, the lawyer who spent his career writing briefs and was now acting as Al's chief tax negotiator.

Capone was indicted by the grand jury, and bail was set at $50,000. He quickly paid $5,000 to remain free pending arraignment and was silent and subdued throughout, leading newspapers to write stories such as the one in McCormick's *Tribune* that said he had been "pushed around so much his power has waned." The Colonel made sure that all stories in his paper treated Capone negatively, and most other papers took their cues from Chicago, for, after all, they were the reporters on the spot and therefore those who should be in the know. Other reporters, from other countries as well as the United States, surrounded Capone to and from the courtroom, but he said nothing as he quickly eluded them.

Because there were so many variables on both sides, a deal did seem the wisest outcome. Information kept filtering back to Capone's attorneys that Johnson had several newly discovered safe-deposit boxes belonging to the Outfit that contained further damaging information. Also, the attorneys learned that he was pressuring fairly high-level gang members to appear as witnesses for the prosecution, and there was even the rumor that he planned to call Johnny Torrio to testify against his onetime protégé. Despite the damaging evidence he was amassing, Johnson was still worried that he would not be allowed to enter one of his key pieces of evidence, the Mattingly letter. He was well aware of the daily rumors about the usual sort of "Chicago influence," a code name for the intimidation that Capone's people would use to ensure the trial outcome they wanted. And in retrospect, there was even the slightly amusing pressure President Hoover was putting on Johnson: he wanted Al Capone in jail to bolster his 1932 reelection campaign and also before the 1933 Chicago World's Fair opened. Hoover decreed that Chicago was to be declared safe for tourists from all over the world, and the only way that could happen was if Al Capone was off the main stage.

Meanwhile, public opinion favored both sides in almost equal part. Capone courted reporters, telling them all he was out of the rackets for good, especially now that it was just a matter of time until Prohibition was repealed. This is when remarks began to be attributed to him about how he should have been in the milk rather than the beer business, for not only was milk legal, but there would always be a demand for it. Perhaps he did say it, but like so many other myths, particularly the one that he was responsible for having "sell-by" dates put on milk bottles and, later, cartons, it can't be verified. However, as he always did when he wanted to present a picture of himself as gentle and home loving, he trotted out references to his mother (the best in the world), Mae (the saintly wife he loved dearly), and Sonny (the innocent son of whom he was justly proud). He said that because of his love for them (true) he would throw himself on the mercy of the court, willingly serve his time, and never violate the law again (patently not true). As if to reinforce how ominous was the dreadful fate awaiting him, he began to repeat what he had told reporters when he left Eastern Pen: "Jail's a bad place under any circumstances, and don't let them kid you."

He expected to be sent to federal prison in Leavenworth, Kansas, where his cohorts were cozily situated and, depending on who told the tale, all but running the place, and when he got out, he vowed to be a model citizen. And oh yes (said he humbly), another equally important reason he planned to plead guilty was the great respect he had for "his fellow tax-payers," who were regrettably footing the bills for his expensive trial. He claimed that because he was imbued with such generosity of heart and spirit, he would not put his fellow Americans through lengthy and expensive appeals but would throw himself on the mercy of the court, try for a plea bargain, and take his punishment. Every newspaper in America printed what he said in one form or another, with half the stories proclaiming his stance heroic while the other half saw it as his way of trying to beat the system. Judge Wilkerson read them all and was not amused.

The streets of Chicago were chockablock with people who had come to see Al Capone on June 6, 1931, for what might be their last chance in a very long time. He came to court in full regalia but here again, it was subject to different descriptions; the *Tribune* called his yellow suit "bilious yellow" while the *Herald and Examiner* described it as "Shrieking banana." His voice was much more subdued than his garb as he replied with a low "guilty" to each indictment. Reporters in the courtroom said the entire encounter was over in approximately three to five minutes. And then the unexpected happened: Judge Wilkerson said he needed time to consider the sentencing and set June 30 for the sentencing hearing. Ahern had asked for this date so that his client's Florida lawyers could deal with the suit brought by his former lawyer Vincent Giblin claiming that he had not been paid his $50,000 fee. Ahern's reason for requesting such a long continuance was an excuse to let the media heat die down before the sentencing in Chicago, for everyone in Miami already knew Giblin had agreed to take Capone's offer of $10,000 in full settlement.

There was an ominous undertone in the discussion leading to Wilkerson's granting of Ahern's request, which neither the lawyer nor his client seemed concerned about. Ahern argued that Capone was not likely to flee Wilkerson's jurisdiction, and besides all the charges in the indictments for conspiracies and tax evasion were relatively minor in the legal scheme of things, as were the punishments meted out for them. Judge Wilkerson replied that there were "conspiracies and conspiracies, and tax violations and tax violations." Of all the reporters in the courtroom that day, only the one from the *Philadelphia Inquirer* paid attention to what he said, and even he did not give it any special emphasis.

With the permission of his attorneys, Al Capone was absent from the courtroom for sentencing on June 30. Judge Wilkerson never spoke or wrote about whether he had already decided how he would sentence the defendant, but there were many factors that probably influenced and ultimately led to his unprecedented decision. The press had turned solidly against Capone after the continuance was granted, mainly because their readers resented that he would only go to prison for slightly more than two years, which he confirmed whenever anyone asked him. Publications like the *Literary Digest, Collier's, Time,* and the *New Republic* had wide circulations and were respected for their editorial positions. They all denounced Capone's grandstanding and interpreted what had happened in Judge

Wilkerson's courtroom as yet another victory in which he had manipulated the law to suit his purposes. Regional newspapers from St. Louis and Louisville, Philadelphia and Boston, did the same, reporting it as the triumph of the crook over the guardians of goodness. Or, as the *New Republic* put it, the victory was Capone's, but the defeat was Chicago's.

———

Al was out and about during the continuance. Mae and Sonny had returned after the school year ended and moved into their old apartment on Prairie Avenue, while he stayed mainly at his headquarters in the Lexington. In one ironic coincidence, he and the prosecutor Johnson went to the same racetrack on the same night: Capone preened to the crowd's adulation from his private box, while Johnson sat anonymously in the stands. Recognition of the two adversaries was one-sided; the band serenaded the defendant, who waved to the audience, so Johnson knew Capone was there, but no one recognized or serenaded the prosecutor, and there was no contact between them. Each man went into the courtroom on July 30 fully expecting a quick end to the case that was linking them so closely together.

Reporters already had their stories written as Capone entered for the 10:00 a.m. sentencing hearing. They were all ready to print the same thing: that Al Capone would serve two and a half years and probably pay $10,000 in fines. The writers were relaxed, thinking they could file their stories quickly and take the rest of the day off. They expected the hearing to be as brief as the one in which Capone pleaded guilty earlier in the month. However, they snapped to attention as soon as Judge Wilkerson began to talk and said the court (meaning himself as the presiding officer) was not bound to accept a plea bargain.

He said it was likely that Al Capone had pleaded guilty because of his agreement with Johnson, and he acknowledged that judges almost always followed the prosecutor's recommendation. However, this case was different, and this particular defendant had no right to determine its outcome. Al Capone could not dictate the punishment he would accept, or as the judge said, he "may not stipulate as to the judgement to be entered."

For prosecutor Johnson, it was a public humiliation for him and his office. For Capone and his lawyers, it was a question of what to do next, for they had no alternative strategy prepared. Wilkerson told the assemblage that he had to end the morning session to attend to another matter and they would have to reconvene at 2:00 p.m. In the few hours until then, Capone's lawyers had to consider what the judge said as he closed the morning session, that if their client expected leniency, he should be prepared to answer any questions the judge might ask about "the matters to which he has confessed by his [original guilty] plea." It seemed he was referring to the Mattingly letter and was prepared to allow it as prosecutorial evidence.

All parties were stunned when they reconvened that afternoon, especially the prosecutor, Johnson, whose voice and hands were shaking as he told the judge the two reasons he had accepted the plea, both of which were obviously based on the orders President Hoover had issued via Elmer Irey: to avoid "the hazards" of a trial and to settle the matter "at an early date." It was doublespeak, a code for his fear that the state's evidence was not strong enough for a conviction. Johnson was an honorable man who was stung to be put in the position of welching on a deal. He said he believed he "owe[d] this further duty to the defense" as he tried to explain that the guilty plea was entered only because he (and the U.S. attorney general and the director of the Treasury) had agreed to the settlement. The judge was unmoved by Johnson's explanation and did not modify or change his decision.

In his response, it was clear that Wilkerson had been influenced by the media coverage to a far greater extent than anyone could have predicted. He named no names as he said press coverage had been "contemptuous in character" and had made a mockery of the federal court system by announcing the outcome of the hearing before the verdict was even rendered. Wilkerson's voice was thunderous as he said, "It is time for somebody to impress upon this defendant that it is utterly impossible to bargain with a Federal Court."

An embarrassed Johnson tried to save face again by offering to produce the informally written letter from the two federal officials regarding the two and a half years as an appropriate sentence. Judge Wilkerson refused to consider the letter and said he would hand down his own sentence—but only after he heard evidence, first from the government and then from Capone himself. Capone's lawyers saw the exchange as Judge Wilkerson's signal that he wanted to use the Mattingly letter to force Capone to incriminate himself, thus freeing the judge to hand down a longer, more punitive sentence. They decided the best recourse was for Capone to withdraw his guilty plea and request a jury trial. The judge agreed to their request and told all the participants to convene the next day to set a trial date. When they reconvened, the judge cleared his docket for the trial to begin on October 6, 1931.

By that time, Capone was mounting another full-court public relations campaign, inviting any reporter who wanted to see him to his Lexington Hotel headquarters. The press was having a field day every time they asked him how he felt. He told them all that he was prepared to throw himself on the mercy of the court, once again assuming the persona of the poor persecuted fellow who was being hounded for crimes he didn't even know he had committed.

Was he worried? they wanted to know. "If I told you I wasn't, I wouldn't be telling the truth," he said, according to the *Chicago Herald and Examiner.* The *New York Times* put it more succinctly, quoting him as saying, "Well, who wouldn't be?"

Chapter 20

"I GUESS IT'S ALL OVER"

U p to the moment the trial began, Capone thought everything was under control. Shortly before the first session on October 6, 1931, he tried to take care of business in his usual way, by summoning some of the prosecution's key witnesses to his office in the Lexington Hotel. When they were called to the stand, Judge Wilkerson concluded that they were "forced by Capone to give perjured testimony" because "their oral testimony [was] entirely unsupported by records of any nature." After the trial ended, the judge said it had been "perfectly clear" throughout that Capone and his Outfit had such a "coercive influence over those with whom it comes in any contact [that it is] nothing less than insurrection against the laws of the United States." He said he would have been "blind indeed" not to have seen "the intimidation practiced on witnesses almost under the eyes of the court."

One of the chief intimidators was Capone's bodyguard Phil D'Andrea, who was sentenced separately for contempt of court on two counts, for false testimony and for carrying a loaded gun into the courtroom. Judge Wilkerson said "the pistol was far less serious than the perjury" and sent him to the Cook County Jail for six months. Throughout the trial, D'Andrea did not take particular care to hide the gun as he sat in clear sight of every witness and directly behind his boss. The gun bulged prominently and was visible as he unbuttoned his jacket and draped his arm over the back of the chair. He glared at witnesses, as did Capone, who carried no weapons other than his celebrated "stare," which he used with great effect to further unsettle witnesses.

Besides "persuading" witnesses, Capone and his men had taken added precautions: they had bribed, cajoled, and threatened enough of the jury pool that even if all the charges were not dismissed, the consequences would be less severe than those he had agreed to in the plea bargain. Unfortunately for him, he had not taken Agent Wilson's unorthodox methods of witness persuasion as seriously as he should have. There was so much information flowing between Capone's lawyers and his adversaries on gossip grapevines so fully entwined that each side knew exactly what the other was up to, not to mention those of sideline players who had their own informants. If Capone and the government had their sources and snitches, so too did journalists and courthouse employees. There were so many offshoots that even the snitches had their own snitches, which made it all the more astonishing that what happened next took place in perfect secrecy.

Easy Eddie O'Hare, still angling to get his son into the naval academy, got wind of the attempted jury fix even before the prosecutor and the judge knew it was in. Through his courthouse sources, O'Hare received a copy of the sixty-person list of those who were in the original pool and were then whittled down to the thirty-nine who would be questioned by the judge and the lawyers during voir dire for the final selection of one dozen with three alternates. He knew that those who were numbered 30 through 39 had the best chance of being selected because they had served on previous panels, and he also knew that they were the ones who had agreed to take Capone's various bribes and/or payoffs.

O'Hare effectively signed the contract for his death warrant (although the Outfit hit that killed him did not happen until eight years later) when he told Wilson, who, in turn, told Judge Wilkerson, who did not know, because the official list was still in preparation. Some time later, when the clerk of the court delivered it and the judge compared his list with O'Hare's, the names of jurors 30–39 were identical. Wilkerson read it in silence and made no comment afterward, so not even Wilson or Johnson knew what he planned to do about it.

The judge's strategically brilliant solution became clear just minutes before his original jury panel was to be brought in one by one for questioning. In muted, matter-of-fact tones, Wilkerson announced that there would be a slight delay before the trial began, until he could swap panels with another judge whose case was to begin on the same day and at the same time. The panels were exchanged, and as soon as the new, uncorrupted members of the Capone jury were selected, the judge announced further precautions against their contamination: they would be sequestered in a nearby hotel, with guards who would escort them to and from the court-room each day and would stand outside their rooms at night. To make another possible method of bribery unlikely, they would have minimal and carefully monitored contact with the hotel staff. They could not use the telephone but could write and receive letters, all of which would be care-fully censored. There were no radios in their rooms, but they could read newspapers and periodicals—only after anything pertaining to Capone and/or the trial was cut out.

Thus, there was no way Capone or any of his associates could make con-tact with members of the jury, but even if he could have, those jurors were not likely to succumb to bribes or threats. The entire jury selected for Al's trial was composed of nonethnic working-class men whose backgrounds were what the sociologist Digby Baltzell called WASP (white Anglo-Saxon Protestant), all of whom lived in rural communities outside Chicago. They were conservative elderly men, which made it unlikely that they had ever had the slightest casual contact with an Italian-American, and like many of their ilk they held the usual prejudices against them. Also, they would have had scant opportunity (and perhaps even the desire) to break Prohibition laws, so the clandestine world of booze was another unknown. And what they knew of gangland violence was only through what they read in the papers.

The distinguished journalist Meyer Berger, then a young reporter cover-ing the trial for the *New York Times,* described them as "rural gentlemen of simple and rather careless habits of dress." Al's erstwhile friend from Florida Damon Runyon, who was there to cover the trial for the Hearst papers, also mocked the jurors, calling them "horny-handed tillers of the fruitful soil, small-town storekeepers, mechanics, and clerks." The lawyer Michael Ahern agreed with both journalists, but he had a far more serious reason for making a formal protest to the judge.

He said they were, in a very real sense, professional jury servers, men who had been called repeatedly and selected to serve on many recent trials that might have prejudiced them against Capone's. He recommended that they all be dismissed and a new and fresh panel selected, one that was more representative of the community at large. The judge denied his request.

What upset Ahern the most was that at least half a dozen of these men had prior involvement in the Capone family's legal affairs: four of them had served on the federal grand jury that heard the tax evasion charges against Ralph and voted for the indictments that eventually led to his prison sentence; another was on the grand jury that investigated Al's violations of Prohibition. Others, probably so numerous that Ahern did not single them out specifically, were men who had made no secret of how they relished their roles in trials that convicted criminals.

After Ahern made his plea, Colonel McCormick's *Tribune* chastised him and the reporters who shared the opinions expressed by Berger and Runyon, editorializing that Capone needed to be tried not by his "peers" but rather by "men who reflect the opinions of the countryside, whose minds are formed in the quiet of the fields or in the atmosphere of wayside villages." In retrospect, with this jury, the defense was already on the ropes before round one of the fight began.

———

The trial began on October 7, 1931, with the U.S. attorney Johnson in charge, alertly attending every session while taking a backseat and letting his team engage in the courtroom gymnastics. Although he had several assistants, the one he was supposed to have relied on most was Dwight H. Green— this according to Green, whose later successful campaign for governor of Illinois was largely based on the exaggerated role he claimed to play in sending Al Capone to Alcatraz. At the defense table sat Michael Ahern and Albert Fink. For reasons still unknown to this day, Thomas Nash, who had defended Al in the past and was expected to lead a spirited defense, was absent throughout. Fink, nervous and unprepared, took the lead.

Wilson's staff began its presentation by submitting records uncovered during raids on various gambling and drinking businesses owned by Capone's gang. To testify as to these records, they called the employee Shumway and the mid-level beneficiaries of the spoils Peter Penovich and the brothers Frank and Ben Pope. The "raiding pastor," Henry C. Hoover, captivated the courtroom as he told of his bravery in 1925, when he refused to agree to an "understanding" with Capone and told him he had to get out of Cicero and all the western suburbs. He described in detail the raid on one of the gambling houses when he claimed this encounter took place. There were many in the courtroom, primarily among the reporters, who found serious contradictions in Hoover's testimony that could have been used to Capone's benefit, but his lawyers did not pounce. They did not question Hoover about these discrepancies, perhaps because the five years allowed for prosecution of the raid had come and gone and the statute of limitations was in effect. The prosecution well knew this, but the jury did not, and lawyers in later years who have studied the trial agree that Ahern and Fink should have made this point. Johnson and his staff held their collective breaths as they waited for them to object to the testimony and ask the judge to advise the jury that Hoover's testimony was inadmissible. But the challenge never came. Wilkerson, who knew it had expired, allowed the reverend's testimony to stand because, if the defendant's lawyers did not object, the judge was not obligated to draw their attention to it. It proved to be severely damaging, a setback from which Ahern and Fink never recovered.

Sworn statements were entered into evidence from Parker Henderson, about how he handled the purchase of the Palm Island estate and funneled other funds to the Capones, and also from the Miami branch manager of the Western Union office, through which many of those transactions passed. There was even a sworn statement from the stenographer who recorded Capone's testimony on the day of the St. Valentine's Day Massacre, testimony he gave far from the scene in the Miami district attorney's office. After that, evidence in the form of documents and invoices was entered, through employees of furniture and jewelry companies, dealers in expensive rugs, interior decorators who worked on the Palm Island house, and managers of hotels who booked whole suites for Capone's friends.

Tailors from posh shops testified about how they had to make the jacket pockets in the custom-tailored suits extra strong so they would hold guns securely. There were bills of sale for luxury Lincoln sedans, a Cunningham sixteen-cylinder Cadillac, and several specially reinforced Chevrolets. In the depths of the Depression, what was probably the most damaging testimony of all was the amount the Capones spent each week on food, usually more than $1,000; it was far more than most middle-class families spent in a year and far more than most struggling working-class families could envision. All these sworn statements were introduced to show how lavishly Al Capone spent money that had to have come from somewhere and how none of it had been declared to the tax man.

Then came the sworn statements of successful men in positions of power, among them the editor of a weekly Miami newspaper and a rich and respected real estate magnate. They and many others testified to being guests at Palm Island parties where liquor flowed and food was never ending. They said these bacchanalia were held several times weekly, always with thirty to fifty guests and with Capone boasting freely about how much everything cost.

On the third day of the trial, October 10, Wilson's team then introduced a different kind of damning evidence to show how Capone tried to hide his assets from government seizure. Wilson called him "the taxpayer" and recommended that a jeopardy assessment be entered against him so that liens could be filed by Florida's collector of internal revenue. He said he felt it was necessary to protect the government's interests after he learned that since July 6 Capone had been trying to sell his Palm Island property and all its contents, the two yachts, and a McFarlan automobile. On that day, Capone had sent a telegram to a Miami Beach realty company saying he would accept a $150,000 cash offer for everything. In front of judge and jury, Wilson then presented Capone with a notice that the government had assessed the value of his assets for the years 1926 to 1929 inclusive at $137,328.16. Unless he paid the bill "within a reasonable time," the local tax office would take "the appropriate steps to foreclose the lien," sell the property, and apply the sale's proceeds to the unpaid taxes.

Even though this was a tax evasion case and not a criminal one, the proceedings moved on to a brief discussion of the Lingle murder, in which the prosecution admitted that there was no concrete evidence to tie Al Capone directly to it. Wilson used the inability to connect Capone with it to introduce the topic of why he had originally thought it wise to accept Capone's decision to plead guilty and take the prison sentence. He said he agreed to go along with Capone's lawyers because he was "convinced that [every important witness] was in deadly fear of the Capone organization" and he could not guarantee they would even identify Al Capone, let alone stand by their grand jury testimonies. Also, Wilson said he felt sure that the attempts to bribe jury members would succeed, "so the trial would have been unsuccessful for the government."

The prosecution then turned to the Mattingly letter and tried to enter it into evidence. The defense immediately objected. The judge denied the defense objection and said he would allow it. Ahern said the letter should not be used against his client because Congress, hoping to unclog the backlogs already overwhelming the courts, was on record as openly inviting citizens to settle claims so that neither criminal nor civil actions could be filed against them. Ahern said that is exactly what the good citizen Al Capone tried to do via the Mattingly letter, to pay what he owed.

Instead of bolstering his colleague's contention or letting it stand on its own, Fink took over and proceeded to undercut Ahern disastrously. He argued that Mattingly had no right to introduce such a letter, even though it was his attempt to free Capone from "criminal liability." As such, Fink said, it was therefore inadmissible in a trial for tax evasion. Fink did not stop there; next he said Mattingly had overstepped his legal boundaries by volunteering to prepare such a letter at all; his task was to defend his client and not give law enforcement the gift of an open admission of criminal conduct. Fink was not yet finished with his damnation of Mattingly when he thundered that he wanted to cross-examine him to ascertain what possessed him to write it.

Fink's attempts to rebut the prosecution's arguments were so weak and ineffectual that they were more like corroboration than disagreement or denial. What he should have done, according to lawyers in later years, was to show how various aspects of Capone's income came from different sources so that his admissions of the part that originated in criminal activity, all made in good faith as an offer to arrive at a suitable taxpaying compromise, could not later be held as admissions of guilt in a prosecution for tax evasion.

A sad comedy of errors ensued as the defense team veered hopelessly off the central subject. Legal experts agree that Ahern was foolish when he argued that every citizen and not just Al Capone wanted to conceal income and evade taxes. When he compared Capone's actions to those of the Boston Tea Party, an incredulous Judge Wilkerson interrupted to ask if he could possibly think the current trial was akin to the earlier political demonstration in Boston Harbor. Ahern then made what was probably the most inane comment of the entire trial: "No, I don't know what it is." Further inane comments abounded as the defense tried to rebut the prosecution with its own arguments.

Many years later in 1990, when the Chicago branch of the American Bar Association staged a retrial based on original transcripts, the biographer Robert J. Schoenberg had the good fortune to interview the judge and several of the lawyers for his book *Mr. Capone.* Terry McCarthy, acting as one of the two defense lawyers, described the original team as "really inept criminal defense lawyers. Certainly, by today's standards they did not know what they were doing." The judge who presided at the retrial, Prentice H. Marshall, concluded that even though most of the laws still setting precedent today were in effect then, "those were simpler days." It was an oblique way of saying that life in Chicago in those years was played fast and loose, even in the courtroom. Both retrial participants agreed that Fink's tack concerning the letter was self-defeating, especially his repeated insistence that he had to call Mattingly to the stand because parts of his letter "indicate the lawyer is crazy." The retrial lawyers believe he should have downplayed the admissions of criminal guilt and concentrated instead on verifying Capone's taxable income and his offer to pay it. Judge Marshall said the letter was "a bona fide offer in compromise," and under the rules of evidence in effect then (and still today) "bona fide offers to compromise are not received in evidence." Judge Wilkerson must have been well aware of the law but almost jumped out of his chair in his haste to admit the Mattingly letter. Such a letter is known legally as a defendant's admission against interests, and the judge said, "When a man makes such statements, he does so at his own peril. He cannot bind the government not to prosecute him." It was the judge's second decision not to be bound by any prior decision, the first being his refusal to honor Wilson's acceptance of the plea bargain.

And so the Mattingly letter was introduced after the transcripts of Capone's April 1930 interviews were read to the jury. This is the one point on which every lawyer who has since studied Al Capone's legal issues agrees with Fink: the very fact that Mattingly took his client to those meetings in the first place and then sat quietly while he gave testimony that was likely to convict him was indeed a clear indication that "the lawyer is crazy."

———

Most of the trial's first week was taken up with one witness after another being called to demonstrate Capone's high living and verify his reckless expenditures, providing reporters with an embarrassment of riches for their articles. One witness testified that he always carried huge wads of cash that would have "choked an ox." Fink's limp attempt to discredit him in cross-examination was the question, "Wouldn't the size of the roll depend on the size of the ox?" Meyer Berger had sheer fun when he wrote about it in the *New York Times,* saying that it was all "too much for the rural gentlemen in the [jury] box," especially when bills for Al's diamond studded belt buckles and soft silk underwear were presented.

Another moment of levity came when one of the prosecutors tried to introduce a witness's statement that Capone's first job had been tending bar at Coney Island. Fink objected, asking what that had to do with the current charges; the prosecutor said it proved he had humble origins and did not inherit his money, so it had to have come from somewhere else. Fink then asked if the prosecutor was attempting to show that Al Capone was a self-made man, "like Abraham Lincoln and Herbert Hoover." "Not exactly," replied the deadpan prosecutor.

———

On October 13, one week after the trial began, Johnny Torrio and Louis LaCava, a mid-level Outfit functionary, were waiting to appear as the last witnesses for the prosecution, both hostile and obstructive and only there under subpoenas. Everyone was shocked when they were never called and the prosecution rested its case. Wilson and his colleagues made the risky decision that the testimonies and documents (Ries's in particular) were enough for conviction. It so startled Ahern that he was heard to shout "What?" Fink was taken off guard by the announcement but recovered quickly enough to ask Judge Wilkerson for a continuance since his team was not prepared to go forward with a defense. Wilkerson could have insisted that they begin immediately but said he would give them until the next morning, October 14.

Fink had not prepared a defense because he and Ahern never thought they would have to use one. During the trial, they simply assumed that the prosecution witnesses were suspect and unreliable, and theirs would offer convincing rebuttal. Ries's grudging testimony for the prosecution's case was one of the clinchers that eventually resulted in the guilty verdict, but the witnesses called by Capone's defense to discredit Ries only tightened the clinch. Fink called Peter Penovich, who had been manager of the Subway gambling house, where Ries had worked as his bookkeeper. Penovich told how he had run it as an independent operation in Cicero until the Capone faction took over the town, and how he found it expedient to throw in his lot with them even though his take was much smaller once he became their employee at the Ship. The retrial lawyer McCarthy rightly described Penovich as "a better witness for the government than any the government put on," and this was only the first of many such unhelpful witnesses.

The lawyer Tom Mulroy, who played the part of the prosecutor in the 1990 retrial, called Fink's witnesses "laughable" since most of them were bookies or gamblers who skirted the fine line separating legal from illegal activity in racetracks and betting parlors. Fink did not try to explain or defend where Al Capone got his money; his questions to various bookies only required them to swear that he was such a lousy gambler that he never had a winning day. It was a "silly defense," for the law then and now stated that gambling losses could only be deducted from winnings. If Capone's largesse in every aspect of his life did not originate in gambling wins, Fink put him squarely in the position of still not being able to explain where or how he acquired the enormous sums he needed to support his extravagant life.

Despite the procession of gamblers and bookies Capone's lawyers trotted out to take the stand and swear that he was a constant and consistent loser, they made a glaring error when they failed to stress the fact that until 1927 earnings from illegitimate activities were not taxable. This was the one time when the Mattingly letter could have worked to their benefit: they should have stressed that Capone did try to pay what he owed and that the government had refused to accept his offer and had chosen to prosecute him instead. A competent defense would have hammered this point repeatedly, and even though the jurors were as determined as Judge Wilkerson to convict Al Capone, the question of reasonable doubt would have at the very least been entered into the record for an appeal.

The prosecutors did their own hammering in closing arguments. They offered summations of the defense witnesses' testimony to show how they corroborated the documents collected by the government. Five years of painstaking paperwork, the boxes of ledgers, journals, canceled checks, money orders, and telegrams, when buffered by witnesses for both sides, all worked in the government's favor because they added up to the same thing: Where did the vast sums of money Al Capone claimed to lose in gambling come from, and how was he able to live such a high life if he never won? The Mattingly letter loomed large in the government's summation, with the prosecutors using it to prove that it was a statement against his own interests wherein Capone had openly admitted culpability. To enforce why the jury should disregard Mattingly's contention that it could not be held against his client, the government's lawyers used the analogy of a murderer who hung a sign on the smoking gun he had just fired and said it could not be used against him. Weak as the analogy was, it impressed the jury.

Then it was the defense's turn. Recognizing the weight of all the evidence against their client, they chose to concentrate on claiming that Capone had not been fairly tried but had instead been unjustly persecuted as well as prosecuted. Ahern said the government's case was based on "inference," "presumption," and "circumstantial evidence" and that it "sought to free itself from the law, to convict him merely because his name is Alphonse Capone." If he had continued to follow this line of argument clearly and succinctly, he might have actually broken through to the largely uncomprehending and therefore unconvinced jury; instead, he chose to launch into dramatic rhetoric by invoking the Roman senator Cato, who (in one of the several Latin versions of the phrase) advocated the fall of Carthage. "Delenda est Carthago," Ahern roared, hovering over the puzzled jury, who had no idea what he was talking about.

Undeterred, Ahern moved forward in historical time from the Roman Empire to Sherwood Forest. He told the jury that the government was seeking to convict Capone for being "the mythical Robin Hood you read so much about in all the newspapers." Certainly, he conceded, his client was "spendthrift" and "extravagant," but he should not be convicted on such "meager evidence." The New York Times, which printed Ahern's impassioned arguments along with descriptions of how he pounded the railing of the jury box so hard that jurors shrank back in alarm, described how a puzzled Capone listened to his lawyer: "There seems to be a reasonable doubt as to whether he grasped the full meaning of it all, [but] it sounded good."

When Fink took over, his voice was shrill and strained, but his oratory stuck to the known facts, primarily that Capone had tried to pay his debt to the government but the government didn't want his money; instead, it wanted to put him in prison. He did not mention that the real reason for a trial on tax evasion was that the prosecution could not be sure of a conviction on criminal charges. Fink kept as strictly silent about Capone's criminal activity as did the prosecution's lawyers. The closest he came to admitting illegal gains was when he tried to put the onus onto the government by insisting that Al Capone was not a "piker" and had never welched on a debt. If he had not paid his taxes, the fault was not his, and the reason had to be something other than an attempt to defraud the government. By the end of Fink's statement, the New York Times noted that Capone had listened so intently and was so deeply moved that his face was suffused with "self-pity." The "poor picked-upon Al" look was ignored by the judge and jury.

George E. Q. Johnson gave the final summation for the prosecution, and he began by turning Ahern's words against him. Johnson said Capone was a strange sort of Robin Hood, for instead of robbing the rich to give to the poor, he lavished diamond belt buckles on friends, put them up in expensive hotels, threw parties overflowing with illegal booze and tables groaning under lavish loads of food in his garishly decorated mansion. And it would seem, the most damning of all for a jury of working-class men, Al Capone wore custom-made silk underwear!

Naturally, Johnson made no mention of the soup kitchens, the handouts to widows and orphans, and the many other good deeds that benefited the poor and indigent. Instead, he told the jury he was puzzled by "the halo of romance and mystery" in which Capone's lawyers tried to envelop him, and to dispel it, he gave a brief chronology of his life in crime. He followed it with rhetorical questions about why Ahern and Fink had not called Jake Guzik, Ralph Capone, and Frank Nitti as witnesses for the defense. Johnson knew that citing other gang lords who were either on their way to or already in prison for trying to defraud the government made an excellent contrast with his final argument, that millions of citizens went to work every day and dutifully paid their share of taxes to keep society functioning.

Johnson presented his summation in calm, controlled, and dispassionate tones. He avoided all references to criminal behavior and heinous deeds with the exception of one blatantly false assertion about the Outfit, that it was created and designed not only to build wealth for Al Capone and his cohorts but, more important, to amass the spoils with only one purpose: to *avoid* paying taxes. Capone's lawyers let it stand unchallenged. If Johnson showed any emotion throughout, it was when he referred to the five years it had taken for him to build the government's case. Capone's lawyers could have used the way he described the process to insist that the entire trial was a personal vendetta, but here again they left it unchallenged. Johnson then said he had begun the case against Capone not because of "public clamor" but rather because "the facts" (in Johnson's opinion) clearly showed how Al Capone was in repeated violation of the laws of the land.

He then unwittingly made what was the most profoundly truthful statement of the entire trial when he said that it was one "future generations will remember." It certainly was, with lawyers having argued its fine points ever since. But Johnson was making this statement in a more specific manner: he meant that he wanted the public to remember the trial not because it was of Al Capone but rather because it established "whether or not a man can go so far beyond the law as to be able to escape the law." The biographer Robert J. Schoenberg summarized Johnson's position succinctly when he wrote, "In other words, can a man get away with murder and not answer at least for *tax evasion*?" What Johnson was really asking the jury to do was: "In other words—remember that this defendant was Al Capone."

—

Johnson concluded the government's case, and Judge Wilkerson began the instructions to the jury. It took an hour, but that length of time was not unusual for a trial with so many resonances. He explained to the jurors that they would be applying the facts (direct and circumstantial evidence and testimony) as they had been presented to them during the course of the trial. Legal commentators have since opined that the instructions more closely reflected the prosecution's case than the defense's. Perhaps, because this was a new area of the law, jury instructions had not yet been completely formulated; perhaps, once again, Capone's defense team had failed to grasp the issues and their severity and thus failed to request instructions that would have been more favorable to their client. Reporters who were not familiar with how instructions were prepared, by lawyers who could request information they wanted to have the judge read to the jury, knew only that Judge Wilkerson's instructions adhered most closely to the prosecution's positions, and most articles agreed that he all but urged the jury to accept everything it presented in order to find Al Capone guilty. This might have been because the defense lawyers were sloppy or in error in what they submitted. In fact, from the Mattingly letter and the question of whether it should have been admitted to the expiration of various statutes of limitations, the prosecution's case was so full of legal holes that it could have been ripped to shreds by a competent defense team.

Capone and his legal team were in his Lexington Hotel headquarters at 11:00 p.m., when they were told the jury had reached a verdict. Because it was returned in nine hours, a relatively short time for a trial of such complexity, Capone and his legal team had the momentary hope that the jurors were rejecting the government's case entirely and had reached a decision favorable to their side. Actually, it was just the opposite, for they had no problem with finding the defendant guilty on most counts. The only surprising information about the jury's swift decision did not come until later, when news leaked out that one juror was unconvinced by the prosecution's evidence and had been holding out for a not guilty plea and the only way the others could get him to go along was with a compromise verdict.

When the verdict was read, the mood in the courtroom was somber despite the palpable tension exuded by the reporters and other spectators who sat on the edges of their seats. There was no outcry, most likely because it was so puzzling that no one really understood it. The jury found Al Capone not guilty on seventeen of the twenty-two indictments, and guilty on only five of them. Newspapers reported that he "smiled nervously" as he listened to the reading. The judge frowned, took several minutes to study the written verdict, and then told the clerk to read it again so that he, the attorneys, the defendant, and everyone else could try to understand what had been decided. The felony guilty verdicts covered the years 1925 through 1927, in which Capone was said to owe $250,000, $195,000, and $200,000, respectively. The two misdemeanors were for failing to file for income tax payments in 1928 and 1929. It was a confusing verdict, for how could Capone be guilty of failing to file tax returns (counts thirteen and eighteen) when he was found not guilty of evading them (counts fourteen to twenty-two)? How could the jurors use the same evidence to find him guilty of one count in a particular year and not the several others within the same indictment? The prosecution team huddled to confer, to make sure they understood the verdict, while Ahern made the judge give him permission to poll the jury to ask each member individually if this was the verdict for which he had voted.

When Ahern finished and the judge officially accepted the verdict, the understanding was that Capone could face prison sentences of five years each for the three felonies and one year each for the two misdemeanors, a total of seventeen years. He also faced several fines starting at $10,000 each, with a maximum of $50,000, plus court costs still to be decided. Judge Wilkerson said he would pronounce sentencing in one week, banged his gavel, adjourned the session, and left the bench. Capone was grimly silent as his lawyers nervously escorted him out of the building and back to the Lexington.

One week later, on a Saturday morning, October 24, 1931, Al Capone stood before Judge Wilkerson to learn his fate. Those who listened to the judge's statement were puzzled until the very end. On the first felony count, Capone received the maximum five-year sentence and a $10,000 fine, which he expected because it was what Jake Guzik had received. Capone received the same sentence on count five, but the judge did not say how it would be served: concurrently or consecutively. He said the same with count nine and then clarified that counts one and five could be served concurrently, but not count nine. All told, Capone was facing ten years in prison, and the two misdemeanor counts were still in play. He was sentenced to serve one of the two years concurrently with the felonies, but he had to serve the other one in full. In short, he would be imprisoned for eleven years if his conviction was not overturned on appeal. And if it were, he would still have to serve two and a half years. If he lost the appeal, ten of those years were to be spent in a federal prison and the last in the Cook County Jail. His fines would total the $50,000 maximum, and the court costs would add an additional $7,692.29.

TOP: Sonny Capone, in a rare public appearance with his father at a Chicago Cubs baseball game in 1931, shortly before Al's tax evasion trial began. Cubs player Gabby Hartnett made a point of autographing a baseball for Sonny while Cubs fans cheered support for Al Capone. *[John Binder collection]*

BOTTOM: Mae Capone, when her hair was still its natural brown color, at Palm Island in Florida, shortly after the property was acquired in 1928. With her are her younger brother, Dennis (always called Danny), and their sister Claire's daughter, Joan. *[John Binder collection]*

TOP: The "other" Capones: Raphael Capone and his wife, Adelina Clotilde Tufano Capone. Al Capone had a deep, private friendship with this family who lived west of Chicago, first in Freeport and then in Rockford, Illinois. Their home became a refuge for him during the height of the gang wars and a convenient location to store various Outfit financial ledgers. *[Courtesy of the Rockford Capone family]*

BOTTOM: The wedding party of Mafalda Capone and John Maritote, December 14, 1930. Everyone was there but Mafalda's beloved brother Al, who thought it best to remain alone in Miami. At the time, his presence in Chicago for any activity, legal or otherwise, would have been dangerous. *[John Binder collection]*

TOP: Albert Duckett, staff artist for the *Chicago Herald Examiner*, attended Capone's 1931 tax evasion trial and the paper printed his daily cartoon. This one shows the principal players and a somewhat nervous Al Capone. *[Albert Bruce Duckett collection]*

BOTTOM: Al Capone on the train taking him to the United States Penitentiary, Atlanta, in May 1932. He sits carefully so that his handcuffs and the chain tying him to the frightened young car thief next to him will not show. *[John Binder collection]*

ue Federal Government Has Proved
Indicate He Was Chief Owner of Ga

DISTRICT ATTORNEY
JOHNSON

DEFENSE
ATTORNEY
AHERN

DEFENSE
ATTORNEY
FINK

AL
CAPONE

CAPONE'S LAWYERS ARGUE—Gang leader, his attorneys and the prosecutor as they appeared yesterday to Staff Artist Al | Duckett during the argument over income in federal court. District Attorney Johnson will close the prosecution this morning.

TOP: The happy Capone family at their Palm Island home after Al's release from Alcatraz in 1939. This photo, taken in the early 1940's, shows left to right: Sonny; his wife, Diana; Al and Mae. Al adored his daughter-in-law, whom he always called by her maiden name, Casey. [Diane Capone, Capone family collection]

MIDDLE: Al Capone being escorted home from the reception after Sonny's marriage to Diana Casey on December 30, 1941. His mental deterioration left him susceptible to outbursts in situations where there were large crowds and strangers, so he quickly left this happy occasion and returned to the sanctuary of Palm Island. [John Binder collection]

BOTTOM: Al and Mae Capone pictured next to the grotto on the Palm Island property. Mae is blissfully happy, while a more relaxed Al holds his daily cigar and his waistline shows the effect of his mother's good cooking in the months after his release from Alcatraz. [Diane Capone, Capone family collection)

TOP: Al and Mae Capone, with their first granddaughter, Veronica (Ronnie), and Jack, their Jack Russell terrier. The first of four daughters born to Sonny and Diana, Ronnie was one of the two grandchildren who were old enough to form treasured memories of time spent at Palm Island with their famous grandfather. *[Diane Capone, Capone family collection]*

MIDDLE: Al Capone, fishing in pajamas from his boat, the *Sonny & Ralphie*, when it was moored at the dock on the Palm Island property. After his death, legends arose that Al was so befuddled in his later years that he cast his lines in the swimming pool, something his granddaughters said never happened. *[John Binder collection]*

BOTTOM: Al Capone with his mother, Teresa, in the last year of his life. His face reflects the ravages of syphilis and hers reflects the tenderness with which she always regarded her son, whom she called "a very good man." *[John Binder collection]*

TOP: Al Capone in his casket in late January 1947 at the Miami funeral home where his body first lay for a private viewing. The photos were taken surreptitiously and a set was given to his physician, who showed them seldom and kept them from publication until his family sold them in 2013. *[Marc and Mary Perkins collection]*

BOTTOM: After the Miami viewing, the casket was transported to Chicago for interment. As gangster funerals go this one was relatively modest, with floral tributes only from his family and closest associates. *[Marc and Mary Perkins collection]*

TOP: The long-lost Capone brother, Vincenzo, who became known as Richard Two-Gun Hart, the fearless fighter of illegal booze in Nebraska during Prohibition. He liked to wear full cowboy regalia, particularly boots with his signature red hearts on them. *[Courtesy of the Hart family]*

MIDDLE: Ralphie (Capone) Gabriel's ex-wife, Elizabeth (Betty) Barsaloux Gabriel Irwin, with their two children, the teenaged Deirdre Marie Gabriel and her younger brother, Dennis Gabriel. After divorcing Ralphie, Al's nephew, in 1945, Betty raised their children as far from the Capone family as she could keep them, fearing the influence they might have on her children's upbringing. *[Courtesy of Brian Gabriel]*

BOTTOM: An older Sonny Capone with his second daughter, Diane, in the late 1980s after he moved from Florida to be near his daughters in California. Sonny and Diana had a turbulent relationship in the years after Al's death, but Sonny was always a loving father and became especially close to his children in later life. He and Mae, who lived until 1985, closely guarded Al's legacy. *[Diane Capone, Capone family collection]*

TOP: Mae Capone with her eldest granddaughter, Ronnie, at Ronnie's high school graduation from Notre Dame Academy for Girls in Miami, June 1960. Mae spent the years between her husband's death and her own in Florida, but she traveled often to spend long visits with her granddaughters, regaling them with her stories of what it was like to be Mrs. Al Capone. *[Diane Capone, Capone family collection]*

BOTTOM: The legend of Al Capone is global: Beyond his appearances in American movies and television series that are popular worldwide, Bulgarian gangs claim to study the Outfit to learn how to conduct their business and Tadjikistan issues postage stamps (seen here) with his face *[Courtesy of Niko Courtelis]*

The lawyers Ahern and Fink asked Judge Wilkerson to release Capone pending their appeal, but he refused. Bailiffs took Capone directly to the Cook County Jail, where he was to be held until his appeals were heard. His lawyers warned him to expect to lose his appeals, so that was where he would be when he learned the name of the federal penitentiary in which he would serve his sentence.

———

Throughout the trial, Al had forbidden Mae and the other Capone women to attend. He didn't even want his younger brothers there, so on the few occasions they attended, they sat quietly in the back and beat hasty exits once the sessions ended. Mae was in Chicago throughout, staying in the Prairie Avenue house with Sonny. She and Al agreed that she would stay in Chicago until the appeals were exhausted and they learned where he would serve his prison sentence. Although Sonny was missing the start of the school year in Florida, they agreed that if the penitentiary was closer to Chicago, she would enroll Sonny there, and if not, she would return to Palm Island, put him in school there, and make her visits from Miami.

Al's edict to Mae was understandable considering that he followed Italian-American traditions toward women, but some of his and his siblings' descendants wonder why he did not want his brothers there for moral support. Al would explain during the prison intake examination one year later. He told the doctor that he had been dealt with "unjustly, especially by the press," and accused reporters of implicating him in all sorts of dastardly deeds he knew nothing about just to increase circulation. Because of this, he claimed that he was defiled and defamed and did not want that opprobrium extended to his family. The doctor also noted that he was "quite bitter toward the [government] officials whom he feels double crossed him."

Al Capone would try hard to be a model prisoner, but he had many reasons for his bitterness toward the press, starting with how he was portrayed during his legal woes. He only succeeded once, and then indirectly, to curb the vividly lurid prose that described his every move: at the March trial for vagrancy, Ahern successfully petitioned the judge in that case to remove all references to "Scarface" or "Scarface Al" from the record. In all instances, he was to be known by his legal name, Alphonse Capone. Except for the occasional slip by a witness in Judge Wilkerson's courtroom, this courtesy was observed there as well.

The campaign to vilify him intensified throughout the last half of 1931, especially in Colonel McCormick's *Chicago Tribune*. A front-page cartoon showed a grotesquely fat Al sitting atop a crushed and downtrodden city of Chicago, while the hand of the attorney Johnson reached out to knock him off it. The caption was "King Alphonse, you are about to lose your throne." When he made his first appearance before Judge Wilkerson, the *Tribune* described his "porcine bulk" and resemblance to "a milk fattened shoat lolling in a mud puddle." *Time* had him enter the courtroom, "greasy and grinning," mopping sweat from his "fat head." In the *New York Times,* he had "thick lips" and "fat powerful fingers covered with dark hair," his face was "thick featured," and he had a "roll of flesh at the back of his neck." Throughout the trial, McCormick did all he could to turn public opinion against Capone by painting him as a man who delighted in making a mockery of the law. His reporters had Capone "grinning at the crowds and tirelessly posing for photographs," thus giving the impression that the trial was all fun and games and "the gangster is enjoying himself immensely."

Every physical description of Al Capone echoed that of Eleanor Medill Patterson, the newspaperwoman and cousin of Colonel McCormick who had interviewed him at Palm Island the previous January. What she wrote became the standard portrait echoed by reporters and feature writers everywhere. Patterson wanted readers to see him as the movies portrayed the stereotypical gangster, a grossly corpulent and ill-mannered Italian thug; she called him "one of those prodigious Italians, thick-chested . . . the muscles of his arms stretched the sleeves of his light brown suit, so that it seemed to be cut too small for him."

The press campaign worked on many levels to turn the hitherto-adoring public against Capone. On the weekend before his trial began, even the Northwestern University student newspaper joined the attack when Capone was roundly booed at the Northwestern-Nebraska football game. "You are not wanted," the editors wrote. "You are not getting away with anything and you are only impressing a moronic few who don't matter anyway."

Meyer Berger, whose reportage in the *New York Times* fluctuated from being perceptive and semi-positive to being downright nasty and negative, was one of the few who tried to be objective in the face of such relentless ridicule. When the silk underwear was the topic of courtroom titters, Berger wrote that he interpreted Al's "passion for colored silk underwear" as a humanizing quality in a man who was indeed a ruthless murderer but who was also "smiling, good-natured, [and] trying to find a place for himself and his wife in a fashionable Florida community." And yet he could not help adding one of those easy stereotypical analogies that reporters use when they can't decide which side of the fence to jump down on: that Capone also seemed like "a jovial Italian opera singer."

Critics did not stop with caricaturing Capone's physical attributes. As usual, his wardrobe was the subject of sartorial scrutiny usually reserved for women. Reporters took such delight in telling readers what he wore when he appeared in court. He wore a different suit every day, but because of his wife's influence and with one or two exceptions they were far more subdued than his usual flashy colors and shiny materials. This, too, reporters found interesting, describing how he stuck to dark gray, dark blue, or dark brown but always with his trademark cream-colored fedora and usually with a crisp white handkerchief carefully folded into points in his breast pocket. Reporters actually wrote of their disappointment when Al wore an ordinary watch and no other jewelry, especially not his diamond belt buckle or ostentatious pinkie ring. When he wore a suit that appeared to be the dark purple known as aubergine, reporters vied to top each other as they strove to explain the color to midwestern working-class readers. Even his footwear came under scrutiny, especially when he appeared in court "collegiate style," without garters or spats or any other support for his socks.

Although most of the newspaper headlines gloated about the downfall of Public Enemy No. 1, some also had the good sense to criticize or condemn the way the world's most famous gangland leader had been herded into prison on charges that, although real, were also sensationalized. In what was described as a rogue court hell-bent on getting a conviction, no matter for what, and alluding to the many criminal and illegal acts for which he was never charged, Washington's *Evening Star* summed up what so many were thinking: the downfall of Alphonse Capone was long overdue, but the charge of income tax evasion was little more than "a technical means to the end of getting him in jail." When all was said and done, and the mountains of ink stopped flowing, the *Evening Star* said it best: "There will remain the sense that the law has failed."

The law failed again in a different way when the Chicago division of the American Bar Association retried Al Capone in 1990 and a panel of fourteen independent and objective jurors listened to all the evidence and found him not guilty. This time, the defense lawyers held fast to the two major contentions: that the government failed to document proof of his income and that, because of ineffective counsel, he was given conflicting information about whether or not he had to file. They mentioned that the government had singled him out unfairly to make an example of him, but they did not dwell upon it; it was enough to plant the idea in the minds of the jurors. As for the prosecution's case, there were clear reasons to question the truthfulness of their witnesses, for it was clear they had been coerced into testifying and then coached about what to say. Judge Marshall, who presided over the retrial, said, "Back then nobody cared whether anybody's testimony was coerced; that's the way the police did it." The defense lawyer Mulroy concurred with Judge Marshall that the 1990 retrial verdict was the one that should have been rendered originally. Mulroy thought that if the case came before a modern-day federal judge, it might never have been scheduled for trial, simply because "even with the Mattingly letter, the government never could establish an unequivocal starting point for a net worth prosecution." If a trial did go forward today, "common sense would take over." Schoenberg, who described his conversation with the retrial participants, concluded much as they did: "Capone *was* guilty, however technically insufficient the government's case."

As for the convicted felon Al Capone, he said, "I guess it's all over," as he was taken from the courtroom directly to the Cook County Jail on October 24, 1931. More photographers were waiting for him at the courthouse exit, and when they asked him how he felt about the sentence, he said it was no one's fault but his own: "Publicity—that's what got me."

Chapter 21

"I'M IN JAIL; AREN'T THEY SATISFIED?"

The indignities did not end once Judge Wilkerson denied bail and Al Capone was hustled off to the Cook County Jail. More reporters were waiting for him there, and the police did nothing to stop photographers from entering the building and crowding around the highly visible holding pen where he was detained while awaiting permanent cell assignment. Reporters jostled to get closest to the bars, hoping for a photograph showing him behind them. He tried to move as far to the rear as possible so that his picture could not be taken unless cameras were pushed through the bars, but that meant he had to cower in the darkest corner among the unwashed and smelly, into whose midst he had been unceremoniously dumped. He begged the relentless photographers to think of his family and not shoot humiliating photographs of him behind bars, but there was so much glee in seeing the king of crime among all the riffraff that of course no one paid attention.

Trying to avoid photographers marked the start of his new attitude toward the press—to avoid it—and yet the same old hubris was still there, particularly after he was moved into the large and private Cell D-5. If the Cook County Jail could be said to have a VIP section, the D block was it, where big-time criminals with clout and connections were housed next to the relatively quiet hospital wing. Once again, the press pounced because Capone was up to his usual behavior, which made for good copy.

Ahern and Fink were busy filing an appeal to overturn his conviction, but they were only partially successful. They won when Capone was granted a stay, which meant that he would be kept in Chicago until all their appeals were exhausted; they lost when Judge Wilkerson refused their request for bail, which meant that Capone would have to remain in jail while pending appeal. The judge's animosity was on blatant display when he also refused the lawyers' request that time served in the county jail should count toward the one-year misdemeanor sentence; Wilkerson's decision meant that Capone's eleven-year sentence would not start until he was in a federal prison, and who knew how long it would be until then? His lawyers were pushing for the appeals process to be fast-tracked, but realistically everyone knew it could take as long as one to two years. Capone thought it best to settle down and make himself comfortable for the duration, and the D block was as comfortable as it got.

Mae was not permitted to furnish Al's cell with the comforts she provided when he was in Eastern Pen, but she did what she could. His mood improved when Phil D'Andrea was confined in the next cell and he had the companionship of a trusted personal assistant with whom to establish schedules for the daily visits of Outfit members. D'Andrea took care of all Al's needs. He arranged for deliveries of Teresa's home cooking, and to ensure that the boss was not bored, he supplemented it with meals brought in from some of Al's favorite restaurants. In short, the daily business of running the Outfit from the Cook County Jail was much the same as when they ran it from the Lexington Hotel. Al appeared unchastened by the courtroom defeat as life went on as usual.

The newspapers soon got wind of the goings-on and lost no time in telling the world. Stories proliferated about the big black sedans that were parked on twenty-four-hour guard duty outside the prison, the errand boys who came and went with telegrams and packages, and the secretaries who arrived to take dictation so that Al Capone could reply to the many letters that came each day from well-wishers. Visitors abounded, mostly his henchmen, and they were allowed in anytime he summoned them, day or night.

The warden, David Moneypenny, was not as enthralled by Capone as was the one in Philadelphia. Stung by newspaper accounts that led the government to make a formal investigation, he invited officials and reporters to come see the convict in his cell and decide for themselves if he was getting special treatment. Moneypenny defended the decision to put him in D block by saying that Capone needed to be near the hospital because he was recuperating, although he never specified from what. When the reporters arrived, Capone made no effort to charm them enough to enlist their sympathy. In keeping with his new attitude toward the press that ranged somewhere between indifference and disdain, he waved dismissively and said, "I'm in jail; aren't they satisfied?" In the vernacular of the times, he could not see anything "swell" about being there.

But despite his circumstances, he was still wielding his extraordinary power. Although the warden was vindicated in the official investigation, there was little he could do otherwise to curtail the steady string of visitors. When he tried to stop them by setting up a system where they had to apply for special passes that were only good during restricted hours, Capone persuaded some of the politicians on the Outfit payroll to issue special permanent passes. Thus, these so-called ordinary friends continued to come and go as they pleased, and the beat reporters who covered the jail took delight in writing colorful stories about some of the biggest names in gangland.

One such story that has been told persistently was that Johnny Torrio came from New York, bringing Lucky Luciano and Dutch Schultz to the jail so that Al could broker a truce between them. It made for a lively story, but there was scant basis in reality to it. Various gangster memoirs and biographies mention that in either 1931 or 1932 Luciano called a meeting in Chicago of the gang leaders who controlled what eventually became known as families. To date, the only verifiable record of Capone having met with Luciano and other New York mob leaders is the home movie taken of them roughhousing and jousting at the Palm Island pool in 1929. If there had been another meeting in 1931 and in Chicago, no doubt they would have visited Capone, but they would have had to do so in deepest and darkest secrecy, for nothing was written about it at a time when every reporter worth a byline had a jailhouse informer to keep him up to date on Capone's activities. It is even more unlikely that Luciano and Torrio would have held such a highly visible meeting in Chicago when their stature could have commanded all the other leaders to come quietly to New York.

Another story from that time, much told in later years, was mostly true. The infant son of Charles and Anne Morrow Lindbergh was kidnapped from his second-floor bedroom in their rural New Jersey home on March 1, 1932. Al, thinking of the care taken to keep Sonny out of the public eye because of Mae's almost-irrational fear of kidnapping, volunteered to help the New Jersey state police find the Lindbergh baby. He said if he was temporarily released from prison, he could all but guarantee the child's return within forty-eight hours. The Lindberghs were sufficiently desperate that they were ready to accept whatever help he offered. The New Jersey state police superintendent, H. Norman Schwarzkopf Sr. (father of the future general of the army who bore his name), decided to proceed cautiously.

Schwarzkopf senior contacted the two federal agents who had been instrumental in putting Capone behind bars, A. P. Madden and Frank Wilson, and they in turn contacted their boss, Elmer Irey, who would have none of it. He told the Lindberghs it was merely Al's ploy to get out of jail so he could flee to a country where there was no extradition. Irey told them to refuse the offer, and they did.

After more than five years of investigating the personal life of Al Capone, the government still had so little insight into the man's character. They knew that in his public life he was the personification of evil, but when it came to families—and especially children—they ignored the evidence that he was the model of rectitude and loving paternal behavior. As proof of his honorable intentions to return to jail, he offered to leave his brother John (Mimi) as his guarantor, and he meant it, for he would never "double cross [his] own brother."

Jail officials also had the opportunity to see for themselves how much family meant to Al Capone, for Mae brought Sonny to see his father; it happened only once, but in the warden's office, where he was able to embrace the boy. It was not the last time he saw his son, for Mae took him to Atlanta several times, and even once to Alcatraz, but after he was transferred to federal prison, there was no physical contact between them until Al's sentence was over.

———

Meanwhile, the appeals process was proceeding swiftly. On February 27, 1932, the U.S. Circuit Court of Appeals for the Seventh Circuit confirmed his conviction by the lower court. That left only the Supreme Court, and on May 2 the justices upheld the appeals court decision by refusing to hear the case. On the evening of May 4, Al Capone was hustled from his cell on his way to federal prison to start his eleven-year sentence. From newspapers to newsreels, every one of them reported that he was on his way to Leavenworth. Besides his destination, the stories made sure to note and describe the circus atmosphere surrounding his departure.

Chicago was having the equivalent of a national holiday as crowds formed everywhere for a last glimpse of the dethroned king of crime being herded into exile. Inside the prison gates, the yard was filled with anyone who had the credentials to wangle getting inside. Reporters and photographers tried to jostle past ordinary policemen, federal agents, and U.S. marshals, many of whom either had been or still were on Capone's payroll but nevertheless had the effrontery to be there and gloat at his send-off. As he passed by, he gave some "the stare" while ignoring others. He was dressed not in prison garb but in his own impeccable clothing; no handcuffs were showing, thus denying onlookers the sight of the broken and humbled man most had hoped to see.

The noise in the courtyard was deafening. Those surrounding him yelled cheers and jeers in equal part, while inmates in their cells shouted through the bars, wishing him mostly good luck and Godspeed. They would miss the happy distraction that his mere presence among them had provided. Reporters had difficulty getting close enough to hear what Al said in response to all the fuss, but most of their stories said he compared the emotional outpourings to those that another *duce* (leader), Mussolini, was inspiring as he passed among the people on another continent.

Once outside the gates, other crowds had gathered all along the route to see Al Capone as he was driven to the station, where he was expected to board a train scheduled to depart shortly before midnight. As night fell, if people managed to see inside the darkened car, they beheld a quiet, subdued, and serious man, with none of the waving and glad-handing that had characterized his preconviction car rides. Capone sat barely moving in the backseat, his face showing no emotion, and seemingly deep in thought.

He had said good-bye to his family the day before, on May 3, when they were all permitted to come together. Mae was there, in a carefully chosen hat and coat with a deep collar, both selected because she could pull them up or down as needed to shield her face from intrusive cameras. Teresa was angry and bitter but mostly silent as she hugged, kissed, and patted her son; Mafalda, who came with her husband, John Maritote, was also angry, venting her spleen loudly to reporters at the injustice she felt had been done to her brother; Matty and John seemed bewildered, as if they still could not comprehend the downfall of their family's leader. There were two noticeable absences among those who said farewell, Ralph and Sonny. Ralph was in prison, and Sonny was not there, because Al did not want the press to take pictures of his son watching him go to prison.

Reporters, who did not have access to the family, resurrected what they wrote when Al went to Eastern Pen: that he had told Mae to tell Sonny he was traveling in Europe on business but would soon be writing lots of letters that would keep them in touch with each other. It was hardly true, because Sonny had visited his father with the rest of the family in the jail and knew where he was going. Mae did not respond to those stories or any other, for the family's strategy was not to confirm or deny but to let reporters write what they wished.

Al Capone's destination was changed at the last minute; because of

Ralph, the Guzik brothers, and Frank Nitti, authorities decided not to place him among the other high-level Outfit officials cozily ensconced in Kansas. Even though Ralph had recently been transferred from Leavenworth to the McNeil Island facility in the state of Washington, the Guziks and Nitti were still running Leavenworth as if it were their own personal fiefdom. They lived in comfortable cells, wore their own clothing, had special meals, and spent time lolling in the garden during clement weather; they even drove the prison superintendent's car just for sport. The possibility of their companionship was one of the main reasons Al was so determined to be a model prisoner before he even got there; with boon companions in such pleasant circumstances, it would be easy to get along just by going along.

Thus, it was a terrible shock after his tearful good-byes to his family when he turned on the radio news in his cell and learned of the change before officials arrived to notify him. He would not be going to Kansas to join his best pals. There was too much opportunity for criminal mischief in Kansas, so Alphonse Capone would be taking a far different route, to Atlanta and the federal penitentiary with the worst reputation for harsh discipline in the entire prison system.

The Capone family learned of the change of location in the same way Al did, over the radio on May 3. When night came on the fourth, they were gathered at the train station to bid him another emotional farewell. The brothers stayed in the background, but it was the women the cameras wanted to film. They tried to hide from the flashing lightbulbs of print photographers and the shoving and cursing of newsreel cameramen who pushed forward for close-ups. Capone arrived in handcuffs, now chained to a terrified twenty-six-year-old small-time car thief whom he had instructed to walk close beside him so that the handcuffs were not visible. Most of the other dozen or so prisoners who were also going to Atlanta walked past the cameras with hats on and heads down, but he lumbered past with his head held high as he looked straight ahead, a mammoth compared with the tiny figure who walked beside him. None of the Capone women were permitted to get near enough to touch or embrace him, but once he was on board the train and out of sight, the cameras focused fixedly on them. Teresa, crying and screaming, lashed out as she ran toward them brandishing her fist in their faces. Mafalda was carrying a small child, probably her brother Matty's, and she, too, waved her fist as she shouted in their direction. Another unidentified woman, probably Matty's wife, stood close to Mae, who was in the background in her typical pose, hat pulled down and collar raised to hide her face. There was nothing left for any of them to do but go home and try to figure out how to live through the next decade.

———

Al Capone traveled to Atlanta on a hard wooden bench in a closed car that became hot and fetid as it rumbled slowly through the South. He was hand-cuffed most of the way but released occasionally for a card game with one of the escort marshals. He entered the Atlanta penitentiary on May 5, 1932, and was diagnosed with neurosyphilis during the three weeks of routine quarantine for medical examinations that were given to all incoming pris-oners. Records show the first clinical indication of the disease was when his eyes responded abnormally to light, a classic example of an Argyll Rob-ertson pupil: the one in his right eye was slightly larger than his left, and it reacted "faintly and incompletely to light." Otherwise, with the exception of slightly elevated blood pressure, his health seemed stable and his behavior well within the range of normal, so no treatment or medication for the disease was prescribed at this point.

A Wasserman (the former test used to identify syphilis) was routinely given to all incoming prisoners, but Capone's results were not yet known when he was taken several days later for his mandatory interview with the assistant warden. It began calmly enough as he answered personal ques-tions about his family, education, and background, but then the warden tried to elicit information about the various vices the Outfit controlled. Capone became furious when his interviewer included prostitution along with bootlegging and gambling. He launched into a diatribe that was both grandiose and irrational, growing increasingly agitated as he insisted that he had too much respect for women to have engaged in anything related to brothels, either as an owner or as a patron.

His anger veered into megalomania as he paced the room, slamming one fist into another and pounding the table. He claimed that he was the chief benefactor of the entire city of Chicago, and if not for his beneficence men would be out of work, crime would run rampant, and families would starve. Were it not for him, he thundered, anarchy would rule the land. Al Capone was a big man when he entered prison, just under six feet tall and well over 250 pounds of well-tempered muscle beneath many layers of fat, and if he had actually attacked the warden, he could have been dangerous. As he ranted on, guards were summoned to escort him back to the quarantine cell. It was a space that made him feel safe, so he calmed down and followed orders.

He was pleasant and lucid when taken for the neuropsychiatric examination given to incoming inmates. This time, he was better behaved throughout. He began by giving his family history, which the examining physician noted was "negative as to insanity, tuberculosis, cancer, suicide, syphilis, and consanguinity." He claimed that he himself "contracted gonorrhea at the age of 24" and was treated for it and cured by an unnamed physician. He told the psychiatrist, Dr. C. R. F. Beall, that his first positive "blood Wasserman" for syphilis was in 1931, when he had been given "several intramuscular, anti-luetic injections." It must have been a private examination, for there is no record that it took place at the Cook County Jail, where he was at the time. When asked if he ever used drugs, he denied it emphatically, admitting only to "the use of beer and wine." He was still lying about the difference in his and Mae's ages, telling the doctor that he "ran away and married at the age of seventeen his boyhood sweetheart," whose age he gave as sixteen. For his work history, he created a sanitized version, saying he quit school at age fourteen to help support his family, and worked as a pin boy in a bowling alley. He gave no starting date for his next job—in the production department of United Paper Box Company—but said he left at age twenty-two to become manager of a dance hall in New York. Six months later, he said, he resigned to accept a similar position in Chicago, where he became "engaged in various business enterprises, including real estate, newspapers, hotels, garages, and security." The examining physician wrote that "he states that he has accumulated considerable money." When the doctor asked if he had ever been arrested, Capone said his arrests were "too numerous to mention, using as a criterion the fact that he was arrested eight different times in twenty-four hours at Miami, Florida."

The one theme that recurred throughout his psychological examination was his bitterness about his trial and conviction. He was bitter toward the officials who "double crossed" him or did "not live up to the agreement" they made. He blamed them for leading him to self-incriminate by pleading guilty, which he would not otherwise have done. Capone was both plaintive and puzzled as he told his version of how he had been railroaded. The doctor wrote that "he does not know wherein he has violated this [federal income tax] law, as no income was proved in his case." Capone told how he had gone willingly to tax officials to offer to pay whatever they said he owed and how they responded only with silence. He summarized the events that followed in a clear and cogent manner, exhibiting "no mannerisms, no evidences of hallucinations or delusions . . . his insight is good."

His other recurring bitterness was toward the press, whom he accused of treating him unjustly, "in that numerous crimes, of which he had no knowledge and in which he was in no way implicated, were laid at his door, merely to increase the circulation of the papers and to add interest to the story." He claimed that this was done in such a way that "caused him to be looked upon as a much more lawless individual than he actually is." Although he freely admitted that he violated Prohibition and gambling laws, he tried to justify his actions with a convoluted explanation for having done so. When Dr. Beall pressed him for details, he became only slightly testy when he said he either could not provide the information or would not because it had to be kept confidential. Dr. Beall concluded that "his judgment, as evidenced by his behavior during the interview, is shown to be good."

As to his medical condition, that was far more worrisome. Dr. Beall noted that his routine admission exam showed "routine blood Wasserman negative; Kahn -2 plus," not yet alarming, but something to watch, especially considering his pupils. A "psychometric examination" showed his mental age to be "15.1 years, with an I.Q. of 95 by Binet test." He was diagnosed with latent syphilis and "Constitutional Psychopathy, criminalism, without psychosis."

Several days later, his Wasserman test results came back, confirming that he had "central nervous system syphilis," thus providing the doctors with a valid explanation for his occasional uncontrollable temper and misbehavior. The Atlanta prison doctors began to treat him but with outmoded bismuth therapy, which had been known to be ineffective since shortly after it was first used in 1916 and by the mid-1920s was widely acknowledged as useless. Thus, to give it to Capone in 1932 did nothing to slow the disease's advance. After he was transferred to Alcatraz and upon his release, the doctors who cared for him were aghast when they read his medical records, condemning his early treatment in Atlanta as "entirely inadequate."

On the outside, before he went to prison, in his public life, Capone had always been gregarious, sociable, and the center of attention among people who catered to him. In his private life at home, he was used to big family gatherings with as many men as could crowd around a table loaded with good food and drink, where everyone talked at once and there was much joshing, teasing, and laughter as the women ferried huge platters back and forth from the kitchen. There was none of this when he entered Atlanta, where prisoners had to conduct their daily lives in strict silence except for brief, specified times.

His disease made him befuddled at times, and his first three weeks of medical isolation followed by the long daily silences compounded his confusion. He was not used to being alone, so he was eager to join the rest of the prison population just to be surrounded by other people. But his judgment was declining enough that he was not aware he could become a highly visible target, and so he made no effort to preserve some distance for himself. He was either naive or impaired enough to think that all he had to do was follow the rules and not get into trouble. He knew that good conduct was often the route to early release, and even before he was incarcerated he resolved that he would practice good behavior so he could get out early. For every forty days of good behavior, ten would be deducted from a prisoner's sentence, and as a former bookkeeper he knew how to count and keep careful track.

However, from the beginning his good intentions were constantly thwarted. Al Capone, the Big Guy, was also the big fish and a target for verbal taunts and physical attacks from other inmates. With his naturally razor-quick temper intensified by his disease, he often could not control himself. Yet when he really wanted something, he still had the ability to present himself calmly enough to ask for a privilege or request a courtesy. His first request came when he sent a prison-approved memo to the "leader of orchestra" asking for the opportunity to play bass in the prison band. If granted, he promised to do his best to learn how to play the instrument so he could be "of use" to the band and thanked the unnamed leader in advance for considering his application.

Another request concerned the five photographs Mae had sent of herself and Sonny. Because prisoners were only allowed one, Al wrote to the deputy warden to ask for the special permission he needed to keep all five. If the warden refused, he asked to be able to destroy them himself in the warden's presence as he was unwilling to take the risk that they might get lost in the mail or, even worse, "go astray as some New's Paper [sic] may get them." The warden confiscated four, and Al kept only one.

Al Capone's mere presence created problems of all kinds for the entire prison system, starting with the deluge of mail that arrived every day. There were times when he received more letters than the rest of the penitentiary's prisoners combined, with people writing to ask for photographs, souvenir autographs, or large sums of money, the last category running the gamut from pleas on behalf of dying relatives to threats against him or his family if he didn't comply. Reporters, members of Congress, and movie stars deluged the warden's office to request interviews, all of which were routinely denied. Publishers who heard rumors that Al was writing "a book on advice to evil doers" clamored to buy the rights to publish it. Even J. Edgar Hoover got into the act when he wrote to ask the warden to accommodate "various members of Congress and other persons" who wished to "see Al Capone." It was Hoover's polite but firm way of telling the warden to go along with his veiled orders to put the prisoner on exhibit; on Hoover's whims, Prisoner 40886 became a specimen to be displayed whenever he or someone else important wanted to curry favor or grant one. Capone's daily life was one humiliation after another for the man who had once held the same sort of ultimate power to humiliate.

Capone's bitterness toward the press intensified in Atlanta. Reporters who were denied firsthand views of what he did each day got past the warden's blockade by courting newly released prisoners and persuading them to spill the beans about the most famous prisoner of them all; never mind that the beans they spilled had scant basis in fact. "Ex-convict No. 35503" got the most coverage as he aired his inventions and allegations in a three-part series on the front pages of the Philadelphia *Evening Bulletin*.

The only verifiable truth in the series was that Prisoner 40886 was intent on living the same flamboyant life he had enjoyed during his earlier incarcerations, first in Philadelphia and then in the Cook County Jail, but what the story omitted was that this did not happen while Al Capone was in Atlanta. Many differing stories were either leaked to reporters or created by them about Capone's circumstances, such as the one that said he was the true ruler of the Atlanta prison, barking commands from a cell that featured all the comforts of home. When reporters asked the warden to comment, he stuck to the official line, that Al Capone was just one among others and subject to the rules that governed them all, and in his particular case a model prisoner who obeyed every order the moment it was given. This story did not make for good copy and seldom saw print.

Fellow inmates, however, were eager to insist that Capone enjoyed luxuries they could only dream of, starting with special shoes costing the then-grand sum of $25, cobbled by hand by sympathetic inmates in Leavenworth with metal arch supports for his flat feet and shipped by express to Atlanta. Where they got the resources to make such shoes and who paid to ship them were not questions ever addressed. This myth could have originated because of his work assignment in the prison shoe shop; he told the psychiatrist he got along well with his co-workers but did not find the work itself "at all interesting."

Reporters eagerly repeated inmates' exaggerated tales of how no one could get near Al Capone because of the phalanx of beefy bodyguards who surrounded him. If such a group existed, they were self-appointed, especially in the beginning, when he was too overwhelmed by the initial isolation, tests, and examinations to be in any condition to organize anything or anyone. There were rumors that he had access to massive amounts of cocaine, which he supposedly imbibed almost as freely in prison as he allegedly did back in Chicago. But here again, this was just another story without factual basis, for no concrete evidence that he used drugs has ever been found and his angry responses when anyone questioned him about it were well documented.

Seven other prisoners shared his eight-man cell, so it must have been crowded in there if the most flagrant group of legends about his daily life were true. The first myth probably originated in testimony from his trial: that he brought his own fine underwear and bed linen when he entered Atlanta, and much more of both than regulations allowed. The next probably came from his time in Eastern Pen, where he did have several albums of family pictures, Oriental rugs, a special mattress and blankets, a typewriter, and the twenty-four volumes of the *Encyclopaedia Britannica*. He had none of these in Atlanta's Cell 3-7. When the press wrote about the few comforts he actually did have, the warden had no choice but to take most of them away, starting with the tennis rackets he used during the brief afternoon periods of recreation each convict was allowed. The tales of the tennis rackets gave rise to stories that they had hollow handles where he stashed wads of cash, as much as several thousand dollars at a time. Sometimes hollowed-out broom handles were reputed to serve the same purpose.

When his rotation in the shoe shop ended and he was put to work swabbing floors, prisoners who wanted to goad him called him "the Wop with the mop." They knew Al would invariably become enraged enough to lash out and then receive punishment for bad behavior. Many volunteers were eager to take his brooms and mops apart, but they found nothing despite insisting that he hung on to the cash and stashed it in other handy places for bribing guards and persuading other convicts to do his bidding. Where or how he could have done this in a cell crowded with seven other men was never considered.

Capone's biggest troubles began when he sassed guards and was obstreperous during his work assignments. He was quiet enough when he worked in the shoe shop, but when he was rotated to other details, he was often physically abusive if he didn't like them. He declared that Al Capone washed windows for no one, and when the guard told him to get busy, he threw his bucket of water at him and demanded to see the warden so he could tell him in person. In his report, the guard noted the prisoner's "insolence" and the "confusion" he caused. No one attributed his behavior to mental deterioration, so no new or different medical treatment was prescribed. All that prison officials could see was that Al Capone was creating a major problem just by behaving as his outsized self rather than as Prisoner 40886. To them, he was acting as if he were still running the Outfit and unbound by the rules of the institution. As he strutted, swore, preened, and proclaimed, none of his grandiose delusions were attributed to his disease.

Al Capone spent two years in the Atlanta penitentiary, and stories of his time there vary widely. He was everything from the de facto warden who ran the prison just as he had run the Outfit to a shambling hulk with lopsided gait (a true sign of the disease) who shuffled along, muttering to himself in his own delusional world. In truth, his unruly behavior lessened not too long after his arrival because disease incapacitated him just enough to keep this side of his nature in check. During his two years in Atlanta, he was a generally good prisoner who followed orders and went along just to get along. He received no special favors, as the warden attested in his official reply to the questions asked during the government's investigation.

Capone had the same privileges as other convicts when it came to writing and receiving letters, and he was allowed the same number of visitors, who for him were usually Mae and his mother. Mae had returned to Florida permanently, and Sonny was once again enrolled in St. Patrick's Catholic School, which he attended until he graduated. His health was dramatically improved, and he was a good student and a generally cheerful and happy boy. For Mae, commuting to Atlanta was difficult but doable, for several of her siblings had relocated to the Miami area and she was able to depend on their help as well as enjoy their companionship. Teresa spent much time at Palm Island, particularly in the harsh winter months, and Al's brothers dropped in whenever they wanted and stayed for as long as they liked— much to Mae's annoyance, but for her husband's sake and peace within the Capone family she put up with it. When Teresa took the train with Mae for her first visit to Al, she took along a massive platter of one of her homemade Italian specialties. Prison rules forbade gifts of food, so she had to leave it at the check-in desk and pick it up and take it home on her way out.

Al Capone received the same monthly commissary scrip of $10 as every other prisoner, and he did indeed pass most of it along to other prisoners. It was rumored that when one or another inmate needed money for family members on the outside, Al could be counted on to tell Mae to ask Ralph to take care of it; here again, no one in the family can (or will) attest that this ever happened. It is unlikely that Ralph intervened directly because he was still in the McNeil Island penitentiary. Thus, Mae, who never took any direct part in Al's business dealings before he went to prison, had to serve as his go-between for anything relating to the family's finances. When Mae knew business subjects would come up during her visit, Mafalda usually went with her. It was often said of Mafalda that, had she not been a woman, she had such business smarts that she could have run the Outfit as well as Al. Mae didn't like her, but until Ralph was released from prison and resumed his role as head of the family, she had no other choice but to rely on Mafalda.

———

Things settled into a routine for Capone in Atlanta, and he would probably have served his entire sentence there without major untoward incidents were it not for President Franklin D. Roosevelt's attorney general, Homer S. Cummings. On August 1, 1933, Cummings submitted a proposal to the Justice Department, saying he dreamed of a "special prison" for the most notorious prisoners in the country, a place so remote that they would not be able to communicate with family, friends, or business associates, where they would be isolated as if "on an island, or in Alaska." The Justice Department liked Cummings's idea so much that one week later, it offered him the perfect site: Alcatraz Island in San Francisco Bay. The army had controlled the island since 1850 but was eager to get rid of it. Because it had once been the site of a military prison, there was already a disciplinary jailhouse that could house prisoners easily and soon.

On August 1, 1934, the Federal Bureau of Prisons took control of Alcatraz Island, thus seizing from Atlanta the distinction of being the most punitive home to the most dangerous outlaws in the country. James A. Johnston was appointed warden, and on August 18 the first contingent of prisoners left Atlanta to begin the arduous train journey across the country. No one was better suited to be among them than Chicago's former Public Enemy No. 1, Alphonse Capone, and he was on the train. The worst was about to come.

Chapter 22

THE MOST INTRIGUING OF

ALL CRIMINALS

W hen Attorney General Cummings declared that Alcatraz would become the prison whose name sent shivers down the spines of hardened criminals, he could not have chosen a more visible example to punish than Alphonse Capone. Almost immediately, his choice was questioned, particularly by the press who had accepted that Capone was trying to be well behaved in Atlanta. Prison officials in Washington and Atlanta had to work hard to find enough excuses to justify why a prisoner who tried to obey the rules was being sent to live among incorrigible criminals. Thinking they had come up with a reason to justify the transfer, Atlanta officials deployed a flimsy excuse that unwittingly reflected badly on them and made it appear that they could not control their inmates.

Based on the outlandish news stories about the luxuries that allegedly filled Capone's cell, they scurried to declare him "too big a problem . . . to handle" and said he had to go because he "comported himself as the king of crime." Through the press, the public demanded proof of all the allegations of Capone's supposedly flamboyant lifestyle and excessive influence on other prisoners. It led the FBI to launch an investigation in 1932 that did not end until 1937, when he had been gone from Georgia for three long years. The agent who wrote the final report sheepishly concluded that no evidence could be found to support a single one of the assertions.

———

Prohibition was over, the Great Depression had reached its nadir, and all over the land out-of-work people gathered along railroad tracks to see the

"Al Capone Special" as it passed by. The train was easy to recognize, three sealed cars carrying fifty-three prisoners who left Atlanta on August 18, 1934, bound for San Francisco. Reports were wired to Washington when the train reached its destination on August 24 that the "fifty-three crates of furniture from Atlanta" were successfully delivered to their destination. Steel bars and wire mesh covered the windows, and guards with guns sat at the end of each carriage in specially constructed cages positioned where they could fire upon any disruptive prisoner who tried to walk toward them. By the end of the six-day journey, it was indeed a fragrant train in those pre-air-conditioning days of summer, so it was probably a blessing that no welcoming committee was permitted to board in San Francisco. The cars remained sealed as they were loaded onto barges and pushed by tugs to Alcatraz Island. Only then were officials allowed to see the incoming prisoners as they detrained, among them No. 85, Alphonse Capone.

Warden James A. Johnston was there to greet him, and according to the highly skewed and self-serving memoir he wrote about his tenure on the Rock, he claimed to have recognized Al Capone immediately. Johnston had undergone a change of character when he took charge of Alcatraz. Previously one of the most sensitive and reform-minded wardens in all the state systems, once he was on the Rock he morphed into one of the most brutal enforcers in the entire history of law enforcement in the United States. The language of his memoir was as stern and unyielding as was his person, and in it he accepted the tales of Capone's egregious behavior in Atlanta as gospel truth. He used them to boast about how he had no fear of a convict like Capone usurping his authority in Alcatraz.

Johnston wrote of how Capone supposedly swaggered off the train and strutted over to him, wearing a big wide smile and making sly comments out of the corner of his mouth as he sauntered by other prisoners. Johnston said his demeanor was meant to show everyone that he intended to take over and run the place, just as he had in Atlanta. If true, it must have been a very brief swagger, because all the incoming prisoners knew that harsh guards were there to enforce the rule of total silence. Also, any prisoner who broke out of the lineup would have been physically beaten back into place, and none dared risk such a furious assault.

Another story followed Al Capone to Alcatraz, this one told by his Atlanta cell mate Morris "Red" Rudensky, an unreliable source who cheerfully contributed highly inventive accounts of Capone's daily doings to any reporter who needed a good story. Rudensky claimed that Capone resisted the transfer, striking angrily and spewing profanities at guards, who had to restrain him in order to get him out of his cell. The calm, resigned letters Al wrote to Mae belie this ugly tale; in them, he expressed his realization that he was powerless to fight the transfer, and his only concern once it happened was for the discomfort she would have to endure on her arduous cross-country train trips each month for the single hour-and-a-half visit she would be allowed. Johnston, who took sadistic pleasure in ignoring his own regulations, made it even harder for her: it took many months and many petitions before he granted the frantically worried Mae permission to make her first visit.

Al Capone had every reason to behave himself on the Rock. Unlike other prisoners, whose sentences ranged from a minimum of twenty-five years to far longer, his ten years were already shortened by the two he had served in Atlanta. He was well aware of "the Good Time Law" in the federal penal code, wherein nonlife sentences could be lessened if the "record of conduct shows that he has faithfully observed all the rules and has not been subjected to punishment." A prisoner whose term was ten years or more could have his sentence shortened by ten days a month for good behavior. In Capone's case, time served in Atlanta and added to good behavior in Alcatraz would have amounted to twelve hundred days, which could have reduced his time to a little over six years and eight months. He would still have a year left to serve in the Cook County Jail, but that was also subject to the Good Time Law, so his entire sentence could have come to something around seven years. He told Mae that he did not intend "to make any moves of any kind, outside of obeying perfect health and respecting them [prison rules], and doing my work." He told her to tell the rest of the family there was nothing for any of them to worry about.

He was able to practice good behavior in Atlanta because he had a supporting group of inmates who had benefited from his generosity. They knew they had a good thing and did not want him harmed, but this was not the case at Alcatraz. One of his fellow prisoners put it best: "Al Capone looms on the horizon of public interest as the most intriguing of all criminals, and to his intimates, he is quite as mysterious and baffling as he is to the public at large." To the prisoners at Alcatraz, his attempts to practice good behavior made it seem that he had been stripped of the authority that derived from being the most feared mob boss in America and had become instead a shambling old man who bowed and scraped to the lowliest guard and who behaved with abject humility toward those in charge. It did not take long before the other inmates, emboldened by his obsequious behavior, singled him out for verbal taunts, teases, and physical attacks, most of them more serious than anything he suffered in Atlanta.

Al weighed around 250 pounds when he entered Alcatraz, and his reputation for mob violence had gone before him. Other prisoners thought his trial had been a trumped-up showpiece substituted for his real crimes, the uncounted ruthless and relentless killings he either committed or ordered. "Clicks" formed quickly in Alcatraz, and there were rumors that most of them were targeting him, to strike eventually in such a way as to enforce their own supremacy in the small confined world of the prison. But in the beginning, they did not dare do anything to arouse him because of his imposing size and his reputation for vicious retaliation. For the first few months of his captivity at Alcatraz, he was mostly left alone because the other prisoners were all afraid of him.

Capone was sincerely trying to be obedient in everything he did. Put to work in the shoe shop, where he built on his work experience in Atlanta, he performed diligently as a "stitcher" during his assignment there. He took his exercise for the daily hour he was allotted by walking in the yard or playing tennis, for which he had developed quite a passion. There were soon stories in the press that whenever he walked onto the courts and saw players he wanted to oppose, those players' partners had to leave and let Capone take over. More likely, they left on their own accord whenever they saw him coming, for there were no records in his prison file relating to any altercations on the courts.

One of the reasons the gangs eventually overcame their hesitation to launch their taunts and assaults might have been related to Capone's unconscious behavior toward Johnston and how the warden reacted to it. Roy Gardner, one of the inmates who was on the Rock from 1934 to 1936, wrote a perceptive study of daily life there that he called *Hellcatraz*. He was an intuitive, if distanced, observer of Capone, particularly of his encounters with Johnston. Gardner wrote that every day was filled with "the hopeless despair on the Rock [that] is reflected in the faces and actions of almost all the inmates." He had few real moments of levity to include in his memoir except for those that involved Capone and Johnston, whose interaction Gardner called "one of the funniest things [he] ever saw."

As he observed Capone from the sidelines, Gardner watched him develop what he called "a condescending attitude" toward the warden, who was so amazed by the prisoner's speech that he went into "a slow burn."

The warden must have been extremely flustered, for whenever he spoke to Capone, his naturally "soft and pleasant" voice "sounded like a cackle from a parched throat." Other prisoners interpreted these exchanges as Capone's getting away with "vanity and arrogance," and he soon became "the most hated man on Alcatraz." By 1936, his enemies began seriously to give "much time and thought on planning a 'no rap' way to kill him."

Meanwhile, Capone was trying to behave as a model prisoner, and if his attitude toward the warden seemed condescending to others, his official communications with authorities were humble and groveling. He got no special privileges at Alcatraz and like every other prisoner had $10 per month in prison scrip to spend as he wished. In addition to the articles of clothing and bedding authorized by the regulations, he was granted permission to keep in his cell family pictures, a world almanac, and the following books: several sets of music instructions and finger control, an instructive course for playing the banjo, a few sheets of paper for writing music, and two books: *The Blessed Friend of Youth* and *Seeing Italy*.

In the summer of 1935, his request to be transferred from the shoe shop to the library was approved, and he was assigned to process the borrowing cards of other inmates. In this work, he became a devoted library patron whose reading ranged widely. Permitted to have three books in his cell at a time, he checked out titles such as *Common Errors in English Corrected,* FDR's *Looking Forward,* and a popular book of self-improvement, *Life Begins at Forty,* which was approximately what his age would be when he was released. He also had travel books about Italy and Brazil and how to sail alone around the world. Most of all, he checked out books about how to enjoy listening to music and how to play it, practical flower gardening, and how to build an American home. He was happily preparing for the quiet life of a family man and property owner once he was released.

If Al Capone's years in prison were ranked for contentment, those he worked in the library would have been highest. When his supervisor wrote Al's "Confidential Work Report," he described his work as "good (not 'excellent')" and his character as "friendly, pleasant, energetic, [and] faithful (neither 'trustworthy' nor 'quarrelsome' or 'skeptical')." He was also "talkative" and "boastful," with the latter word encircled with the handwritten qualification "somewhat." The evaluator was "pleasantly surprised" by Prisoner 85's positive attitude toward his work, and he had only one objection to his conduct: "too great readiness upon his part to offer unasked advice, or to make suggestions as to when or how things should be done."

In conclusion, the supervisor said he would "very much dislike to lose him from the library force."

Despite such positive appraisal, Prisoner 85 (for they had no names in Alcatraz and were known only by dehumanizing numbers) was rotated to a stint in the laundry room. It was hard, hot, and mindless work, a setting ripe for provocations and outbursts of all kinds. On one occasion, he was the passive victim of a physical assault that had to be broken up by guards, who nevertheless assigned as much responsibility for the fracas to him as to the provocateurs.

He spent eight days in solitary confinement in "the Hole," a darkened cell of complete sensory deprivation in which night and day were indistinguishable. He never knew what time it was until silent guards shoved trays through slots in the door, with the daily ration of all the water he could drink and four slices of white bread. Twice a week, he got small portions of whatever was served in the dining hall, minus dessert or beverages. There was no mattress or bedding, so he spent his days and nights on the bare concrete floor. He had applied for parole before this incident, but now it was unlikely to be considered.

Life in Alcatraz was so grim and inhumane that there was scant chance he could stay out of trouble. There were prison strikes that he refused to join, leading to taunts of cowardice. Other prisoners tried to extort him for huge sums of money in payments he was supposed to authorize to their contacts on the outside. One informer wrote to Ralph, who by 1936 had been released from McNeil Island but as a convicted felon was barred from visiting his brother. The informer told Ralph of how Al's enemies planted a knife under his dining hall seat because he refused to go along with a $5,000 extortion attempt. Another told Ralph that Al would be killed because he refused would-be escapers the $15,000 they needed to buy guns to break out and a speedboat to whisk them away. He lost weight by eating very little after his coffee was poisoned with lye, and from then on he only tasted the interior sections of the food portions that were dumped onto his tin tray. By 1936, he had lost more than fifty pounds and weighed just under two hundred. He had also lost most of his hair and had sores on his face, declared later to be signs of advancing syphilis.

Although most incidents of violence were not in official prison records, inmates who served time with Al Capone and who told their stories or wrote memoirs after their release gave many different versions of the attacks and assaults. Everything they claimed as true appeared in some form or another in newspapers, magazines, and subsequent biographies. The one account of an assault that can be verified in its entirety came in the form of a report from the prison's chief medical officer to Warden Johnston.

Just after breakfast on June 23, 1936, as Capone was working at his next rotation in the clothing room, James Lucas (No. 224), an inmate in search of the glory that would come from "taking out Scarface," seized a pair of scissors and stabbed him repeatedly in the back and chest. That much was true, but all other accounts of this event were wishful exaggeration, such as the one about how Capone was strong enough after the stabbing to break his banjo in shards while using it to beat Lucas repeatedly. There was no way he could have taken his banjo to work, nor was there any truth in the tale of how he roared in uncontrolled rage as he used it to hammer Lucas into submission.

The medical examiner's report was accurate: Factual and succinct, it described how Capone was brought to the hospital in a state of semi-shock after first being medicated to stabilize him for the transport. There was a small puncture wound in his left posterior chest that was deep and bleeding heavily but did not penetrate the chest cavity, a puncture wound on his left thumb, and several superficial wounds on each hand, inflicted as he raised them in self-defense. Further examination revealed a possibly contaminated scissor blade that had broken off and was deeply embedded in his left thumb and that required local anesthetic to remove. The wounds were not life threatening, but the removal of the scissor blade was so difficult and possibly infectious that he had to spend three days in the hospital to see how he responded to the massive units of tetanus antitoxin the doctors prescribed.

When the family learned of the stabbing, Ralph sent another in the series of letters he had been writing to the director of the Federal Bureau of Prisons, Sanford Bates (whom he addressed as "the Honorable"). They were models of perfect English that covered all the legal bases, and because Ralph was barely literate in speaking, let alone writing, they were obviously prepared for his signature by the lawyers. They were written at the beginning of Al's imprisonment by the lawyer Ahern and later by the wily Abraham Teitelbaum, the Chicago lawyer who served Al for the rest of his life. The letter sent two days after the stabbing confirmed what Ralph had said in an earlier phone call, that he, his mother, and his brother's wife would "gladly assume all responsibility for [Al's] safety and responsibility" if he could be transferred to another prison.

Anticipating the excuses for why this request might not be honored, Ralph's letter said that if the transfer were granted, he would "personally assume full responsibility and guilt for any bribes of officials or guards, also other prisoners, seeking any special privileges, favors, etc., and in fact anything of any nature whatsoever in violation of your prison rules." To reinforce his point, he repeated that he would assume "full responsibility and the guilt thereof." He concluded with the family's concern that his brother's life was in constant danger and his health impaired by his "extreme nervous condition [and] mental worries . . . being at all times fearful of criminal attack." This request, like those in the many other letters the lawyers sent, was denied.

The Capone family lived in a similar state of anxiety and fear as their beloved Al. In Alcatraz, visits were limited to one per month from the loosely defined "members of your family" and lasted from 1:30 to 3:10 p.m. In an undated letter, Al wrote directly to Johnston to ask for special consideration so that he could at least see Mae and his mother on two consecutive days. Al asked that if the warden refused this request, would he grant Mae and Teresa the privilege they had enjoyed in Atlanta, of three visits on three consecutive days? In return for such a tremendous favor, he promised not to see them for the three months that followed. He explained that the trip was long and expensive and he would forgo the pleasure the visits brought him in order to spare them from having to travel so far for only a little over an hour with him.

His letter was a model of humility, yet filled with the verbosity that characterized all his correspondence and marked by the simplicity of language that came from his sixth-grade education. Repeatedly, he wrote how "we will more than appreciate it, sure hope you will consider this condition, for the sake of my family, as it sure mean's [sic] plenty to able [sic] to see them for a few hour's [sic] a month, thanking you in advance, and sure hope and pray that you will consider this favorably."

His lawyers made the same request in succinct perfect English, in a letter addressed to Attorney General Cummings and asking for the same visiting privileges as the Capone family had had in Atlanta. Interestingly, the letter was signed not by Mae but by Teresa (here signing her name as Theresa). As she had always done, Mae stayed quietly in the background and let others do the legal petitioning. When all their appeals failed, no matter how difficult it was to make the journey, Mae never missed a visit, even though she had to make her own appeals to apply for each one and then to wait for long and capricious periods of time to receive what should have been routine permission. Sometimes she had to wait as long as three months for it to be granted, but she never missed any visit she was allowed.

Mae took trains across the country, always in private compartments, usually accompanied by Teresa and/or one of Al's brothers and occasionally by Mafalda. Sonny was happily in school at St. Pat's, and Mae's siblings living in the area of Palm Island were available to help look after him as needed. When Sonny was fourteen, he met Ruth Diana Casey (who later reversed the order of her given names to Diana Ruth), his classmate and the woman he would marry. He, Mae, and her sisters and brother became friendly with the large Irish Catholic Casey family, so Sonny had the companionship and support of a network of caring people whenever his mother was away.

Because the journey was so arduous, the Capone contingent usually booked a suite in a quiet San Francisco hotel where they could count on their privacy being respected. They always tried to arrive a few days before and to stay on for a few more after the visit, mostly to recuperate before making the exhausting journey back. Tension before the visit was high, and time was needed afterward to decompress. In later years, Sonny told his daughters about how, when he accompanied his mother on such visits, he and Mae filled these hours at the movies, which had the added benefit of letting them lose themselves in anonymous, dark rooms and Hollywood make-believe. Mae was adept at eluding press coverage, even though she always traveled under her own name, so reporters and photographers only occasionally learned she was there.

Because visits were so frustratingly short, Al and Mae stayed in touch through letters. He was allowed to write two per week and to receive seven (and she wrote every day), but only after prison officials approved the prisoner's list of correspondents. On Mother's Day, they were allowed to mail a third letter for the week, and at Christmas four cards; on Christmas, Easter, Father's Day, and their birthdays, they were allowed to receive unlimited greeting cards. Letters Capone wrote had to be presented in unsealed envelopes, and those he received were opened and read by censors. Mae saved all the letters they exchanged until the last years of her life, when she made a bonfire and burned them, along with family photographs and every other document that related to her life with Al Capone. She told her granddaughters that she did not want to leave anything behind that might result in salacious public scrutiny.

Anything No. 85 wrote that appeared to be related to the conduct of illegal activity in or out of the prison was deleted before being released or sent. Al was careful to couch any instructions to Ralph that he sent through Mae in the vaguest language he could manage, but he still occasionally crossed the line. When his beloved Frank Rio died unexpectedly at the age of thirty-nine, felled by a coronary occlusion and not by a mob hit, Al asked Mae to instruct Ralph to see that his widow and two children received monthly stipends from the Outfit. He praised Mae for going to Chicago to comfort the widow even as he expressed his doubts about the cause of death: "Ask Ralph how sure he is that it was heart trouble as Honey, you know Frank was at all times real healthy and strong and really I can't understand it and for Ralph to find out and let me know."

The letter, which made it through the censors unedited, set off a flurry of exchanges between Johnston and the national director of the Federal Bureau of Prisons, Sanford Bates. Besides asking that Ralph see to Mrs. Rio's needs, the letter asked Mae to send a lavish, attention-grabbing floral tribute to the funeral. Newspapers of course gave it headline coverage, thus alarming Bates, who insisted that Johnston explain what was going on and justify how he was running Alcatraz. Johnston rushed to convince Bates that he was firmly in control and that Al was not running the prison. The warden explained that even if Ralph did make all the arrangements for money and flowers, the request from Al was not necessarily mob business: "If the money . . . represents charity, it is one thing, but if the deceased was one of a gang or mob, it may be looked at differently." Johnston recommended that if Bates remained unconvinced of his control, he launch an investigation that would, Johnston knew, clear him of any wrongdoing. His letter must have satisfied Bates, for there is no record that he did anything at all.

Al's exchanges with Mae represented a lifeline to the outside world, one that buttressed his resolution to steer clear of prison politics and keep to the straight and narrow of good behavior. He always knew what a remarkable woman he had married, but being alone and having to maintain silence for such long stretches of time, the naturally gregarious Al began to think about her worth in ways that he might not have previously done.

Al's continuing discomfort with solitude is evident in his letters to Mae, where he expressed his love for everyone, from Ralph's current wife, Valma, to Mafalda's infant daughter, Dolores. He yearned to be among them all. His pre-prison life had consisted of long periods of time spent in his hotel headquarters, away from his family but always surrounded by a contingent of his men. When he was on the run, they were there with him, too. If he went for long stretches of time without seeing Mae, he still had female companionship whenever he wanted. In prison, he was deprived of all these encounters, and the sheer aloneness made him cling to Mae in an almost childlike fashion. His letters were poignant expressions of love and devotion, and when he was not calling her "Sweet" several times in almost every sentence, he referred to her as "Mom" and himself as "Dad." Sonny was their "beloved son," the fine young man of whom he was so proud that only the cliché of a father busting his buttons can describe Al's emotion. Sonny was eighteen years old and about to begin his freshman year at Notre Dame, something unimaginable for the man who started out as a small-time Brooklyn hood, and especially unreal for the broken gangster who had once been on top of the world.

They were both still so young—Al was thirty-eight and Mae forty—but the events of their lives before he went to prison had contrived to make their relationship seem one of people far older and greatly removed from the youthful days of passionate love. From Alcatraz, Al repeatedly told Mae, "I love and adore you more now than ever and my love is increasing more and more each day . . . when your dear dad gets lucky and comes home again into your wonderful arms it will be a new daddy, and yours alone, so please believe me dear, as I sure will prove it to you later." Without referring to the mysterious Jeanette DeMarco by name, he tried to dispel her shadow by concluding, "Dear, I love you alone and have forgotten all about the other party."

The tone and content of Al's letters to Mae changed around 1936, when the syphilis began its insidious inroad toward his brain and he turned toward religion. Whether a sincere conversion or a desperate prayer for a cure, Al embraced the lifeline offered by Mae's unwavering love for him and devotion to their marriage, and because she was a devout practitioner of the Catholic faith, he began to follow it himself. His letters told her of his frequent participation in the sacraments of Mass, confession, and Communion. He was fond of the priest who ministered to the prisoners every week, Father Joseph Mahoney Clark, S.J. If they discussed anything pertaining to Al's life in crime, the priest maintained the silence of his calling and never told, nor did he write anything in the extensive archives he compiled. The priest did share a love of music with Al, who had become proficient on the mandolin (he called it the mandola). He used his library privileges to study all sorts of literature on the history of the instrument and how to play it, and he also composed his own songs for it. Mae was graced with one written especially for her on Mother's Day, as was Teresa with another, but for Father Clark he wrote out the words and music and signed a copy that the priest was allowed to take with him as a souvenir and gift from Al. The priest provided comfort and serenity around 1938, when the syphilis became rampant.

Capone appeared to have settled into a quiet life in Alcatraz by that date. Johnston's rules and regulations were so harsh that in their helpless frustration inmates retaliated by lashing out with murders, suicides, and every sort of violent attack. But when it came to Capone, for the most part his tormentors had moved on to other targets and victims; except for taunts and insults, proximity had become indifference, and he was pretty much left alone. He was more a symbol of their mockery and laughter, particularly for his shambling and lopsided gait. Even though it was a direct sign of his disease, it was of no real concern to officials. Occasionally, he mumbled as he shambled, saying something that had no connection to his current circumstances; less frequently but still often enough to be noticed, he uttered gibberish. Still, he seemed healthy, and because he was well behaved, officials found nothing to worry about until the end of January 1938.

Mae made her usual request for the monthly visit in February and this time with Mafalda. Johnston granted this one more quickly than usual but with his usual strict directives: she was to board the ferryboat that left San Francisco at precisely 10:00 a.m. on Monday, February 28. She knew that if she was not on that particular crossing, he could refuse to let her see her husband at all, so she was making arrangements to follow his instructions when the most serious incident to date occurred.

It was a Saturday, February 5, and Capone had trouble arising that morning. Instead of dressing in his workday coveralls, he dressed in the blue suit he was only allowed to wear on Sundays and holidays. The guard chastised him and made him change, after which he followed the guard to breakfast but was unaware of the time or the meal he was to eat. He was allowed to return to his cell, where he was unsteady and delirious, gagging and trying to vomit. The prison doctor was summoned, and he realized immediately that something serious had happened. Capone was taken to the prison hospital, and a specialist was summoned from San Francisco.

By Tuesday the eighth, headlines to lead stories in daily papers around the world read, "Al Capone Goes Berserk," "Al Capone Loses Mind in Prison," and "Al Capone Goes Insane." All over America, listeners were glued to evening news broadcasts to hear the details, most of them highly exaggerated. Capone did resist the guards who took him to the hospital, but "the paunchy scar-faced immigrant" was never "strapped in a madman's strait jacket." No doubt he did hum the occasional Italian aria or spout incomprehensible gibberish, but he didn't spit at inmates, nor did he spend hours making and remaking his cell bed because he was not there but in the hospital and in isolation. While in medical care, he was neither comatose nor at death's door, even though he slept a lot and was often unaware of his surroundings.

Johnston did not have the good grace to inform Mae of Al's breakdown, so the Capone family received the news the same way as the rest of the world, through newspapers and radio. Mae sent a telegram to Johnston on February 9 from Miami that began, "Due to the rumors," for she had not been given any facts. One of the main rumors being bruited by the newspapers was that Al would be transferred to another facility, most likely in the East, where he could receive the care Alcatraz was not equipped to provide. Mae begged Johnston to tell her if this was true before she began the slow cross-country journey, because he might be long gone to the East while she was still in transit going west. She signed it "respectfully yours," but Johnston gave her no courtesy or comfort, replying in his usual hard-nosed and disrespectful fashion: her husband was stable and unrestrained; no transfer was necessary, but one might occur in the future. He told her not to make the visit she had been promised but to stay in Miami and "await further advice." He said he would not send her further reports about Al's condition but would communicate his information to the director of the Bureau of Prisons in Washington. "In the meantime," Johnston told Mae, if she wanted to know anything, she should contact Director Bates, and— although he left it unstated—she should hope for the best because he had no intention of trying to ease her anxiety. Johnston was a strict moralist who believed that inmates deserved the most serious punishment he could mete out, and he extended this view to include those who loved them.

———

There were other stories about Al Capone's breakdown, but they were given far less space in newspaper accounts. Most of them concerned two separate petitions by his new attorney, Abraham Teitelbaum. The first was to the Bureau of Prisons to ask that Capone be transferred to a facility where he could be given the treatment he could not get at Alcatraz.

Although unnamed, it probably meant Atlanta, where the prison hospital was far superior. The second and equally important petition was to ask the Supreme Court to cancel the one-year sentence in Cook County Jail. Capone had enough deductions for good behavior in Alcatraz to make him eligible for parole on January 19, 1939, after which he was to be escorted directly to Chicago to begin serving the sentence there. Everyone in authority who was monitoring his case knew how ill he was and that a transfer to another prison hospital should have been granted immediately, but it was not.

He stayed on at Alcatraz for the rest of 1938, in the hospital rather than in his cell, undergoing treatment consisting mostly of weekly injections of the useless bismuth and tryparsamide and once even a lumbar puncture that confirmed tertiary syphilis. The medications were all given by injection, which should have put to rest the myth that he never sought treatment for syphilis when he first had it because he was so terrified of shots. He had injections throughout his remaining year at Alcatraz, and there is no record then or afterward that he did anything to avoid needles. The lumbar puncture also confirmed other signs of syphilis, both physical and mental. At times, his speech was slurred and he stumbled when he walked. Mentally, he had periods of grandiosity wherein he was going to reform the world and end the Depression by giving money and jobs to all who needed them. His devotion to Catholicism sometimes had him speaking directly to God and the angels.

And yet within days of the attack, he was still capable of clear and defined periods of lucidity, as can be seen in the letters he wrote to Mae and Sonny. Leaving Alcatraz in January 1939 was uppermost in his mind, as was reassuring Mae that he was completely recovered. But he also told her how he prayed to "God above to make me well, which *she* has and I thanked *her* for making me well and sure am in perfect health again." In a letter to Sonny, whom he called "Junior," he praised Mae for her devotion to them both and then told Sonny how proud he was of him at Notre Dame. Al was lucid enough to realize that Sonny might have had questions about his father's career that for any number of reasons he was reluctant to ask. Al told him, "If you've got something on your mind that you want to keep between you us two [sic], not to hurt your dearest mother . . . what I'm trying to get at is this, maybe you've got something on your mind about your future. Son all I want you to do is not hold it back as your Mother and your dear dad will go to the limit for your health and future."

Teitelbaum was kept busy during Al's last months at Alcatraz. Financial concerns weighed on the family, and money had to be found to pay the fines and costs associated with the federal felony counts, which were now assessed at a whopping $37,617.51. The weakness of the government's case for his conviction was shown once again when it could not find any assets to attach. The Prairie Avenue house had been in Teresa's name from the beginning, as Palm Island was in Mae's. Nevertheless, the government served papers on Mae's house, which Michael Ahern had unwisely told her she could ignore, and that bad advice then allowed the government to proceed toward foreclosure. Mae endured the strain of possibly losing her home from 1936 until two days before Al was due to be released in January 1939. By that time, Ralph had fired Ahern and hired Teitelbaum, who helped him arrange a $35,000 mortgage. Headlines described him as a "mob lawyer" because he had represented quite a few gangland figures; however, he was shrewd and thorough and served all his clients (but especially Al) well. Al's brother John Capone (now officially John Martin and in Chicago at the time) took Teitelbaum a cashier's check for that amount plus an additional $2,962.29 in cash. Teitelbaum submitted it to federal officials in Chicago in full payment of the debt. The final amount included an extra $74.78, which was loosely categorized as "processing fees." The government got its every last penny, but Ahern and Fink were not so lucky when they submitted their final bills: Ralph told them, in effect and in far more colorful language, to go away. And they did.

By the end of 1938, prison officials decided that Al Capone was too ill to be returned to the Cook County Jail after he left Alcatraz, and besides security there was too lax to house him. Federal officials overruled Judge Wilkerson, who wanted him back, and decided to keep him on the West Coast in a federal prison where he could receive good medical treatment while serving his last year in a strictly monitored setting. They decided on Terminal Island, a facility in Southern California just south of Los Angeles.

Getting him there involved laughably complex security designed in response to bizarre rumors. During the night of January 6, 1939, Capone was incoherent and rambling when he was awakened and taken from his hospital bed. The prison staff was on high alert because word had spread of the possibility that he would be abducted during the transfer, by either the Outfit, various regional gangland groups, or even bands of drunken kids out for a lark. All were supposedly ready to spirit him away to an undisclosed destination, but it appears that no one considered why any abductors would want him in his present condition or what they might do after they got him. Nevertheless, authorities were convinced the kidnapping might be carried out by someone who just wanted the thrill of trying to get away with it.

An associate warden headed the contingent that was put in charge of getting Capone to the Oakland train station across the bay from San Francisco, in darkest night and deepest secrecy. Two guards stood on either side of the befuddled prisoner, whose arms were handcuffed and legs were shackled to each of them. Other guards carrying machine guns surrounded them as they all got on board a night train going south. Still maintaining excessive secrecy, they left the train the following morning at the Glendale station north of Los Angeles and got into black cars that sped them to the prison, where A-85 became TI-397.

Beginning with his time in Atlanta, Al Capone's medical condition was of particular interest to the doctors who worked for the prison system and were routinely rotated throughout the various institutions. The chief physician at Terminal Island, Dr. George Hess, had not previously been his primary doctor but did examine him in both Atlanta and Alcatraz and now was in charge of his care. He saw to it that Capone was not put through the usual processing for incoming prisoners but was taken immediately to the hospital, where he stayed until he was discharged on November 16.

Throughout his time at Terminal Island, the treatments that were begun at Alcatraz continued. Besides the injections of bismuth and tryparsamide, injections of malarial fluids were added to his treatment, for it was thought that inducing high fevers in patients would kill the syphilis. None of these pre-antibiotic remedies worked, and the disease typically progressed to the tertiary stage of dementia called neurosyphilis. His periods of lucidity continued to alternate with those of delirium. Guards who talked to reporters were happy to report that he was "nutty as a fruitcake" and gave florid descriptions of his behavior; visitors who were let in to provide various services to inmates told stories of how Al had found Jesus. And yet at the same time, Secret Service agents from Chicago who were sent to assess whether the decision not to return him to Cook County Jail was justified told reporters that he was in perfect health. Granted, all these stories were told by people who had self-serving reasons for telling them, but there was probably a modicum of truth in all of them. One above all rings true: Mae, who visited faithfully, told family and friends that her husband was just fine—which he was when in her company. Just being with her was enough to bring him back to reality.

———

The longed-for day of his release finally arrived on November 16, 1939, but even then there were strings attached to keep him from going home to Palm Island. Instead of being discharged directly from Terminal Island, he had to make the cross-country trip by train to the federal penitentiary in Lewisburg, Pennsylvania, where his release papers were processed. Afterward, Mae had to agree that he would continue inpatient treatment in a medical facility. Because he was released early for good behavior and because his full sentence did not officially end until May 1942, he had to accept the stipulation or else remain in prison. Mae had no problem agreeing with his prison doctors, who wanted him to go to Baltimore for treatment with Dr. Joseph Moore, one of the most respected physicians in the treatment of neurosyphilis.

Al Capone left Terminal Island on November 13 under the same cloak of secrecy as he had arrived. To bypass members of the press, who had gathered at Los Angeles's Union Station, he was driven to San Bernardino and put on a train that headed east through St. Louis—not Chicago, for there was still a lingering whiff of fear that his men might abduct him. After everything legal was signed and sealed at Lewisburg, Al was put into a car with several gun-toting officials who took him to a spot on a highway near Gettysburg where Mae and Ralph were waiting in a car of their own.

The memorandum written for the Bureau of Prisons detailing the swap stated only that the exchange took place. There was nothing about the intense emotionalism of the reunion, when husband and wife, who had only seen each other through glass, embraced for the first time since 1931. The agents did not write about how the happy and tearful people inside the Capone car took off so swiftly for Baltimore, as if fearing that at any moment their happy reunion might be rescinded.

Chapter 23

THE ENDGAME

A l Capone was admitted to Baltimore's Union Memorial Hospital directly after he was released to his family, and he stayed there until just after the 1940 New Year. Dr. Moore reluctantly agreed to take charge of his treatment only after making inquiries to the Bureau of Prisons about who would pay his fees. James V. Bennett, the new director of the Bureau of Prisons, advised him to be wary, because the government still could not find any assets to attach for payment of Capone's back taxes. The family was financially hard-pressed, but they had hitherto found the money to pay for every fine the government levied. Mae and Ralph both assured Dr. Moore that he would be paid, and thus Al's treatment began.

Dr. Moore had admitting privileges at Johns Hopkins Hospital and wanted Capone to be treated there. The hospital administrators were worried about the publicity such a notorious patient might generate and refused to take him. Moore also had admitting privileges at Union Memorial, so that was where Capone went. He was put into a private room with a connecting door to a two-room suite that Mae rented, one for her to live in and the other for visiting family. Mae also rented a large brick Georgian colonial house in a quiet neighborhood, where Teresa stayed, and she and Ralph often joined Mae in the hospital.

Here again, exaggerated rumors abounded: reporters claimed the family rented the entire floor of the hospital so they could empty it of all other patients (they could barely pay the $30 a day for the small suite); Al was said to have brought in a food taster because he was sure his food was being poisoned (he was often in states of unreality, but food was not something he obsessed about); he supposedly kept bodyguards, a barber, and a masseur on steady call (if his brothers could be called bodyguards, they were indeed there; the hospital barber came at regular intervals; and a masseur was part of the physical therapy program).

During his early examinations, Dr. Moore concluded that the disease had been in the advanced "paretic psychosis" stage since 1936, or perhaps even earlier. In notes that he knew other doctors might consult, he initially described the treatment in Atlanta and Alcatraz cautiously but firmly as "inadequate." The Alcatraz doctors were the focus of his scorn as he noted that it took them until August 1938 to begin the "fever therapy" (malarial injections), even though Capone had presented behavior to suggest that he was "insane" six months before that. And when they eventually did get around to inducing malarial fevers, the treatment was administered with flaws, leading Dr. Moore to call it more strongly "entirely inadequate." It was not until Capone arrived at Terminal Island that serious treatment was begun, but by that time it was too late to slow the progress of the disease.

When Al Capone entered Union Memorial, he had deteriorated to the mental age of a seven-year-old. Dr. Moore described him as boisterous, physically and mentally overactive, and with "grandiose ideas, a marked tendency toward confabulation, euphoria, and lack of insight." Ralph exacerbated Al's behavior when he made the uninformed, grandiose decision to tell him to disregard what Dr. Moore prescribed because he was "a quack and [then made] a multitude of other nonsensical statements." Ralph told Al not to worry because he would soon spirit him away to be treated by vaguely described "other doctors." Al became irrational, angry, and violent, and Dr. Moore had a difficult time quieting him down; he had an even more difficult time relieving his patient's ongoing anxiety as Al brooded and brought it up for the next month or so. Each time, he became agitated and uncontrollable in varying degrees.

Eventually, Dr. Moore stabilized Al Capone, but he had observed his patient long enough to state conclusively that he would never regain full mental cognition: "The evidences of his mental deterioration will persist . . . he will remain in his present condition indefinitely." When he left Baltimore at the end of March, Dr. Moore's ministrations had rejuvenated his mental age to fourteen, but he was still "silly, childish, and mentally deteriorated." That was the husband Mae would take home to Palm Island.

Al had been given outpatient status in mid-January, but he had to stay in Baltimore and continue treatment for at least another six weeks. They all lived in the house in the quiet Mount Washington neighborhood that was large enough for Teresa and her other children, most of whom came and went, with the exception of Ralph, who generally stayed. In gratitude to the hospital, Mae donated two weeping cherry trees in Al's name, and both were planted on the grounds. For the most part, the six weeks passed tranquilly except for Al's occasional bouts of irritability and the anger he had begun to direct toward family members, as he had earlier done when hospital personnel who were new to him entered his room. Anyone he did not recognize was likely to provoke a violent reaction, so everyone had to tread carefully. The doctor told Mae there would be a steady decline in his ability to reason, so she needed to establish routines to keep him from erupting and acting out and also to screen him from encounters with strangers who might upset him.

Mae listened carefully to everything Dr. Moore told her and she followed all his directives, but she was still not willing to accept his diagnosis that Al was in an irreversible decline. The doctor tried repeatedly to make her see reason by describing how other mainstream researchers might have pronounced patients "cured" when they were really only slowing or altering the progression of the disease. Sometimes the patient lived for a long time, often to old age, and eventually did die of something else. This, he said, would be the optimum outcome for Al. Dr. Moore made sure Mae knew how rare such outcomes were because he did not want her to become desperate enough to put a charlatan in charge who would promise Al's complete recovery. In mid-March, he told Mae she could take him home, but he must be put under immediate medical observation as soon as they arrived, and every six months he must be checked for "standpoints . . . blood and spinal fluid also."

The family entourage bundled themselves into a car to drive straight through to Miami, stopping only for gas and food, with Mae stubbornly refusing to accept that Al would not make a full recovery. Dr. Moore continued to worry that her attitude might possibly create two major problems in the future, one of which he concealed from her. He revealed his first concern only to the Capone family's physician in Miami, Dr. Kenneth Phillips, who took over Al's care and with whom Moore continued to collaborate. Again being truthful but tactful, Moore told Phillips that, as he saw Mae, she was so desperate for a complete cure that he feared she would disregard both doctors and hire a "relatively unscrupulous physician." He urged Phillips to help him make sure this did not happen.

Moore did tell Mae his second reason for concern: he warned that she would have to be constantly on guard to make sure Al had full "social adjustment . . . to his environment," because anything he could not comprehend could throw him into a violent tantrum, and being confronted with people he did not know was often the trigger. If, for example, Al were to make "an unprovoked attack upon a stranger," Moore said he could very well be arrested for disturbing the peace, and there was a justified fear that an unsympathetic judge might commit him to a psychiatric hospital.

Dr. Moore hoped that Dr. Phillips could persuade the Capone brothers to prevent Mae from making bad medical decisions and help her to keep Al under control. He encouraged them to help her find "a thoroughly experienced and psychiatrically well trained male nurse." To soothe any anxiety Al might express at having a stranger come into his house, he asked them to introduce the nurse as "a chauffeur or companion." They did not follow Dr. Moore's advice, for shortly after he gave it, Al attacked his brother John, and there was severe "physical violence." After this unprovoked attack upon a family member, they decided they could not risk introducing a stranger to the household.

Mae and the brothers decided they would have to control Al by themselves, and no one but family was allowed in the house. Both physicians worried about the entire family's long-term welfare because Al could live a very long time, as much as ten to thirty more years. The doctors thought it would be impossible for "his wife, his son, and his brothers [to] give up their entire interests and time to the maintaining of this patient in the capacity of personal attendants to him. They too are human beings." The doctors concluded that "it may be confidently anticipated that some of them will be in psychiatric difficulties, to say nothing of the financial difficulties" that were likely to arise if some or all of the brothers had to remain in full-time attendance in case he needed to be restrained.

Dr. Phillips digested all his colleague's information and advice and then contributed a piece of his own. His most immediate problem was one he would deal with for the rest of Al's life: Ralph. Ralph had taken charge of everything—at least in his own mind. Mae had always disliked him, but now she detested him, arrogant bully that he was, and not a very intelligent one at that. Fortunately, Abe Teitelbaum had his measure, and between the lawyer and the wife they managed to bypass Ralph and make most things happen in ways that were best for the patient. Correspondence between the two physicians shows how Dr. Phillips sometimes asked Dr. Moore for advice about how to deal with Ralph and how both doctors sometimes wrote letters or made phone calls in which they dispensed platitudes they hoped would calm him down.

Ralph still refused to listen to reason and found ways to interfere. After his release from the penitentiary in Washington State, Ralph had set up several businesses in Wisconsin's far north, among them a roadside joint in Mercer called Billy's Hotel and Bar. He was also involved with the Waukesha Water Company in ways that are still unclear, and he was seen making trips to Chicago, where he was in frequent contact with fellow members of the Outfit. He created a major crisis when he told Al, without consulting Mae or the doctors, that he would take him first to Chicago for a long stay and then on to Mercer. It had the unfortunate effect of making Al wildly excited and convinced that he would soon be returning to Chicago to take command of the Outfit. Although it was beyond the realm of possibility, anytime anyone changed the subject or tried to distract him, it triggered one of his worst outbursts.

Dr. Moore decided on an intervention and asked Ralph to stop in Baltimore on his way back from Mercer, where he usually was when not at Palm Island. Ralph refused to understand that allowing Al to return to Chicago would be the worst possible decision, so to mollify him and pacify Al, Dr. Moore was trying to find a compromise to satisfy them both. His first suggestion was for Ralph to find some way for Al to occupy himself with the "minor details" of Waukesha Water: "for example an attempt at keeping a set of books." If that did not satisfy Al, he suggested that the family purchase one of the adjoining vacant plots of land abutting Palm Island and "let the patient run it as his personal garden, either flower or veg." The easily distractible Ralph lost interest in both suggestions, and because the family income consisted of whatever the new leaders in the Outfit doled out as Ralph's share and Mae's for her upkeep, purchasing new property was not an option. Mae's only option along these lines was to find a spot on the Palm Island property where Al could plant a garden. The best they managed was going for walks on the property, where she taught him the names of the luscious plantings, which he enjoyed reciting as he cleaned off dead leaves or pulled the occasional weed.

———

A year elapsed, and by March 1941 Al was calmer and his periods of lucidity were greater, which made him more determined than ever to go to Chicago. Mae had come around to thinking it might be good for him to live most of the year in Cicero, where he could have the kind of male (that is, Outfit) companionship he did not get at Palm Island. She had gradually been able to introduce outsiders into Al's daily environment, and he was at relative ease with most of them. Every day she had a trustworthy jack-of-all-trades on the property named Brown and called Brownie, who served as general family retainer and companion to Al. Rose, an equally trustworthy maid, came each day for a few years, but when she either quit or retired, Mae was left to do the housework herself.

Two reasons led her to this decision: the first was that the entire Capone family was living on the weekly $600 the Outfit sent Ralph, which had to support Mae, Teresa, and any other family members who needed help. It meant that Mae could not afford a maid or cleaning woman. The second reason was far more important: she could not trust anyone other than family and close friends not to talk to reporters, who camped out at the end of the driveway and, when no news was leaked, invented their own. Family members knew they had to keep Al as secluded as possible because he had frequent periods when "he said things he should not have. He talked to dead people and told them why they had to die. Sometimes he gave away Outfit business. We couldn't take a chance that any of this would get out."

Mae and the family did all they could to shelter Al from situations where he might be subjected to unpleasant encounters. Occasionally, they took him to a movie, which he enjoyed enormously, or to a restaurant with sympathetic management where they knew they would have a secluded table. They kept him busy with gardening, swimming in his magnificent pool, and fishing off the end of the dock. Totally untrue were the stories of how he sat beside the pool in his nightclothes and cast his fishing rod into it because he thought it was the bay. There were false stories of how he was so weak he could not get out of bed and how all physical activity was forbidden, and false stories that he had resumed holding large parties where he regaled guests with tales of his past exploits and assurances that he was now back in command of his illegal empire. He looked much the same as before he entered prison. His physical appearance gave the illusion of good health and total recovery; within several months of being at home, he regained the fifty pounds he had lost at Alcatraz.

But during the day, besides the few trusted retainers, family members attended to their own activities, and except for Mae, Al was often alone. Sonny had left Notre Dame after his first year and enrolled in the University of Miami to study business administration and to help Mae care for Al. Here again, another untrue rumor dogged Sonny for the rest of his life.

He did not leave because of harassment when it got out that Albert Francis was really Albert Francis Capone; Sonny had enrolled at Notre Dame under his full name and was always known during his time there as Al Capone's son. He transferred because he was needed to help out at home and also because he was seriously dating his high school sweetheart, Diana Ruth Casey, whom he married on his parents' twenty-third wedding anniversary, December 30, 1941, in the family church, St. Patrick's.

Al attended the ceremony, pausing on the church steps for photographs, responding to the good wishes shouted by onlookers, and looking fit and smiling for the cameras as if he had never spent the unpleasant ten-year interlude in courtrooms and prisons. But shortly after those photographs were taken, he was led into a small private room away from the main celebration, and soon after that he was taken back to Palm Island. No one wanted to risk an outburst, and thankfully there was none because the wedding coincided with one of his good periods. He enjoyed his brief participation in the festivities because he liked the vivacious redheaded Boogie (pronounced "Boo-ghee," with a soft g). He was always happy when she was in the house. Al called her by the nickname, but to Sonny and Mae she was always "Casey."

Mae's sister Muriel and her husband, Louis Clark, had relocated to Miami, and they were also living in the house to give Mae the help she desperately needed. Of her four sisters, Muriel was the one closest to Mae, and Al liked her as well, so he was always happy for her company. Through Sonny's wife's family, Gertrude F. Cole came into the Capone household and became a good friend, trusted confidante, and unofficial nurse to Al.

Cole (as she was called) had originally been hired to care for Diana's grandmother, and after her death she stayed on to care for her mother, Ruth Casey, who was a severe alcoholic. Cole liked Sonny, but she still worried about her dear Boogie marrying into such a notorious family. After they married and she saw how happy they were, she became close to the extended Capones, just as she had been to the Caseys. Cole was a large, physically imposing, and headstrong woman, and Al had great fun with her. She claimed to be psychic and used her gift to pick winning racehorses, which Al marveled at despite continuing his losing ways. By now, though, his losses were imaginary: Cole helped him choose horses through racing forms because he could not go to the track, and she pretended to place bets but did not actually do so.

He was losing more than made-up bets on horses, as could be seen in the note he wrote to Cole that has come to be called "Al's Grocery List."

He began by calling himself "Your dear old pal, Al," but his once distinct and flowing handwriting had degenerated into an illegible scrawl, and in run-on sentences he asked Cole to bring him "three decks of pennucle [*sic*] cards" and a bottle of Bayer aspirin. Mae took care of all the household needs, so he must have been in one of his delusional periods for he also asked Cole to "get some Borax or Lux or any kind of soap you can get the more the better." His remarks about how he would pay her were equally convoluted, and he ended by wishing her a "real good happy new year." It was only October.

Sonny and Casey were often at Palm Island in the early years of their marriage, coming to dine with Mae and Al as many as three or four times each week. In quick succession, Casey gave birth to four daughters: Veronica and Diane Patricia (who called themselves "the older kids") and Barbara and Theresa (whom the older two called "the little kids"). Each one would become a lifelong source of great joy to their grandparents, who in turn are well and lovingly remembered by their granddaughters.

The Palm Island house had a long porch, a shaded veranda where Mae liked to serve meals and Al liked to sit and relax. It was large enough for grandchildren to run around the seated adults and play. The two older girls spent the most time with the grandparents, particularly after Casey gave birth to the two younger daughters. She much appreciated how Mae helped by keeping Veronica and Diane for several days at a time so she could concentrate on the two littlest ones.

They especially liked their sleepovers with "Mama Mae," as they called their grandmother. Grandfather Al was "Papa," which in their pronunciation sounded much like "paw paw" (accent on the second syllable). Of him, they remember a loving, happy presence. Al and Mae were the ideal grandparents in the early years of the granddaughters' lives, and in their adult years their childhood memories were reinforced by their grandmother's stories: "Mama Mae loved him dearly, and she painted every picture of him with a very loving brush." This was what they knew of their grandparents, and this is what they treasured.

These domestic details were a source of much comment for the FBI. The bureau never stopped watching the house and filing reports about everything, especially family activities, for the rest of Al's life. All the FBI's spying memos were written as if they were imparting news of world-shaking importance, and the most pompous were usually about the family. In one, the agent who watched the house wrote of the "extremely close bond" between the parents, their son and his wife, and their daughters: "It is known that one of the paramount interests in Al's present life is the welfare of Albert's two children, for whom he is constantly purchasing gifts. This feeling, of course, is equally shared by Mae." The memo went on to say that Boogie was expecting another child and Mae sometimes gave her small gifts of money to supplement Sonny's income. Also, that Al left the house each day, sometimes to "attend to the shopping," but mostly to be driven by Mae to Sonny's home "for frequent visits."

While this kind of surveillance was innocuous enough, the government was still actively pursuing Al for payment of back taxes. In 1941, Abe Teitelbaum wrote to Dr. Phillips asking him to verify that his client's mental condition prevented him from attending a court session in Chicago "in aid of execution of a law money judgment." Perhaps because he had been burned when he swore all those years ago that Al was ill with the flu and unable to travel, Dr. Phillips deflected the decision to Dr. Moore, saying he was the official supervising and attending physician. Dr. Moore wrote the letter, and Teitelbaum did not have to take Al into the courtroom. As before, there were no assets to attach, and the back taxes remained unpaid.

An exchange followed between the two doctors in which Dr. Moore offered to transfer responsibility to Dr. Phillips and stay on in a consulting capacity. Both parties agreed in principle to this arrangement, but it took some time before it was put into effect. Dr. Moore wanted to examine Al, but he also agreed with Dr. Phillips that their patient was not in good enough mental health to travel to Baltimore, so arrangements were made for the family to pay Moore $500 plus expenses to come to Miami for one examination.

From the day Al was released from prison to the day he died, Ralph created numerous crises in his brother's life, usually by bringing up trips to Chicago or Mercer. Al kept insisting that he wanted to return to Chicago and live in Cicero, and Ralph kept pestering the doctors to let him go. Mae was so content with the way Al had adjusted to life in Miami that she now wanted him to stay there. However, Ralph was in full bully mode and was so insistent on moving Al that he was upsetting her and the entire rest of the family.

Dr. Moore convened the entire family and told them that "Mr. Ralph did not show very much horse sense in telling the patient any such thing," but there was little he could do to stop Ralph, for he had appointed himself the head of the family and the person in charge of all medical decisions concerning Al. When Al first became his patient, Dr. Moore told Dr. Phillips that "Mr. Ralph and Mr. John [were] both extremely intelligent and cooperative," but by now he had ample reason to change his mind entirely. Dr. Moore was wise in his subsequent dealings with everyone in the Capone family: he simply cut Ralph out of most loops, telling him only what he wanted him to know. He advised Mae and Dr. Phillips to do the same, and they followed his advice.

But Ralph was seemingly unstoppable when it came to causing controversy. He found ways to question one doctor, then repeat a version of what he had been told (actually, what he *wanted* to hear) to the other, thus creating a round-robin of distrust and suspicion between the two primary physicians over who said what to whom. It exacerbated the tension between them because Dr. Phillips complained about Dr. Moore's inability to decide whether to assume full responsibility for Al or to transfer it to him or to another physician. Dr. Phillips insisted that only one of them could be in charge, even as Ralph huffed and puffed about firing them both.

For his part, Dr. Phillips was generally afraid of the men in the Capone family and had said several times that he would be relieved to pass his notorious patient on to another doctor. To explain, he told Dr. Moore he had been the family doctor since 1928, and he described the men's dynamic as he knew it. Ralph was a "much less pleasant person to deal with than John," but despite his "occasional rudeness" he and John had "a clear understanding of the gravity of Al's illness." Of the two younger brothers, Matthew (Matty) and Albert (whom he called Alfred), he said they were "more or less nonentities who either have nothing to say or are not allowed to say it."

Dr. Phillips was frustrated by Dr. Moore's indecision, and he asked a third physician, Dr. George W. Hall, to intercede and persuade Dr. Moore to make up his mind about what he wanted to do. He finally surrendered authority to Dr. Phillips, and he did so in obvious frustration. Based on the condition Al was in, Dr. Moore said it didn't matter where they made him live; if he wanted to be in Cicero to be in closer touch "with friends and acquaintances," Ralph's job was to ensure that "in doing so he did not get into trouble." For the time being, the question of a permanent move was postponed, and in the spring of 1941 a monthlong fishing trip to Ralph's Wisconsin lodge was proposed instead.

Al's mental age at this stage of his treatment was somewhere around ten, and when he was told he could go fishing, he exhibited the joy of a boy being told he was about to get the treat of his dreams. He could not wait to get started, but they did not actually go until midsummer. They drove through to Chicago, stopping only once at the Prairie Avenue house, where they stayed just long enough to rest, recoup, and prepare for the rest of the journey. There was no opportunity for Al to encounter any of his old cohorts, so his mood remained stable and calm. At Ralph's lodge, he wrote a letter to Dr. Phillips in which his language demonstrated a general, albeit childlike, command of his faculties. He began, "Here is your friend Al Capone, writing you this letter from here," after which he wished the doctor and his family well in convoluted language with words missing in crucial instances. He said that after he left the lodge, he planned to stay in Chicago until mid-October, and "then I'll be back there at our home and have something nice for you which I will bring back home for you Dr please send me 2 bottles of them red pills for bowels movement. Send to this address it's the address I'll be until I leave."

Al spent a good healthy month from mid-August to mid-September in the sun, mostly fishing, eating his catch, playing cards at night, and sleeping long and well. Sonny was there for a time, and long afterward Al could not stop talking about the pleasure he had as they fished together. Ralph was still (to put it loosely) in contact with his Outfit associates, but none were invited to the compound, nor did any show up uninvited. While they were probably curious to see what had become of the once feared and respected "Big Guy," no one dared to go against the ferociously protective Mae, who did not want them there.

On the way home to Palm Island at the end of September, both Dr. Moore and Dr. Phillips commanded them to make a medical detour to Baltimore. Dr. Phillips had been treating Mae privately in Miami for a serious recurrence of syphilis, and Moore agreed with him that she should be admitted to the hospital in Baltimore for a complete checkup because the risk of leaks to the press was too great in Miami. She refused to be treated in either city; she was in one of her Candide moments, when it was the best of all possible worlds and nothing could be wrong with her life. It left Dr. Moore no choice but to write to Ralph and give him firm instructions to make the detour: "Recheck examinations are essential on Mrs. Capone and on Albert [and] as with Al, it will not be necessary for Albert to go into the hospital." Mae stubbornly refused to be hospitalized, so Moore agreed to a compromise: "Mrs. Capone should plan on remaining in bed at the hotel with a nurse and attendants for forty eight hours. This should take the place of a hospital admission since I know that she is opposed to that."

All this time, Mae remained unwilling to accept that Al was never going to be entirely well, holding her hands over her ears and walking away when the doctors tried to talk to her. In the past, both Dr. Moore and Dr. Phillips had resorted to getting information about one family member by asking some of the others to tell what they knew. Usually they asked Mae, but for a time after she refused to stop in Baltimore, they had to ask Ralph and John to report. Ralph told them that Mae was urging Al "to regard himself as a perfectly normal person and to resume his position of ascendancy in the family." Dr. Moore acknowledged this was only hearsay, but he did know that all the while Al was in Alcatraz and Terminal Island, Mae "felt nothing was wrong with him that release from prison would not cure." He was astonished when she told him, insistently, that she had kept the truth of Al's condition from Sonny until after he returned to Miami from Notre Dame.

"If he reads the daily press, he can hardly fail to be aware of it," Dr. Moore wrote, and Dr. Phillips told him he was right: Sonny had known since Al's first crisis in Alcatraz, when he had accompanied his mother on one of her trips. The doctors never mentioned if he was actually able to see his father, only that he went with Mae and they spent most of their time waiting to make their visit by going from one movie to another. Dr. Phillips thought it unnecessary to follow Dr. Moore's request that he persuade Mae to accept that Al was never going to get well and then broach a full and open discussion with Sonny. Neither happened, especially the full and open discussion, for that was not how Italian-American families conveyed information among themselves. Everything had to be cloaked in veiled and oblique exchanges, and with rare exceptions that was how they all discussed Al.

———

When Al was originally discharged from prison, Dr. Moore and Dr. Phillips had agreed to dispense a certain amount of factual information through a single press release, one that would contain general information while still honoring their professional responsibility to shield the patient's medical history from public scrutiny. They thought the announcement of Al's peripatetic travels from Terminal Island to Lewisburg, Baltimore, and then home to Miami would be enough to quell the flood of outrageous stories that were filling the void of official medical news. They were naive to think that after several weeks "the world-wide flurry of publicity" would end and all parties could resume their private lives, but they were medical men who had no idea of the staying power of the press.

They were not left alone, particularly Dr. Moore, who was hounded day and night after Al was released, until he made it clear that Dr. Phillips had taken charge of the case and he was no longer the spokesperson. After the first year or so, reporters bothered the two doctors less, even though the stories continued in a steady stream. American and foreign reporters still camped outside the gates at Palm Island in search of a sudden spontaneous interview; they would continue to hang around there until mid-1946. Generally speaking, the family disregarded them.

The FBI continued to linger near Palm Island as well. Knowing that Ralph was supporting Al, and rightly surmising where the money was coming from, they questioned Mae from time to time to see if she might let something slip. She was always careful with what she said, and they learned nothing from her. Her nerves were strained by being constantly on the alert over what Al might do or say; she lost weight and had trouble eating and sleeping. Al was the center of life for everyone, and everything else was on permanent hold; sadly, there was no way to change it.

———

By 1945, there was a large enough supply of penicillin for Al to be among the first nonmilitary people to receive it. The drug did little to slow the disease because his condition was too advanced for it to have a positive effect. The FBI had its sources in the Dade County Medical Society, and the memos local agents sent to Washington often contained the latest medical information about Al Capone. In the one noting the penicillin treatment, it describes the decline in his ability to speak clearly, his increasing gibberish (which the agent interpreted as "a slight Italian accent"), and his difficulty controlling bodily tremors or walking a straight line. "He has become quite obese," the memo read, and "he is of course shielded from the outside world by Mae."

Al himself might also have been controlling the image he presented to the outside world. His granddaughters think there were times when he deliberately exaggerated his condition whenever he knew he was being observed. Those who were with him in the house knew another man in the last three years of his life, one entirely different from what the public observed. News stories described how he played cards using his own set of unusual rules, often erupting if not allowed to win; in the privacy of family life, he taught Diana's brother, Jim, to play cards in the conventional way, carefully instructing him how to count those still in play and suggesting mental tricks to use for keeping the count in mind. The papers related incidents of irrational outbursts connected with gambling bets; at home, Cole did not place real bets, and she joshed with him about horse races and boxing matches as he made his usual skewed observations about various outcomes of winners and losers. While stories were told of how he lay in bed most of the day muttering to himself, barely able to walk, his greatest delight was to walk his older two granddaughters around the garden, pointing out the names of flowers, butterflies, and birds. The stories of Al in pajamas fishing in his swimming pool originated around this time, but Al never did any such thing, and the pool was never stocked with fish for the catching.

A few visitors to Palm Island made disparaging remarks about Al's mental state, but the validity of such observations is subject to interpretation. Jake Guzik allegedly proclaimed Al "nutty as a fruitcake." Perhaps Guzik made the comment as a way to throw off the FBI, for one of Al's brothers' descendants who was old enough to have clear memories of life in the house said, "I would not put it past any of them to give out misinformation just for the hell of it."

Descendants of Al and his brothers who remember him recall the merriment that went on around the table at family dinners. He loved having everyone there, as he did at holidays. Christmas was especially festive, with the lights, decorations, and large tree. As presents were chaotically unwrapped, Al sat in the middle of it all, beaming at everyone and thoroughly enjoying the good cheer. In recent years, a story has surfaced of how he dressed up in a Santa suit, but "that *never, ever* happened," said the granddaughter who was always present for Christmas. "Papa was *never* dressed like that in his life."

———

Shortly after the start of the penicillin injections in the summer of 1945, there was a second trip to Ralph's lodge. This one was pleasant in its way, although quite different from the first in 1941 now that the decline in his physical health was becoming more noticeable. His mental age had deteriorated to that of a seven-year-old, even though he still had occasional periods when his doctors said he seemed more like ten. He had to be supervised like a small child, for there were times when he did not know how to stay out of harm's way and other times when he had to be instructed about what to do ("eat your peas," "wash your ears"). He still enjoyed fishing, but someone always had to be in the little boat with him. Mostly, he was sweet-tempered, particularly when children were around. There is a family photograph that shows him pushing the one-year-old son of one of his brothers in a baby buggy, and the expression on his face shows his clear delight. The family had managed to spirit Al to Wisconsin quietly without the press getting wind of it, and information about it stayed private until one year later, when a rash of stories appeared that raised genuine concerns about more government scrutiny of the family's affairs.

There were many telephone calls between Miami and Chicago, all made by Ralph but nevertheless originating in Al's house. The FBI agents followed Ralph's movements as closely as they studied Al's, which brought the Wisconsin trip into focus as they monitored the subsequent activity in the Palm Island house. Ralph often received so-called vacationers from Chicago who just happened to be swarthy men in dark suits that hid possible underarm bulges. In late June 1946, a reporter jokingly asked a Palm Island groundskeeper if Al was in the house. The man joked right back, saying he was not there because he was "up north doing business." This incident, paired with the press's knowledge of the government's increased interest in Ralph's activities, led to an explosion of stories that Al really was back in charge of the Outfit and that was why he had gone to Wisconsin in 1945. Reporters had their own sources in medical offices and government agencies, so a great deal of rumor, invention, and speculation was printed as hard-and-fast fact. Al himself added fuel to the fires of these rumors, for he was overheard on his few public outings in Miami boasting that he was in charge and once again directing everything that happened in Chicago. Whether he was doing this deliberately or whether his mental impairment had progressed to such a delusional point, it did not matter; no one checked the facts because anything about him still made good copy.

The media frenzy grew when James M. Ragen, who took over the horse-racing wire services after Moe Annenberg went to jail, was gunned down in Chicago in June 1946. He survived the injuries long enough to accuse Al of being back in charge of the Outfit and of having him killed in order to take over his business. The frenzy that erupted in Miami was so intense that Dr. Phillips, "in the face of recent publicity given Mr. Al Capone, and on behalf of the family," released a formal statement of denial to all the national and local press services shortly after the initial stories appeared. He did so after he received a telegram signed by the three major news agencies, AP, UP, and INS, "urgently recommending" that he hold a press conference.

In a veiled threat of what would happen if he did not, the telegram said it would "save you many possible headaches such stories futurely suggest." Dr. Phillips gave in and spoke to the press, truthfully telling the assemblage that Al was in his Miami home and had been since he went "north" during the summer of 1945; since then, "he has not been taking any active part in business whatsoever."

Dr. Phillips then got himself in serious trouble with the local medical society throughout the last half of 1946, when he continued to provide occasional medical details of the situation in the Palm Island house: "Capone's physical and nervous condition remains essentially the same as when last officially reported. He is still nervous and irritable and is advised against assuming any responsibility or engaging in any work or business activity." In an effort to make the reporters go away—which he should have known would only make them forge relentlessly onward—he also described Mae: "Mrs. Capone has not been well. The physical and nervous strain placed upon her in assuming the responsibility of his case is tremendous. A plea is, therefore, requested that she not be annoyed or molested." The concluding sentences of such statements only guaranteed that she would continue to be stalked and hassled: "I shall cooperate in an effort to obtain any pertinent news desired in order to avoid her being subjected to further strain."

In January 1947, the wrath of the Dade County Medical Society came crashing down on him, with board members demanding an explanation of why he had violated doctor-patient confidentiality. He traced the situation back to his response to the three American news agencies, which he mistakenly thought had agreed to honor his request that all further announcements of Al Capone's health would come through the medical society and not from Dr. Phillips himself. He insisted that all the hysteria that domestic newspapers and radio were dispensing did not come from him but rather was repeated from international news agencies who were not required to follow American rules. In his defense, he wrote, "The balance of the rather colorful stories was constructed from records already within their possession plus information obtained directly from the family." Among themselves, the family thought Ralph was probably responsible, for he often boasted that he knew how to handle reporters.

———

Once the 1946 summer media frenzy died down, the long and lazy days established a pattern that hewed to the earliest predictions of Al's doctors:

nothing much would change, and he would continue to live for many years to come.

During the last months of 1946, his outbursts and tantrums had lessened. He rarely lashed out at anyone who had the misfortune to do something innocent that displeased him. Strangers still agitated him, so callers to the house were strictly controlled. Except for trips to the drugstore or Sonny's house, his days were quiet ones under Mae's devoted attention and the care of whoever else was at home. Daily life revolved around his fluctuating moods, but as long as he was happy, the household was content. In his last year, Al spent many days wearing pajamas and wandering the grounds, often sitting in a chair where he could see the pool and have delusional conversations with people long dead whom he might have killed or had killed. It was another reason to keep strangers away from him. For entertainment, the family supported his childlike pursuits, taking him to an occasional dinner in a quiet restaurant (which he usually thought was one of the snazzy nightclubs he had frequented in Chicago) or to a movie, but only if it was a harmless fluff comedy and several hefty men went along to keep him calm. He had developed a passion for Dentyne gum and licorice Sen-Sen breath fresheners, and it was a great treat when one of the brothers took him to a drugstore where he was allowed to buy them himself.

His doctors were aware that the Capone family's financial reality was straitened now that others had taken control of the Outfit and the Capone brothers no longer had access to unlimited sums of money. The brothers (usually Ralph) scrutinized every bill that was submitted and questioned every item on it, with the doctors trying to manage Al's care while keeping enough distance to avoid acknowledging where the money came from. Ralph was supporting Palm Island, Prairie Avenue, and his Wisconsin businesses. His share of the Outfit's intake barely covered all these expenses, and sometimes it did not. Sonny wanted to help, but he had a wife and three (soon to be four) daughters to support. During the war, his impaired hearing had made him ineligible for the draft, so he took a job in an airplane depot; after it ended, he bought a partnership in a restaurant and was working long hours to make it successful. The help he could offer was limited.

Occasionally, the financial uncertainty would become too much for Mae, and she would indulge in wishful thinking and say that it was only a matter of time until Al got better and could take his place at the head of the Outfit he had led for the six brief years from 1925 to 1931. The entire family vacillated between refusing to accept that Al would never again be the man they once knew and resigning themselves to a new life highly constrained by financial realities.

Al was aware that Ralph had taken charge of his financial affairs, and he seemed both relieved and content that he no longer had to deal with what some family members called "business." In retrospect, they believe he had gone through "a major transformation" and was serenely happy to be free from his past professional life. He reveled in being a family man, a husband, father, and doting grandfather, and in his periods of lucidity he had no regrets about leaving the Outfit behind and seemed relieved to be free from it. The remarks he made during his glory days, of wanting to put that life behind him, were now actually possible, and even with diminished mental capacity he found enjoyment in his every day.

———

Perhaps it was because of the many years of confinement in a tiny jail cell that Al was no longer comfortable in the large bedroom he had always shared with Mae. His sleep was disturbed, thus disturbing hers, until by chance they discovered that he was calmer and more likely to sleep through the night if he was in one of the two single beds in a small bedroom at the back of the house. He slept fairly well there, but Mae did not, so she was still in the master bedroom, where her husband sometimes joined her. He was with her there on the night of January 21, 1947, when she heard the unusual sound of what Dr. Phillips later called "stertorous" (labored) breathing. She knew at once that Al was dying and the endgame had begun.

Chapter 24

THE END

The end, when it came, was sudden and unexpected. In the psychological tests given at the start of 1947, Al had demonstrated a small improvement in mental age to somewhere between twelve and fourteen. Mae continued her loving ministrations, the rest of the household provided distractions that amused him, and the three brothers (Ralph, John, and Albert) were there to do the heavy work of soothing and calming him after an outburst and protecting him whenever he was out in public. No major changes appeared likely.

Thus it came as a shock to Mae Capone when she was awakened around 3:30 in the early morning hours of January 21, 1947, by her husband's respiratory distress. The day just ended had unfolded like any other. Al had recently undergone a routine examination, and the doctors pronounced his health good and stable; he was active and had no physical complaints, and his laboratory test results were unchanged. When Dr. Phillips later pressed Mae for details of Al's day, she told him that only one thing had been different: he was unusually "melancholic and disinclined to talk." Mae reluctantly admitted that Al had tried to make phone calls she described in the vaguest terms as to "some of the relatives" and that he had "some difficulty" with them so he slammed down the phone. She was used to his moods fluctuating from one moment to the next, so she wasn't concerned about his silence and depression, even though he had not exhibited these traits before.

In the last weeks of his life, Al had been free from the panic attacks that drove him to sleep in the small secluded guest room, so he was in his own big bed in the master bedroom next to Mae in the early hours of January 21, when she heard him gasping and snorting. She tried to prod him awake enough to drink some water, but he "strangled" when he tried to swallow it. Within minutes, he went into "a clonic type of convulsion" that came and went every several minutes. The rest of the household was awakened by her shouts to call Dr. Phillips, who arrived at 5:00 a.m.

By the time he arrived, the convulsions were occurring every three to five minutes. Al's "limbs were spastic, his face drawn, pupils dilated, and eyes and jaws were set." After medications were given, his body immediately relaxed, and within the next hour and a half he was awake and aware of his surroundings. Dr. Phillips engaged several nurses for round-the-clock care, and as Al's condition stabilized, everyone began to relax. Two days passed, and by January 23 the seizures had stopped entirely, he was mostly conscious, and the paralysis on his face and in his arms and legs had abated. The only dangerous symptom he still had was the deep chest congestion that indicated bronchial pneumonia.

At first, no one was seriously worried that he would die, but despite oxygen, penicillin, and the newest and best medications to treat his heart failure, he grew steadily worse. The next day, his doctor called in cardiac specialists to confirm for his family, particularly the belligerent Ralph, that Al was being given the best possible treatment. Besides penicillin, he was given digitalis and Coramine, and there was nothing else to do except wait and hope that the medicines would cure the pneumonia and slow the progression of his heart failure.

Al Capone drifted in and out of consciousness several times on January 24, just long enough to recognize those attending him and give hope to his wife and family that he was going to get better. He was cognizant enough for the two older granddaughters to be brought into his room to say good-bye to the Papa they loved. It was one of the last times the two older girls walked up the grand staircase, holding a hand on either side of their mother. Mae took the precaution of having her parish priest, Monsignor Barry Williams, on call, and on January 21 he administered last rites and prayed with the family. It was good she did so, for on January 25 at 7:25 p.m., "with no warning whatsoever, he expired."

On the death certificate, Dr. Phillips described the "primary cause" as "bronchial pneumonia 48 hours contributing apoplexy 4 days." Al Capone's death certificate also stated that he was "retired" from his "usual occupation." With the exception of an occasional mention buried deep in the obituaries of a "paresis, a chronic brain disease causing loss of physical and mental power," there was no mention of the underlying neurosyphilis, either on the death certificate or in any of the accounts that filled the front pages of newspapers around the world.

Over the years, rumors of what killed him have grown, with the one most often cited claiming he did not have syphilis but diabetes, which had been deliberately ignored during his years of imprisonment. His family, reluctant to feed the public's appetite, did not bother to deny or correct this rumor when it emerged. If his syphilitic condition was mentioned, it, too, was couched in rumors that Al had been actively and punitively denied proper treatment in prison, the implication being that it was exactly what such an evil criminal deserved. The family did not deny or confirm that rumor either, but it was at least partially true: treatment had been slow in coming and was sometimes not the most modern or the most effective available at the time.

After her beloved husband died, Mary Josephine Coughlin Capone never went up to the second floor of her Palm Island house again, choosing to sleep in the bedroom of the garage apartment. She covered the living room furniture with sheets, never served a meal in the dining room, and took all her meals on one of the three long porches on the house's exterior (two of which have since been removed). Her granddaughters have fond memories of eating on the porch, for they were often with her. "Mama Mae seemed to need our company," one recalls. "It's as if the house died when he did. Even though she lived to be eighty-nine and was only forty-nine when he died, something in her died when he did."

———

As expected, the death of Alphonse Capone, former Public Enemy No. 1, was worldwide news. It is not known how word initially got out—perhaps the contingent of reporters who routinely camped out at Palm Island saw Dr. Phillips's early morning arrival on the twenty-first—but what had been a small group ballooned to the point of bursting. Their ranks were swelled by "tourists and the curious . . . a virtual parade of rubberneckers [who] strolled by or stood around, chatting, some laughing." Anytime someone came or left the house, reporters and photographers swarmed the visitor's car to shout questions and take pictures, so during Al's last days Ralph decided to give them periodic bulletins that were always upbeat, with the basic theme that his brother did have pneumonia but was going to recover. To try to stop them from writing dire prognostications and to demonstrate how relaxed he was (and by extension, everyone else), he brought them cold drinks. They photographed him holding bottles of beer and quoted him as their source, but they still wrote inflammatory stories about Al Capone's imminent demise. All over the world, almost every story was front-page news, with only a few exceptions like the *Miami Daily News,* where the publisher, James Cox, instructed his editors to treat the death like any other obituary. "I don't want that son of a bitch on my front page," he said.

When Al's death happened, Dr. Phillips thought he was helping Ralph to defuse the situation, but in his typical clumsy fashion he only fueled the fires. He told the press that Al Capone's death was sudden, coming after the several days when he was "stricken with apoplexy," most likely his way of describing a stroke. He unleashed reporters' imaginations when he continued with "his wife, Mae, collapsed and is in very serious condition." Some wrote that she was in such serious distress that news of Al's death had to be withheld from her until she could be stabilized. In reality, Mae was at his bedside and indeed devastated; she did break down in sobs, but she was a strong woman who quickly recovered her equilibrium and shared with Ralph the task of deciding how to bury Al's body with dignity and without creating a media circus.

Meanwhile, reporters were combing newspaper morgues, as their libraries were called, for every possible reference to Al Capone's life in crime. Haste made for poor fact-checking, so from the beginning multiple myths were created. Things that happened in Brooklyn were transposed to Chicago and vice versa. Stories of where and how he acquired his facial scars all vied to be the most sensational as each one gave a different time, place, and assailant. Even the paper of record, the *New York Times,* made egregious errors such as the one it reprinted from an Associated Press story, misstating that he had been born in Naples and brought to New York as a child. From the public to the private, nearly everything written about him was wrong: when family members were listed by name, his brother Erminio (John) was identified as his father, and his son, Albert, was "Alfred." The household was under siege, and the family braced for further onslaughts, particularly when it came to making funeral arrangements.

Teresa and Ralph wanted Al's body to be interred in Chicago, next to the remains of his father in the plot the family owned at Mount Olivet Cemetery. It is not known if Mae agreed to this because it was what she wanted or because she was too exhausted to oppose them, but that was what eventually happened. A local undertaker, the Philbrick Funeral Home in Miami

Beach, took charge of the body, and here again versions of events prolifer-ated. The most prominent and lasting account held that the body had to lie in the small back bedroom for four days because the funeral home's hearse could not get near the house. Some newspapers said the crush of sleek black limousines crowding the causeway as people came to pay respects kept the hearse from getting in; others said the family did not want photographers to take pictures of the dead Al, so an empty hearse came and went until one dark night a few days later when the crush of rubberneckers had lessened. While some papers accepted this fiction, the reality was far simpler: the hearse came the day after his death, January 26. It took Al Capone's body to the Philbrick Funeral Home, where it was prepared for between three hun-dred and four hundred selected guests to see it and pay their last respects.

Al Capone was buried in a dark blue suit, black tie, and white shirt. The funeral directors secretly took photographs of him in his casket without the family's knowledge, and in them he looked remarkably the same as he had in life. Dr. Phillips was given a set and kept them until his death. Phillips wanted the family to consent to an autopsy so his brain could be studied, but the family refused and Al Capone went to his grave with his body intact. The Miami undertakers liaised with a firm in Chicago, and on February 4, a brutally cold day, he was laid to rest beside his father.

It was a relatively modest send-off compared with the mob funeral extravaganzas of the past because the bosses of the Outfit decreed that only those who had been close to Al Capone should attend. There were flowers from others, but they were relatively discreet wreaths and bouquets. On the casket was a gardenia blanket with orchids on top of it from Mae and the family. Reporters still pressed for advantageous positions to photograph any mob figures in attendance, but whether Ralph's glowering looks or the big strong men who stood guard over the invited members deterred them, they did hang back. At the graveside service, the *Tribune* reported that most surviving members of the Outfit had gathered under the tent erected next to the burial plot, "hiding their faces, cursing photographers, and elbow-ing aside all except the few who were allowed under the awning." The old-timers were there: the Fischetti brothers, Jake Guzik, Murray "the Camel" Humphreys, and Sam "Golf Bag" Hunt, along with "half a hundred of the smaller fry from the vast areas which once comprised the vice empire of prohibition." The Capone cousin Charlie Fischetti was heard to say, "I'll kill any son of a bitch who makes any pictures." Matty Capone made the same threat to a reporter who tried to take his mother's.

The entire burial ceremony was a brief one of less than an hour. The Archdiocese of Chicago forbade a requiem Mass but allowed a brief graveside ceremony because Al had repented of his sins in his last years by going to confession and receiving Holy Communion and often went to daily Mass with Mae or his mother at St. Patrick's. It was said that the graveside service was only permitted because of Teresa's piety. Al Capone (as his black granite tombstone read, not his full and legal name, Alphonse) was buried next to his father and brother Salvatore (Frank).

One could say that Capone's death marked the true end of that era: Prohibition had long been repealed (1933), but in a strange congruence Andrew J. Volstead, the Minnesota congressman who gave his name to the act, died on January 20, 1947, just five days before the outlaw who arguably profited most from it.

All the coverage after Capone's death concentrated on cataloging his rise and fall, with emphasis on the latter. Many stories were pompously self-righteous, with a tone of "he got what he deserved." Even the staid *New York Times* hoped that someone would send a wreath to put on his open casket that read, "The wages of sin is death." Much was made of the more than seven hundred killings (a hotly contested figure) that happened during the few brief years of Al Capone's reign and of the fourteen or so witnesses who were murdered so they could not testify at various trials. Of all the carnage that took place in those years, the writers grudgingly admitted that Capone was "officially . . . tied up with only two slayings."

None asked how he could have risen so swiftly, and at such a young age, to the pinnacle of such power that he held an entire city in the palm of his hand and every time he squeezed, he made it do his bidding. In retrospect, the unasked question might have been one of the reasons for the worldwide fascination with his flamboyant life and outsized career.

———

As if to dispel any remaining myths about Capone's enormous wealth and vast empire, Abe Teitelbaum (who did much to arrange the secret transport of his body from Florida to Illinois) felt compelled to address the continuing question of what happened to Al Capone's money. Rumors were brewing of how he had squirreled vast stashes of cash in various places that in his senility he could no longer remember. Several days after his death, Teitelbaum told reporters those stories were not true and that Capone had died penniless, totally dependent on "the generosity of his brothers and other members of his family." He added that the government was still pressing for unpaid back taxes and there were serious problems with trying to find enough money for Mae to hang on to the house. He only implied that the Outfit was still footing the Capone family's bills, but the implication was enough to sustain the rumors of the lost or forgotten bundles of cash.

Besides the public's fascination with the whereabouts of Al Capone's alleged money, there was an equal fascination with the location of his remains. The Capone descendants are not sure which story is true about why the remains of the three Capone men buried in Mount Olivet were removed in 1950 and reinterred in the Mount Carmel Cemetery. The fact that the stones in Mount Olivet of Al's father and brother gave their full names and dates of birth and death while his only read "Al Capone" with no other information on it leads some family members to think the plan to move the three was in place even before Al was first buried. Others think all three were moved because of the many curiosity seekers who trampled the graves and took whatever souvenirs off Al's they could, while at the same time leaving crumpled papers, empty bottles and cans, or worse.

Mount Carmel is on Chicago's far west in the suburb of Hillside. The Capone family plot is an imposingly tall structure of white granite surrounded by shrubbery designed to hide the names of those buried beneath it. Each of the three graves is marked by a simple granite stone, and even though the cemetery staff does not tell the public where the plot is located, Al's stone has twice been vandalized and replaced. On it, there is a simple cross next to his full name and the dates of his short life. Beneath them is the simple phrase "My Jesus Mercy."

The simplicity of Al Capone's tombstone belies his brief, florid, and dramatic life. The legacy he left behind is equally colorful and outsized. One wonders, if he had lived longer in full command of his intellect, what he would have made of it. But he was gone, which meant that so many others who were close to him had to deal with the unfillable void of his absence.

Chapter 25

———

THE LEGACY

The world as Al Capone's family had known it ended abruptly when he died. For so many years, he had been the center of their lives; now, without him to set their course, they were all moving into uncharted territory, unmoored and adrift. During his glory days, his presence was electrifying, and they basked in the warm and affectionate familial encounters. As they shared his beneficence and generosity, the family was secure in the knowledge that whatever they needed, Al would take care of it.

During his years in prison, they clung to each other, ostensibly gathering to support Mae but in reality to comfort and support each other. In Al's post-prison years, the Palm Island house was the family's center, each member holding the illusory hope that he or she could be the catalyst that would bring him back to full health. A mostly unstated but deeply held hope pervaded, that he would fully resume his position in the Outfit and, with it, his grandiose and extravagant life, which by extension they had shared. After his death, everyone had to adjust to the new reality. With him gone, and with the new generations of Capones growing up, moving away from their parents, and not adhering so closely to "the ways of the old country" and Italian-American traditions, reasons for staying close diminished, and the family drifted off into largely separate lives, seeing each other only on ceremonial occasions.

Mae and Sonny remained in Miami, with Mae doggedly clinging to the Palm Island house until 1952, when she could no longer afford it. There were mutterings that she sold it because those who had taken command of the Outfit refused to give her the money such a house required for upkeep.

Also, some said she could no longer depend on Ralph to meet her household expenses because the Outfit had marginalized him as well, to the point where he could barely meet his own needs. Capone descendants affirm there is truth in both rumors, and in the one claiming the Outfit turned Sonny down when he asked for a loan for his restaurant, because, although it did help widows in varying degrees, it did not assist children.

When Mae left Palm Island, she took the things that mattered most to her and sold the rest of the possessions, along with the property, to a real estate developer who was an early practitioner of "flipping." He kept the house as she left it for several years until it was free from the "Capone Curse" and then sold it for a handsome profit. To maximize his profit, he also sold off piecemeal the furniture and objects Mae had lovingly collected, and some of these items still appear from time to time in auction houses and on Internet sites. They usually command high prices from collectors who want "a piece of Al." The house went through several owners until 2014, when a real estate consortium bought it. After serious refurbishing, it is now available for rental functions and film and television shoots.

After Mae sold Palm Island, she moved to Hollywood, Florida, to live with Muriel, the sister to whom she was always closest, and Muriel's husband, Louis Clark. Eventually, she bought her own small house in Hollywood, where she lived modestly until her last years, when she went into a nearby nursing home. She spent the rest of her life in privacy and seclusion, seeing her family and friends, attending daily Mass, and in later years making joyful visits to the homes of her granddaughters in California. She enjoyed good health until her last few years, and she was eighty-nine when she died on April 16, 1986. Mae never held a job, wishing to avoid public display at all costs. She was helped by Sonny and as years passed occasionally by Ralph, who was allegedly able to do so because of his ties with the Outfit, but in reality the money came mostly from his northern Wisconsin businesses.

Teresa died on November 29, 1952, in the Prairie Avenue house where she had lived since she came to Chicago in 1923. The house was sold shortly after she died, but the primary benefactor of the sale varies depending on the source. Some writers cite Mae as Teresa's co-owner who received the profits; others claim that Ralph was the seller and the beneficiary; others say Teresa willed the house to Mafalda, who lived there for a short time before selling it. The truth is that the house had been put in Mae's name as co-owner with Teresa, and after Teresa's death she had every right to sell it and pocket the proceeds. Instead, she allowed Mafalda and her family to keep on living there, because they had been in residence since shortly after their marriage twenty years before. Sometime in the early 1980s, Mafalda made irrational phone calls to Mae, saying the house should be hers and she should be allowed to sell it. The always-gracious Mae gave her the deed and allowed her to keep the proceeds from its sale.

The Prairie Avenue house's several subsequent owners have kept it much the same as it looked when the Capone family lived there. The exterior could serve today as the location for a film set in the 1920s and 1930s, and the interior is largely unchanged as well, with two full-floor apartments and numerous small bedrooms in the basement. In the 1980s, a movement began to have the house listed on the local historic register. It was the first of several such attempts, still ongoing in the twenty-first century, but every petition has been rejected. The century-old house, like Palm Island, is not one that buyers clamored for: as of 2014, when it was again up for sale, the owner cut the price by half and still had difficulty selling it. In early 2016 it was listed again, this time with online photos showing the interior in appalling disrepair. The desire for "a piece of Al" does not seem to include real estate.

Even before Al died, most likely around 1941, Ralph's role in the Outfit was severely diminished, so even though he continued to play the role of his brother's swaggering right-hand man, he no longer had his brother's access to unlimited amounts of money. After Al died, he stayed briefly in the Chicago area, managing a dance hall, controlling cigarette machines that were also a front for slot machines and other gambling materials, and holding "interests" in water companies that sold and maintained filtration systems. Eventually, he drifted north in a permanent move to the Wisconsin area where he and Al once had their lavish retreats, both long since sold. Al's Couderay property was turned into a restaurant known as the Hideout. It closed in 2009 for lack of patronage, went into bank receivership, and has been for sale on and off ever since. Ralph's RaCap retreat has had several owners who remain largely out of the public eye, even though the latest keeps a large portrait of Al hung over the fireplace. Every now and again, something surfaces at auction purportedly from the house. Recently, a collection of twig porch furniture came to market without provenance and with an asking price ten times or more than what the chairs are really worth.

One of the most dramatic turns in Ralph's life in the years leading up to and after Al's death was the return of his long-lost older brother, Jimmy (Vincenzo), who appeared out of the blue around 1940. Throughout his adult life, he appeared to live on the right side of the law as Richard "Two Gun" Hart, a figure straight out of the legendary Old West, a sheriff who captured criminals, demolished bootleg stills, and smashed hijacked booze shipments.

But Jimmy's path was not always straight and narrow; there were several episodes in his mostly law-abiding life where he was prosecuted for theft and sanctioned for cruelty. In recent years, his descendants commissioned a biography in which the author took great pains to incorporate revisionist family myths of his fearless crusades to uphold Prohibition laws. There are, however, enough documented sources to verify that Two Gun's life was sometimes troubled and somewhat sad.

He lived mainly in Homer, Nebraska, ending up there according to family lore for a variety of reasons: First, it was where the train stopped to refuel when he was on his way west to Hollywood to become a star like one of his two heroes, William S. Hart. They said he liked the looks of Homer, so he hopped off and thought he would stay awhile. The other hero his family thinks might have induced him to settle there was General Black Jack Pershing, whose daring leadership Two Gun greatly admired and who he mistakenly believed was a native of the state (he was actually from Missouri). Although there are no records to show that Vincenzo or James Capone, or James or Richard Hart, served in the military, the family bases its contention that he served in Europe during World War I on several photographs and a cache of medals and souvenirs. They say he enlisted as James Richard Hart, the name he had used since leaving Brooklyn; however, there is no record of his service under his real or assumed names because all the records in the St. Louis military repository were destroyed in a massive 1973 fire.

Hart married a local girl, Kathleen Winch, the daughter of a grocer, in a romance that blossomed when he saved her and some others during a flash flood that enveloped the car in which they were riding. They had four sons: Richard Leo; soon followed by William, named for his father's first idol and killed in the Pacific in World War II; Sherman, who went to work for Ralph Capone in northern Wisconsin, where his descendants live today; and Harry, the only one still alive and now in his late eighties, who remained in Nebraska. Harry vacillates between thoroughly enjoying telling one version of his father's myths and legends, only to refute it with another before lapsing into grouchy silence and berating those who ask questions. There are numerous descendants of the three sons who survived to old age who all live in states near to Nebraska: they lead respectable lives in public professions; they all bear the name Hart, and mostly keep their Capone heritage private.

Two Gun Hart never made it to Hollywood, but that did not stop him from playing the role of a colorful cowboy character. He enjoyed wearing full regalia: the ten-gallon hat, the holster with two pistols he was adept at quick-drawing with either or both hands, and hand-tooled cowboy boots that had large hearts emblazoned on them to call attention to his adopted surname. His great-grandsons tell family stories of how, even in the 1920s and 1930s, the mere sight of him in costume was enough to turn hardened criminals into quivering messes. He wore only cowboy clothing when he worked throughout several western states for the Bureau of Indian Affairs. Because he was a gifted linguist who spoke several Native American languages, he was welcomed among the people he supervised. At times, he was a champion of Native Americans' rights and their protector on their reservations, but, at other times, he condoned corruption and was an arbitrary and capricious tormentor and prosecutor, particularly when it came to enforcing Prohibition. Eventually, he and the bureau parted company, and back in Homer he became the town sheriff, where he was accused of theft from hometown stores.

As sheriff, he had passkeys to all the town shops and businesses. Charged with protecting them, he was also accused of using the keys to steal food and household supplies. Granted, this was in the depths of the Depression, when the Hart family was so poor that they lived in a shack by the river where they had to catch fish if they wanted to eat. Also, the so-called theft has to be viewed in light of how the town economy worked, for barter was big in Homer and farmers, tradesmen, and merchants often exchanged goods for services. The biography commissioned by the Hart descendants does not address this murky issue, which was the real reason why a desperate Richard Hart returned to Chicago as Vincenzo "Jimmy" Capone. Quite simply, his family was destitute, and he had nowhere else to go.

Richard became Jimmy when he returned to the Capone family. They were beyond ecstatic to see him, with the exception of Mafalda, who resented him for being on the opposite side of the law from her revered brother, Al, during Prohibition. The Hart family believes that even as an adult she continued to see herself as the family's princess who resented having to share any attention at all, even with a long-lost brother. She was the only one who did not welcome him.

Once Ralph was convinced that Jimmy was truly his brother, he took care of everything. People in Homer could not help but notice the new suits Two Gun wore when he returned from his frequent visits to Chicago or the wads of money that now filled his wallet. Naturally, his true identity as an Italian Catholic shocked his conservative midwestern Protestant wife and sons, but they and the townspeople eventually grew accustomed to the stranger who had lived among them for so many years. Even though there was a certain amount of embarrassment, if not actual shame, among the Hart family, they were so grateful for the security Richard's revelation provided that they accepted their Capone identities when it suited them.

Mae and Al invited Jimmy and Kathleen to Palm Island, but Al could barely comprehend who he was. Jimmy and two of his sons, Sherman and Harry, were in Mercer when Al made his second (and last) visit in 1945, and from time to time they have contributed various versions of their memories to the lore of how Al spent his time there. After he died, Mae continued to send Christmas cards to the Hart family every year.

Ralph was generous in helping the Hart family, but he was not above using his brother when the need arose. The Kefauver Crime Commission called Ralph to testify in 1950 about his ties to organized crime, and in early 1951 the IRS was once again investigating him for tax evasion. The government agents were especially interested in the sale of RaCap and where the money to buy it came from and then went. Although the date of the actual sale was murky and had taken place long before his lost brother resurfaced, Ralph asked Two Gun "Hart-or-Capone" (as the *Chicago Tribune* named him) to swear under oath that he, not Ralph, was the buyer and seller. Two Gun testified before a grand jury for almost five hours and stuck to his story throughout: after thirty-five years of total silence, he said he wanted to see his mother, so he revealed himself to her and his brothers. He claimed that she gave him most of the money to buy the $40,000 property and Ralph put him on the payroll of his business at the time, listed in the commission's proceedings as "a suburban cigarette company," so that he could use his own earnings to pay for the rest. It was an obvious untruth, but no prosecution was begun at that time, although Ralph spent most of his remaining years trying to find enough money to pay off the IRS and keep himself out of jail.

When "Hart-or-Capone" came to Chicago to give testimony, he brought his wife of thirty-three years. Photographs show an elderly couple, with him nearly totally blind, suffering from diabetes, and so obese he could hardly walk. One year later, in October 1952, at the age of sixty, he died of cardiac arrest.

———

While Ralph was dealing with government agencies, a personal tragedy struck when his only son, Ralphie, committed suicide on November 9, 1950. He left a note beside his "whiskey-soaked corpse" saying he could not live without Jean Kerin, who was identified by the *Chicago Tribune* as "a night club singer." Ralphie was thirty-three, and his life had been one of failure and personal disappointment. He was an infant when his mother abandoned him to Teresa, who took him into her Prairie Avenue home. Despite being raised by Mae as a brother to Sonny, Ralphie was aware of the differences between them when he went to grade school and Sonny was privately schooled at home, or when Sonny and Mae went to Palm Island and he had to stay behind.

Both young men began their college careers at Notre Dame, but when Sonny left for Miami, Ralphie transferred to Chicago's DePaul University, from which he graduated. In both, he was known by his birth name, Ralph Capone Jr. From various campus sources, it appears there was no onus attached to the name, for he was popular at both universities. He took part in drama department productions at Notre Dame and was a member of the editorial board and a reporter for the DePaul yearbook. He graduated with a bachelor of science degree, but contrary to claims made by his daughter, he never attended Loyola University School of Law or took the Illinois bar exam.

Shortly after he graduated, he married Elizabeth Marie "Betty" Barsaloux and began to use his middle name, Gabriel, as his surname. Betty gave birth to two children: a son, Dennis, and a daughter, Deirdre Marie, whose birth certificates were both registered under the name of Gabriel. At his daughter's birth on January 25, 1940, Ralph Gabriel was twenty-two, and Betty Gabriel was twenty. On her birth certificate, he gave his occupation as "Service Man, Cigarette Machine Company," and she as housewife.

Ralphie was supporting his family by working for his father's business of slot machines and other gambling paraphernalia as well as cigarettes. From there, he drifted into another job found for him by his father, working for a company that manufactured prefabricated homes for what was alleged to be a mob-related gambling resort. Next, he became the operator of a used-car lot, and by the time of his death he was a hopeless alcoholic who tended bar in one of Chicago's seedier Rush Street dives. His marriage to Betty ended around 1945, and when he died, he was living alone in a shabby apartment where his body was discovered next to a half-empty bottle of whiskey, an empty bottle of cold medicine whose label warned against taking it with liquor, and the note to Jean Kerin (who professed amazement when reporters contacted her, implying that the relationship must have meant more to him than it did to her).

In the five years between his divorce and his death, he seldom saw his children because Betty did not allow them to be anywhere near a member of the Capone family. They were never present at any of Teresa's Sunday lunches, nor were they ever with their grandfather Ralph in Wisconsin. They were kept away from the Capones not out of spite but rather out of Betty's fear that the entire family's ties to the mob and Ralph's particular influence would not be positive for impressionable children. They were so sheltered by their mother that their father died without their knowing him or anyone else in the Capone family.

Ralphie's son, Dennis Gabriel, was the father of sons who in turn fathered sons, most of whom still live in the greater Chicago area. Ralphie's descendants insist that everything good about them is because of Grandmother Betty's careful and loving influence. They remember her with great affection, and one grandson in particular credits her with turning his life around when he was a troubled and troublesome teenager. He remembers "nothing but warmth and love and lots of good family stories."

Ralph and his three surviving brothers stayed in touch, although they were never in each other's company as much as they had been when Al was alive. Mimi (John Martin) drifted between various businesses in Chicago and Miami, and of all the brothers he lived the longest, into his eighties. He stayed closest to Ralph and Mae, so his one son, Michael, has strong memories of family occasions in Prairie Avenue and Palm Island.

Matthew had a fractious marriage that produced one son. He had several run-ins with the law during Al's last years, when he began to live under several different aliases. He suffered from a heart condition for several years before his death in 1967 at the age of fifty-nine. His one child took an altogether different name and retreated into a deeply private life that denied all connections to the Capone heritage.

Albert also used a string of aliases until 1942, when he changed his name to a variant of his mother's maiden name, Rayola. He surfaced in newspapers from time to time: once in 1953, when he bought one of the first gambling stamps after the federal government required professional gamblers to get them; another time when he paid a small fine for wife beating; and again in 1969, when he was identified as "the principal syndicate man" in a new wave of gambling in Chicago's southwest suburbs. He died in June 1980, at the age of seventy-four. He also fathered one son, whose family remains deeply private. Interestingly, the three younger brothers all changed their surnames, and they all did so during Al's lifetime. Ralph was the only brother who kept the Capone name.

Ralph ended his days in Mercer, where he owned a roadhouse called Billy's Hotel and Bar, where he could usually be found sitting on a stool observing the goings-on. Townspeople still speak of him with a combination of awe and fear. To some, "he became Santa Claus, the Easter Bunny and the tooth fairy all rolled into one. Others were less enchanted with the old mobster's presence in their community." He was generous to anyone who needed help, financial or otherwise, and was generally good for a donation to local causes; he routinely bought bicycles for children whose families could not afford them; and he contributed generously to the committees that mounted the annual holiday parades. Still, townspeople who frequented his bar trod carefully when they encountered him.

His several marriages ended in divorce, and newspapers that covered the proceedings usually cited domestic violence as the primary reason. In his last years, he and his third wife, Madeleine (who subsequently took the name Morichetti when she married again), lived in reduced circumstances on a much smaller property in Mercer, in an apartment above a garage. Ralph died in a nursing home at the age of eighty on November 22, 1974. Madeleine, several decades younger, made headlines from her nursing home in 2014 when she allowed a gun to be auctioned that supposedly belonged to Al and was used by him (in matters not specified). The only provenance for the weapon was Madeleine's letter asserting that Ralph told her Al had used it. In 2015, her granddaughters auctioned a collection of jewelry and other objects, some of which they claim belonged to Al.

Mafalda lived to be seventy-six, weakened by dementia before dying in a nursing home in Oscoda, Michigan, on March 25, 1988. Her husband, John, survived her into the twenty-first century. They lived in Chicago for most of their married life, owning and operating a succession of delicatessens and pizza parlors until they retired in the mid-1960s. Mafalda never conquered her swift and violent temper, and over the years there were stories of how she insulted customers and once did not hesitate to throw out (physically) a policeman who she claimed was hassling one of them. Reporters wrote about her in modes that ranged between hilarity and sarcasm, and whenever they teased her by asking if she was related to "Scarface Al," she always replied, "Yes, and I'm proud of it." She grew closer to her husband's family than her own after Al died, and, ironically, she was known among them as Mae Maritote, the name of the sister-in-law she never forgave for taking her beloved brother's attention away from her. She was interred according to her instructions, right next to him in the family plot.

Mafalda's daughter, Dolores Teresa, grew into exemplary womanhood. She attended Aquinas Dominican High School in Chicago, where she was a model student, active in extracurricular activities and an officer in any number of them. When the school presented its annual music festivals, she twirled batons in time to the music. At Purdue University, she majored in science and was secretary of the Pan-Hellenic Council and a member of the queen's court, one of the highest honors for women students. After her graduation, she also retreated into anonymity, eventually marrying, having one child, and settling in a small town in Northern California.

In her private life and under another name, Dolores was doing what most of the children of Al's siblings did: they worked hard to establish their own lives and distance themselves from their fathers and especially their (in)famous uncle. Quite a few have had high-ranking careers under different names, everywhere from Hollywood and the movies, to Florida and the leisure industries, and even in the greater Chicago area in a variety of businesses and professions. They continue to think it best not to draw attention to their Capone heritage.

Most of their children and grandchildren, particularly those of Al's great-grandchildren who are reaching young adulthood, think "how cool" it is to have such a famous ancestor in their backgrounds, while their mothers say quietly, "It's different for them; they never had to endure the disparaging remarks we heard whenever we said our last name." They say their children can think this way because enough time has passed that Al Capone has become a legend so large that they cannot conceive of him as the actual person who was once a very real part of their family.

———

The four daughters of Diana Casey and Sonny Capone were born into a world of love and spent their childhoods basking in it. Diana's family became close to Al and Mae, and to Mae's siblings as well. It was a warm and loving conglomeration, all of whom doted on the four little girls. Al and Mae loved their daughter-in-law and were delighted with her accomplishments, of which they considered the granddaughters the most spectacular.

Diana came from a background entirely different from the Capones, well-off, refined, and upper-middle class. She was a fiery redheaded Irishwoman with a temper to match and tremendous willpower. Her daughters remember her "deep abiding faith and an absolute conviction, a belief in God." A devout Catholic, Diana led her daughters every night in family prayer as they said the rosary together. She was an excellent golfer who played with her merely proficient husband, the patient son who often took his father (who was not even that) to hit balls down the fairway. She and Sonny were also excellent marksmen who competed in various shooting contests, with her often placing higher than him. Reporters delighted in writing about the skills the younger Capones displayed with weapons. They were a popular young couple among their peers in Miami, and life seemed good.

Unfortunately, things did not remain on that even keel. The restaurant did not do well, and eventually it failed. Contrary to popular legend, Sonny never worked as a cook or a maître d', and Mae was never a cashier or hostess there. Sonny tried hard to save the restaurant, reportedly going so far as to ask members of the Outfit for a loan, which they declined to give. Although the Outfit was known for not giving financial support to the children of members, the reason generally cited in the crucial instance of Al's son is that Sonny was involved in a rather public affair and the Outfit frowned on visibly dishonoring wives. The marriage frayed when he became involved in what is loosely called the Miami Beach scene: "night life, heavy drinking, and deep sea fishing with wealthy sportsmen from the north east." He himself was a teetotaler who managed to be part of the scene while not participating in most of it, but when Diana learned of his affair, she "literally had a fit." She confronted him but did not immediately file for divorce.

Because she needed to get away and think, she took her children to the San Francisco Bay Area in 1961 to stay with Winnie, her younger brother Danny's wife, who lived in Palo Alto. She did not look at it as a permanent move; she only closed up the Miami house rather than listing it for sale. In retrospect, her daughters believe that she hoped Sonny would come after her so they could resume the marriage. He did not, and when she returned for her older brother's wedding, she found there were too many unsettling aspects of life in Florida to deal with and decided to make the move to California permanent.

Diana never filed for divorce, but Sonny did, in 1964, when he went to California to tell his daughters that he was planning to marry for the second time. He did not see Diana on that trip, because relations between them were so strained, but he wanted his daughters to hear directly from him that he was dropping the name Capone and would henceforth be known by his middle name, Francis. "There will never be another Mrs. Capone," he told them.

After that, things between Sonny and Diana were "complicated, complex." When the divorce was finalized, he gave her the proceeds from the sale of the house and all its contents, and he did the best he could to support her and their daughters. Diana made a good life for herself in the Bay Area. She worked because she had to, first doing office work in the electrical and insurance fields before finding her true calling, real estate. As soon as her daughters graduated from high school, they did what they could to contribute to the family. Born on Thanksgiving Day 1919, Diana was about to turn seventy in 1989, when her birthday would once again fall on the holiday, and she was looking forward to the lavish birthday celebration dinner her daughters were planning for it. She had been ill throughout most of the year, diagnosed six months earlier with the blood disorder acute myeloblastic dysplasia, a type of leukemia, and she had been debilitated by the treatment. By Thanksgiving week, she was hospitalized, and she died on Thanksgiving Day, the holiday on which she was born. Sonny and her daughters surrounded her, while their husbands and his third wife were in the lounge area waiting to support them.

The four daughters grew up, married, divorced, remarried, had children of their own, and became stepparents to their spouses' children. They attended college and took graduate degrees, had professions in which they excelled and careers they enjoyed. All their lives they have been close, and they all settled in Northern California near each other. When they gather to celebrate holidays, just under two dozen are the direct descendants of Mae and Al Capone and the three surviving granddaughters who bore the Capone name at birth.

When they describe themselves, they remember the oldest, Veronica (Ronnie), as the one who most resembled the Capone family; Diane is the most like Mae and her family, the Irish Coughlins; Barbara takes after the fiery, strong-willed Caseys; and Theresa (Terri) is the composite of them all.

Ronnie died on November 17, 2007, also of leukemia, her loss still mourned by her sisters to this day. The three who survive remember growing up as Capones and during their formative years feeling "saddled with a certain amount of responsibility to the name. There's no doubt that we were all given rose-colored glasses to wear when we were born into the family—everyone does that to a degree no matter who their family. But I suppose ours were rosier than others."

In the last years of Mae's life, Ronnie and Diane told her of their childhood memories and pressed her to tell them stories about their heritage, which they in turn passed on to their two younger sisters, Barbara, who was an infant, and Terri, not yet born in the last years of their grandfather's life. Mae's stories all concentrated on the good qualities of the husband she adored, so Diane says she and her sisters must now "work through all of this. I have to admit, Mama Mae's stories told us the reality that she wanted them to be."

Mae stayed on in Hollywood, Florida, but she made frequent visits to be with Sonny and the granddaughters until she became incapacitated by extreme old age. She almost always stayed in Diane's home, because during the early years of Mae's visits she was mostly at home caring for her three young sons. Mae might have been reserved and retiring in public, but with friends and family she was vivacious and funny, outgoing, full of life, and a nonstop talker. Diane remembers sending her children off to school in the morning and settling at the kitchen table to have coffee with her, only to look up to see the boys returning at the end of the school day while she and Mae were still in their nightclothes and chattering away.

Throughout the years after Al's death, when offers came for Mae to sell the story of her marriage for large sums of money (which she certainly could have used), she always refused, preferring to cherish her memories in private. Only once did she relinquish her privacy, when she and Sonny waged a losing battle to keep his high school classmate Desi Arnaz Sr. from filming The Untouchables, the 1987 movie that wrongly glorified Eliot Ness's role in bringing down Al Capone. It was the occasion of Mae's last argument with Ralph, who refused to join her in the lawsuit, where she asked for $1 million in damages. Mafalda, ever ready to defend or support her brother, was the only one of Al's siblings who participated.

In 1985, Mae had a stroke and was diagnosed with the early signs of Alzheimer's disease. She was taken to live in a nursing home in Hollywood, Florida, and from then on was in a wheelchair until she became bedridden.

She drifted into a coma in her last days, but when her granddaughters came, she had periods of lucidity. "She had a good life and she loved her life," her granddaughters recalled. She was cremated, and they held a memorial Mass for her in California. Her ashes rest privately. Shortly after Mae died, Sonny moved to be near his daughters. He was completely distraught at the time: within a two-month period, he had lost his mother and his second wife, who died of lung cancer, and also his beloved dog. All those tragedies might have contributed to an otherwise unexplainable incident in his local Miami grocery store. Having done his shopping, he picked up several small objects and walked out of the store without paying for them. Police told reporters that when asked to explain, Sonny told them "everyone has a little larceny in him." The grocery store's manager described him as a "real good customer" and said he hoped Sonny would shop there again. His daughters helped him to move near them, where he lived the rest of his life and died in Cool, California, on July 8, 2004, survived by his third wife. He, too, was cremated, and his ashes rest privately.

To the end of his life, he told his daughters that he deeply regretted the affair that had split up their family, but by then there was no going back. For a number of years after the divorce, they thought "he kind of bailed on his family," but they explain this attitude by saying it was a pivotal time in their lives, when they were in their teen years and concentrating on their new surroundings. In retrospect, they think he made many more overtures than they responded to, and they were probably just as responsible for the "ups and downs" in the relationship as he was. However, it was still a striking contrast to the years when he had been "absolutely the most loving father, when he thought all his girls were just perfect." They still hold fast to memories of how he boosted and bolstered them when they were all a united family.

After Sonny moved to be near them in Northern California, they all became close again and to this day, they are close to his widow, America. The daughters have many stories from their father about how he adored his father and how his father doted on him. "Even as an old man, he [Sonny] never got over the loss. We'd be sitting at the dinner table talking, and all of a sudden he'd start to cry over his dad." They realized that he had raised them with the same love his father had always given him. When they consider this aspect of their grandfather, they wonder "how the same person could be so admirable and still be guilty of the terrible things he did." They call it the conundrum they are still trying to resolve.

While most of the Capone descendants prefer to live privately, many have decided that they must now break their silence long enough to tell what they call "the real truth" about their family.

The catalyst for the group decision to "go public" came about when one descendant broke the family's vow of silence. Ralph's granddaughter, Deirdre Marie Gabriel O'Donnell Griswold, who now calls herself Capone, published a memoir in 2010 that can only be described as sheer fantasy. In it, she declared, "I am the last person of Al Capone's family who was born with the name Capone. I am the last of the living Capones." Obviously, it is a specious claim, as are many others she made in her book concerning her closeness to her famous uncle. No such relationship existed.

"It has become her truth," said one of Al's three surviving granddaughters as she explained why so many other Capones have decided to break their lifelong silence: she laughingly gave the "credit" for the family's willingness to reveal the Al Capone they knew to her first cousin's fabrications.

Others have a more dynamic interest in attaching themselves to the name of Al Capone, like the current generation of the Rockford descendants of Raphael and Clotilde Capone, who just wanted to know whether, as family legend had it, one of their fathers was Al Capone's illegitimate son. Through the research for this book, they were introduced to members of two branches of Al's family: the grandsons of Sherman Hart in Wisconsin, and Dennis Gabriel's family in Chicago. Both agreed to have DNA testing with the Rockford Capones, and it proved that they were not Al's progeny. At best, they may be distant cousins.

When the Rockford family discusses "the Oath" they swore so solemnly after the death of their patriarch, their positions diverge. Many still insist that despite the DNA evidence what their elders told them about their heritage is still valid: "They told us, 'You don't know how close you are' [to Al], and then they said for our own protection they couldn't tell us which one was his son. I just have to believe they didn't lie to us." An equally large number thinks otherwise: when one who speaks for this faction refers to his grandfather, he says, "If we ever asked about Al, he would get so mad, he would tell us, 'You don't fuck around with those people.' He would scare the shit out of us if we made him mad. And when he got mad, you steered clear of him." To this young man, his task is to convince his family to accept that "the Oath" is nothing more than its principal myth. With the DNA test results for both the maternal and the paternal lines, it now seems certain that whatever the reason for the deep bond forged between Al and Raphael Capone, it was not one of paternity.

Another major reason why people connect themselves to Al Capone involves a knotty question: Where does wanting reflected glory end, and where does wanting to cash in begin? In 2009, a thirty-seven-year-old man named Christopher Knight declared that he was the legitimate grandson of Al Capone and that his deceased father, William Knight, was Al's legitimate second son. He says his father's parentage is a "touchy subject," and he bases his contention on two points: his father's say-so and a 1927 newspaper article that said after Al had been summarily kicked out of Los Angeles, he returned home to his "two" children. Calling Mae by her birth name, Knight claimed that "Mary and Al" were his father's parents. When asked why they would have put him out for adoption, to be raised on a farm "outside Chicago," he said it was "because Sonny was so much older and already known. By the time my dad was born, Al was on his way to prison and they had to hide him." Knight received extensive publicity after he made his claim. Newspapers took him seriously and did haphazard investigations. Even so, there were so many inconsistencies in the stories he told about his parentage that he hired a genealogist to sort them out. Her conclusions were as vague as those he gave in the book he self-published in 2008, *Son of Scarface: A Memoir by the Grandson of Al Capone*.

That book appeared shortly after he went to court to have his name legally changed to Chris Knight Capone. With all the publicity generated by both his memoir and his name change, he contacted several of Sonny's descendants plus those of Al's siblings to ask them to submit to DNA testing. In one of the versions he offered about their responses, Knight said they refused: "I always wanted paper proof but they wouldn't give me any." In another version, he claimed, "I did test with some Capones who are not Italian, but I am." And in yet another version, he claimed that although he has the legal right to call himself Knight Capone, he no longer does because one member of the family told him, "If the mob and Al were still in business, you would be at the bottom of the river. You deserve what you're gonna get." He claims this last encounter happened just after he had a lawyer file a legal motion in 2009 asking the Archdiocese of Chicago to agree to exhume Al's body so that DNA samples might be obtained. His lawyer said Knight wanted "to proceed through less invasive means but wants to keep disinterment as a possible option should those fail." The archdiocese denied his request, and Knight said he decided to end the matter there. In actuality, his quest for proof of his identity ended far less dramatically: when two children of Al's brothers offered to take a DNA test with him, "he just disappeared into the woodwork."

Not surprisingly, Chris Knight ran afoul of Deirdre Marie Gabriel O'Donnell Griswold, who has called herself Capone since the 2010 publication of her book, *Uncle Al Capone*. "He has absolutely no proof of anything he says," said Griswold. "My proof is my blood," Knight retorted. David Kesmodel, who wrote about the sudden emergence of people who claim relationships to Al for the *Wall Street Journal* in 2010, described the Capone family as long having desired to "keep a low profile, forgoing the opportunity to cash in on their infamous relative's name. Most live modest, middle-class lives. No living relative has been linked to organized crime." This was the situation, he continued, until "some Capones—authentic or not, [began] bickering. And money may be at stake." Kesmodel reported on Griswold's efforts to set up a company to license rights to Al Capone's name and his likeness in California, where state laws are favorable toward "asserting publicity rights for dead celebrities." He quotes Knight as saying he wants them, too: "I want to get what my family deserves."

After that fiasco, when Knight stopped using the Capone name and retired from the scene, and with Griswold continuing her campaign of self-promotion, there was a flash of publicity announcing a reality television series on the ReelzChannel called *The Capones*. The premise of the show was to follow a family named Capone who own a pizza parlor in Lombard, Illinois, and who made the claim that they were related to Al through a "great-great-grandfather who was Al's uncle" (via several unspecified "greats" on his family tree). Supposedly, one of the Lombard Capones had an aunt (a non-Capone) several generations earlier who married into this branch, but neither the family nor the sponsors of the series offered any proof of relationship to Al Capone on either side.

Knight jumped into the fray, asserting that the program should "sleep with the fishes," and demanded that its creators hire a genealogist to prove the relationship. Griswold threatened vague legal action, claiming that she controlled the rights to the use of Al's name and that she had hired lawyers to enforce "Illinois's 'deceptive practices' law." When asked to explain this, she declined to answer. Both were ignored by the sponsors, and the program went on, a mess of vulgarity and stupidity. When it was canceled for low ratings and lack of viewers, the rented mega-mansion in which it was filmed was returned to its owners, and Dominic Capone, the "star," went back to his real job as a parking enforcement officer in Cicero.

Meanwhile, throughout all these shenanigans, claims, and counterclaims, the descendants of Al and Mae stay silent, content to get on with their satisfying private lives. Nevertheless, things happen almost daily to keep their famous ancestor omnipresent. Vince Gilligan, who created the television series *Breaking Bad* and who gives credit to Al Capone for inspiring much of it, made the comment in a television documentary that "kids who can't name the last three presidents can tell you who Al Capone was." One of Al's granddaughters can offer proof of this. One of her friends, a docent at a Bay Area museum, was taking a group of fourth graders on a tour and was astonished when one of them asked, "Don't you have some more exciting stuff than this, like—about Al Capone?" The child's request supports the biographer Schoenberg's contention that "given today's educational trends and the debate over what should be included in the canon, the day may come when there is only one name that writers and speakers dare allude to with perfect confidence that their entire audience will get the point. Al Capone may become America's last allusion."

The question remains: When did he graduate from person to myth, and from myth to legend? The legends may not be true, but they are definitely real to the world at large. His granddaughters agree that he is a riddle to be solved but wonder whether it is possible. Gilligan wonders how Al Capone could have become the major cultural figure that he is today. He suggests the phenomenon is something akin to the 1962 film *The Man Who Shot Liberty Valance*, "where the legend outran the man." Perhaps a line from the film itself describes the phenomenon best: "When the legend becomes fact, print the legend."

Chapter 26

―――

THE LEGEND

Al Capone's brief life was florid and dramatic, but his afterlife is even more colorful and outsized. His reign as the king of crime lasted for six short years, and even after he was stripped of power, the public still could not get enough of him. In the almost seven decades since he died, the frenzy of publicity he inspired during his lifetime has increased exponentially and shows no sign of slowing down. He died in 1947, and in 2016 the daily Google alert still records at least half a dozen new hits per day.

New books and films appear almost every year, including novels, biopics, documentaries, and even mockumentaries, such as the recent one about an annual festival dedicated to his memory in Árborg, Iceland. There are memoirs purporting to tell the "real truth," along with biographies for specific audiences that include young adults and very young children, so even eight-year-olds can tell you how "he killed bad guys and that was okay because it let him feed poor people." The television series *Boardwalk Empire* has made him, surprisingly, not an antihero but a genuine hero to avid younger viewers.

His name appears on all sorts of lists, including one from the *Smithsonian* magazine that in 2014 named him one of the hundred most influential Americans in the entire history of the country. Websites are devoted to him, and the Mob Museum in Las Vegas gets its best crowds when exhibits feature him. The Madame Tussauds wax museum in San Francisco has captured him after his disease took over, in a life-sized statue that sits in his Alcatraz cell playing the mandolin. "Gangsterologists," as those who are fascinated by criminals have been dubbed, and professors who proclaim themselves

"Capone scholars" debate every aspect of his life and (if it can be called so) his work. Law schools study his court case, bar associations reenact it, and academic institutions from the most august to the most local offer courses: the Harvard Business School examines the Chicago Outfit as a case study, and the Lifelong Learning Institute at Kankakee Community College in Illinois holds a course titled simply "Al Capone." When first given, it was so popular that it was oversubscribed and two more sessions had to be scheduled to accommodate the demand.

Restaurants claim he ate there, cocktails and sandwiches are named for him, hotels claim that he slept there, and there is even the laughable contention that he often sneaked off anonymously to play golf on Scottish courses. One reporter said it best: "If Capone frequented even a tenth of the places that he's said to have, the notorious mobster hardly would have had time to build his Chicago crime empire, let alone run the thing."

From musical groups to young adult novels, just his name in the title can command far more interest than most of them merit. Cats and dogs on Internet postings, especially the countless pit bulls who bear his name, are sure to be quickly adopted. His name alone can secure a good table, as a young woman in San Francisco who bears the same surname finds every time she tries to reserve one in a posh restaurant. His face is on postage stamps in Tajikistan (where they even made one of Mae, hiding her face behind a fur coat) and Kyrgyzstan (where his image is centrally placed among other notorious gangsters' mug shots). In Romania, websites and meet-up groups proliferate, while writers and journalists seek contact with Americans who write about Capone's life in crime. In Bulgaria, gangs claim they study the Outfit to learn how to conduct their business. In England in the 1960s, the Kray brothers, notorious for murder and extortion, modeled themselves after that "upper class criminal, Al Capone." In Iceland, the entire town of Árborg is allegedly obsessed with its weeklong Al Capone Festival, where all the residents are devoted to "the scourge of Chicago." When the Mexican drug lord El Chapo escaped from prison, the comparison to Al Capone was immediate, and El Chapo was quickly dubbed "the new Public Enemy No. 1."

Reporters don't stretch their intellects when writing stories about tax-dodging hedge fund managers: they just make the immediate comparison to Capone, and the public gets the message. "Amazing," mused a criminal defense lawyer in Chicago, "how often his name is used to spice up a story." Without any reference to who he is, was, or might have been, Al Capone's name is the one to grasp when making comparisons with everything from the 2016 presidential election, to the finale of the immensely popular television series *Downton Abbey*. A reader wrote a letter to the Midland, Michigan, *Daily News* comparing Donald J. Trump to Al Capone, who also "understood the 'average' person and used them to his advantage." In an overwrought contribution to the *Jewish Journal*, a writer who denounces Trump supports his argument with Freud, continues with a reference to Erik Erikson, and touches on Hitler and Himmler before attesting that Al Capone "was America's contemporaneous lawless contribution to this tradition." On the other side, bloggers wonder whether "Hillary's emails [are] the same deal as Al Capone's tax records." And the *New York Times*, summing up the six seasons of the PBS serial, wrote that the hapless servant couple, Bates and Anna, who were each charged with separate murders, "have spent more combined time in jail than Al Capone."

People from Chicago who travel abroad usually have a tale or two to tell of the response they get when asked where they come from: the questioner's recognition comes with the shout "Al Capone!" followed by pretending to fire a tommy gun and mimicking the sound it makes. Most Chicagoans just sigh and say they have gotten used to it, but the topic led to an extensive conversation in 2015 on the Internet site Reddit. "I get sick and tired of tourists wearing Al Capone t-shirts," said the originator of the exchange. One of the more thoughtful replies said the fascination continues because "idolizing Capone just gets easier as time goes on and we get more and more disconnected from what he actually did."

It is precisely this disconnect that has contributed to the unending questions of what there was about this man to turn him into an international cultural icon and why the mere mention of his name sets up a chain of immediate associations. Writers have long pondered the questions of why this particular man became the über-celebrity among so many other colorful gangsters and mobsters and why the legends that grew up around both halves of his life—the violent and the benevolent—became so shrouded in myth. How did he, of all the other outsized criminal characters of his era, become an internationally recognized cultural reference, while their names often go unrecognized today?

When he was at the height of his criminal career in 1931, Katharine Fullerton Gerould wrote a profile in which she concluded that "it is not because Capone is different that he takes the imagination; it is because he is so gorgeously and typically American." Speaking in a 2014 television documentary, Vince Gilligan carried the analogy much further, saying he is not only a "major cultural figure" but a "truly Shakespearean" one. One of Capone's numerous biographers, Robert Schoenberg, took another tack in a 2015 post on his website, when he used Capone to make the distinction between a "celebrity" and an "allusion." He describes celebrities as those whose names appear in headlines or commentaries only when the story is directly about them, whereas a person becomes an allusion when his name is so instantly recognizable that the use of it conveys meaning without any need for further explanation.

His family seeks answers, too, beginning with a vested interest in stripping away the myths that cling in order to find the actual person whose life has so dominated theirs. After trying to ignore or evade their famous ancestor and fade into obscurity, going their separate ways for so many decades, they have been led by the public's unending fascination to make their first hesitant steps toward examining their heritage and trying to connect with one another. As the older ones share their memories and impressions of their grandfathers and uncles, sorting through the family stories that have been handed down, the younger ones who did not know Al Capone find themselves sorting through the reminiscences of others in search of their own reality.

During the many years they tried to hide their connections to Al Capone and to each other, a curious thing happened: they were so determined to stay hidden that many did not know some of the others existed. Their search for truth has resulted in meeting relatives they did not know they had and forming solid friendships among themselves. However, instead of these meetings letting them refine or refute the many myths about Al Capone, when they put all their conversations together and try to create a whole person, they find themselves shaking their heads in amazement at the many new parts of the puzzle that just won't fit.

One of their first questions to each other was where, from the public image to their personal memories to the stories that were handed down, is the man they knew: the one who loved his wife and son; phoned his mother every day; loved to sing, play, and write music; was happiest when fishing, enjoyed swimming and golf, and took pride in being able to support finan-cially too many people for an accurate account to be made? They are proud of the good things they know about his public life, about how he fed the hungry, gave lavish amounts to charity, was alleged to be responsible for the dates on milk bottles, and always made sure to provide for the widows and orphans of his men. When describing him, one member of the extended family repeatedly intones several sentences intended to be both a solemn pronouncement and a vindication: "Was he a mobster? Yes. Was he a monster? No." Actually, he was both, and most of the Capone family admits what he did and accepts that he was. Al Capone was a gangster and racketeer whose illegal and immoral activities ran from selling booze to running gambling places, selling women's bodies, and selling drugs. Like the rest of his cohorts, he had no reservations about doing all these things if he thought they would make money.

"I don't see much goodness in the heart of Al Capone," said the psychotherapist Charles Strozier in a 2014 documentary. He shares the view of many who see Al Capone's public acts of beneficence and charity as the behavior of a brutal thug who needed to perform good deeds in order to convince himself that he was a good man. "Mild disassociation served his purposes," Strozier added. "He attains internal self-cohesion when he persuades himself that he only does bad to enable himself to do good." Dale Carnegie, he who wrote of winning friends and influencing people, said much the same thing in 1936 when he compared Capone to the criminals in Sing Sing prison: "Few . . . regard themselves as bad men. They are just as human as you and I. So they rationalize, they explain. They can tell you why they had to crack a safe or be quick on the trigger finger. Most of them attempt a form of reasoning, fallacious or logical, to justify their anti-social acts even to themselves, consequently stoutly maintaining that they should never have been imprisoned at all."

Al's descendants do not accept such a premise; to them, it implies a falsity of character they do not believe he possessed. They refuse to accept that he presented himself as a loving family man who cared for the public's well-being in order to maintain the fiction that murder and mayhem were necessary evils he had to perform so that he could spend the rest of his life living as the good man he was at heart. Most of them insist that such behavior was not a self-deceiving ruse and that he never wanted to be on the wrong side of the law. They insist that the mantle of criminal greatness was thrust upon his unwilling shoulders.

The family believes that he might have become the lifelong businessman he always claimed to be had it not been for his father's death and the need for him to become the main breadwinner for his extended family. If he was indeed working as a bookkeeper in his only honest job, and if his father had lived, they think there is every possibility that he might have risen through the ranks of accounting and financial affairs to the top of the legitimate corporate world. But after he was called back to Brooklyn and drawn into criminal circles, he stepped willingly into the unknown. When he was sent to Chicago, by his own admission he went because no other option was available.

To reinforce the view that he was a reluctant killer, they point to the many times he told reporters that he wanted to get out of the Outfit and retire to a quiet private life. They argue that for Italian-Americans of Al's generation the options for legitimate advancement were few. They are correct in one sense but not in another, larger one: not all Italian-Americans found the life of crime the only route to success.

Katharine Gerould was correct to identify Al as "gorgeously and typically American," because his rise to fame paralleled a most unusual moment in American history, one that could well fit the same description: Prohibition. It was a curious early form of political correctness that was imposed when a small number of fanatics convinced the national government that laws mandating universal behavior could be enforced. It was a weirdly schizophrenic time, when magazines like the fervently dry *Ladies' Home Journal* could quote the former president and later chief justice of the Supreme Court William Howard Taft (a wet who became rabidly dry once the law was passed), as he observed with regret that the strongest tendency of human nature was "the desire to lay down rules of conduct for other people."

Unlike others who had wealth and social station and used them surreptitiously to defy the unpopular law they were often charged with enforcing, Al Capone ignored it and told the truth about why he did so. Capone openly admitted that he sold illegal alcohol to the "best people" as "a public service [to] supply a demand that was pretty popular." For most Americans in the Roaring Twenties, he was an American hero because he did publicly what most of them had to do in hiding: he defied the law and got away with it.

It is an accepted truism that cultural norms underwent seismic changes at the end of World War I. Women got the vote, shortened their skirts, and went to work; jaded and disillusioned men refused to join the traditional workforce and took off for foreign climes to create the great American novel or revolutionize the art world, and their opting out of the traditional "American way" gave rise to the glamorous myths that have since surrounded European expatriates. The rich, who always got richer, suddenly found they had lots of company as the economy soared and the middle classes found themselves with lots of disposable income. The time was right for thumbing one's nose at what constituted acceptable social conduct, and with a flamboyant bootlegger leading the way, many others were as eager to break all the smaller prohibitions and constrictions on their private lives as they were to disobey the large one forced upon them by the Eighteenth Amendment.

Al Capone led them on, and the public loved him, even though he was largely responsible for washing the streets of Chicago in blood. For most Americans who did not experience such sights directly, newspaper photographs and movies that portrayed sprawled and bloody dead gangsters and bullet-ridden cars were only entertainment and far removed from real life. Evil was appealing, even enticing, as long as it did not touch them directly. It had become entertainment, disconnecting the public even more from the violence of the gang wars and Al Capone's part in them.

To a lesser degree to be sure, blood was flowing all over the country. Colorful figures were robbing banks, kidnapping, and going on shooting rampages that were so frequent and frighteningly antisocial that they made the violence dictated behind the scenes by Capone seem almost dignified and "upper class," as the British criminal Kray twins described him. He was the 1920s version of the Teflon man; nothing stuck to him. He waved his hand and brutal killings and hideous butchery happened while he stayed cannily removed, far enough away to make sure there was never solid proof that he actually participated in any of the heinous acts.

James O'Donnell Bennett, one of the first journalists who tried to explain the phenomenon that Al Capone has become, described how "with no conscious effort he emanated menace while saying please." He was the criminal version of a foppish dandy in his luridly colored but exquisitely tailored suits, with the handkerchief neatly folded in his breast pocket and ready to be whipped out to cover the disfiguring facial scars whenever he needed to smile for the cameras. Everyone knew to beware of that smile, for it could turn sinister in a moment.

He was, in short, the perfect human paradox and the counterpoint to the political paradox that was Prohibition. He was so wildly charming, so blatantly outsized in everything he did, and so fully in the public eye that it was hard to believe such a good fellow and one so highly entertaining, he of the pithy quotation and catchy phrase, could be all that bad. And as for Prohibition, it might have been the law of the land, but nobody took it seriously, so why not have that drink. That was how Al Capone filled the public's imagination, and that was how he was regarded—at least until the market crashed.

Once that happened, public opinion reflected the changed new world of the Great Depression. Although Capone was still a figure of envy because he had the wherewithal to dress and eat well, wear diamond jewelry, drive in chauffeured limousines, and live in a spectacular mansion, he was no longer a figure of unquestioned approval. People were hungry, out of work, and losing their homes. Fun time was over, and the repeal of Prohibition reflected the new sobriety of the nation. The working class no longer had the jobs that gave them the income to pay for drinking and gambling, and admiration for Al had given way to deep resentment for how he lived the high life.

Public opinion, easily diverted and fickle at best, turned against him, not entirely, but just enough for people to feel self-righteous satisfaction to say in one breath that he got what was coming to him and in the next that he got that comeuppance in a shaky trial on trumped-up charges. Even as they passed righteous judgment, they remained alert for every scrap of information about his life in prison, and as tales of his mental decline seeped out, they were ghoulishly avid for news, the more bizarre the better.

By the time he died in 1947, the United States had been through a second world war, Prohibition was a distant memory, and Al Capone had become the nation's antihero. The violence of his era had become watered down, glossed over, the stuff of fiction and film rather than the blood and gore of actual torture and trauma. The generation who had been through the war was more interested in the existential rather than the actual hero—or antihero. In contemporary times, the current generation puts its thoughts about Al Capone into a simpler, more direct context: Where does the existential hero of myth and legend end and the antihero of his historical time begin? Perhaps the legacy of Al Capone is that he will become permanently slotted into the category of "mysteries that aren't going to be solved, that are too sacred to be solved." This is how most of Al Capone's descendants would like to leave the discussion, even as they admit that it will never happen. When handsome film idols take on the roles of the dastardly menacing and truly evil criminals of the 1920s and 1930s, the aura of allure they project is so far removed from the reality of what actually happened that nothing remains but myth and legend. It is interesting to make comparisons between these movies and the 2015 film *Black Mass* about Whitey Bulger and starring the chameleon actor Johnny Depp. The question has been raised whether Depp's protean performance will begin the process of elevating Bulger to the status of Al Capone, but as quickly as it is asked, it is dismissed, for Bulger never had the international name recognition that Capone had and still has. So the ultimate question remains: Why is Al Capone the lodestone for so many different kinds of discussions, and where does he fit into the contemporary reality?

The stories written about him during his lifetime are flawed in both content and interpretation, so arriving at the factual certainty of public events is difficult. All the traditional methods of determining the historical accuracy of his personal relationships are mainly nonexistent, because Capone, his cohorts, and his family were not the sort of people who wrote letters or kept diaries. Even the record books of the Outfit cannot provide certainty, because they lie and obfuscate in order to conceal illegal gains. After contemporary enthusiasts sort through the scant documentation available and combine it with personal memories and recollections, the consensus is that arriving at anything approaching a definitive interpretation of the man who was Al Capone remains elusive. All that we have are speculation and probability, and they lead only to endless possibilities.

"God knows," Oscar Wilde said of himself in his oft-quoted response to the question of what posterity might make of him. Wilde's answer is something Al Capone might have said as well: "Somehow or other I'll be famous, and if not famous, I'll be notorious." Wilde envisioned himself as leading "the life of pleasure for a time and then—who knows? . . . Perhaps that will be the end of me, too."

For now, the only certainty is that as time passes and the man who was Al Capone recedes into history, the legend shows no sign of stopping.

ACKNOWLEDGMENTS

———

Books come into being for a variety of reasons. Mine usually began with an idea I wanted to explore or a question for which I wanted an answer. This book did not fall into either category. It began when my friend, Jane Kinney Denning, told me her lawyer brother, Kevin Kinney, worked with a man named Andy Capone, who had grown up hearing family stories that they were so closely related to Al Capone that one of them might have been his illegitimate son. He thought the time had come to find out what his elders meant when they said "you don't know how close you are," and then refused to tell him anything more. When Jane asked how I would advise Andy to find the truth of his family's myth, I was intrigued. One thing led to another until I found myself writing a book that explored the private Al Capone, the man behind the public legend.

As I began the research, I met many people who were members of various families named Capone, some directly related to Al, others not at all. One man's father was one of Al's brothers, but he changed his name during Al's lifetime so his children would not bear the onus attached to Capone. This man told me how his uncles, three of Al's four other brothers, had changed their names for the same reason. Now, two generations later, he did not know any of his cousins, who they were or where they lived. He knew that some of his generation had gone one step further, changing their birth name to ensure they could never be identified by a prying public. He was eager to connect with these cousins, to meet them and explore their mutual family histories. Through this book, I was able to put many of them in touch with each other for the very first time, and to watch them forge friendships as they compared notes about their family's history.

I also met the granddaughters of Mae and Al Capone and learned that they, too, were wary of outsiders. They were curious about their heritage but still wanted their identities to remain private. Here again, through my research, I was able to introduce them to relatives they did not know they had, and to see the pleasure with which they formed friendships among themselves. In a very real sense, this book has been responsible for any number of Capone family reunions.

I wish I could thank each family member who helped me by naming them all, but only some consented to let themselves be identified. I will respect their confidentiality as I thank those who wish to remain private by saying how much their testimonies have enriched this exploration of their illustrious ancestors' lives. I know how hesitant they were to reveal anything about themselves, and I am deeply grateful that they trusted me to tell the stories they grew up hearing and those they experienced themselves.

There were others who bore the Capone name who have allowed me to thank them by name. The senior direct descendant of Al and Mae Capone is their eldest (of four) granddaughters, Diane Capone, who was a generous friend as she shared her memories of the beloved "Papa" and "Mama Mae." I look forward to her forthcoming memoir. By extension, I thank her sisters, Barbara and Theresa, whom she consulted on my behalf. They all lovingly remember their eldest sister, the late Veronica (Ronnie), who was a living presence in all our exchanges. Mike Martin was judicious in relating his memories. Brian Gabriel was generous with family stories and photographs, and Richard Corey Hart did the same. Ralph Hart cooperated in matters of genetic testing.

In Rockford, I thank Andy Capone and his wife, Sang, for uncounted hours of research and archival assistance and for too many personal kindnesses to name. I thank the matriarch of that particular family, Phyllis Sciacca, who holds the key to "the Oath." Her nephews, the sons of the late Joseph (Pip) Capone, tracked down photos and documents and often enlisted friends to help them. I thank the late James, Joseph Edward, Gary, and Gennaro (Jeep), all surnamed Capone. Their wives, Beverly, Chris, and Kathi (respectively), were generous with hospitality. Other Capone cousins contributed memories and documents, and I thank John (J.J.), John (Opie), Paula, Christine, and Naomi (all surnamed Capone), and Adele Anderson Mittlestat and Andy Sciacca.

For photos, documents, archival information, and research, I wish to thank Bobby Eaton and Bobby Livingston of RR Auctions, and Marc and

Mary Perkins for contributions from their impressive Capone collection. Albert Bruce Duckett donated his father, Albert Duckett, Sr.'s, drawings. Bill Papenhausen and Brett Schrieber, Esq., conducted genealogical research; John Alessio did so in Baja, California. June and the late Bob Kinney told me about life in Northern Wisconsin when Al had the Hideaway and Ralph had RaCap. Joanie Stern and Lynne Rossetto Kasper added to my knowledge of the area and its Italian-American people. Jeff McArthur contributed information about Two Gun Hart (Vincenzo Capone); Jan Day Gravel about Al Capone's friend Gertrude Cole; Jessica Daugherty, of Las Vegas Pawn TV, investigated the provenance of a mistress's prized necklace.

Research assistance came from Deborah Cannarella through the Research Internship Program of the Graduate Writing Program in the School of the Arts at Columbia University. I thank Patricia O'Toole for putting the two of us together. Among those who write about Al Capone and who shared their significant knowledge of gangland and gangsters, I thank William J. Helmer, John Winkeler, William Balsamo, Laurence Bergreen, Andrew Pappachristos, Robert J. Schoenberg, and Charles J. Strozier. I owe a special debt to John Binder, who contributed his extensive knowledge of Chicago's beer wars by letting me read his forthcoming book in manuscript. Mary Lawrence Test, Esq., read the manuscript with an eye toward all things legal and medical. Leon and Myrna Bell Rochester provided everything from good cheer to photographs, calendars, and online research. Karen Nangle alerted me to collections that held Capone documents in Yale's Beinecke Library, as did Kenneth Nesheim. Good friends, Ken and the late Roberta (Bobbi) Nesheim, were invaluable allies throughout the long process of making a book. Walter Donahue made sure I had enough miles for research travel. Thomas Henderson has saved me from scams and computer glitches time and again; for that I am exceedingly grateful, and also for the friendship he and Deborah offer.

Theodor Itten and Evelyne Gottwalz-Itten contributed interesting observations about character and personality, as well as warm and welcoming friendship in Switzerland. Within the Jungian community, I benefitted from conversations with Suzanne and the late George Wagner, Jean and Thomas Kirsch, and Andrew Samuels.

I am fortunate to be a member of the Women Writing Women's Lives seminar at CUNY, the New York University Biography Seminar, and the New York Institute for the Humanities. Through conversations at lunches and in seminars, many friends helped this book. I thank Betty Boyd Caroli,

Gayle Feldman, Anne Heller, Dorothy Helly, Laurence Lockridge, Dona Munker, Jill Norgren, Joan Schenkar, Alix Kates Schulman, Will Swift, and Aileen Ward. Three friends who wrestle with biographical issues contributed wisdom, expertise, encouragement, and especially commiseration in our gang-of-four dinners: Marion Meade, Diane Jacobs, and Sydney Ladensohn Stern. I received the same support from Lisa Corva, Patricia DeMaio, Allison Stokes, and Judith Steinberg Bassow. My agent, Kristine Dahl, and her assistant at ICM, Caroline Eisenmann, have smoothed my way repeatedly, as has Gary Johnson at the Markson Thoma Literary Agency.

It is an honor to be published by Nan A. Talese, whose vision led her to take a chance on a most unorthodox subject for a so-called literary biographer. Daniel Meyer has been an extraordinary hands-on editor. Ingrid Sterner painstakingly copy edited the manuscript. Pei Koay designed the text and Michael Windsor created its jacket. Victoria Chow has shepherded the book through its public reception and Lauren Weber has supervised its marketing. I am grateful for the care and attention they all gave to it.

I am the most fortunate of women to have a close and loving family. I would need to write a separate book to describe all that my children have done to make this one happen. Vonn Scott Bair and Katherine (Katney) Bair have put up with my shenanigans all their lives; my granddaughter, Isabel Courtelis, makes my feminist heart glow through her adventures at the University of Oregon; her father, Niko Courtelis, provides everything from advice on design issues to postage stamps bearing Al Capone's likeness. My "Swedish son," Bjorn Lindahl; his wife, Nina Kjølaas; their son, Sebastian Kjølaas; and his wife, Siri, provided hospitality in Oslo and an introduction to Al Capone's legend in the Scandinavian countries. My sister, Linda Rankin, is there for all things medical, and my brother, Vincent J. Bartolotta, Jr., takes care of the legal, while my sister-in-law, Judith, takes care of everything else.

This book is dedicated to one of the great editors of our time and a publishing legend, John R. Ferrone, whom I met when I was writing about Anaïs Nin, whose editor he had been. In the years until his death on April 10, 2016, we forged a deep friendship through daily telephone conversations in which I poured out my trials and tribulations while he listened carefully before offering perceptive opinions and solutions. He was always right, the best editor I never had, and, best of all, he always listened.

NOTES

INTRODUCTION

1   "all families are closed narratives": This eloquent sentence is Rosemary
     Sullivan's, in *Stalin's Daughter: The Extraordinary and Tumultuous Life of
     Svetlana Alliluyeva* (New York: HarperCollins, 2015), 561.
2   "You who only know him": *Chicago Tribune*, May 18, 1929.

CHAPTER 1: THE EARLY YEARS

5   Gabriele Capone was twenty-nine: To trace the genealogy of the Gabriele
     Capone family (and almost every other Italian family who came to the United
     States before or even after Ellis Island) is no easy task. Nothing is consistent,
     from the spelling of their names to the accuracy of ships' passenger lists and,
     later, official U.S. government census records. Earlier biographers of AC have
     struggled to arrive at consensus but often cannot find it. To read the notes
     of—to give but three of the most recent examples—Kobler, Schoenberg,
     and Bergreen is to be aware of the diligence they applied to the task and the
     difficulty and sheer frustration in each attempt to arrive at the truth. My own
     attempts were compounded by the lack of documentation in Italy: Naples and
     its environs suffered massive destruction during World War II, and many civic
     and religious records and archives were either destroyed or dispersed to places
     that I and the researchers who assisted me were unable to find. Richard Corey
     Hart, the great-grandson of Vincenzo Capone, traveled to the family village
     in 2014 and learned that he was several months too late because the ninety-
     six-year-old parish priest had just died and everything that could be known
     about the villagers was in his head. Betty Boyd Caroli, whose dissertation was
     on immigration and return among Italian-Americans, advised me that often
     the families have the information but are unwilling to share it for a variety of
     reasons, most of them having to do with issues of secrecy and privacy. As for
     archival records, Jerre Mangione and Ben Morreale in *La Storia: Five Centuries
     of the Italian American Experience* (New York: Harper Perennial, 1992), 79, quote

the mayor of Racalmuto, Sicily, who when asked about them in 1972 replied, "What archives? They fled here without regrets and most of them clandestinely. What records? . . . They were dying of hunger." He could have added that most immigrants were also illiterate and could neither read nor write. I have also relied on family history and legends, most of which have come from the current generation of AC's descendants, whose information is based mostly on tales told to them by their parents and grandparents. I am able, therefore, to present only this brief account of what I believe (at least for now) to be accurate.

5   With him were his wife: Here again, there is disagreement about how the Capone family came to America. Some sources have them sailing separately and state that Gabriele arrived before Ellis Island was opened, for there is no record of his arrival between 1885 and 1895; other sources have Teresa and the two children arriving on the ship *Werra* on June 18, 1895, not as some sources have stated in 1893 or 1894. However, Gabriele's descendants believe that he arrived with his family and the confusion was probably caused because they traveled in separate classes on the same ship: Gabriele might have been in steerage, where record keeping was often haphazard, while Teresa and the children were in second class, where as a pregnant woman she would have been more comfortable and where better records were kept. Apparently, this was not uncommon among families who paid their own passage, and it sometimes resulted in the omission of some of their names.

5   Gabriele was unlike his countrymen: He did have distant cousins, the Fischetti family, who might have come before Ellis Island was opened in 1892 because no record of their arrival has yet been found. Three of the Fischetti sons, Rocco, Charles, and Joseph, later followed AC to Chicago and became trusted employees in the Outfit. They, too, settled first in Brooklyn.

5   A rumor surrounding his arrival: Each immigrant was assessed an entrance fee that varied from fifty cents in 1875 to $2 to $4 later. In 2015, $4 would be approximately $85.

6   "We can't get along": Mangione and Morreale, *La Storia*, 138.

7   Alphonse was followed by: AC's descendants think there were miscarriages between Teresa's pregnancies and perhaps even other children who died at birth, particularly two boys who might have been the first Erminio and Amedoe. The surviving son's name was probably meant to be Amadeo and misspelled on his birth certificate. He used the incorrect spelling until he was an adult and changed it to Matthew. It was not uncommon for Italian families to use the name of a child who died for the next one who lived.

7   and the daughters Erminia: There is some uncertainty about this child's name and dates of birth and death: John Kobler calls her Rose and gives 1910; John Binder cites New York City death records that give her name as Erminia and dates of 1901.

7   "seven or eight hundred thousand": John Quinn to Jacob Epstein, October 21, 1920, NYPL, quoted by Kevin Birmingham, *The Most Dangerous Book: The Battle for James Joyce's Ulysses* (New York: Penguin Press, 2014), 157.

8   They were even more crowded: Their names were given on the Twelfth Census of the United States, Kings County, Borough of Brooklyn, as Michael Martino and Andrea Callabrese.

9   With the exception of shopping: Monsignor William J. Gorman, who conducted the graveside ceremonies at AC's burial, said of Teresa Capone, "So

far as I know, she never missed mass a day of her life or missed communion of a Sunday." Attested to by some of her great-grandchildren, and as quoted by George Murray in *The Legacy of Al Capone: Portraits and Annals of Chicago's Public Enemies* (New York: G. P. Putnam's Sons, 1975), 13.

10   "I'm no Italian": Mangione and Morreale, *La Storia*, 258.

10   "*existence* presented a challenge": Schoenberg, *Mr. Capone* (New York: Harper Perennial, 2001), 22.

10   Nothing in that version of the story: William Balsamo knew the daughter of the woman in question, whose name was Maria Adamo. He interviewed her daughter, Mary Savarese, when she was in her nineties. With him were Vanni Capelli and Laurence Bergreen, who chose to write a different story in his biography, *Capone: The Man and the Era* (New York: Simon & Schuster, 1994). I am grateful to Balsamo for telling of how this meeting took place and for providing a copy of the taped interview.

12   This last version seems least likely: Richard Gambino, *Blood of My Blood: The Dilemma of the Italian-Americans* (Garden City, N.Y.: Doubleday, 1974), 13.

14   He would have dressed as a cowboy: Vincenzo Capone (a.k.a. Richard Hart), testimony given at Ralph Capone's income tax evasion trial in 1950, Sept. 21, 1951, National Archives at Chicago, p. 1 (of 8), v. 4 and v. 5.

15   He was well-known on the streets: Jacob Riis deplored the situation in which immigrants lived, writing, "The Italian has nevertheless the instinct of cleanliness but it is drowned by the nastiness of the tenements." See *How the Other Half Lives* (New York: Seven Treasures Publications, 2009), chaps. 5 and 6.

15   "something of a nonentity": Daniel Fuchs, "Where Al Capone Grew Up," *New Republic*, Sept. 9, 1931, 95–97.

16   Don Balsamo: William Balsamo and John Balsamo, *Young Al Capone* (New York: MJF Books, 2001), 93. The authors are the grandsons of Batista Balsamo. The authors based the information in their book on many firsthand accounts of people who knew AC and the Capone family when they lived in Brooklyn, accounts that include both truth and possible revisionism: there is a basic veracity to these tales, but there is also a caveat about accepting them in their entirety, for many of the people who shared their memories did so long after the events actually occurred. Throughout the book, the authors tell a story that is replete with dialogue purportedly said by AC, much of which has found its way into so many different accounts of his life and work that it is now taken for the truth. However, the authors themselves wrote in the introduction that "the dialogue in this book is written with *the hopeful intention of providing a plausible discourse* to the events as defined by the historical record" (emphasis mine).

16   Al observed the don's minions: Ibid., chap. 2.

16   Ralph Capone left Ralphie: She gave up the child to Teresa, and Ralphie moved with the rest of the family when they relocated to Chicago. Teresa had charge of him, but Mae Capone raised him along with her son, Albert (Sonny).

17   Soon he was part of a loose affiliation: Torrio had begun what later became his permanent move to Chicago as early as 1909, when AC was ten. He made periodic returns to Brooklyn, but by the second decade of the twentieth century he was no longer active in the borough's crime scene.

17   "dominated his swollen-muscled thugs": Schoenberg, *Mr. Capone*, 24. Schoenberg is too harsh on Torrio, who was actually quite a good-looking man, when he completes this sentence with the following phrase: "all seated in

a puny, flaccid body, with chipmunk cheeks, a little potbelly, and dainty soft hands and feet."

18 "probably the nearest thing": Herbert Asbury, *Gem of the Prairie: An Informal History of the Chicago Underworld* (DeKalb, Ill.: Northern Illinois University Press, 1986), 320. (Originally published by Knopf, 1928.)

18 "an organizational genius": Virgil W. Peterson, *The Mob: 200 Years of Organized Crime in New York* (Ottawa, Ill.: Green Hill, 1983), 156.

18 "for the development of modern corporate crime": Bergreen, *Capone*, 37.

19 "What Torrio, with his brilliant, analytical mind": Ibid., 38.

19 Al learned about women: RC's file in the Federal Bureau of Prisons, under the heading "Notorious Offenders."

CHAPTER 2: MAE

22 Mary Josephine Coughlin: After they moved to Chicago, MC began to lighten her hair to blond, a color she kept for the rest of her life.

22 But why would a young woman: Personal information in this chapter about the relationship of their grandparents comes from the descendants of AC and his siblings.

28 allegedly Frank Gallucio: William Balsamo, interview, May 22, 2015, calls him Charles Gallucio. When previous biographies were under way, Gallucio insisted that his sister, whose real name was Teresa, be given the pseudonym Lena.

28 The scars were real, but how Al got them: William J. Helmer, in a personal communication, July 16, 2013, said he regrets using Balsamo's "second- or thirdhand account of Capone's scarring at Yale's place . . . even if he did talk to an aging Gallucio. One or the other or both embellished it . . . Evidently he and Capone did tangle at Yale's dive, but that's all I trust anymore." Bergamo, in telephone conversations, July 2015, stands by the story as he wrote it.

28 Al and Mae were so attracted to each other: Diane Capone has written this in her forthcoming memoir, *Tales My Grandmother Told Me*.

28 Albert Francis Capone: There were multiple errors on the birth certificate: AC was not residing in the Coughlin house but was living in his parents' home; his name is wrongly given as Albert rather than Alphonse; both his age and MC's are incorrect.

29 she was adamantly against: Nathan Glazer and Daniel P. Moynihan, in *Beyond the Melting Pot* (Cambridge, Mass.: MIT Press, 1970), 204, write, "Today [1963] a more significant symbol of rising social status [for an Italian man] is marriage with a girl of Italian descent, who has gone to a good Catholic school, and who seems to young Italians to represent the older American society much as Protestantism did a generation ago."

31 He was supposed to have taken: Mike Aiello, as quoted by Bergreen, *Capone*, 57. AC's granddaughters find it difficult to accept this period of their grandfather's life. Diane Capone, telephone conversation, Sept. 22, 2015, said her grandmother told many stories of her early married life but this was never one of them. John Binder, who has studied AC's life extensively, agrees with Diane Capone that AC was never in Baltimore.

CHAPTER 3: THE NEED TO MAKE A LIVING

33   he collapsed and died: Death Certificate no. 21742, New York City Department of Health, Records Bureau. It read Gabriel Caponi. He was buried first in Calvary Cemetery, Queens, New York; later reinterred at Mount Olivet, Chicago.

34   From the very beginning: Correspondence between Drs. Kenneth Phillips and Joseph Moore concerning AC's and MC's medical history. I am grateful to Bobby Livingston of RR Auction for calling it to my attention and to the Marc and Mary Perkins Collection for permission to use it.

34   "spoiled brat family princess": Almost every descendant of AC and his brothers used this expression or a version thereof when speaking of the young Mafalda.

35   her symptoms erupted: I refer here to the medical correspondence between the two physicians who cared for AC after his release from Alcatraz. Further information will be given where appropriate in later chapters.

36   Torrio's frequent trips to Chicago: The relationship between Torrio and the Colosimos is unclear. Bergreen, *Capone*, 81, says Torrio was neither Victoria's nor Jim's cousin and that the relationship was "spiritual rather than physical." Schoenberg, *Mr. Capone*, 48, says Torrio was Victoria's cousin. John Kobler, in *Capone* (Cambridge, Mass.: Da Capo Press, 1992), 52, says Colosimo was Torrio's uncle. The oldest of the current generation of AC's descendants say they have always believed that Torrio was Victoria's cousin, and she insisted that Jim bring him to Chicago. Italian scholars and journalists in Italy who attempted on my behalf to find records in Calabria pertaining to both men were unsuccessful. As happens with so much else of Italian-American genealogical history, my researchers and I reached a dead end.

36   "the premier madam": John Binder, personal communication, Sept. 2015, said the 1910 census of the brothels in the Levee district lists fewer than a hundred and that the count usually given of two hundred is highly inaccurate.

36   a much younger man: For the most informative account of the Moresco-Colosimo activities, see Gus Russo, *The Outfit* (New York: Bloomsbury, 2001), 16–19.

37   Lovett was a sharpshooter: William Balsamo believes that "the most important murder AC took part in" was that of Wild Bill Lovett's brother-in-law, Peg Leg Lonergan, on Christmas Eve, 1925. Balsamo believes AC was "a hired killer employed by Frankie Yale." He adds that, "at that time, Italian gangsters were no match for the Irish" (Balsamo, telephone conversation, May 21, 2015). John Binder, in his forthcoming *The Beer Wars: How the Capone Gang Came to Rule Chicago's Underworld*, echoes Balsamo's belief.

37   But the domestic benefits: His surviving eldest granddaughter says it is not clear if he went alone on his first trip to Chicago and returned to Brooklyn later for MC or if he took her with him the first time. From my interviews and conversations, I have chosen to write the version here.

38   "I thought I needed more": William J. Helmer, "The Wisdom of Al Capone," TS, gift of the author.

38   "Capone would go": Russo, *Outfit*, 25.

CHAPTER 4: AL COMES TO CHICAGO

40   "maneuver of the fates": Richard T. Enright, *Capone's Chicago* (Rapid City, S.D.: USM, 2000), 35. (Original publication: 1931).

43   He was also alleged: In 2015, the house's owner claimed that he found three secret tunnels and was sure he would find bullet holes upon further excavation. Upon investigation, nothing of the sort was found. Tim Schroeder, "Learning Leadership at Capone's Hideaway," *Kelowna (B.C.) Daily Courier,* Aug. 16, 2015.

43   It was sold shortly after Teresa died: The house was sold twice, once in 1953 and again in 1963. After four or five years of trying to sell the house for $445,000, the owner reduced the price in 2014 to $225,000.

44   Al moved them into a quiet middle-class neighborhood: In a private communication, John Binder described the locations of the four southern Italian neighborhoods in the 1920s in Chicago: Twenty-Sixth Street (near South Side); Taylor Street (near West Side and associated with the Rockford family of Capones); Grand Avenue (near Northwest Side); and Division Street (near North Side).

44   There are even stories: The first to start these stories was Fred D. Pasley, in his *Al Capone: The Biography of a Self-Made Man* (Garden City, N.Y.: Garden City, 1930), and they have been accepted and enlarged upon ever since. My interpretation considers them but with skepticism. Information also comes from interviews and conversations with AC's descendants and the descendants of some of his associates.

44   "I am a property owner and a taxpayer": Helmer, "Wisdom of Al Capone."

45   Chicago's city government: Each of the two major political parties, Republican and Democratic, had a committeeman who was the ward's political boss and who determined each party's candidate for alderman. Sometimes the committeeman also ran for alderman and, if elected, served on the city council. John Binder, in private communication, 2015, wrote, "The committeeman in each ward was the political powerhouse and not a figurehead. He received and dispensed various patronage positions."

45   "For the gangsters": Russo, *Outfit,* 15.

46   "he was a Republican": Testimony of Phil D'Andrea before the Kefauver Committee, formally known as the Special Committee to Investigate Organized Crime in Interstate Commerce, pt. 5, "Capone Syndicate."

46   "burned with the reckless optimism": Bergreen, *Capone,* 104. All quotations by Robert St. John are from Bergreen's interview with him.

48   Nearly everyone who wrote about Al's role: Some of the differing sources include Asbury, *Gem of the Prairie,* 334; Russo, *Outfit,* 26; Murray, *Legacy of Al Capone,* 119; Bergreen, *Capone,* 106–9; Schoenberg, *Mr. Capone,* 109; Kobler, *Capone,* 112–16.

48   "gun blazing in each hand": Asbury, *Gem of the Prairie,* 334.

48   "an unusual 'hood'": Edward Dean Sullivan, *Chicago Surrenders* (New York: Vanguard Press, 1930), 157–58.

49   Dean O'Banion: I follow Rose Keefe in her biography of O'Banion, *Guns and Roses* (Nashville: Cumberland House, 2003), who writes that he was called Dean by those who knew him, as do all official uses of his name (such as his tombstone).

49   Hot Springs, Arkansas: Michael Wallis, in *Pretty Boy: The Life and Times of Charles Arthur Floyd* (New York: St. Martin's Press, 1992), 315, writes that visitors

"came to cure ailments ranging from syphilis to rheumatism . . . Huey Long, Herbert Hoover, and Al Capone were among the highly disparate guests."

49 Al wasted no time acquiring: There is some debate about whether the Thompson submachine gun was used in this attempt. Russo claims it was, Schoenberg has it as pistols and "shotgun," John Binder merely points out the discrepancy.

50 In an extremely sloppy and error-filled copy: Quotations that follow are from "Statement of Alphonse Caponi, 7244 Prairie Avenue, Vincennes 9360, Relative to the Shooting of John Torrio in Front of 7011 S. Clyde Avenue, About 3:30 p.m. January 24, 1925." Document in the Marc and Mary Perkins Collection, generously made available via Bobby Livingston of RR Auction.

50 when he was on his way to buy tickets: There were two versions of the movie, 1930 and 1942. The first was not made at the time of this incident. There was a play of the same name showing in New York, but I have not been able to verify that it played or was playing at that time in Chicago.

CHAPTER 5: THE OTHER CAPONES

52 There was already a family named Capone: Much of this chapter is based on interviews and conversations, as well as documents provided by members of the Rockford Capone family: Joseph Edward, Gary, James, Gennaro, Andrew, and John. Also, Adele Anderson Mittlestat; Phyllis Sciacca; Beverly, Paula, Chris, and Cathi Capone; and the compiler of the "family history," Nancy Capone.

52 "cousin on Taylor Street": From Ellis Island passenger records for Vincenzo Piccolo, Gennaro Capone, Raffaele Capone, and Clotilde Tufano and from conversations and interviews with the branch of the family I will call the Rockford Capones.

53 The father Gennaro was a poor landless peasant: The senior Gennaro Capone was known as January Capone when his sons brought him to Chicago in 1923, after the death of his wife earlier that year in Acerra. He died in Chicago in 1939. The reader may find some confusion as this book proceeds, for in the traditional Italian fashion, the Capone family used the same names over and over. There was always at least one or possibly more Gennaros, named after the patron saint of Naples. Gennaro sometimes became January or Jann; other frequently used names were Ralph, James, Joseph, and John. In succeeding generations, as each son used these names for his sons, all those who bore them acquired nicknames, which was also a common way of identifying individual men. It was much the same for women, and certain names were common in families. Annunziata became Nancy, and Philomena usually became Fanny or Phyllis. These are only some that the various Capone families used, but all will be given with their appropriate nicknames as the family's saga unfolds. For an interesting explanation of why the same names were used over and over and how nicknames came into common parlance, see Richard Gambino, *Blood of My Blood*, 55–56.

53 Clotilde (as she was known): Anna Maria Tufano, aged ninety-eight in 2016, who knew AC and was a close friend of this branch of the Capone family, insists that she was always called Adelina. Her descendants are divided, but most agree that she was "Grandma Clotilde."

55 Vincenzo Piccolo, in whose house her brother: He was actually living at 727

Morgan Street, Chicago's Ward 19. Shortly after, Vincenzo Tufano disappears from the narrative of the Rockford Capones. He may be one of the significant number of Italians who returned to their native villages, but no documentation has yet been found to verify this. The current generation of this family believes that he told Clotilde he had received a letter from Italy saying everyone in her family was dead and she was to inherit their property but she had to claim it in person. Because she could not leave her family, he asked her to authorize him on her behalf. He went to Italy, and never returned to Chicago. The current generation believes he claimed the land and stayed there.

55 on December 18, 1906, she married him: Marriage license no. 44781, State of Illinois, Cook County, shows that they applied for a license on December 17, 1906, and were married the following day by a Catholic priest, the Reverend John [looks like] Chenier, but no church name is given. For many years, until this document was found, their descendants thought they were never legally married but simply declared themselves as such.

55 he had set himself up as a "storekeeper": Nancy Capone, untitled and unpublished family history. Both the 1910 and the 1920 census records list Raphael's surname as Caponi and his wife's first name as Lena (possibly a nickname for Adeline, although she was always known as Clotilde). In some shipping and census records, her maiden name is misspelled as Pufono or Gufano.

56 She left behind the two older children: They did not know they had a sister until she contacted them when they were all middle-aged.

57 Raphael was offered the plum manager's job: His grandsons always use the title "president" when they speak of the B&K job offer, but because they were well on their way to building the fifty-some movie houses, it is more likely he was being offered a mid-level managerial position.

57 gang leaders always put their people on the inside: Schoenberg, *Mr. Capone,* 303.

57 "*Chi lascia la via vecchia*": Gambino, *Blood of My Blood,* 2–3.

60 although this story has doubters: John Binder, personal communication, 2015, wrote, "This vignette of Raphael striking Al and living to tell about it is very hard to accept. AC's bodyguards would likely have shot him before AC could have called them off." Perhaps, but not if they were aware of AC's respect for Raphael.

60 First they told the tale among themselves: For an interesting and relevant discussion of memory, see Theodor Itten and Ron Roberts, *The New Politics of Experience and the Bitter Herbs* (Monmouth, U.K.: PCCS Books, 2014). Itten and Roberts argue that a telling such as this one "is thus an historical one of recovering not just family memory but collective social memory in all the collective social settings in which we live. Profoundly modernist in character, the intention behind the method is to reveal something of how we as human actors engage with each other *in reality,* reconstructed from their *memory in action.*" See also their original sources, upon which they base their conclusions.

61 "When he got as far as Elgin": Standard Certificate of Death, State of Illinois, no. 9361, March 29, 1929.

CHAPTER 6: THE ROAD TO POWER

66 "official graft disbursements": Russo, *Outfit*, 27, 34.

66 "would dare to go out": AC's immediate family members (his grandchildren, a great-grandchild, a child and a grandchild of his siblings) all told this story during interviews and conversations, all using exactly the same expression as one they say Mafalda often said.

66 until he was arrested: "Matt Capone, Al's Brother, Dies at Age 59," *Chicago Tribune*, Feb. 1, 1967.

68 He always used a tailor: Daniel R. Schwarz, *Broadway Boogie Woogie: Damon Runyon and the Making of New York City Culture* (New York: Palgrave Macmillan, 2003), 123–24; Richard Rayner, "His Wit Was Hard-Boiled," *Los Angeles Times*, May 25, 2008.

68 depending on who told the tale: Most books and articles use the 11-carat figure; in 2015, the granddaughters of Ralph Capone's last wife, Madeleine Morichetti, were offering a 4.25-carat ring purporting to be AC's for sale at auction through ATR Estate Sales, Kenosha, Wisconsin.

69 "more or less constant friction": Dr. Joseph Moore (who treated AC in Baltimore and Miami after his release from Alcatraz) to Dr. Kenneth Phillips (AC's family physician in Florida), March 20, 1940, Marc and Mary Perkins Collection, via RR Auction.

70 "I can't tell you": Helmer, "Wisdom of Al Capone."

70 "Your father broke my heart": Because this appears in various versions in so many different sources, I simply mention how common it is and cite none here.

71 in order to get the boy to New York: William Balsamo holds the opinion that AC was in New York on other business as well: to participate in the assassination of Richard "Peg Leg" Lonergan; Schoenberg, *Mr. Capone*, 142–44, describes the event with Al present and in charge.

72 she began to exhibit some alarming symptoms: Phillips to Moore, who writes that he is "pluck[ing] the essential details" from "an enormously voluminous" record. This is from what appears to be either a second letter or a separate postscript of March 20, 1940. Information about MC's illness and treatment comes from the correspondence of Moore and Phillips.

72 This led Dr. Moore to conclude: Moore to Phillips, March 20, 1940.

CHAPTER 7: THE FORTUNES OF WAR

73 Harvard Business School case study: Tom Nicholas and David Chen, "Al Capone," Harvard Business School Case 809-144, April 2009 (rev. March 1, 2012).

74 twenty-two brothels were operating openly: The figure of twenty-two brothels is from ibid.; while researching *The Beer Wars*, John Binder found no references to prostitution in Cicero during the 1920s–1930s. In a personal communication, 2015, he wrote, "Cicero was so intolerant of brothels during Prohibition that Torrio and Capone located them in Stickney, Lyons, Forest View, and other nearby suburbs."

74 there were roughly 700 gang-related deaths: For a partial list of Capone-ordered killings, see Nicholas and Chen, "Al Capone," exhibit 6. See also Asbury, *Gem of the Prairie*, 355, where he estimates that "more than 500 died. Just how many of these killings Al Capone was responsible for was never known, but estimates

ranged from twenty to sixty." Asbury also cites the *Chicago Tribune*, listing "thirty-three persons who were described as 'Capone's victims' . . . and many others about whom definite information is not available." For further detailed information, see Dennis E. Hoffman, *Scarface Al and the Crime Crusaders: Chicago's Private War Against Capone* (Carbondale: Southern Illinois University Press, 1993), esp. 26–30. The Chicago Crime Commission listed 1,239 murders during 1922–25, with 209 gangland-style killings.

74 "I am getting too prominent": Guy Murchie Jr., "Capone's Decade of Death: Prohibition's Crime Reign," *Chicago Daily Tribune*, Feb. 16, 1936, D5. John Binder's forthcoming book, *The Beer Wars*, will provide the most complete and authoritative account of this historical period.

75 "Capone's Castle": Asbury, *Gem of the Prairie*, 362.

75 a small apartment building: Pasley, *Al Capone*, 114–17, describes the building.

75 The body was covered: Ibid., 78; Asbury, *Gem of the Prairie*, 320.

76 where he inhaled so much cocaine: Bergreen, *Capone*, 116, cites an author's interview with Roy Kral as the source for the description. He is the only author to date to make the claim about cocaine.

76 There is nothing in Capone's voluminous: Ibid., 116n, cites the "Neuro-psychiatric Examination, June 4, 1938," in the Bureau of Prisons file for U.S. Penitentiary, Alcatraz, which says only that AC had a "perforated nasal septum." I find his argument to be based on speculation because I have been unable to find other evidence to corroborate it. Also, Bergreen, *Capone*, 292, writes that "he was far more sensitive to a new threat to discipline in his ranks . . . heroin." He quotes AC as saying, "I love the son of a bitch but if he ever goes back on that stuff he'll wind up in a cement overcoat." This is hardly the reaction of a man who used drugs himself. AC's physicians, Moore and Phillips, who wrote extensively about his medical conditions, treatments, professional contacts, and family relationships, never mentioned the use of drugs. His own descendants and those of his siblings recall how horrified any of their elders were whenever the subject of drugs was mentioned.

76 "a solid week": Polly Adler, *A House Is Not a Home* (New York: Rinehart, 1953), 79.

77 "double-walled fortress of meat": Alva Johnston, "Gangs à la Mode," *New Yorker*, Aug. 25, 1928.

77 His decorating choices: Reference to the bulletproof chair is from John O'Brien and Edward Baumann, "Recalling Life as Wife of a Capone Gangster," *Chicago Tribune*, April 13, 1986, quoting Rio Burke, whose husband was Dominic Roberto: "When Al moved into the Metropole, Dominic and Jimmy Amaratti (Roberto's nightclub partner) gave him [the chair]. The back was bullet-proof. It came up over Al's head"; reference to drawing of Big Bill Thompson is from Pasley, *Al Capone*, 152–53; reference to the portrait of AC is from Howard Vincent O'Brien, *All Things Considered* (New York: Bobbs-Merrill, 1948), 61. Hoffman, *Scarface Al*, 47, writes that Frank Loesch was "flabbergasted" to see "two great presidents alongside a buffoon like Thompson."

78 "all kinds of traps and escape routes": Vern Whaley, interview with Bergreen, *Capone*, 291.

78 "responsible for everything": This and quotations that follow, until otherwise noted, are from Helmer, "Wisdom of Al Capone."

79 "soft, fat, sentimental features": Johnston, "Gangs à la Mode."

CHAPTER 8: IN HIDING

80   Cranberry Lake: John Dettloff gives the location as "Pike Lake, a thirty-seven acre lake that feeds into the [Chippewa] Flowage." Dettloff, *Three Record Muskies in His Day: The Life and Times of Louie Spray*, with Louis Spray (Couderay, Wis.: Trail's End, 2004), 99.

80   Edward J. "Artful Eddie" O'Hare": O'Hare was gunned down on November 8, 1939, allegedly because AC wanted revenge for O'Hare's testimony in helping to convict him for tax evasion. In the years since AC's conviction, O'Hare had continued to be an informant on the mob. Ironically, the O'Hare name graces Chicago's principal airport but for the son and not the father: Edward "Butch" O'Hare Jr. was a graduate of the U.S. Naval Academy and a hero who gave his life in World War II when his plane was shot down.

80   a way station for contraband booze: Later, it became the Barker Lake Lodge and Golf Course.

81   where a local resident was the conductor: Dettloff, *Three Record Muskies in His Day*, 99, notes that Bob Cammack (the train conductor) built one of the first resorts in the area, Treeland Pines.

81   Residents of the little town: I am grateful to Bob and June Kinney, who told me their childhood memories of AC and provided interviews and documents concerning the Couderay property. Gennaro "Jeep" Capone introduced me to Joanie Stern, who graciously provided information and photographs. Richard Corey Hart supplied information about Ralph Capone's relationship to his grandfather Vincenzo, Richard "Two Gun" Hart, and to Hart's sons Sherman and William. Other descendants of AC's brothers, among them Ralph Hart, contributed their memories of visits to the property.

81   the Hideout: In 2009, the Hideout was in foreclosure and listed for sale after being appraised at $3.7 million.

82   "Al must have never gotten anywhere": Bill Farmer, "Mystery Still Cloaks Capone's Old Hideout," *Sawyer County Record*, June 4, 1978.

82   "big black cars, with the motors running": Personal interviews with residents of Hayward and Couderay, Wisconsin. Also, Terrell Boettcher, "Bank Has 'Interested Buyers' for Al Capone's Hideout," *Sawyer County Record*, Oct. 14, 2009, 1, 10A.

83   "a room where the gang lords": Mary Ann Pattison, "Father Kinney and the Hideout," unpublished MS, graciously made available by the author and June and Bob Kinney.

83   "He is the most-shot-at man": Pasley, *Al Capone*, 60.

83   In other attempts: Ibid., 171, lists 1927 "as the banner year for plots against [AC's] life." This is another instance of his suspect chronology, which should have begun a year earlier, around the time of the McSwiggin murder.

84   "Of all Chicago's gangland killings": Bergreen, *Capone*, 354.

84   McSwiggin had the misfortune: The northern part of Cicero was either granted to or already under the control of the West Side O'Donnells, who might have been given it in return for their help in the 1924 election. Binder provides further information in his forthcoming *The Beer Wars*.

84   flat out blamed Capone: Asbury, *Gem of the Prairie*, 357.

84   "murder cases are tried in the newspapers": Pasley, *Al Capone*, 131–32.

85   "It's a waste of time": Ibid., 128, quoting Chief Morgan A. Collins.

85   "spread Chicago's evil renown": Asbury, *Gem of the Prairie*, 354, 355.

85 a lieutenant in the Outfit: The term "Outfit" (capitalized) was seldom in use before the 1960s. Until then, Chicago newspapers generally used "the Old Capone gang," the "Nitti-Guzik-Capone gang," and several other terms that strung leaders' names together. Schoenberg refers to the Capone gang as "the outfit" (lowercase), while Binder and others reserve "the Outfit" (upper case) for the gang led by Frank Nitti after Prohibition, which merged other entities into the Capone gang. Given that the Nitti-led crime family is the direct outgrowth of Capone's gang, I use the term "Outfit" to describe both.

85 Al was very fond of Roberto's wife: Sources include Bergreen, *Capone*, 172; O'Brien and Baumann, "Recalling Life as Wife of a Capone Gangster"; John O'Brien, "2 Memorial Services Will Be Held for Capone Confidante, Rio Burke," *Chicago Tribune*, Dec. 9, 1994. Rio Burke, ninety-one, died on November 1, 1994, from burns suffered in a fire in her apartment. She divorced Dominic Roberto in 1927 but remained on good terms with him while he was in Leavenworth prison, sentenced for perjury. Released in 1933, he went to Italy. She had no contact with him after that. Her second marriage was to a Hollywood florist, Jack Burke, whom she also divorced. Two months before her death, she told the reporter O'Brien, "I have had Al Capone up to my ears. I'm tired of Al Capone. I have given over 100 interviews [about him]. No more." I have read many (if not most) of them and find her remarkably consistent in her many retellings.

86 Tony Lombardo: Tony Lombardo was a power in the Taylor Street neighborhood where Raphael Capone had one of his stores. That branch of the Capone family remained close to Lombardo's widow after he was assassinated on September 7, 1928. Descendants of both families settled in or near Rockford, where they remain close to this day.

87 When the Lansing patriarch worked for the Outfit: The embers of this family who contributed reminiscences remain in and around the Lansing area today and wish to retain their privacy. Bergreen, *Capone*, 176, says the family patriarch left Chicago after a "deadly altercation." His family members dispute this assertion. My own efforts to verify either contention were unsuccessful.

88 Indeed, on the Fourth of July: "Capone Enjoyed Fireworks at Round Lake Hideaway," *Lansing State Journal*, June 9, 1987.

90 "I paid McSwiggin plenty": Sources include "Al Caponi [sic] to Give Up Today, He Announces," *Chicago Tribune*, July 28, 1926; "Capone 'Mum' on McSwiggin Case," *Chicago Daily News*, July 28, 1926; "Caponi [sic] Taken Before Grand Jury," *Chicago Evening Post*, July 28, 1926; "Caponi [sic] Gives Up but Gets Jail Instead of Bail," *Chicago Tribune*, July 29, 1926.

90 "supreme on the west": Pasley, *Al Capone*, 144. Binder, in *The Beer Wars*, provides an accurate and realistic description of the territory controlled by the Outfit.

CHAPTER 9: THE GLORY YEARS

91 "czar-like power": John Stege, "Stege Exposes Chicago's Killers," *Chicago Herald and Examiner*, Jan. 16, 1927.

91 "I'm the boss": Helmer, "Wisdom of Al Capone."

92 "This definition may seem": William J. Helmer, *Al Capone and His American Boys: Memoirs of a Mobster's Wife* (Bloomington: Indiana University Press, 2011), 71.

92   Capone was turning the Outfit: Nicholas and Chen, "Al Capone," Exhibit 2, "Capone's Criminal Organization." Original source is Guy Murchie Jr., "Capone's Decade of Death: Prohibition to Blame for Al's Rise," *Chicago Daily Tribune*, Feb. 9, 1936, D1; also available from the FBI under FOIA, "Capone, Alphonse: Sub. A—News Articles," pt. 2.

92   "His body guards were legion": Sean Dennis Cashman, *Prohibition: The Lie of the Land* (New York: Free Press, 1981), 81–82.

92   Guzik: Guzik's birth name was probably Jacob. He preferred to be called Jack but is usually known as Jake by those who wrote about AC in later years. He is Jack on his World War I draft registration card and on his 1907 marriage license is Jack Cusik. Because most other sources call him Jake, that is the name I use here.

92   Edward J. O'Hare: O'Hare was the co-inventor of the mechanical rabbit in dog racing and was the owner of the Hawthorne Race Course. He was murdered years after he betrayed AC by testifying against him at his trial.

93   All told, there were several hundred: The Harvard chart gives a partial listing; a full list of names and positions is in Cashman, *Prohibition*, 81–82, but his accuracy is disputed both in a private communication with John Binder, 2015, and in *The Beer Wars*.

93   "a supertrust operating": Pasley, *Al Capone*, 70.

93   At its most robust: Binder, *The Beer Wars* and private communication, 2015.

93   By the end of 1928: Harvard and Cashman represent the high number, Binder the low.

94   "between seven hundred": Cashman, *Prohibition*, 96. Binder, private communication, 2015, puts the number at five hundred.

94   "You know what will happen": Helmer, "Wisdom of Al Capone."

94   "He's the boss": Elmer I. Irey and William J. Slocum, *The Tax Dodgers* (New York: Greenberg Press, 1948), 36.

95   Money was no object: Schwarz, *Broadway Boogie Woogie*, 124.

95   His betting was even more: Original source is Timothy Sullivan (via John Kobler), "Caddying for a Man Who Never Shot Par," *Sports Illustrated*, Nov. 6, 1972. Luciano Iorizzo, *Al Capone: A Biography* (Westport, Conn.: Greenwood Press, 2003), 65, writes, "At first, he seldom broke 60 for 9 holes; he eventually increased to playing 18 holes, though there is no evidence that he was ever anything but a hacker on the golf course. His rounds were devoted to having fun with his gangster friends, who drank plenty on each hole, gambled recklessly on the stroke of a ball, and carried loaded weapons in their golf bags for eventual uses in emergencies."

95   Some accounts say: The first version is from the *Chicago Tribune*, Sept. 21, 1928; the second is from Timothy Sullivan, who gave his version of caddying for AC and his sister Ida Mae's involvement with AC to Kobler in "Caddying for a Man Who Never Shot Par." AC's nephew, the son of his brother John, described some of the revels that took place, including this one, which happened in a fit of temper. Other members of the extended Capone family provided information about Mae's reaction. The official version is from AC's medical records taken at the Atlanta penitentiary on September 12, 1932, now in the National Archives at San Bruno, California.

96   Under Al Capone's direction: The first quotation is Kobler, *Capone*, 200; the second is Pasley, *Al Capone*, 148.

96   "a steady stream": Kobler, *Capone*, 200, 202.

97 "when I sell liquor": Helmer, "Wisdom of Al Capone."
97 "gangster chic": Schwarz, *Broadway Boogie Woogie,* 53.
98 Sophie Tucker's biographers: Joanne Palmer, "Filming Sophie Tucker: Rockland Couple Researches, Tells Story of Last Red-Hot Mama," *New Jersey Jewish Standard,* March 21, 2014; Sophie Tucker, *Some of These Days: The Autobiography of Sophie Tucker* (Garden City, N.Y.: Doubleday, Doran & Co., 1945). Tucker makes cursory mention of AC and writes nothing about playing cards with him.
98 Joe E. Lewis ran afoul: Because so many different versions of this event exist, I will cite two of the most different here: Russo's restrained factual retelling in *The Outfit,* 124n1; Bergreen's more creative account in *Capone,* 251–54.
99 Their buskers guided white voyeurs: Thomas Brothers, *Louis Armstrong: Master of Modernism* (New York: W. W. Norton, 2014), 226.
99 "more or less a Robin Hood": Terry Teachout, *Pops: A Life of Louis Armstrong* (Boston: Houghton Mifflin Harcourt, 2009), 163. The filmmaker Richard Larsen, producing *Capone's Treasure of the Heart* (with the expected release date of Valentine's Day 2015; as of that date, 2016, it has not yet appeared), tells the unsubstantiated story that AC rushed to Hinton's hospital bedside when he was threatened with the loss of an index finger in a car accident. AC allegedly forced doctors to repair the injured finger and then paid for all Hinton's medical costs. Mina Bloom, "Filmmaker Seeks to Show a Softer Side of Capone," *DNAinfo Chicago,* Oct. 6, 2014.
99 "had all the black guys": Milt Hinton, video recording in the Hamilton College Jazz Archive, Hamilton, N.Y., May 31, 1995. Portions also quoted by Iorizzo, *Al Capone,* 69, 70n4.
100 "first exposure to gangsters": Brothers, *Master of Modernism,* 226.
100 "because we kept their clubs": Ibid., 227.
100 Benton Harbor: In later years, he did visit Dempsey's camp at Benton Harbor, and the town itself became one of his favorite spots for the times when he needed a quick nearby getaway and Tony Lombardo's house provided sanctuary.
101 Everyone came to it: Adler, *A House Is Not a Home,* 79; Louella Parsons, *The Gay Illiterate* (Garden City, N.Y.: Garden City, 1944), 108; Roger Kahn, *A Flame of Pure Fire: Jack Dempsey and the Roaring '20s* (New York: Harcourt Brace, 1999), 402.
101 "your friend . . . Jack Dempsey": Kahn, *Flame of Pure Fire,* 412–13.
101 All forms of governance: Hoffman, *Scarface Al,* 30.
102 He knew how to quell this: Asbury, *Gem of the Prairie,* 102; John Landesco, *Organized Crime in Chicago,* Part III (copublished by the Illinois Association for Criminal Justice in cooperation with the Chicago Crime Commission, 1929), 132; Hoffman, *Scarface Al,* 30; Binder, *Beer Wars,* 56.
102 "I told them we are making a shooting gallery": Helmer, "Wisdom of Al Capone."
102 Before the truce, he said, he needed: "Capone Happy as Peace Reigns," *Chicago Herald and Examiner,* Oct. 23, 1926.

CHAPTER 10: INVENTING AL CAPONE

104 "educated the guy in this respect": Berardi senior is usually described as being on staff at the *Tribune,* although his obituary in that paper did not say

he was. His son, Anthony Berardi Jr., was, however, that newspaper's chief photographer.

104   "I knew what he was": Berardi, interview with Bergreen, *Capone*, 148.

105   There was the man who somehow: From a press conference reported in the *Chicago Tribune*, Dec. 6, 1927.

105   When Tony Berardi invited him: Tony Berardi, interview with Bergreen, *Capone*, 150.

106   "allowed his imagination to take over": Schoenberg, *Mr. Capone*, 188–89. He uses a personal system for his sources. For their provenance, see notes, 416, and "Explanations," 366–69.

107   Capone tried to put a good front: *Chicago Tribune*, Dec. 17, 1927.

108   Tijuana, Mexico: Information about AC and Tijuana is from John Alessio, Sophia Alessio, Dominic J. Alessio, Maria Eugenia Bonifaz de Novelo, and Roberto Valdez. Also from the Sociedad de Historia de Tijuana, A. C., and the Instituto de Investigaciones Históricas UNAM-UABC. Signora Bonifaz de Novelo, a historian of Ensenada and Baja California, provided the following information in a letter of April 9, 2013: "The hotel casino was disbanded by the government and replaced by the Hotel Playa Ensenada (now Hotel Riviera de Ensenada) in October, 1930. U.S. investors developed these hotels due to the Prohibition in the United States. I do not know of Al Capone having anything to do with any of this. The story of the tunnels is a legend made up by the tourist guides . . . the name of Capone is being used by the tourist guides. If he was indeed here, there are no records of it. What we can suppose is that the [U.S.] Mafia sent the liquor from possible distilleries in California but from this to the fact that Al Capone was here in Baja, it's a stretch."

108   The cheering hordes: Information that follows is from stories in the *Los Angeles Examiner*, Dec. 13 and 14, 1927.

109   "a citizen with an unblemished record": *Chicago Herald and Examiner*, Dec. 17, 1927.

109   "You'd think I was Jesse James": From articles in the *Chicago Herald and Examiner*, *Chicago Tribune*, *Chicago Journal*, all Dec. 16 and 17, 1927.

110   "Capone's Son Finds Sins of Father Heavy": *Chicago Herald and Examiner*, Dec. 15, 1927.

111   Al Capone thought he had found: Newspaper articles in the *Chicago Tribune* and *Chicago Herald and Examiner*, Jan. 9 and 10, 1928.

114   "Capone Hunted": *Chicago Tribune*, Jan. 12, 1928.

116   They were close friends as children: Their closeness was lifelong: when Ralph Gabriel's daughter, Deirdre Marie Gabriel, was born in 1940, Sonny became her godfather.

116   members of the Capone family never met there: Deirdre Marie Griswold, Ralphie's daughter and Sonny's goddaughter who now calls herself Capone, has made this claim on various television programs. She is also the source of the myth that fish swam in the swimming pool.

116   And then there was the interior: Information about the interior furnishings is from interviews and conversations with AC's descendants, photographs of the property during AC's residency and when it was being sold in 2013–14, and from the Auction Bulletin, April 15, 1992, Leslie Hindman Auctioneers, Chicago.

117   "curiosity, dare-deviltry": Kobler, *Capone*, 285.

118   a staple of local lore: The first, and probably the version closest to the truth, was given by Pasley, *Al Capone*, 85; another, and probably the most susceptible to

the biographer's interpretation, was given by Bergreen, *Capone*, 284. These are only two of the many variants.

120 "you can get a man's arm broken": Kobler, *Capone*, 221.

121 Bombs continued to burst: Enright, *Capone's Chicago*, 78, wrote that AC, "supposed to be in Florida, cast his vote at his Chicago home." Perhaps someone else cast the vote for him because all other evidence that I have consulted has him remaining at Palm Island throughout this election.

121 "Gentlemen, the King!": Damon Runyon, "Gentlemen, the King!," *Collier's*, April 25, 1931.

121 "as a bomb such as these Guineas": *The Damon Runyon Omnibus* (Garden City, N.Y.: Sun Dial Press, 1944), 238.

121 "gangster chic": Schwarz, *Broadway Boogie Woogie*, 53.

121 "womanizing narcissist": Ibid., 9.

123 These two were just the beginning: Kobler, *Capone*, 309, estimates there were seven. Some of the most important (and lasting) besides Pasley's were Walter N. Burns, *The One-Way Ride: The Red Trail of Chicago Gangland from Prohibition to Jake Lingle* (Garden City, N.Y.: Doubleday, 1931); Edward Dean Sullivan, *Rattling the Cup on Chicago Crime* (New York: Van, 1929); Richard T. Enright, *Al Capone on the Spot: Inside Story of the Master Criminal and His Bloody Career* (Fawcett, 1931; reprinted by USM, INC., Rapid City, S.D., 2000).

123 "Journalists took the leading role": David E. Ruth, *Inventing the Public Enemy: The Gangster in American Culture, 1918–1934* (Chicago: University of Chicago Press, 1996), 119.

123 "Sunny Jim": A character created by advertisers as early as 1902 to sell two separate products: a breakfast cereal and peanut butter.

124 "the toast of Chicago": Russo, *Outfit*, 37.

124 "a wonderful person": Kobler, *Capone*, 229.

124 "It is a curious fact": Pasley, *Al Capone*, 83–85.

124 "Gangland King": Pasley was referring to a newsreel photograph showing AC with the prizefighter Jack Sharkey and the all-American football player Bill Cunningham and captioned "Gangland's King." What is interesting about the photograph and the story that accompanied it is the focus on AC the criminal and not on the revered athletes.

125 "to spend some money": Sullivan, *Chicago Surrenders*, 86–87.

126 He claimed that he could not recognize himself: O'Brien, *All Things Considered*, 61. O'Brien mistakenly spells Pasley's name as Paisley. Information that follows is from ibid., 60–66.

127 O'Brien told the story: Ibid., 58–66.

CHAPTER 11: LEGAL WOES

134 a necklace she wore all the time: According to her caregivers during her last years, neither Jeanette nor Vincent DeMarco ever married but always lived together in Florida. He died before her, and both were cremated. A search of state records for their death certificates found no documentation for either, leading to the supposition by people who knew her that both she and her brother used DeMarco as a pseudonym and were buried under their legal names. Her caregivers also state that her possessions were inherited by "a niece" who "showed up one day and removed them from the house." Jeanette

always wore a necklace that featured a large ruby pendant at the end of a long and thick gold chain that, shortly after her death, the niece allegedly put up for auction with a Las Vegas pawnshop that was supposed to have advertised it on television. To date, no pawnshop has any record of this incident, and if the necklace exists, it has not been found. According to Jessica Daugherty in an e-mail of June 19, 2014, the only two items purporting to belong to AC that were ever auctioned on television were his "[unspecified] jail cell keys and his guitar." Also, in photographs DeMarco showed to her caregivers during the years she claimed to be with AC, she was bleached blond because he wanted her to be, but as soon as he went to prison, she reverted to her natural color, which was black. She also claimed AC never allowed a photograph of them to be taken together because he feared Mae would see them. According to the caregivers, all photographs disappeared with the niece who inherited her estate.

134 "I love you alone": AC to MC, March 3, 1935, reprinted in Michael Esslinger, *Letters from Alcatraz* (San Francisco: Ocean View, 2008), 56. Also, copies in National Archives and Record Administration and/or U.S. Library of Congress Historic Records Collection, and copies and some originals of correspondence in possession of AC's descendants.

135 He also took Dr. Phillips, who was reluctant: Dr. Phillips mentions throughout his correspondence with Dr. Moore of being wary, if not actually frightened, of Al's brothers and how reluctant he was to disobey any of them, but most particularly Ralph because of his violent temper and frequent eruptions.

137 "Cicero mobster in the public's mind": The quotation is from William J. Helmer and Arthur J. Bilek, *The St. Valentine's Day Massacre: The Untold Story of the Gangland Bloodbath That Brought Down Al Capone* (Nashville: Cumberland House, 2004), 101, whose contention differs from most other writers and biographers.

137 "the death knell of gangdom": *Chicago Daily News,* March 19, 1929. Quoted in Hoffman, *Scarface Al,* 51.

138 "each agency [having] its own agenda": Helmer and Bilek, *St. Valentine's Day Massacre,* 105.

139 "a Volsteadian paradox": Pasley, *Al Capone,* 87.

139 "broncho-pneumonia pleurisy": A copy of the affidavit is in the Phillips/Moore collection. The original is dated March 5, 1929, and is in the FBI's "Permanent File, Al Capone," Washington, D.C.

140 "only Capone kills like that": There are various versions of this remark in newspapers and books, but it has been questioned from the beginning whether Moran actually said it. It falls into the category of when truth can't be printed, print the legend.

141 "possessor of one of the keenest": Daniel Okrent, *Last Call: The Rise and Fall of Prohibition* (New York: Scribner, 2010), 138. See ibid., 137–41, for further biographical information.

141 "If Mabel had worn trousers": Mary L. Clark, "Women as Supreme Court Advocates, 1879–1979," *Journal of Supreme Court History* 30 (2005): 47, 52. I thank Jill Norgren for these references.

141 George Emerson Q. Johnson: As all writers have noted, the initial Q stood for nothing; Johnson took it to distinguish himself from the many other George Johnsons in the world.

141 "not within his authority": Johnson to Willebrandt, memo, March 13, 1929, in selected documents relating to AC's trial.

141 "it is impossible to find": Willebrandt published a memoir in 1929 at the same time as (depending on who has written of this) President Hoover either fired her or she resigned her position: *The Inside of Prohibition* (Indianapolis: Bobbs-Merrill), 121.

141 "something devotees of dime novels": Okrent, *Last Call*, 140.

142 "brilliantly original": Bill Bryson, *One Summer: America, 1927* (New York: Doubleday, 2013), 405.

142 "mild, middle-aged": "Mary Ann Johnson—Tied to Chicago History Including Case vs. Al Capone—Dies at 82," *Chicago Sun Times*, Feb. 3, 2015.

142 "a personal matter of great importance": Willebrandt to Hoover, memo, May 14, 1930, in the FBI's "Permanent File, Al Capone," Washington, D.C.

142 President Hoover's way of dealing: William E. Leuchtenburg, *Herbert Hoover* (New York: Henry Holt, 2009), 84–85.

142 "a vehicle of joy": Herbert Hoover, *The Memoirs of Herbert Hoover: The Cabinet and the Presidency, 1920–33* (New York: Macmillan, 1952), 276.

142 "reign of lawlessness and terror": Bascom N. Timmons, *Portrait of an American: Charles G. Dawes* (New York: Henry Holt, 1953), 4–16; Hoffman, *Scarface Al*, 25.

143 Did Mellon "get Capone" yet?: John H. Lyle, *The Dry and Lawless Years* (Englewood Cliffs, N.J.: Prentice-Hall, 1960), 249. Hoover began his day tossing a medicine ball with members of his cabinet, during which he usually asked Mellon, "Have you got that fellow Capone yet?" Jonathan Eig used the phrase "Get Capone" for the title of his 2010 book.

143 "that a man guilty of inciting": Hoover, *Memoirs*, 277.

143 "like the hoodlum he is": "Capone Ready to Say Nothing at Quiz Today," *Chicago Tribune*, March 20, 1929.

CHAPTER 12: ATLANTIC CITY AND AFTER

146 "a crime so hideous": Tony Berardi, quoted in Biography Channel documentary.

146 an embarrassing black mark: The social historian Humbert S. Nelli's remark appears in Cashman, *Prohibition*, 78.

148 "political showmanship": Ibid., 100.

149 "the account generally accepted": Kobler, *Capone*, 257–58.

149 A far more florid and garish tale: Burns, *One-Way Ride*, 256.

151 He compared Capone's life to a whodunit: Cashman, *Prohibition*, 77–78.

152 Home movies taken at Palm Island: In possession of Diane Capone, who found the film among her father's effects and had it restored.

153 Each gang controlled its own fiefdom: Robert T. Loughran, *Literary Digest*, June 15, 1929.

155 "No more brass bands": Quotations are from Helmer, "Wisdom of Al Capone."

155 Unfortunately, it didn't work out: Newspaper articles and biographers differ on what actually happened as AC worked to get himself arrested. My account takes them all into consideration but also relies on the Capone family reminiscences and the stories they handed down to their descendants.

CHAPTER 13: IN PRISON

157   When one looks at the barrage: To write the following account, I have consulted newspapers in Chicago and New York (primarily, among many others), the biographies of AC, and the testimonies of elderly family members who remember what their parents said about the resulting publicity.

158   "gangsterologists": John Kobler coined the term for "the house crime expert" employed by most large metropolitan dailies. *Capone,* 287.

161   John Kobler had the good fortune: Kobler, whose biography was published in 1971, had the opportunity throughout the 1960s to talk to many of AC's visitors, fellow inmates, police officials, and Pennsylvania government employees and elected officials. His account, ibid., 261–65, remains one of the most accurate and complete.

162   His insight into Napoleon's failings: Loesch held this meeting in November 1928, but the account of it was not printed until March 25, 1931, in the *Chicago Tribune*. Hoffman gives a detailed account from Loesch's perspective in *Scarface Al,* 47.

CHAPTER 14: "THE ELUSIVE 'SCARFACE' AL"

164   "the grand mogul": *Chicago Tribune* and *Chicago Herald and Examiner,* respectively, both March 18, 1930.

164   "aided by perfect cooperation": *Philadelphia Bulletin,* March 18, 1930.

164   "'Scarface Al' Capone": *Rockford Daily Republic,* March 19, 1930.

165   The story reported: *Belvidere Daily Republican,* March 19, 1930. Although there are still a number of people named Phillip Vella in northern Illinois, none were aware of this alleged connection to AC. AC's descendants never heard the name until I told them about this news article.

165   As for Mrs. Lombardo: Helmer, *Al Capone and His American Boys,* 77, writes that Lombardo's killing was in retaliation for the slaying of Frank Yale and that at the time of AC's release "the underworld was making an elaborate pretense at mourning for the departed gangster [Lombardo]."

166   "grilling by 'them ignorant coppers'": *Belvidere Daily Republican,* March 19, 1930; it was repeated in various forms in newspapers throughout the United States.

166   The last surviving member: Phyllis "Fanny" Sciacca, interviews and conversations, 2013–14.

168   The bad news continued: Binder, *Beer Wars.*

168   The wiretappers learned he was there: Kobler, *Capone,* 265, tells of a drunken party on the night of March 18. There was indeed a drunken party, but it would have been impossible for it to be held on that date. The drive between the two cities took much longer, so it was most likely held around the twentieth.

168   "You're the only one": Ibid.

168   While he was throwing furniture: Kenneth Allsop, *The Bootleggers and Their Era* (Garden City, N.Y.: Doubleday, 1961), 312; "Capone Gives Up to Stege," *Chicago Evening Post,* March 21, 1930. AC's earlier biographers repeat various versions: Bergreen, *Capone,* 355; Eig, *Get Capone: The Secret Plot That Captured America's Most Wanted Gangster* (New York: Simon & Schuster, 2010), 271; Schoenberg, *Mr. Capone,* 252–53.

169   The first interview he granted: Genevieve Forbes Herrick, "Capone's Story by Himself," *Chicago Tribune*, March 22, 1930.

169   "tirade of self-justification": Kobler, *Capone*, 268.

169   Later the same day: "Al Capone Relates His Own Story of 'Racket' in Chicago," *Chicago American*, March 22, 1930.

170   First, he got in touch: Schoenberg, *Mr. Capone*, 252, quotes Berardi as saying he and Harry Read, the editor of the *Chicago American*, "convinced" AC to make the call on Stege. Because AC was doing exactly and only what he wanted during this period, he might have listened to the suggestion, but taking the action was most likely his own independent decision.

170   Miami police had raided the Palm Island house: *Chicago Tribune*, March 21, 1930. Six men were arrested altogether, including "Machine Gun" Jack McGurn, who had been responsible for the search warrant when he fired a machine gun at cans floating in the bay behind the house. The article described the liquor seized as whiskey and champagne.

171   "without reference to popular opinion": *Miami Daily News*, March 28, 1930. See also Schoenberg, *Mr. Capone*, 255.

171   In Monticello, Iowa, voters went beyond: *Chicago Tribune*, April 2, 1930.

171   "the [name of] the Scarface is as well known": *Chicago Evening Post*, May 16, 1930.

173   "political influence or otherwise": Summary of the report prepared by Special Agent Frank J. Wilson, Dec. 21, 1933, for Elmer Irey (chief of the Bureau of Revenue's Intelligence Unit, Washington, D.C.). In "IRS Historical Documents Relating to Alphonse (Al) Capone," available under FOIA.

CHAPTER 15: A NEW DAY FOR CHICAGO

175   Scholars of the Capone era: As of 2015, Tom Barnard is researching the Secret Six, aided by John Binder. Both have reservations about the composition of the committee as given by Hoffman in *Scarface Al*. Tom Barnard cites the scrapbook of his grandfather Harrison Barnard, in which he names himself as a member of the Secret Six, which would make the membership seven at the least. Barnard's research is ongoing, and his list is forthcoming. Hoffman, ibid., 10, names seven men: McCormick, Dawes, Robert Isham Randolph, Loesch, Burt A. Massee, Calvin Goddard, Henry Barrett Chamberlin. On ibid., 68–69, he names Julius Rosenwald as a member and Edward E. Gore and George A. Paddock, both of whom held joint memberships in the Secret Six and the CCC. John Binder, in the forthcoming *The Beer Wars*, names Harrison Barnard, Rosenwald, Samuel Insull, Paddock, Gore, Loesch, and Randolph.

175   Dawes most certainly qualified: This is Hoffman's contention, *Scarface Al*, 11.

175   He was a banker: Sources include Timmons, *Portrait of an American*; M. O. Hatfield, *Vice Presidents of the United States, 1789–1993* (Washington, D.C.: Senate Historical Office, U.S. Government Printing Office, 1997).

175   the only vice-president and Nobel Peace Prize winner: Joel Whitburn, *The Billboard Book of Top 40 Hits*, 6th ed. (New York: Billboard Publications, 1996).

175   "one of the last anachronistic citadels": *Time*, Aug. 29, 1955.

176   "bitterly attacked": "Debates Swirled About McCormick," *New York Times*, obituary, April 1, 1955.

176   McCormick conveniently forgot: Herbert Asbury, *Gangs of Chicago: An*

Informal History of the Chicago Underworld, (New York: Thunder's Mouth Press, n.d. Last copyright year given is 1968 by Northern Illinois University Press), 76, describes Lingle thus: "Ostensibly Lingle was a police reporter . . . earning sixty-five dollars a week, but death revealed him as possessing an income of more than sixty thousand dollars a year. He drove a big car, owned an eighteen-thousand-dollar summer home, plunged in the stock market, bet heavily on the races, and maintained an elaborate suite of rooms at one of Chicago's most expensive hotels. He was also disclosed as an intimate friend of Al Capone, as an occasional visitor [in Florida], as the proud owner of a diamond-studded belt given to him by Capone." The list of Lingle's "underworld connections" continues here and in most other books about AC.

176 Harrison Barnard: John Binder, *The Beer Wars* (unpublished 2015 MS), cites Tom Barnard's contention that the Secret Six members were "most likely" his grandfather, the "merchant Prince" Julius Rosenwald, the "public utility magnate" Samuel Insull, the "investment banker" George Paddock, the "accountant" Edward Gore, and Loesch.

177 Chicago Crime Commission: James Doherty, "History of the Chicago Crime Commission," *Police Digest*, December 1960.

178 "ice water smile": As described by Okrent, *Last Call*, 133.

178 "dictatorship in politics": Hoffman, *Scarface Al*, 25.

178 "sixty percent of my police [force]": Dominic J. Capeci, "Al Capone: Symbol of a Ballyhoo Society," *Journal of Ethnic Studies* 2, no. 4 (Winter 1975): 36.

178 "Chicago has shown it means": *Chicago Daily News*, Nov. 7, 1928.

179 However, when it actually came to curbing crime: Asbury, *Gangs of Chicago*.

179 "a crazy man": Hoffman, *Scarface Al*, 13.

179 One of his first acts: Much of the account that follows is based on Binder's *The Beer Wars*.

179 "the 'rackets' which have pestered": Ibid., quoting Swanson in the *Chicago Tribune*, Feb. 26, 1929.

180 "notorious in these activities": John H. Wigmore, ed., *The Illinois Crime Survey* (Chicago: Blakely, 1929), 1066.

180 "intelligent and affable": *Chicago Tribune*, Aug. 1, 1930, cited by Hoffman, *Scarface Al*, 177n12.

180 Many reasons have been offered: *New York Times*, May 19, 1931, 5.

181 "They dwell in a twilight zone": "Law Enforcement by Stigma," *New York Times*, April 25, 1930.

181 "vice monger, business manager": Chicago Crime Commission, Jacob Guzik file, nos. 21700 and 21700-1, quoting the *Chicago News* and *Chicago Examiner*, respectively. John Binder provided this reference.

181 the Hollywood movie: *The Public Enemy*, released in 1931, starred Jean Harlow along with Cagney.

181 How such a street-smart man: Binder, *Beer Wars*, names, besides the CCC and the Secret Six, the Juvenile Protective Association, the Committee of Fifteen, the Better Government Association, and the Employers Association.

182 "the free advertising": *New York Times*, June 8, 1931, 16.

182 "soft blues": *New York Times*, March 21, 1929, 14.

182 "supplying a huge public demand": W. R. Burnett, "The Czar of Chicago," review of *Al Capone*, by Pasley, *Saturday Review of Literature*, Oct. 18, 1930, 240.

182 "an ambidextrous giant": Mary Borden, "Chicago Revisited," *Harper's Magazine*, April 1931, 542.

183   "I'm no angel": Burns, *One-Way Ride,* 210–12. AC's comments about retirement are from this text.

183   "That's Al Capone speaking": Dale Carnegie, *How to Win Friends and Influence People* (New York: Simon & Schuster, 1952), 20.

183   "Once in the racket": This version of the oft-made remark is in Helmer, "Wisdom of Al Capone."

185   "If Al Capone is not murdered": *Chicago Daily News,* April 26, 1929.

CHAPTER 16: ON THE ROAD TO JAIL

186   "most strenuous efforts": Wilson, report, Dec. 21, 1933. All quotations are from this until noted otherwise.

187   "without a doubt": Report prepared by the Bureau of Internal Revenue agents W. C. Hodgins, Jacque L. Westrich, and H. N. Clagett, for the "Internal Revenue Agent in Charge, Chicago," July 8, 1931. In "IRS Historical Documents Relating to AC," available under FOIA. All quotations are from this until noted otherwise.

188   Now that Guzik was in prison: Chicago Crime Commission, Jacob Guzik File, no. 1688, quoting *Chicago Daily News,* Sept. 9, 1929. John Binder called this to my attention.

189   It was a decision that led most lawyers: When the American Bar Association's annual meeting in 1990 included a staged re-creation of the trial, both the prosecuting and the defense lawyers agreed that Mattingly should never have taken his client to the hearing.

189   The recorded remarks showed: Transcript of the April 17, 1930, interview is from IRS files and is quoted at length in Schoenberg, *Mr. Capone;* Kobler, *Capone;* Bergreen, *Capone;* and Eig, *Get Capone.*

190   In one of his most dramatic: Frank J. Wilson and Beth Day, *Special Agent: A Quarter Century with the Treasury Department and the Secret Service* (New York: Holt, Rinehart and Winston, 1965).

190   Depending on who tells that tale: Bergreen, *Capone,* 393, accepts it as fact, giving as his source Alan Hynd, *The Giant Killers* (New York: Robert M. McBride, 1945), 49. Schoenberg, *Mr. Capone,* 258–59, disputes Wilson's claim, made in *Special Agent,* 43–44. Kobler, *Capone,* 282, accepts Wilson's story. Although Kobler does not provide source notes, his bibliography confirms that he used Wilson's memoir.

191   "seize, arrest, kidnap": John Kobler's eloquent description in *Capone,* 284.

191   A city ordinance had been passed: *Miami Herald,* May 15, 1930; also quoted and with further detail in Schoenberg, *Mr. Capone,* 269.

191   The police were waiting: The following account is based on articles in the *New York Times,* the *Chicago Tribune,* the Associated Press, the *Miami Herald,* and the *Miami Daily News,* all between April 20 and June 15, 1930. Various versions that rely all or in part on these accounts can be found in Kobler, *Capone;* Schoenberg, *Mr. Capone;* and Bergreen, *Capone.*

193   "newspaper war": To write the following account, I have used the *Chicago Tribune,* stories throughout July 1930; Allsop, *Bootleggers and Their Era;* John Boettiger, *Jake Lingle* (New York: E. P. Dutton, 1931); Hoffman, *Scarface Al,* 102–5; Kobler, *Capone,* 297–98; and Schoenberg, *Mr. Capone,* 282.

194 As he had threatened: AC's denial was printed in the *Chicago Tribune,* July 20, 1930.

195 Once again, Mae was careful: *Miami Herald,* May 18, 1930, said fifty children were there; *Miami Daily News,* June 11, 1930, put the number at seventy-five.

196 Trucks wended their way: From confidential report prepared by the Bureau of Internal Revenue agents W. C. Hodgins, Jacque L. Westrick, and H. N. Clagett, "Computation of Income and Tax on Basis of Partnership," Treasury Department confidential memorandum, July 8, 1931.

196 In reality, Al paid Giblin: Schoenberg, *Mr. Capone,* 312, 445n. Citing American Bar Association trial documents, Schoenberg adds that the $10,000 was generous because AC's Philadelphia lawyers had charged far less for much greater representation.

197 At that time, the Outfit controlled: Binder, *Beer Wars,* 172–73.

198 "an assault on the Pie Handlers' Union": Ibid., 193–94. Information about labor racketeering is from this, until noted otherwise.

198 Mattingly sent the long-delayed letter: Mattingly to Herrick (Bureau of Internal Revenue, Chicago), Sept. 30, 1930.

199 Mattingly's letter worked against: Wilson, report, Dec. 21, 1933.

200 "they evaded, lied, or left town": Wilson, as quoted by Douglas O. Linder, "Al Capone Trial (1931): An Account," http://law2.umkc.edu/faculty/projects/ftrials/capone/caponeaccount.html.

CHAPTER 17: LAW ENFORCEMENT BY STIGMA

201 "Law Enforcement by Stigma": *New York Times,* April 25, 1930.

202 "a lean, long-faced grump": Schoenberg, *Mr. Capone,* 300. All quotations from this until noted otherwise.

202 "persons who neglect": *Chicago Tribune,* Sept. 10, 1930.

202 "bombinated from the bench": *Chicago Tribune,* Feb. 18, 1931.

203 When a reporter: *Chicago Tribune,* Sept. 17, 1930; Hoffman, *Scarface Al,* 120.

203 "who feed, fatten, and thrive": *Chicago Tribune,* Sept. 24, 1930; Hoffman, *Scarface Al,* 122.

204 "abnormal crime situation[s]": *Chicago Daily News,* Nov. 23, 1928.

204 "cool effrontery": *Chicago Daily News,* Nov. 3 and 4, 1930.

205 He eluded arrest: *Chicago Tribune,* Oct. 5, 1930.

206 Al pulled out all the stops: To write about the wedding, I have consulted the standard biographies (Kobler, *Capone;* Schoenberg, *Mr. Capone;* Bergreen, *Capone*) and the following newspapers: in Chicago, the *Herald and Examiner, Tribune, Post, Daily News, Daily Times.* Also, the *New York Times.* Members of the Capone family have contributed both personal memories and stories they were told by their elders.

207 "blubbering jungle hippopotamus": *Chicago Tribune,* Feb. 22, 1931; *Chicago Herald and Examiner,* Feb. 24, 1931.

208 "a sumptuous blue suit": The quotations are from Schoenberg, *Mr. Capone,* 305, 306, 310; Kobler, *Capone,* 320; Bergreen, *Capone,* 418.

CHAPTER 18: JAIL IS A BAD PLACE UNDER ANY CIRCUMSTANCES

211   Wilson sent impassioned requests: Wilson to Irey, March 27, 1931. I have been told by several lawyers, including Mary Lawrence Test and Vincent J. Bartolotta Jr., that several thousand documents are not really very many in a trial such as this. I, and the lawyers I have consulted, consider this another of Wilson's exaggerations.

211   Wilson and his team gathered: Wilson, report, Dec. 21, 1933.

211   Wilson described how he stumbled upon them: Wilson, "Undercover Man," *Collier's*, April 26, 1947; Chicago Tribune Archives, June 14, 1959, p. 284.

212   "prowled the crummy streets": Ibid., p. 33; Linder, "Al Capone Trial (1931*)*."

212   "Hanging an income tax rap": Frank J. Wilson, as told to Howard Whitman, "How We Caught Al Capone," *Chicago Tribune*, June 14, 1959, a reprinted but abridged and slightly changed version originally from *Collier's*, April 26, 1947.

213   "wash their own dirty linen": Kobler, *Capone*, 276.

214   "took him to task": Chicago Crime Commission, Jake Guzik file, no. 1688, Nov. 14, 1920. John Binder provided this information.

214   "cocky, beady eyed, cop-hating": Wilson, as told to Whitman, "How We Caught Al Capone."

216   "Scarface Al, [sitting] with a jeweled moll": Ibid.

216   "merely shake . . . He rattled": The connection to the 1954 song "Shake, Rattle, and Roll" is irresistible in the context of Wilson's wording. One hopes his co-writer and/or editor for the 1965 memoir had the grace to shorten it for publication.

216   Wilson tracked down one other witness: *Chicago Tribune*, March 6, 1931; *Berkeley Daily Gazette*, June 17, 1931.

217   "bedraggled veteran in her fifties": Wilson, report, Dec. 21, 1933; retold in Kobler, *Capone*, 279.

218   Malone's role as Lepito: Irey and Slocum, *Tax Dodgers;* Wilson and Day, *Special Agent*.

218   "the greatest undercover agent": Wilson's report to Irey, December 31, 1933; Wilson as noted above; David Porter, "Gun Owned by Agent Who Toppled Capone Headed to Vegas Museum," Associated Press, March 28, 2015. Porter is quoting Paul Camacho, former head of IRS Criminal Investigation and "unofficial agency historian." The story relates that Malone's Smith & Wesson .38 special was part of a social exhibition at the Mob Museum. The gun is now owned by his nephew, who said his mother found it under Malone's pillow after he died in 1960 in Minnesota.

218   "why kill him?": Schoenberg, *Mr. Capone*, 296.

218   High-level gamesmanship existed: Wilson, "How We Caught Al Capone," *Chicago Tribune*, June 14, 1959.

CHAPTER 19: "WHO WOULDN'T BE WORRIED?"

219   "an admission of large taxable income": Wilson, report, Dec. 21, 1933.

220   "the backroom brief writing partner": Schoenberg, http://www.alcaponebio .com/al_capone_outline.htm (this site is no longer active).

220   they thought he should have been aware: Members of the Capone family who ask not to be identified hold the first opinion. Robert J. Schoenberg believes that AC was fully competent mentally in 1931 despite his seeming indifference

to the case (telephone conversation, May 21, 2015; see also *Mr. Capone*, 255–56). John Binder believes that AC might have initially "'gone along' to an extent" with his lawyers in the belief that the plea bargain would result in a reduced sentence. Binder also believes AC was mentally competent but that there was incompetence on both sides: AC's lawyers, who should have known many charges were unenforceable due to statutes of limitations; AC "should have been aware of legalistics" governing the Terrance J. Druggan, Frank "Frankie" Lake, and Frank Nitti trials that applied to his case and should have conferred with his lawyers about them. E-mail and telephone conversation, May 27, 2015.

225 "pushed around so much": *Chicago Tribune*, June 6, 1931.
226 "Jail's a bad place under any circumstances": *Philadelphia Bulletin*, March 15, 1930.
227 "conspiracies and conspiracies": *Philadelphia Inquirer*, June 30, 1931.
228 the victory was Capone's: *New Republic*, July 1, 1931. Eig, *Get Capone*, 342, accepts the veracity (unproven) of George Murray, a reporter for the *Chicago American* who had strong ties to underworld informants. He had covered the trial and wrote in a column of July 23, 1956, that the main reason Judge Wilkerson was so intent on bringing AC to trial was that he was visited "two days before Capone was to come to court . . . by the confidential secretary of the man [President Hoover] in Washington." Murray claimed Wilkerson emerged from the meeting "visibly shaken." Eig comments, "The wonder is that Wilkerson never told it to Johnson." The entire account, both by Murray and by Eig, is highly suspect. Judges are expected to be impartial, but one wonders if this one would have subjected the prosecuting attorney to such public humiliation, which was certainly harmful to the government's case.
228 He said it was likely: To write the following, I have primarily consulted (among many others) the *Chicago Tribune*, July 31, 1931, transcript of the proceedings; *Chicago Daily News*, transcript of the opening statement; Schoenberg, *Mr. Capone*, 314–15; Francis X. Busch, *Enemies of the State*, 201 (New York: Bobbs-Merrill, 1954); Robert Ross, *The Trial of Al Capone*, 42 (Chicago: Robert Ross, 1933); Wilson, report, Dec. 21, 1933; Hoffman, *Scarface Al*, 160–64; Iorizzo, *Al Capone*, 73–88; personal communications with John Binder and Robert J. Schoenberg.
230 "Well, who wouldn't be": Both stories were Oct. 7, 1931.

CHAPTER 20: "I GUESS IT'S ALL OVER"

231 "forced by Capone": Wilson, report, Dec. 21, 1933.
233 And what they knew of gangland violence: To write the following, I have relied primarily on newspapers, most notably the *New York Times* and in Chicago the *Tribune, Herald and Examiner, Daily News, Evening Post,* and *American*. Also, personal communication with Robert J. Schoenberg, who conducted several important interviews with trial observers and participants and who will be cited separately. John Binder contributed information through useful conversations and e-mails. I have also consulted the books cited throughout of Kobler, Bergreen, Iorizzo, Hoffman, and Binder.
234 Thomas Nash, who had defended Al in the past: Schoenberg consulted Nash's son, who had no knowledge of why his father, still representing AC, was never present at the trial.
237 "really inept criminal defense lawyers": Schoenberg, *Mr. Capone*, 317.

238 "When a man makes such statements": *Chicago Herald and Examiner,* Oct. 9, 1931.

238 "Wouldn't the size of the roll": *Chicago Daily News,* Oct. 10, 1931.

238 "too much for the rural gentlemen": *New York Times,* Oct. 13, 1931.

241 "There seems to be a reasonable doubt": *New York Times,* Oct. 17, 1931.

242 "In other words, can a man get away": Schoenberg, *Mr. Capone,* 323.

245 "unjustly, especially by the press": U.S. Public Health Service, U.S. Penitentiary, Atlanta, Neuro-psychiatric Examination, 40886-Alphonse Capone, May 18, 1932. Mental examination by C. R. F. Beall, psychiatrist, 4.

245 Except for the occasional slip: *Chicago Tribune,* March 21, 1931.

246 "King Alphonse": *Chicago Tribune,* June 15, 1931.

246 "porcine bulk": *Chicago Tribune,* Feb. 26, 1931.

246 "greasy and grinning": *Time,* Sept. 21, 1931.

246 "thick lips": *New York Times,* Oct. 8, 1931.

246 "grinning at the crowds": *Chicago Tribune,* Oct. 8, 1931.

246 "one of those prodigious Italians": *Chicago Herald and Examiner,* Jan. 18, 1931.

246 "You are not wanted": *New York Times,* Oct. 3, 1931.

246 "passion for colored silk underwear": *New York Times,* Oct. 18, 1931.

247 "collegiate style": *New York Times,* Oct. 14, 1931.

247 "a technical means to the end": *Washington Evening Star,* Oct. 24, 1931.

248 "Back then nobody cared": As quoted by Schoenberg, *Mr. Capone,* 324.

CHAPTER 21: "I'M IN JAIL; AREN'T THEY SATISFIED?"

249 Once again, the press pounced: Some of the sources I have consulted include the Chicago papers: *Tribune, Daily News, Daily Times, Herald and Examiner,* and *Post.* Also, *New York Times.* Books include Bergreen, *Capone;* Binder, *Beer Wars;* Busch, *Enemies of the State;* Hoffman, *Scarface Al;* Iorizzo, *Al Capone;* Kobler, *Capone;* Ross, *Trial of Al Capone;* and Schoenberg, *Mr. Capone.* Others will be cited where appropriate.

251 It made for a lively story: Schoenberg, *Mr. Capone,* 327–28, 448n, cites Kobler, *Capone,* 351, where the only mention of this possible incident is that AC's brothers brought him news that Torrio had formed a partnership with Schultz. I was unable to find verification of Schoenberg's contention, and none of my other research confirmed that this actually happened.

251 Various gangster memoirs: Among them, Joseph Bonanno, *A Man of Honor* (New York: St. Martin's Press, 1983).

252 It was not the last time: Diane Capone said she knew of one visit to Alcatraz because her father talked about how he and Mae would go from one movie theater to another, basically killing time until they could see AC.

254 They tried to hide from the flashing: "Government Takes Capone for Ride to Leavenworth," Universal Newspaper Newsreel, n.d., https://www.youtube.com/watch?v+p8wF2FJOGEY.

254 Another unidentified woman: Besides Ralph, Matthew was the only brother then married. He was twenty-four and the father of one child. Mafalda might have been holding his child, because she had just given birth to her daughter on April 26, 1932. Although Dolores Teresa weighed more than eight pounds, the child Mafalda carried appeared to be at least a year old.

255 a card game with one of the escort marshals: See the photograph in Mark

Douglas Brown, *Capone: Life Behind Bars in Alcatraz* (San Francisco: Golden Gate National Parks Conservancy, 2004), 18.

255 He entered the Atlanta penitentiary: May 4 is the date generally given, but it was actually the fifth, because the train took well over twenty-four hours on the journey from Chicago.

255 Otherwise, with the exception: Information that follows is from AC's medical records and correspondence exchanged from 1939 to 1947 between his two physicians, Dr. Kenneth Phillips in Miami and Dr. Joseph Moore in Baltimore. The complete medical history is in the Marc and Mary Perkins Collection.

255 Capone became furious: In her memoir, Polly Adler writes, "Gangsters in general have a very low opinion of prostitutes . . . A big-time gangster regards a 'prostitution man'—that is, a man who makes his money through procuring, even indirectly—as the lowest thing there is." *A House Is Not a Home*, 173.

256 He was pleasant and lucid: Neuro-psychiatric Examination, May 18, 1932. Copy graciously provided by John Binder. Partial copy is reprinted in Brown, *Life Behind Bars*, 16–17.

257 "entirely inadequate": Dr. Joseph Moore to Dr. Kenneth Phillips, Jan. 15, 1941, Perkins Collection.

258 "go astray as some New's Paper": Bureau of Prisons documents, June 22, 1932, to the orchestra leader, July 26, 1932, to the deputy warden. Both reprinted in Brown, *Life Behind Bars*, 18.

258 There were times when he received: Information that follows until noted otherwise is from Brown, *Life Behind Bars*, 19–25, where some of the letters are reprinted.

259 three-part series on the front pages: The first installment appeared on Jan. 23, 1932. Others followed on consecutive days.

260 "at all interesting": Neuro-psychiatric Examination, May 18, 1932.

260 no concrete evidence that he used drugs: Of his many biographers, only Bergreen, *Capone*, 513, alleges that AC used cocaine. He is the originator of the theory that AC used it beforehand and had withdrawal symptoms in prison. AC family members tell the story, only to insist it is entirely false. Drs. Phillips and Moore make no mention of drugs, and to date they provide the most intimate details of AC's habits.

260 The first myth: Schoenberg, *Mr. Capone*, in notes to p. 332 on p. 450, describes how AC had everything shipped to his mother in Chicago except for the encyclopedias, which he shipped to Mae in Miami. Kobler gives variations of these stories in *Capone*, chap. 26; Bergreen's version is in *Capone*, 510–16.

261 Al Capone spent two years: AC's cell mate at Atlanta Morris "Red" Rudensky (along with Don Riley) wrote a memoir, *The Gonif* (Blue Earth, Minn.: Piper, 1970); a 250-page manuscript allegedly written by an anonymous convict who served time with AC was sent by him to the Federal Bureau of Prisons, where it is now in the AC Permanent File. It is generally discounted because of the wildly inaccurate accounts it contains.

261 He received no special favors: Warden A. C. Aderhold to director, Bureau of Prisons, Jan. 24, 1932, BOP document files, reprinted in Brown, *Life Behind Bars*, 22–23.

262 "on an island": Homer Cummings, *Selected Papers of Homer Cummings: Attorney General of the United States*, 1933–39 (New York: Scribner, 1939).

CHAPTER 22: THE MOST INTRIGUING OF ALL CRIMINALS

263   "too big a problem": James V. Bennett, *I Chose Prison* (New York: Alfred A. Knopf, 1970), 99.

264   none dared risk such a furious assault: Cory Kincade (the pen name of Jolene Babyak, who lived at Alcatraz as a young child) wrote this in her highly suspect book, *Alcatraz Most Wanted: Profiles of the Most Famous Prisoners on the Rock* (Berkeley, Calif.: Ariel Vamp, 2008), 7. To be fair, in this instance she is both quoting and paraphrasing what James A. Johnston wrote in *Alcatraz Island Prison* (New York: Charles Scribner's Sons, 1949).

264   Another story followed Al Capone: Schoenberg, *Mr. Capone*, 332n, quotes Kobler (who did not give citations in his book), *Capone*, 358, saying he (Kobler) talked to Rudensky, who told it to him and also allowed him to read about it in an unpublished version of his published book *The Gonif*. Because Rudensky was a known contributor to inflated newspaper stories, and there is no other documentation to support the account Schoenberg gives on p. 335, I consider it highly suspect until proven otherwise.

265   The calm, resigned letters: Information about AC's attitude from Diane Capone in telephone conversation, June 5, 2015. Information about visits from Paul J. Madigan, *Institution Rules and Regulations: United States Penitentiary, Alcatraz, California, Revised* 1956, 18.

265   "the Good Time Law": Revised Title 18 of the U.S. Code, sec. 4161, as noted in Madigan, *Institute Rules and Regulations*, 18–19.

265   "to make any moves of any kind": Letter dated only "Feb." Internal evidence suggests one of the last years of his incarceration.

265   "Al Capone looms on the horizon": Roy Gardner, unpublished MS, in Esslinger, *Letters from Alcatraz*, 48.

266   "Clicks" formed quickly in Alcatraz: This was the spelling used by inmates for prisoners who had been members of, among others, the Machine Gun Kelly and Barker gangs and the rival Chicago gang the Terrible Touhy bootleggers.

266   "the hopeless despair": Information that follows is from Gardner's *Hellcatraz*, written in 1938 and originally self-published. Republished in book form in 2000 after editing by Tom Ryan, as Douglas/Ryan Communications.

267   "good (not 'excellent')": *Confidential Work Report to the United States Board of Parole*, Aug. 8, 1935, reprinted in Brown, *Life Behind Bars*, 33.

269   The medical examiner's report: George Hess (surgeon and chief medical officer) to Johnston (warden), June 26, 1936, Bureau of Prisons document in the file of Alphonse Capone, No. 85, reprinted in Brown, *Life Behind Bars*, 39.

270   In an undated letter: AC to Johnston, n.d., Bureau of Prisons documents, reprinted in Esslinger, *Letters from Alcatraz*, 53–54.

270   Interestingly, the letter was signed: AC's letter is undated; Teresa Capone's is Dec. 3, 1934, Bureau of Prisons documents, reprinted in Esslinger, *Letters from Alcatraz*, 53–54.

272   "Ask Ralph how sure he is": AC to MC, March 3, 1935, Bureau of Prisons documents, reprinted in Esslinger, *Letters from Alcatraz*, 56–57.

272   The letter, which made it through the censors unedited: Johnston to Bates, March 6, 1935, Bureau of Prisons Archives, reprinted in Esslinger, *Letters from Alcatraz*, 55.

273   "I love and adore you": Esslinger, *Letters from Alcatraz*, March 3, 1935, 56–57.

273   He was fond of the priest: Father Clark was a member of the Society of Jesuits,

and he left his papers to the California Jesuit Archives, Santa Clara. Boxes 2 and 3 contain pertinent information about AC. Diane Capone remembers MC speaking of a seminarian AC liked to talk to, "whose name ironically was Casey."

274 By Tuesday the eighth: Headlines are (respectively) from *International Herald Tribune Asia, El Paso Herald-Post,* and *Oakland Tribune,* all Feb. 8, 1938.

275 Capone did resist the guards: *Oakland Tribune* and *Bakersfield Guardian,* both Feb. 8, 1938.

275 "Due to the rumors": MC's telegram and Johnston's of the same date are among Bureau of Prisons Archives for Alphonse Capone, No. 85. Schoenberg, *Mr. Capone,* 343, reprints the entirety of each.

276 The second and equally important petition: *New York Times,* Feb. 8, 1938.

276 "God above to make me well": AC to MC, Feb. 1938, emphasis mine.

276 "If you've got something on your mind": AC to Mr. A. Capone Jr., Feb. 17, 1938.

279 The memorandum written: Bureau of Prisons, memorandum of Nov. 9, 1939. Because this happened on November 16, the date is obviously wrong.

CHAPTER 23: THE ENDGAME

280 Dr. Moore reluctantly agreed to take charge: James V. Bennett (director, Bureau of Prisons) to Dr. Joseph Moore, Dec. 21, 1939.

280 Mae and Ralph both assured Dr. Moore: Information that follows is from the medical records and correspondence exchanged between Dr. Kenneth Phillips in Miami, the Capone family physician from 1928 until AC's death in 1947, and for the family afterward, and Dr. Joseph Moore, in Baltimore, who cared for AC after his release from Alcatraz in 1939 and who consulted with Dr. Phillips until AC's death.

280 Here again, exaggerated rumors abounded: Welcome to Baltimore, Hon!, http://welcometobaltimorehon.com/al-capones-cherry-tree.

281 "inadequate": Moore to Phillips, History and Summary of AC's condition, Jan. 15, 1941.

281 "grandiose ideas, a marked tendency": Moore to Phillips, May 27, 1940.

282 Mae donated two weeping cherry trees in Al's name: One was cut down in the 1950s to make way for a new addition; the other split in half after a heavy snowfall in 2010, and the wood was given to a craftsman, Nick Aloisio, who turned it into bowls and other objects that were sold on eBay in 2012 as a fund-raiser for the hospital. Still standing to this day are trees alleged to have been created from the one felled, all listed on the national registry of historic landmarks.

283 The doctors concluded: Moore's March 20, 1940, initial assessment, to Phillips.

285 the entire Capone family was living on the weekly $600: Information about money received is from the massive files the FBI maintained on AC during the last years of his life.

285 "he said things he should not have": Three separate members of the older generation of the Capone family are the source of this information. All asked to remain unidentified.

285 Totally untrue were the stories: A scene in the 1975 movie *Capone,* which starred Ben Gazzara as AC, showed such a scene and reinforced the continuation of the falsehood.

286   Diana Ruth Casey: She was born Ruth Diana, but after her divorce when she moved to California in the 1960s, she reversed the names and became known as Diana Ruth Casey.

286   Boogie: The nickname was given to her by her younger brother, who could not say "Ruthie," as she was originally called by her family. His pronunciation stuck, and that was how she was known throughout her life.

286   Mae's sister Muriel: Some biographers claim that "Daniel" Coughlin and his wife, "Winnie," lived in the house as well. Mae's brother, Dennis (called Danny), was the youngest of her six siblings, and he was not in residence during AC's final years. He lived in Miami on and off during World War II but afterward moved to California in the late 1940s. Information about life at Palm Island is from Diane Capone and other members of the extended Capone family.

286   Gertrude F. Cole: Information about Gertrude Cole is from her granddaughter, Jan Day Gravel, Aug. 7, 2013, and from Bobby Livingston of RR Auction, who sold "Al's Grocery List" that same month.

287   "Mama Mae loved him dearly": Diane Capone, telephone conversation, June 5, 2015.

287   All the FBI's spying memos: FBI, Al Capone file.

288   "in aid of execution": Teitelbaum to Phillips, Feb. 10, 1941.

288   Dr. Moore wanted to examine Al: Moore to Phillips, Dec. 16, 1940. Actual visit took place January 10–12, 1941.

289   "Mr. Ralph and Mr. John": Moore to Phillips, June 11, 1940.

289   Dr. Phillips was frustrated: Dr. George W. Hall practiced in Chicago and for a time was asked to consult by Dr. Moore. In a letter to Moore, April 12, 1940, he said he had seen AC when he was at Alcatraz, "as a visitor, but had nothing whatever to do with recommending treatment in his case." Hall appears from the correspondence to have been the go-between until Moore and Phillips resolved AC's supervision.

290   "Here is your friend Al Capone": AC, handwritten letter to Phillips, Aug. 25, 1941, Hurley, Wis. I have reprinted it exactly as he wrote it.

290   "Recheck examinations are essential": Moore to Ralph Capone, Sept. 2, 1941. In a telephone conversation, June 5, 2015, AC's granddaughter said that to the best of her knowledge her grandmother was never treated during the years she was adult enough to have been aware of illness or hospitalization; she said the same about her father.

291   going from one movie to another: Diane Capone, e-mail letter, Sept. 24, 2015.

292   "He has become quite obese": FBI AC File, memo of April 13, 1945.

293   his greatest delight was to walk: Veronica was born in 1943, Diane in 1944. Diane learned to walk at age ten months. Being with "Papa" in the garden is one of her cherished memories. Telephone conversation, July 12, 2015.

293   The stories of Al in pajamas: The claim that the pool was stocked with fish was made in various television interviews in 2014–2015 by Deirdre Marie Griswold, who now calls herself Capone, recorded at the time the Palm Island house was undergoing renovations. AC's granddaughters and all others who were in the house during AC's lifetime agree that she was never there during his lifetime.

293   "that never, ever happened": Diane Capone, July 12, 2015. She is referring to a photograph in the self-published book Uncle Al Capone: The Untold Story from Inside His Family (n.p.: Recap, 2012), 169, by Deirdre Marie Griswold, who now calls herself Deirdre Marie Capone. She is the granddaughter of Ralph Capone

and the daughter of his son, Ralphie (Ralph junior). The photograph shows a girl on the lap of a man in a Santa suit. It is not Al Capone.

293   Shortly after the start: The only evidence to date that AC made this second trip to Ralph's lodge is the mention in Phillips's letter to the Dade County Medical Society, June 23, 1946. Diane Capone (telephone conversation, July 12, 2015) thinks she might have heard her grandmother Mae speak of other, earlier, summer trips but says she has no written evidence to support it. Harry Hart, the son of Vincenzo "Two Gun Hart" Capone, claimed AC was there on several other occasions between 1941 and 1945. John Binder consulted his files and found no reference to the 1945 visit or any other after 1941. None of the biographies write of any other trip than 1941, except for Bergreen, who quotes Hart in *Capone*, 592–93. Because AC's summer trips to Wisconsin are a matter of continuing speculation, I offer the above to add to the mix.

294   "up north doing business": Information that follows is from Phillips to national and local press services, June 23, 1946.

294   He survived the injuries long enough: *Chicago Daily News*, June 25 and 26, 1946.

295   "save you many possible headaches": The telegram is among the Moore-Phillips archives, now owned by Marc and Mary Perkins.

295   In January 1947, the wrath: Phillips to Dr. Elmo D. French (chairman of the Press Relations Committee, Dade County Medical Society, Miami), Jan. 22, 1947.

296   he bought a partnership in a restaurant: He was in partnership with Ted Traina, who owned the popular Ted's Grotto. Sonny eventually took full control and changed the name simply to the Grotto.

297   a small bedroom at the back of the house: This is a correction AC's granddaughters would like to make regarding the small bedroom: "There was also a beautiful blue satin chaise longue in that little bedroom that Mama Mae made into a sitting room off the third guest bedroom [where AC allegedly died]. He *did not die* in that little room with the twin beds. He died in his own big bed in the master bedroom. Maybe Mama Mae slept there [with him] sometimes, but he was not in that room when he died. He was in the master bedroom, in their big bed." Telephone conversation, Aug. 7, 2014.

297   "stertorous": Phillips to Moore, "Death Report," entries dated Jan. 21–27, 1947. Mark and Mary Perkins collection.

CHAPTER 24: THE END

298   The end, when it came: Unless otherwise noted, information about AC's final illness is from the Phillips-Moore correspondence, particularly the Death Report, Jan. 21–27, 1947. Also, from members of the Capone family who do not wish to be cited by name.

299   It was one of the last times: Diane Capone shared this memory in telephone conversations, June 5 and July 12, 2015.

299   "paresis, a chronic brain disease": "Al Capone Dead of Heart Attack," *Baltimore Sun*, Jan. 26, 1947.

300   "tourists and the curious": "Al Capone Dies in Florida Villa," *Chicago Tribune*, Jan. 26, 1947.

301   "I don't want that son of a bitch": Schoenberg, *Mr. Capone*, 354. A note on p. 455 gives the source as a Milt Sosin interview.

301 When Al's death happened: Among the many sources with different versions of his life and death were "Capone Dead at 48; Dry Era Gang Chief," Associated Press, Jan. 26, 1947; "Al Capone Dead of Heart Attack," *Baltimore Sun,* Jan. 26, 1947; "Apoplexy, Not Gun, Kills Al Capone," *Los Angeles Times,* Jan. 25, 1947. Like most others, these were front page.

301 Even the paper of record: "Capone Dead at 48; Dry Era Gang Chief," *New York Times,* Jan. 26, 1947. The *Times* was one of the few papers that did not run the story on the front page; it was on p. 7.

302 "hiding their faces": Of all the graveside stories, this is the only one Phillips kept. Phillips-Moore Archive, Marc and Mary Perkins Collection.

302 "I'll kill any son of a bitch": Schoenberg, *Mr. Capone,* 355.

303 "The wages of sin is death": *New York Times,* Jan. 27, 1947.

303 "officially . . . tied up": "701 Gang Deaths in Capone's Time," *Los Angeles Times,* Jan. 26, 1947.

303 "the generosity of his brothers": Abraham Teitelbaum, interview with *New York Times,* Jan. 27, 1947.

CHAPTER 25: THE LEGACY

306 "a piece of Al": Private 2013 correspondence with a collector who does not wish to be identified.

306 The house was sold shortly after she died: Schoenberg, *Mr. Capone,* 360, is among the first; Deirdre Marie Griswold (who now calls herself Capone) is among the second; various Capone scholars (including William J. Helmer) are among the third. The many newspapers who wrote about the sale are so contradictory that I cite none of them here.

307 The desire for "a piece of Al": The *Huffington Post,* June 20, 2011, cited NBC Chicago as the source for the $16,500 sale of an autographed photograph of AC and an autographed $5 bill at $9,500. At the time, Christie's London was selling a 1929 model .38-caliber Colt Police Special revolver for $80,550, with sale price expected to be in the range of $112,000 or more.

307 Recently, a collection of twig porch furniture: Meghan Edwards, "Wright Launches Style Sale Concept with Blackman Cruz," *Interior Design,* April 3, 2015.

308 his descendants commissioned a biography: Jeff McArthur, *Two Gun Hart: Lawman, Cowboy, and Long-Lost Brother of Al Capone* (Burbank, Calif.: Bandwagon Books), 2013.

309 Quite simply, his family was destitute: Richard Hart, great-grandson of Two Gun Hart, e-mail, Dec. 19, 2014, stated that the family discussed the allegations with the author, who "watered it down." Richard Hart believes the rumors of stealing were started by Kathleen Hart's brother, Richard Winch, "who never really got along with Richard [Hart]. On occasion, Richard did not pay for items, but they were traded for services given his skill as a handyman."

310 The Kefauver Crime Commission called Ralph: John (Mimi Capone) Martin was also called before the Kefauver Committee, but like Ralph he told them very little of substance. They gave testimony to the Kefauver Committee, formally known as the Special Committee to Investigate Organized Crime in Interstate Commerce, in September 1951.

310 "Hart-or-Capone": "Capone Tax Quiz Turns Up Long Lost Brother," *Chicago Tribune,* Sept. 20, 1951.

310 Two Gun testified before a grand jury: Information contained in the eight-page testimony of "Richard J. Hart," to the grand jury for his brother's income tax evasion trial, given September 21, 1951, National Archives, Chicago, v. 4 and v. 5. The charges were dismissed after the 1952 trial.

311 "whiskey-soaked corpse": I am grateful to John Binder for providing information from his personal archives about Ralphie's college career, marriage, change of name, and the birth of his children. Other information comes from *Chicago Tribune, Daily News, Sun Times.*

311 Ralphie was thirty-three: Ralphie was the name by which he was known in the family. The *Chicago Sun Times,* Nov. 10, 1950, gave him the nickname Risky, which Schoenberg, *Mr. Capone,* 361, repeats. The paper invented the nickname, and he was never called by it.

311 there was no onus attached to the name: Contention made by his daughter, Deirdre Marie Gabriel O'Donnell Griswold (who now calls herself Capone). An article in the *Chicago Tribune,* "Capone Kin's Ex-wife Gets Name Changed," Sept. 21, 1960, states that Elizabeth Marie Capone, forty-one, and her son, Ralph Dennis Capone, seventeen, had their names officially changed "to give [Mrs. Capone's] son a better chance." She stated that they married in March 1938, before Ralphie's graduation, in Warren County, Indiana, with his name given as Ralph Gabrail Caponi Jr. (*sic*) and his father's as Ralph James Caponi (*sic*). Elizabeth Capone told the judge they divorced in 1945 and Gabriel was the name they used throughout their marriage and under which they registered the births of their children. By the time of the official legal name change, her nineteen-year-old daughter, Deirdre, was not involved, because she was married in 1959 to her first husband, Thomas O'Donnell, and was using his name legally. Deirdre Griswold, calling herself Capone, told the *Chicago Tribune* that her father "got his law degree from Loyola, but the Chicago Bar Association wouldn't allow him to practice because his last name was Capone." "Deirdre Capone Softens a Notorious Icon," *Chicago Tribune,* Dec. 29, 2012. A search of the Loyola University Alumni Directory by John Binder revealed no listing for the name Gabriel or any variant of Capone. There are no other university records to confirm that he ever attended, graduated, or took the bar exam. A letter from the Law Registrar of Loyola Law School to John Binder, Nov. 4, 2015, stated that the school had no record he was ever admitted, attended, or was graduated from the law school.

311 At his daughter's birth: From Certificate of Birth, no. 2896, Chicago, Central Hospital, Cook County, for "Diedre" (*sic*) Marie Gabriel. It marked the first time Deirdre Gabriel was ever called by that surname.

312 the note to Jean Kerin: "Find Capone Jr., Nephew of Gang Chieftain, Dead," *Chicago Tribune,* Nov. 10, 1950. "I was astounded when I was called about Ralph's death," she said. "I talked to him Saturday and we were on good terms."

312 "nothing but warmth and love": Brian Gabriel, telephone interview, Aug. 13, 2014.

313 Ralph ended his days in Mercer: For information about Ralph Capone in Mercer, I am indebted to Jane Kinney Denning, Bob and June Kinney, Kevin Kinney, Gennaro "Jeep" Capone, and Joanie Stern. Also "Time Rewards AC's Brother with Luxury of Obscurity," *Milwaukee Sentinel,* May 1, 1972; "Bygones," *Duluth News Tribune,* Nov. 24, 1972; McKevitt-Patrick Funeral Home Inc., Ironwood, Michigan: obituary for Sherman W. Hart, Oct. 16, 2010.

313 "he became Santa Claus": *Milwaukee Sentinel,* May 1, 1972.

313   her granddaughters auctioned a collection of jewelry: Madeleine Kozup was
       a nurse and chairwoman of the Iron County Republican Party when she
       married Ralph Capone. After his death, she married his business partner,
       Serafino "Suds" Morichetti. As of 2014, she was in her nineties and was living
       in a nursing home in Hurley, Wisconsin. In August 2015, her granddaughters
       consigned various jewelry, photographs, and objects (one alleged to be a 4.25-
       carat pinkie ring owned by AC; all other sources give the carat weight of AC's
       ring as 11) to ATR Estate Sales, Kenosha, Wisconsin.

313   Mafalda never conquered: Charges against policeman by Mae Maritote,
       Freeport Journal-Standard, March 26, 1958.

315   Diana came from a background: Diane Capone provided information about
       her parents in numerous telephone conversations throughout 2013–15.

317   Only once did she relinquish: They asked Ralph to join them in the suit, and he
       refused. It was the last time Mae did battle with her brother-in-law. According
       to most Capone descendants, she never forgave him and only communicated
       with him when she had no other choice. For an excellent overview of the legal
       dispute, see "Suit Brought by Capone Heirs Dismissed: Judge Sees Need for
       Remedy in Such Cases," *Chicago Tribune,* June 17, 1964. The judge ruled that
       the defendants did "unjustly enrich" themselves, but the law was vague about
       whether the right to privacy continued after the death of the injured party,
       and he had no choice but to dismiss the Capone family's suit. Earlier, in 1962,
       Mafalda Maritote lost a separate $9.5 million suit in which she tried to assert
       that an Allied Artists movie had violated property rights to AC's name and
       private life.

318   Having done his shopping: News stories differ about what these objects were;
       most say bottles of aspirin and packets of batteries.

318   "everyone has a little larceny": From stories in the *Miami Herald,* the *Miami
       Daily News,* and the *Chicago Tribune,* Aug. 7, 1965.

318   July 8, 2004: He died on July 8, but by law the certificate had to be dated when
       the doctor signed it, and he did not do so until after midnight, which made it
       July 9.

319   The catalyst for the group decision: Deirdre Marie Capone, *Uncle Al Capone.*
       So many statements in the book are false that I do not list them here, but there
       are some allegations that particularly offend AC's granddaughters, who would
       like to have them addressed. They believe the photograph in the frontispiece
       has been Photoshopped. Deirdre Griswold denied it in an exchange with
       me on March 23, 2015, via e-mail. In the photograph, p. 169, she claims she is
       sitting on AC's lap while he is dressed in a Santa costume. AC's granddaughters
       insist vehemently that he never dressed in costume and would not have
       been mentally capable of doing so around Christmas 1944, when the picture
       must have been taken and when he spent the holiday with his wife, son, and
       granddaughters. The photograph of two persons in front of a car on p. 174 is
       not, as the subtitle has it, of Mae and Sonny outside his restaurant. The couple
       are Diana and Sonny Capone, and the house in the background is where they
       lived with their four daughters.

319   "I am the last person": Blog by adelesymonds, "At Home with Al Capone,"
       Oct. 19, 2012. She further alleged, in a series of remarks beginning with "no one
       else still alive" that she is the only one who has family photographs, documents,
       and archives, sat on Al's lap as a child, was taught by him to play the mandolin,
       helped prepare the large Sunday meals served at Prairie Avenue, and can

"describe the exhilarating highs and depressing lows of my childhood and adulthood as Capone."

320   Christopher Knight: Unless otherwise noted, information about and from Christopher Knight comes from interviews with him, June 19 and July 1, 2013.

320   a 1927 newspaper article: "Hollywood Too Lonesome So Scarface Goes Home," *Atlanta Constitution,* Dec. 17, 1927.

320   the book he self-published: Chris W. Knight, *Son of Scarface: A Memoir by the Grandson of Al Capone* (New York: New Era, 2008).

320   "to proceed through less invasive means": "Al Capone's 'Grandson' Wants DNA Samples," Associated Press, March 13, 2009. The lawyer quoted was David M. Hundley.

321   Chris Knight ran afoul: Information and quotations that follow are from David Kesmodel, "Growing Up Capone: Mobster's Kin Go to the Mattresses," *Wall Street Journal,* July 20, 2010.

321   a reality television series: The series ran for one season on ReelzChannel in 2014.

321   Knight jumped into the fray: "Al Capone—War Brewing over New Reality Show," TMZ.com, April 17, 2014.

321   When asked to explain this: In a telephone conversation, June 1, 2013, Griswold said the following: "I'm trying to get it stopped. I have lawyers on the case right now . . . What they are doing here is breaking the law." I asked, "What law are they breaking?" She replied, "Illinois has a deceptive practices law, and I'm going to get it enforced . . . I sent two certified letters, and those people refused to accept them. Now I am sending letters to owners of the studio [channel]." I asked how she thought she could stop the program from going forward. She replied, "Because of the publicity I am generating about them. I have reached out to the Italian community, and they are all behind me." At this point, she became angry, said I did not know what I was talking about, and changed the subject. Later in the same conversation, she said if the sponsors "could come to an arrangement" with her, she might withdraw her objections.

322   "kids who can't name": *Al Capone: Icon,* PBS documentary, 2014.

322   "where the legend outran the man": *The Man Who Shot Liberty Valance,* 1962. Directed by John Ford, starring James Stewart, John Wayne, Lee Marvin, Edmond O'Brien, and Vera Miles.

CHAPTER 26: THE LEGEND

323   mockumentaries: "A Town, a Gangster, a Festival," an episode of *Documentary Now!,* IFC, Sept. 2015.

323   "he killed bad guys": Aiden Capone, July 27, 2013.

323   *Boardwalk Empire:* Several friends who are nonfiction writers marvel at how their college-age and slightly older children relish the events of this program and how the AC character is their particular hero.

323   The Madame Tussauds wax museum: I thank Anne Heller and Will Swift for alerting me to this.

324   a course titled simply "Al Capone": Offered by Jorie Walters, who described the original offering as "people's oral histories of how he may have come to Kankakee during Prohibition when there was a local brewery here. This time, the emphasis will focus on 'Gangs, Rivals, and Al Capone in the 1920s.'"

324   he often sneaked off anonymously: A contention expressed during various television appearances by Deirdre Marie Griswold.

324   "If Capone frequented even a tenth": Dave Wischnowsky, "Where in the World Wasn't Al Capone?," *Daily Journal,* Aug. 11, 2012. This is a charmingly whimsical article that collects the spurious claims of hotels that AC slept there. "The Golffather's Secret Trip to Scottish Courses," *Sun,* July 31, 2012: interview with Deirdre Marie Griswold where she invents the totally false story that AC made frequent secret trips to play golf in Scotland.

324   His name alone: Vonn S. Bair provided this anecdote.

324   His face is on postage stamps: I thank Niko Courtelis, philatelist, who gave me copies of the stamps.

324   In Romania, websites and meet-up groups: William J. Helmer put several Romanian scholars in touch with me.

324   In England in the 1960s: Cole Moreton, "Legend: An In-Depth Look into the Violent History of Ronnie and Reggie, the Kray Twins," *Independent,* Aug. 30, 2015.

324   Al Capone Festival: "A Town, a Gangster, a Festival," broadcast Sept. 17, 2015, on IFC.

324   "Amazing," mused a criminal defense lawyer: Robert Schoenberg website, "Al Capone as ALLUSION," posted May 20, 2015. He is quoting Julius Lucius Echeles.

324   Al Capone's name is the one to grasp: "Tuesday Reader's View: Puzzling Decisions," Midland, MI, *Daily News,* Feb. 23, 2016; Harold Brackman, "Dr. Freud Dissects Donald Trump," *Jewish Journal,* March 4, 2016; "Is Hillary's emails the same deal as Al Capone's tax records," posted on *Godlike Productions* and *Done Health,* March 7, 2016; "Cheerio, Then," *New York Times,* March 4, 2016, p. 4.

325   "it is not because Capone": Katharine Fullerton Gerould, "Jessica and Al Capone," *Harper's Monthly,* June 1931.

326   "major cultural figure": *Al Capone: Icon.*

327   "Was he a mobster?": Deirdre Marie Griswold repeats this in almost all of her many appearances.

327   "I don't see much goodness": Charles Strozier, who participated in the documentary *Al Capone: Icon.* His comments here are from a telephone conversation, Aug. 5, 2015.

327   "Most of them attempt a form of reasoning, fallacious or logical": Carnegie, *How to Win Friends and Influence People,* 20.

328   "the desire to lay down rules": *Ladies' Home Journal,* May 1919, quoted by Schoenberg, *Mr. Capone,* 56.

329   "with no conscious effort": James O'Donnell Bennett, *Chicago Gangland* (Chicago: Chicago Tribune, 1929); Schoenberg, "Quotes by and About Al Capone," http://www/mistercapone.com/quotes.htm, May 9, 2014.

330   "mysteries that aren't going to be solved": Justin Kaplan, quoted in Fox, "Justin Kaplan, Prize-Winning Literary Biographer, Dies at 88."

331   "God knows": Wilde's quotation is in Sir David Oswald Hunter-Blair, *In Victorian Days and Other Papers* (New York: Longmans, 1939), 122.

INDEX

—

Deirdre Bair received the National Book Award for *Samuel Beckett: A Biography*. Her biographies of Simone de Beauvoir and Carl Jung were finalists for the *Los Angeles Times* Book Prize. Her biography of Simone de Beauvoir was a *New York Times* Best Book of the Year, and her biographies of Anaïs Nin and Saul Steinberg were *New York Times* Notable Books.

A NOTE ABOUT THE TYPE

This book was set in Minion, a typeface produced by the Adobe
Corporation specifically for the Macintosh personal computer and
released in 1990. Designed by Robert Slimbach, Minion combines the
classic characteristics of old-style faces with the full complement of
weights required for modern typesetting.